International Public Policy Analysis

International Public Policy Analysis is the first textbook to take a truly comparative and cross-cultural approach, organized around policy issues, to examine important policy "lessons" that affect the everyday lives of citizens. Authors George M. Guess and Thomas Husted demonstrate that incremental, marginal changes in sectoral policy systems using cross-national lessons can lead to larger changes in country policies, democracy, and better governance.

Jargon-free and using a cross-cultural approach, the individual chapters in this book utilize a three-level analysis to review the policy issue areas, present analytic tools and frameworks, and provide cases/exercises for practice in applying the methods and frameworks. *International Public Policy Analysis* is an essential upper-level undergraduate textbook for courses on comparative public policy, policy process, political economy, and international policy analysis, and may also be used as required reading in introductory policy and public affairs courses at the graduate level.

George M. Guess is Adjunct Professor in the School of Policy, Government, and International Affairs at George Mason University, USA.

Thomas Husted is Professor and Chair of the Department of Economics at American University, USA.

International Public Policy Analysis

By George M. Guess and Thomas Husted

Routledge
Taylor & Francis Group

NEW YORK AND LONDON

First published 2017
by Routledge
711 Third Avenue, New York, NY 10017

and by Routledge
2 Park Square, Milton Park, Abingdon, Oxon OX14 4RN

Routledge is an imprint of the Taylor & Francis Group, an informa business

Library of Congress Cataloging in Publication Data
Names: Guess, George M., author. | Husted, Thomas, author.
Title: International public policy analysis / by George M. Guess and Thomas
Husted.
Description: New York, NY : Routledge, 2016. | Includes bibliographical
references and index.
Identifiers: LCCN 2016000888| ISBN 9781138673946 (hardback : alk. paper) |
ISBN 9781138673960 (pbk. : alk. paper) | ISBN 9781315561585 (ebook)
Subjects: LCSH: Policy sciences.
Classification: LCC H97 .G843 2016 | DDC 320.6–dc23
LC record available at http://lccn.loc.gov/2016000888

ISBN: (hbk) 978–1-138–67394–6
ISBN: (pbk) 978–1-138–67396–0
ISBN: (ebk) 978–1-315–56158–5

Typeset in Times New Roman
by Saxon Graphics Ltd, Derby

Contents

Tables, Figures, and Cases

Tables

Figures

Cases

Acknowledgments

The authors would like to thank Suzanne Flinchbaugh for her initial editorial support of this book and her continuing advice on how to proceed. We also thank Rob Grosse, Dean of the School of Business at American University, Sharjah, in the UAE, for his insights as initial reader for the book and excellent suggestions for its improvement. We hope we satisfied his concerns as well as those of the manuscript reviewers. Of course, the book in its present form could not have been completed without the energy, foresight, and enthusiasm of the Routledge publisher, Laura Stearns, and editorial assistant Brianna Ascher.

George M. Guess would like to thank his former students at American University in Washington, DC, during the initial offerings of his comparative public policy course (2011–2012). Their incisive questions and critical comments led directly to the development of our book. Since then, he wishes also to acknowledge the ideas gained from his graduate MPA/MPP students at George Mason University in Fairfax, Virginia, to focus its final drafts. As for its content, his former colleagues at IMF, World Bank (especially Mike Smith and Malcolm Holmes), and Development Alternatives, Incorporated (DAI in Bethesda, Maryland) can decide whether he learned and applied international public finance and policy lessons from them properly. He would like to thank his mentors for demonstrating the importance of sector policy analysis in international political economy during his graduate work: David Porter, Ron Chilcote, and the late Mike Reagan at the University of California, Riverside.

As always, George M. Guess wants to thank his wife, Regula, and their two sons, Andy and Marty, for their encouragement, patience, and understanding. Their continued support has made all things happen.

Thomas Husted thanks his wife, Ines, and their two sons, Lucas and Tomas, for their help and support throughout the writing process.

Preface

The intent of this book is to generate valid policy lessons that can improve results in important non-defense sectors that affect the quality of life. For most people, this means life in the cities. Most people live in metropolitan areas of the world, which include suburbs, or are headed to them from rural areas. Governments spend most of their budgeted funds for social security, social assistance, health care, education, energy, environmental protection, and transport infrastructure. Most of the beneficiaries of these sectoral or functional policy expenditures live in urban areas. Two supporting sectors that attempt to generate growth via increased jobs, investments, incomes, and revenues are the financial sector and the fiscal sector. The banking and financial sectors are key in providing capital for economic growth that translates into profits, investments, and tax revenues that finance public budgets. The fiscal sector focuses on public budgets that should be the result of sound expenditure and revenue policies and forward macroeconomic planning. The capital budget is part of the fiscal sector and provides the infrastructure that is needed to stimulate the economy. Because of their importance to growth and quality of life, we focus on these sectors in this book. Our target audiences are advanced English-speaking students around the world in internationally focused public policy, political economy, management, and administration programs.

An aim of this book is to devise best practices in each sector and encourage their transfer to other locales that must adapt them to improve policy performance in contexts that will differ. The best practice approach has been derided for being cookie cutter, providing the same prescriptions for widely different contexts. For instance, the good governance approach to international assistance advocated such Western values as rule of law, democratic policy-making, capable bureaucracies, property rights, official public accountability to citizens and minimal corruption. The major defect of this approach is the assumption that "all policies and institutions are potentially movable and can be aligned to fit some pre-specified blueprint" (Levy, 2014: 8). Thus, as we shall see later in *Chapter 2*, balanced budget and tight fiscal policies, or austerity, were part of the Washington Consensus of the 1980s and were presumed to apply everywhere under all circumstances. But tight fiscal policies evidently fail under recessionary conditions and do not restart growth or increase employment. Often, due to public resistance, they actually cause political instability and weaken growth further. Often the policy contexts are not so different and what is different can be modified by incentive packages that reward conflicting stakeholders—that is, Washington Consensus fiscal policies can be made to fit. But the opposite mistake from the hubris of one-size-fits-all best practices is to assume that every country is unique and there is nothing to be learned from one setting that is helpful in another (Levy, 2014: 8), or that there are no best practices that can be transferred elsewhere.

To avoid these twin mistakes, we propose a set of requirements or approaches in an overall framework for comprehensive international policy analysis. The framework seeks to alert users to the cultures and institutions that affect the incentives of policy-makers and ultimately the results of particular policies. In an effort to avoid "narrow economistic thinking" (Levy, 2014: 8), economists often add other variables to deepen their explanations of policy results. Hirschman, for example, believed that understanding the "disagreeable phenomenon" of authoritarian regime change in Latin America required more than a purely economic interpretation. He included: ideology, politics, culture, and even personality (1981: 134) in his innovative and eclectic approach.

Less eclectic perhaps, we propose that three levels of analysis are necessary to avoid the twin mistakes noted above: Western universal policy hubris and the opposite notion of local singularity. At the first level, one needs to find the relationship between inputs, outputs, and outcomes for each policy, program, or project. Often the relationships are straightforward: laws and operating regulations that limit air emissions from power plants, industries, and motorized vehicles; monitors that measure air quality (outputs) and the health effects (outcomes) of these rules. Since outcomes are often hard to attribute to such laws, more variables might need to be added, making the empirical task more complex. More simple policy relationships can be found at the operational level, such as: funding for conditional cash transfer programs; promulgation of eligibility requirements; and resultant changes in poverty levels. The use of conditional cash transfer programs to reduce poverty in global contexts of all types is an example of an operational level component that has been successfully transferred in programs in dissimilar contexts found in most regions of the world.

At this operational level, more opportunities exist for valid transfer of lessons. That means, many policy components (e.g. financing methods, IT management systems, and program incentives) and delivery institutions can be transferred successfully even if the overall contexts are different. At this technical level, policy analogies are also useful for designing systems and improving results. For example, voting systems require common basic activities: accessible registration, effective polling organizations, valid counting, timely reporting of results, and auditable data and information. Vote processing is similar to the routine and repetitive processing of checks and deposits by banks: accounting, tracking, reporting, and auditing of each transaction. In fact, IT systems designed for processing orders, deliveries, payments, and receipts of goods and services have been used to improve voting systems and electoral performance. Analogous systems can be found for almost all operational processes at the sectoral level that provide transferable lessons to improve policy efficiency and effectiveness. Similar contexts are more important for valid transferability at the strategic level; less so for transfer at the operational level.

If the input, output, and outcomes relationships vary widely by locality, region, or country, more variables must be added and analysis must be taken to a second level. Thus, at the second level we propose our political economy approach that, in addition to economics, brings in variables of: institutions, political culture, organizational structures, and regime support. There are logically two parts: political and economic. The political dimension provides insights into how groups use technical, financial, and social linkages as resources to influence policy processes. These are often exchanges of favors, e.g. funds for election or influence on laws and appointments; and funds for government contracts. These exchanges occur in every country and are situational, varying by regime and election. These types of political exchanges are often the source of economic inefficiency. While the particularities of each transaction and set of procedures are important to explaining results, they are less important to our book than systemic elements that determine policy design and implementation. These are the structural-legal features of governments that provide (or do not provide) rules of law and processes for conflict resolution. These systems provide the most important foundation of policy-making and results.

The economic dimension is vital to analysis at the second level. The incentives surrounding policy design and generated by rules and procedures will affect its results. Effectively implemented policies can realign incentives. In response to a U.S. Supreme Court decision to reduce prison crowding, California adopted a "realignment" policy that shifted the costs of dealing with relatively harmless prisoners to counties and cities. The result was that two-thirds of them were released from prison into supervision programs (*Economist*, 2015b: 26). This diminished the perverse incentives of a policy that tended to make hardened criminals out of minor offenders. Other perverse incentives, such as across-the-board budget cuts to achieve austerity targets, work against efficiency and effectiveness by penalizing economic growth and good service performance, and rewarding underachievement. Another example might be tax credits that target poor families. Roughly half the recipients of tax credits in Britain have incomes below $15,000. To encourage work, the current law allows a single mother of two to work 22 hours per week before welfare benefits start to fall. A proposed new law would reduce the number of hours to 10, which likely would encourage shirking behavior: working less and subsisting on welfare payments (*Economist*, 2015c: 56). Economic theory and applied research on the design of core policies such as education and health provide the clearest insight into what works and what doesn't in varying contexts. Other variables in our political economy framework—such as institutional design, demography, and political culture—affect policy results and need to be tested further empirically. For example, the cultural practice of open defecation instead of the use of latrines by Hindus in India has been known to keep infant mortality rates high because the practice has been a public health disaster for groups in close contact with each other (*Economist*, 2014c: 35). Despite clear empirical linkages between latrines and public health, the intervention of political culture prevents the construction and use of better sanitary facilities from improving health conditions.

With empirical guidance from the first level of analysis, deepened with additional explanatory variables through political economy analysis, the question then is where can lessons be applied? As an aid to providing answers, this book provides a simple comparative method or framework to guide where and how lessons can be transferred. Throughout the book, we distinguish policy lessons at the strategic and operational levels; some operational level lessons were noted above. But if the intent is to transfer whole systems, such as budgeting and financial management or health care, the strategic contexts should be similar. Cultures and institutions must be similar enough to avoid the oranges-to-apples problem. The rationale for first ensuring systemic similarities is that one can then hold constant other effects on the target policy or dependent variable. For example, supposed health care measures improve in country X with a performance transfer system that provides budgeted funds and sufficient discretionary authority for primary health care officials to spend them. To provide transferable lessons, one would first have to attribute policy results to the transfer program. The comparative case would be country Y, similar in culture, demography, and institutions but with no such transfer system. If this comparison were made, one could demonstrate that the differences in fiscal mechanism for health care delivery and its immediate context were likely determining most of the performance results. The idea of our level three analysis method is to control for rival explanations such as demography. To permit lesson transfer at the strategic level, this means that governmental systems, such as centralized unitary versus federalist structures with autonomous subnational governments, and cultures, such as European, Latin American, or North American, should also be similar. Because of the methodological difficulty and lack of available data, transfer of lessons for whole policy systems, such as health care, is often hard to do beyond the local or regional context.

The need for a comprehensive approach to international policy analysis is clear from the fact that examples abound of policies that are successful in one or more contexts. For instance, driven largely by applied overseas lessons from experience at the sectoral level, current reforms in India are focusing on the financial sector: state banking, education, social assistance/ welfare, infrastructure planning/financing, and education. Ultimately, implementation problems may stall reforms in India for lack of political will, meaning the laws will not take. This is not uncommon in many countries in which lessons are not applied for cultural or institutional reasons. Yet there are some spectacular successes. Elimination of tropical forests for farms or fuel has been an international environmental degradation problem in many developing and transitional countries for nearly 60 years. Loss of forest cover has led to flooding, loss of soil, and loss of carbon emissions savings. But now a combination of policies, some more effective than others in particular countries, has reversed this process. In the 1980s, only 20 percent of Costa Rica was covered in trees; now more than 50 percent is. Though reduced population pressure on the land and successful efforts at replanting explain some of reduction in deforestation, research has demonstrated the superior importance of certain types of policies: improvements in agricultural modernization, such as the green revolution in Brazil; imposition of blanket, country-wide bans on cutting in countries such as India; enforcement of moratoria on the sale of food from cleared land in countries such as Brazil; elimination of corruption in official bodies such as the Indonesian forest ministry; and provision of payments for economic services related to forest production such as the Mexican and Costa Rican income support schemes. These diverse country policies, some with international donor support, have worked to slow the rate of deforestation globally (*Economist*, 2014b: 50). Applying our analytic frameworks can identify transferable lessons, contexts, and explanations for differences in policy results, e.g. Indonesia versus Costa Rica. In that the strategic and policy-making contexts in tropical developing and transitional countries are to some extent similar, lessons can be tentatively drawn at that level. But at the programmatic and operational levels, there is evidence that systems and design lessons have been even more successfully transferred between these countries: from forest monitoring MIS and satellite mapping to aid enforcement to fiscal incentive programs for forest dwellers and small farmers managing fast-growth plantations.

Another policy area is policing strategy where lessons are paradoxically not applied between cities, regions, and countries. The impact of policing strategy on rich-country crime has been the subject of much empirical, political economy, and comparative analyses. For example, police records and victim surveys have shown that crimes against persons and property are falling in wealthy countries such as France and Great Britain. Applied research has eliminated explanations such as: lower youth exposure to leaded gasoline and its supposed link to violent crime and higher incarceration levels. Instead, the more robust explanations for lower crimes point to a combination of better policing policies with community contact, and targeting of crime hot-spots through data-driven methods which increases the risk of being caught (*Economist,* 2013: 21). The international policy question then is which design works best? As in the example of forest policies, it turns out that some of the policies or programs are transferable at the operational level despite national income differences and important contextual dissimilarities at the strategic level. In Brazil, for example, urban crime rates continue to fall in the wake of police reforms and better community policing strategies (*Economist,* 2010: 42).

At the macroeconomic level, monetary policies in response to low growth have varied in design and so have the results. The central banks of Japan, England, and the U.S. adopted stimulus policies of quantitative easing (QE), or purchasing government bonds with newly created money. The intent was to counter deflationary tendencies and encourage growth expectations by stimulating demand through artificial creation of inflation. The policies were designed according to standard theory of monetary economics. But the European Central Bank (ECB) and the German Bundesbank opposed QE, arguing that existing labor market rigidity, excessive taxation, and repressive regulations were structural or supply-side problems and could not be corrected by monetary policy. Nevertheless, the three economies using QE policy have grown steadily without inflation increasing; the Euro area has not, and German growth has stalled. Political economy analysis of institutional constraints in Europe suggests that structural reforms are long-term policies, while QE-like changes in tax policies could work quickly to restore confidence. The successful stimulus policies of these three countries suggested that QE can compensate for overly tight fiscal policies and still keep deflation at bay (*Economist,* 2014a: 11). In fact, a growing comparative literature exists on the fiscal and monetary policy impact on growth, many in response to the Great Recession or economic collapse of 2007–2009 (e.g. Baldacci and Gupta, 2009; Dethier, 2010). In 2015, based on growing empirical evidence that QE in the three countries was working, belatedly the ECB adopted QE policy. Early impact evidence, such as declining yields on Italian 10-year sovereign bonds, suggests that the new policy has driven down long-term interest rates as intended. It has also reduced lending rates for mortgages and other loans in southern Europe. Finally, loosening monetary policy through QE has contributed to pushing down the value of the Euro which has helped exporters. From our perspective, earlier action on existing technical analysis and comparative lessons could have stimulated growth earlier (*Economist,* 2015a: 71). Depending on whether the focus is strategic or operational, international policy analysis should include both the comparative and political economy frameworks to analyze the results of policies and where their lessons might be applied.

It should be noted that this is not a book on economic or political development; those subjects are covered by many high quality offerings. To the extent that we focus on development, it is at the sector level to improve the policy design and results of functional policy area. Transfer of valid lessons should make them more efficient and effective in serving users. Nor is this a book on the politics of international policy-making. Interest group contexts and regime power structures offer differing incentives to policy-makers. These variables are particularly important in analyzing why policy processes differ across sectors, such as the Indian nuclear policy and forest policy sectors (Gupta, 2014). But in this book, we eschew inter-sectoral coalition contexts despite their importance perhaps in predicting the composition and results of certain policies. Coalitional structures, strategies, and the current political contexts of any country are largely "givens" and cannot be changed by more rational advice grounded in economic research in the short run.

Our focus is on the institutional and management systems that affect policy results and that we believe can make a difference in the short run, especially at the operational level. We also avoid the more in-depth country analyses that are available in many comparative politics texts. Country institutions are discussed as part of particular sectoral policies. Some regions of the world are given more attention than others. The major rationale for our country and regional choices was data, informational quality and author expertise. As technical aids in empirical and political economy analysis, we provide a few introductory methods of economic analysis applicable to each sector. More advanced discussions of econometric modeling and statistical methods for use in solving the problems provided at the end of each chapter can be found by reference to such works as Finkler, 2010; Dunn, 2008; Schroeder et al., 1986; and Gujarati and Porter, 2009.

There is a wealth of local applied policy cases and exercises waiting to be written and used as supplements to a book like ours. For example, the senior author helped organize an incentive program for local government practitioners in selected Romanian cities to develop cases and teaching notes from their particular management and policy experiences and to demonstrate their use to peers. In response, they developed these experiences into cases and were given packages of non-financial (e.g. more vacation) and financial incentives (e.g. bonuses) for their fine efforts. As an operational level training and education program, modified versions of this effort can be easily transferred to other countries. Please contact us on your efforts here and for any advice on program design: gguess@gmu.edu and husted@american.edu.

References

Baldacci, Emanuele and Sanjeev Gupta, "Fiscal Expansions: What Works," *Finance and Development*, 46, 4 (December 2009): 12–15.

Dethier, Jean-Jacques (2010) "Measuring the Effectiveness of Fiscal Policies in Stimulating Economic Activity in Developing Countries: A Survey of the Literature," Washington, DC: World Bank.

Dunn, William N. (2008) *Public Policy Analysis: An Introduction*, 4th ed. (Englewood Cliffs, NJ: Pearson Prentice Hall).

Economist (2010) "A Magic Moment in the City of God," June 12, pp. 42–44.

Economist (2013) "Where Have All the Burglars Gone?" July 20, pp. 20–23.

Economist (2014a) "Be Bold Mario," August 23, pp. 11–12.

Economist (2014b) "A Clearing in the Trees," August 23, pp. 50–52.

Economist (2014c) "Sanitation in India: The Final Frontier," July 19, pp. 35–36.

Economist (2015a) "The ECBs Medicine: Raising the Dose," March 9, p. 71.

Economist (2015b) "The Right Choices," June 20, pp. 23–26.

Economist (2015c) "Welfare: Credit Crunch," October 31, pp. 55–56.

Finkler, Steven A. (2010) *Financial Management for Public, Health and Not-for-Profit Organizations*, 3rd ed. (Upper Saddle River, NJ: Pearson/Prentice-Hall).

Gujarati, Damodar and Dawn Porter (2009) *Essentials of Econometrics* (New York: McGraw Hill/Irwin).

Gupta, Kuhika, "A Comparative Policy Analysis of Coalition Strategies: Case Studies of Nuclear Energy and Forest Management in India," *Journal of Comparative Policy Analysis, Research and Practice*, 16, 4 (August 2014): 18–27.

Hirschman, Albert O. (1981) *Essays in Trespassing: Economic to Politics and Beyond* (New York: Cambridge University Press).

Levy, Brian (2014) *Working with the Grain: Integrating Governance and Growth in Development Strategies* (New York: Oxford University Press).

Schroeder, Larry D., David L. Sjoquist, and Paula E. Stephan (1986) *Understanding Regression Analysis: An Introductory Guide* (Beverly Hills, CA: Sage).

1 Development and Application of International Policy Lessons

Introduction

A number of years ago while living and working in Costa Rica, the senior author was impressed by how well the population was served by the national health service. From reading about and visiting the region, it was clear that the national health services of neighboring countries were hardly functioning. That was evident from the influx of patients from Nicaragua and Panama seeking to use Costa Rican clinics and hospitals and to obtain medicines and other health-related services. Even the Cubans he met were impressed by the system's effectiveness and adapted for their own health care reforms many elements of the largely free, decentralized Costa Rican model that required doctors to work outside the capital city of San Jose in exchange for their study subsidies. How did the author know the Costa Rican system was efficient and cost effective? Were there valid performance metrics? Were there larger structural variables that explained why health care policy worked in Costa Rica and not in neighboring countries? Was it regime? Or culture? Adequate financing? Institutional systems that properly aligned patient-system incentives? Was the successful health care system but a reflection of the political regime and Costa Rica's long-standing inclusive democracy? If so, are there at least parts of this health care system that could be transferred to work in neighboring countries? Could they be transferred to similar countries in other regions such as Africa and Asia? Conversely, what explains the resistance by countries needing health care that have resources (their own and/or from international aid) to adapting successful lessons from countries like Costa Rica? Are these same questions applicable to other key policy sectors such as education, urban transport, and environmental protection?

The International Flow of Applied Policy Lessons

Since that perplexing experience in Costa Rica, much has changed in the policy world. It is now clear that the flow of inter-country policy lessons at the sectoral or functional level is immense and growing. For example, U.S. analysts reviewed health care financing of systems in Switzerland, Canada, and Germany to use as inputs in the design of the final Affordable Care Act of 2010. Switzerland has a market-based system of health care that uses private insurers, covers everyone, and does so at a much lower cost than the American system. Other important health care models were available from regions such as Latin America for adaptation by OECD countries contemplating reforms. Conversely, Brazilian policy-makers have been examining German fiscal federalism for lessons on how to redesign their system in order to strengthen fiscal discipline. New York City poverty policy analysts reviewed the successful performances of conditional cash transfer programs in several Latin American countries, including Mexico and Peru, in order to develop their own cash transfer system. In fact, Mexico's pioneering policy—to make cash benefits targeted to poor families conditional on behavioral changes such as getting children vaccinated and sending them to school—has been copied by almost 50 countries (*Economist*, 2014: 58). And a wealth of reports from the World Bank, the IMF, and other donors offer lessons from multiple countries on how to improve particular country sector policies. In short, generation and adoption of applied policy lessons on what works and what doesn't is proceeding at a brisk pace.

Unfortunately, less research attention has been paid to the favorable contexts needed for successful systems adaptation and institutionalization of policy lessons. Policy design, implementation, and results lessons from Germany, for example, do not neatly apply in Brazil or Nigeria. But comparative studies often proceed as if they do. The literature seems replete with almost random transfer of policy lessons across international boundaries. Like the problems noted with transferring lessons from Costa Rica, where lessons ought to apply to nations such as developing countries in Asia or Africa, there may be cultural and institutional reasons why they have not been transferred. Kenya, for example, has 15 million mobile phone users that use their phones to transfer money and make payments. About 25 percent of GNP flows through mobile phones. Despite this, countries like India, China, Sudan, and Somalia ignore these lessons, largely to protect their state phone monopolies. Instead, they reinforce policy ignorance by smothering attempts at mobile start-ups in red tape. The enormous opportunity cost of ignoring the telecommunications policy lessons from countries like Kenya is clear from the few countries that have adopted positive lessons: Tanzania utilizes mobile phone systems to receive tax payments; the Philippines uses them to deliver welfare or social assistance payments; Afghanistan uses them to pay salaries. Corruption and turf protection by powerful ruling groups probably explain much of the reluctance to permit mobile phone systems competition.

In this book, we cannot offer tested methods to change such entrenched systems in the short run. Instead, we provide substantive policy issues in each sector from which lessons can be *generated*, *explained*, and *adapted* for use elsewhere than the home country. This will be done through (a) review of the policy issue areas in the following chapters, (b) presentation of analytic tools and frameworks, and (c) provision of cases/exercises for practice in applying the methods and frameworks.

In this chapter we review basic concepts of public policy, including policy-making and implementation cycles, formulation processes, and performance results measurement. Familiarity with these well-known concepts is important to define and distinguish the policy stages and to facilitate the focus "on" sub-policies in the form of programs and projects. We then provide a comprehensive approach to international policy analysis. This consists of three frameworks for (1) empirical validation of policy inputs-outputs-outcomes; (2) explanation of performance variations through a political economy approach; and (3) adaptation and transfer of lessons consistent with a comparative methodological guide. Finally, in each chapter, we offer introductory economic tools relevant for the analysis of the particular policy area, and we provide opportunities to apply them to international cases. Particular sectors and policy areas lend themselves to particular methods and tools. For example, urban rail-bus transport policies are really a combination of current spending for operations, maintenance, and capital investment for facilities and rolling stock. These methods may or may not be sufficient to identify options and preferences that make the best use of available financing to achieve service efficiency and effectiveness. Urban transport policy-makers need to know tools and methods to forecast passenger demand, design optimal pricing strategies, analyze costs and benefits of investment projects, and to assess the cost effectiveness and performance of whole transport systems. Such practical and mostly economic tools as these are essential for policy analysis in the urban transport sector.

To refine the use of our frameworks, we offer the opportunity in each chapter to apply some of the standard tools in each policy area to international cases. As an aid to understanding, our approach can be used as a checklist or policy-audit framework to review such important performance determinants as: (a) application of tools and methods (e.g. Were demand forecasts inaccurate because of data and method problems? Did pricing ignore income or demand elasticity?); (b) incentive effects of institutions and context (e.g. Do the internal routines and micro-rules create perverse incentives, such as those with flood insurance policies? Are there urban transport governance problems that require structural changes at the strategic level?), and (c) design of the policy and its financing (e.g. Were subsidies not properly targeted to clients or users?). It may be that incremental changes can be made in one or more of these areas to improve policy results. If so, transfer to other countries might be more feasible and likely to produce the expected results. If there are deeper contextual problems, such as an adverse political culture and lack of regime support, and if they can be remedied only over the longer term, transfer of policy lessons at the strategic level should either not proceed or should be transferred with the understanding that success will require long-term political and resource commitments.

Sectoral Policy Focus

We have selected certain sectors from a large list of candidates on the basis of three criteria. First, these are non-defense and security sectors. While analytic tools would be similar for this sector for weapons systems procurement in the defense sector, the bases for their need, demand, and utilization in tactical or strategic contexts is beyond our expertise. Second, these sectors affect the majority of people in most countries, those who reside in metropolitan areas and their suburbs. While over 50 percent of the world's population live in cities today, by 2050 this proportion is expected to grow to 66 percent (Ramirez-Djumena, 2014: 42). Third, they represent the bulk of budgeted funds for programs and services in most countries and their financing depends on both fiscal policy and the performance of the financial sector. Thus, we selected macroeconomic and fiscal policy because budgets finance policies and their macroeconomic impact on growth needs to be estimated carefully and controlled. We focused also on urban transport and infrastructure supply because it is a growing problem in many countries; in response, innovative models of alternative urban transport service delivery and financing are being tried with many transferable lessons. Health care financing and service delivery are also important problems with many transferable lessons available from around the world at both the strategic and operational levels. Education policies are in the midst of an international revolution in cities and countries, particularly in Europe and North America. Social assistance and poverty policies offer a wide range of policy implementation and reform lessons learned, particularly from Latin America, that have already been transferred successfully. Global demand for clean energy is growing and the persistence of coal and petroleum sources continues to require smart environmental regulation and control of air, water, and solid waste pollution. A superb example of comparable policy lessons not learned is provided in *Chapter 7* (*Cases 7.6* and *7.7*) by the failure of Japan to learn the costly errors of recent German solar energy subsidies. Finally, the banking and financial sector affects every citizen. We have separated fiscal policy from the financial sector just as they are in the national accounts of every country. Fiscal policy refers to governmental expenditure and tax policies. They are the major macroeconomic tools that target aggregate demand within the broad limits of fiscal discipline. The financial sector refers to institutions that facilitate saving, facilitate the accumulation of wealth, and minimize risk. Example of financial sector institutions include: Banks, pension funds, savings banks, mutual funds, and financial products such as money market funds and collateralized debt obligations. Since financial collapse can wipe out incomes, savings, and jobs, threatening macroeconomic stability, maintenance of a stable financial sector is an important regulatory function of public policy. Failure to do this at the country level, as evident in the 2008 economic meltdown, can jeopardize the performance of the entire world economy.

In short, our selected sectors serve mostly urban people and reflect general urbanization trends across all regions. Each sector offers examples of controversial policy design and implementation. They are all non-defense sectors, since that sector often eschews economic methods in the name of strategic concerns of national security. They all can be subdivided into programs and projects that may be analyzed for lessons which can be transferred to or from the national and sub-national levels. They are all directly linked to the general welfare of most people. One might argue that agriculture and natural resource policies affect more people in some countries. That is certainly true, but our focus is on urban policies of national import affecting most countries.

Policy Concepts: Cycles, Processes, and Systems

Any attempt to analyze, compare, and transfer international policies should recognize the initial fault line in the foundation of the field of public policy. Public administration and policy is expressed in laws, rules, and regulations. Their significance and use for achieving the public welfare is thus critical. The two main traditions view rules and regulations differently, as applied to public sector management of policies and programs. With its civil law system and culture of detailed statutory public law tradition, in Continental Europe public administration and policy is a sub-field of law. The role of administrators is rational application of statutes; the statutes are promulgated by decision-makers seeking the most rational approach to problem-solving. The only question is what "rational" means? This contrasts with development in the Commonwealth countries and the U.S. where public administration and policy studies reflect the common law tradition of precedent and interpretation of laws by managers. Managers act unless expressly forbidden (Wright and Nemec, 2002: 20–21) and the unwritten but utilitarian norm is to act on what works or is likely to work.

By contrast, in the state-centered public law approach to public policy and administration, managers are forbidden to act without statutory authorization. That constraint means that management tools such as financial information systems and budget reforms including such items as program formats require authorizing laws first. These IT and budget systems are not economic or management tools—but rather legal issues. In the U.S. and Germany, politics in principle is separated from policy formulation and implementation. But in practice this rarely happens in the U.S. common law system because of need for managerial flexibility and the necessity of ensuring political accountability of institutions to voters and publics. In Germany, and to a large extent in countries following the civil law tradition, policy is strictly a matter of law. The cultural and political belief is that nothing works except through law. For instance, the suggestion that the European Central Bank (ECB) should create new money to buy sovereign bonds in fiscal crises, a practice called quantitative easing (QE), is viewed as illegal. It would be illegal according to the German Constitutional Court as a violation of the public finance norm that central banks should stick to monetary policy and not perform quasi-fiscal policy acts such as financing. Further, applying QE would be illegal because such actions exceed its narrow mandate to manage the money supply. This would break the rules and destroy trust in government (*Economist*, 2014e: 61). For these reasons, in the U.S. tradition, policy-making and implementation are highly politicized processes to some extent compensated by institutional checks and balances and separation of governmental functions. Country settings where comparative lessons are to be applied will fall into one of these legal traditions, with some mixed examples in unitary Commonwealth countries such as the UK, where managerial accountability is combined with a deep legal-regulatory tradition of policy-making and administration. This legal tradition distinction is important in identifying constraints to both policy formulation and implementation. It also can serve as a constraint on policy analysis or appraisal before enactment and implementation.

Public policies are defined as intentional public actions reflected in laws, regulations, and executive orders approved by governmental bodies to accomplish goals/objectives in response to perceived needs and demands. Policies are not just planned actions; they are made into actual laws, or regulations and administrative actions are implemented to achieve their stated aims. In all countries, policies are made and analyzed through four stages in a continuous cycle.

As indicated in *Figure 1.1*, first, in response to data and information indicating that problems exist, e.g. environmental damage, low quality education, poor urban transport, or growing regional poverty, policy proposals are put on the public and, finally, the legislative agendas. Some proposals become policies; others stay on the agenda, such as gun registration in the U.S. because of "imbalanced politics" (Marmor, 2000). In such cases, issue zealots or concentrated groups of passionate minorities can guard the status quo to prevent contrary action by a less-intense majority of diffuse opponents. In this initial phase, policies are proposed in response to perceived and measurable problems. But suppose there are alternate definitions of the problem that lead to major differences in proposed remedies? For example, the 2008 financial crisis was defined as a problem of inadequate supply of banking system credit. That led to the solution to bail out banks in response. But suppose the cause was excessive household debt or falling net worth from loss of homes and jobs? That would cause diminished demand for bank credit at almost any price. A key remedy instead would be to write down mortgage principal as an alternative to foreclosure (*Economist*, 2014b: 71). Failure to define the problem properly in 2008 may have led governments such as the U.S. to lose time in responding to that major financial and economic crisis.

Second, policy proposals reach the legislative or executive branches and, depending on constitutional laws and practices, may become policies enacted by parliamentary statute, rule, or executive order. At this formulation stage, interest groups, issue networks of policy experts in sectoral areas, and elected officials work out the final details of each policy. Powerful groups exert pressure on lawmakers to craft legislation favorable to their interests. This is also the major stage at which analytic techniques are applied and critiqued by proponents of different versions of the final policy. It is where economic principles and political self-interest rarely coincide.

"If you want change, you have to take political action to get it" (Follett, 2014: 383). That commonsense maxim suggests the need to pull the levers of power using available resources to get intended results. But the issues, participants, and dynamics of political action will vary according to country circumstances. Though it is unusual for a political economy text to de-emphasize politics and policy processes, we suggest that these are granular processes often unique to countries and hard to compare for policy-level lessons. Power mapping may be of some use and many analysts engage in such exercises in country settings for particular issues. Our view is that generalizations across the governance machinery of legislatures, executives, and judiciaries are largely abstract and of little use to practitioners in the shorter term. Our

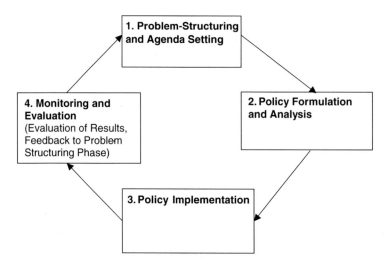

Figure 1.1 The Policy Cycle and Process

intent is to improve operational results by function. Lessons at this level can be drawn and transferred as noted in the preface, e.g. conditional cash transfers. Even lessons on policy design at the strategic level can be drawn if one is cautious.

Third, the policy is implemented. Policy implementation differs from budget cycle implementation in that the former can last for years or decades. Policies remain in force until formally repealed. More commonly, they persist and are modified through legislative amendments and regulatory actions over many years. In principle, this makes it easier to monitor results and to measure the impact or results of policies rather than monitoring public budgets because the time frame is much longer. In practice, implementation is often more complicated than formulation. Pressman and Wildavsky (1984), for example, recounted the problems of implementing the Great Society Program's anti-poverty and economic development programs in Oakland for the U.S. Economic Development Administration. The process of negotiating agreements with local groups, regional-local officials, and agencies all competing for turf—and then allocating loans, loan guarantees, and grants to applicants—involved multiple steps and major unforeseen obstacles based on a larger number of interdependencies, decision points, and participants than was anticipated (Pressman and Wildavsky, 1984: 93). The anti-poverty policy response was a messy program for a messy problem that involved two contradictory objectives: more business and industrial jobs for economic development and reduced poverty for poorly trained and uneducated clients.

Despite the legal tradition governing civil law countries, policy implementation in any country is more than applying the technical details of authorizing laws and regulations. If possible, implementation should be made easier by sorting out perverse incentives in advance during policy formulation. Because of special interest pressures to pass favorable laws, this is often not possible. Perverse regulatory incentives create problems for managing budgets as well as for implementing laws as intended. For instance, flood insurance programs exist in many countries such as: France, the UK, and the U.S. Common risks are pooled and subsidized to prevent losses. But the programs, such as Flood Re in the UK and the National Flood Insurance Program (NFIP) in the U.S., create incentives to build in risky areas that are later flooded. The NFIP has a current deficit of $24 billion (*Economist*, 2014a: 76).

Finally, in the fourth stage of the policy cycle, policies are evaluated for results achieved. The two evaluative dimensions are (1) actual physical impacts on intended clients, and (2) the financial or efficiency (least cost or cost/unit) and cost effectiveness (cost/result) of the policy. Evaluation is performed by official institutions on a regular basis, e.g. national audit offices; or in response to specific requests by legislative committees with jurisdiction over those sectoral areas, e.g. environment; or by non-governmental watchdog groups, e.g. for fiscal transparency.

While this four-stage cycle appears intuitively obvious, country policy-makers may not follow it for two reasons. First, basic baseline data from which to define the policy problem or problems may be missing. For instance, the Colombian president and agricultural policy-makers have been developing options and preferred solutions despite missing data. An agricultural census has not been conducted there for 40 years, during which time recent studies suggest about 5.7 million people have abandoned the countryside and 16 million acres of farmland has been seized illegally or abandoned. One predictable effect of the long-standing armed conflict between Colombia's leftist guerillas, right-wing paramilitaries, and the armed forces is that remaining farmers prefer to grow subsistence crops that turn profits quickly. This means that long-term productivity on a national scale has been limited by fear of investing in permanent crops such as coffee or citrus trees without security or the availability of finance (*Economist*, 2013: 45). Use of the policy-cycle framework suggests that basic data such as an agricultural census is needed first to focus on priority problems for the sector before moving to options and solutions. To summarize, within this policy cycle, the emphasis of our book is on the use of evaluative information to improve policy design and implementation by sector or function.

The second reason for not following the policy-cycle phases is that there may be a lack of clear policy alternatives or options to choose from. The functional policy areas selected for this book offer solid baseline data and relatively clear lessons from tested results in a variety of contexts. But in areas such as foreign policy this is not the case. In many conflicted areas of the world, it is difficult to define an actionable problem, specify an achievable goal, or to know how serious a threat these conflicts (e.g. Iraq, Syria, Ukraine, and Afghanistan) pose to American national security (Krasner, 2014: 42). The expectation is that states and political regimes can and will adapt the relatively clear options and solutions from the menus of each sectoral policy. That presumes legitimate states and central governments with legitimate authority and professional and financial resources to spread policies to all within their borders. But regime legitimacy in such regions as the Middle East and Asia may be in short supply, conferred neither by popular mandate (e.g. elections) nor by the achievement of order, stability, and growth (e.g. China but not Pakistan). Under such conditions of state weakness, the development of options informed by political economy analysis and comparative research, and being able to implement them, is unlikely.

For countries with reasonably legitimate and professional regimes, the job is easier. This is so as each functional area has only so many types of problems and solutions. The problems have all been faced in some country and assessed for workability. But even legitimate and professionally competent governments everywhere: "have been organized to seek the interests of rent-seeking elites who are intent on staying in power and furthering their own material interests. Their elites might sometimes adopt policies that incidentally have wider benefits for society as a whole, but they will not adopt initiatives that as far as they can foresee, will undermine their own base of political support" (Krasner, 2014: 42). Therein lies the political constraint to cross-border transfer of policy lessons: the political sources of economic inefficiency that should be the core of political economy analysis. Fiscal austerity policies, for example, can threaten that power base; fiscal decentralization and universal education policies can also be threatening to regimes. The undemocratic feature of many governments in transitional and developing countries means that the path to policy reform in most places will be incremental, building on existing institutions to the extent that political cultures allow, and pulling whatever political and policy levers that will appear to improve results. But as noted by Sunstein, "incremental improvements should not be disparaged, especially if they help hundreds of thousands of people. And if the goal is to produce large-scale change, behaviorally informed approaches (to reform government operations) might accomplish more than we think" (2015: 9).

Distinguishing Policies and Measuring Results

Moving from the discussion of cycles and constraints to formulation of the major types of policies, we can distinguish four types. First, we focus on sectoral or *functional* policies. This book covers mainly sectoral policies such as education. Policies at this analytic level are complex and affect many sub-systems and levels of government. Functional policies often run parallel to budget functions. Functions can be defined as groups of activities aimed at accomplishing a major service or regulatory program (Strachota, 1994: 164). The nine functions and many sub-functions of the U.S. budget, for instance, relate budget authority, outlays, loan guarantees, and tax expenditures to national needs. Congressional budget resolutions target these needs (Mikesell, 2011: 284), and via *cross-walking* (inter-format reconciliation), every cent of functional expenditures can be translated into objects of expenditure, programs, or organizations. Functions are also independent of the government organizational structure (Schiavo-Campo and Tommasi, 1999: 70). Fourteen major ones are recognized in the United Nations Functional Classification of the Functions of Government (COFOG). There are also 61 groups and 127 sub-groups (Schiavo-Campo and Tommasi, 1999: 70). For example, the Social Service function includes the sub-group of Education and the sub-groups of Primary, Secondary and Tertiary Education. Transparency and comprehensiveness are obtained by cross-walking expenditures objects across organizational units into combined functions. Consistent with this classification, as noted, we focus on international sectoral or functional comparisons and analyses of the major policies such as transportation, health, and education. Ministry and departmental structures often follow functional lines in allocating jurisdictional responsibilities for these policies.

Second, *policies* can be broken down administratively and financially into *programs,* which are like sub- or micro-policies. For example, a national transportation policy might have an urban transportation program that could be dis-aggregated into sub-programs for rail and bus transit. *Programs* can be defined as groups of related activities performed by one or more organizations (like functions). The purpose of the program is to carry out the function (Strachota, 1994: 166).

Third, each functional policy will have many *projects* which are even smaller in scope (but perhaps not in cost) than programs. Most of these are capital investments, e.g. schools for education, hospitals for health, and rail systems infrastructure for urban transport. Projects are often financed by multiple sources: vertically by national and state level budget appropriations, policy grants (i.e. fiscal transfers), and loans, and horizontally by local private and public sources. All three policy types can be analyzed, monitored, or regulated at the strategic and operational levels, e.g. oversight of contractual performance for construction at the operational level or regulatory control of elderly and handicapped transportation carriers at the strategic level.

Fourth, actual policies may be distinguished from *policy mechanisms*. The latter are legally authorized policies but serve as implementing mechanisms at the sub-system or operational levels. For example, conditional cash transfer programs in multiple Latin American countries are national intergovernmental transfer policies but operate narrowly as technical mechanisms. They are simple, flexible, transferable devices that affect few other sub-systems. But they contribute significantly to the results of anti-poverty, health, and education policies. Similarly, capital project and program financing techniques such as public–private partnerships and social impact bonds (which will be discussed in *Chapter 3* and elsewhere) require legal authorization and are therefore policies. But they would also be *policy mechanisms* in that they are narrowly prescribed mechanisms for the execution of functional policies at the strategic level. They affect few policy sub-systems other than the narrow purpose for which they are used, e.g. financing of an airport, highway, or commuter (inter-urban) rail system.

As noted, two analytic levels can be distinguished within these four policy types. At the *strategic* level, the unit of analysis is the law or constitutional requirement and their contents. The goals, objectives, and expected results in sectoral terms are strategic policy issues, e.g. an educational policy to achieve greater school competition, teacher competence, and student choice of schools. At the *operational* level, policies at the school level (often consisting of procedures or regulations), for instance, cover teaching schedules, building maintenance, and the principal's fiscal discretion and management authority to deal with security and teacher competence issues. For comparative purposes, it is critical that policies be compared at the same level, e.g. operational level of principal discretion to plan and execute budgets in the UK, Japan, the U.S., and the Netherlands. Often, operational policies will vary not just by country but widely within countries at the provincial, local, and state levels. Such features of decentralized fiscal and political systems offer significant opportunities to measure variation in results and to apply explanatory tools and methods.

One might also add a super-strategic or an ideological level to this distinction. Operational levels exist for all sectoral policies, and the issues deal mostly with technical, incentives, institutions, laws, and structural constraints. Where national economic conditions worsen, policy debates often move to a more abstract level. In Indonesia, for example, macroeconomic instabilities (i.e. low GDP growth, high unemployment, inflation increasing to 6.8 percent, and lower commodity prices for copper and other ores) shifted the policy debate to this level. Politicians up for re-election in 2014 appealed to voter nationalism by bashing foreign capital and targeting "neoliberal" solutions to economic development, such as the reduction of fuel subsidies (*Economist*, 2013a: 37).

Policy authorizations or approvals in many countries include expected results and performance measures for monitoring and evaluation. The analytic task is to try to link or attribute inputs to outputs and outcomes. As indicated in *Figure 1.2*, *inputs* consist of resources: legal, budgetary, personnel. They are measured in financial terms by object of expenditures or budget line-items, e.g. salaries, supplies, and equipment. The objective should be first to connect inputs with *outputs*, the measures of workload and efficiency. Often they are expressed as ratios of budget outlays or costs/expenditures to common industry output measures, e.g. cost per passenger mile and cost per patient. Or, they might be ratios of either fiscal or physical performance measures, e.g. debt service to total expenditure and student to teacher ratios. Further still, they could simply measure workload, e.g. the number of student contact hours, the average patient stay in days, and the length of prison terms in years. The final link should be with *outcomes* to assess the impact of policies, programs, or projects, and to measure their effectiveness. Outcomes are the impacts or changes in the target population that are consistent with policy objectives. Examples would be the health effects of air quality regulations and

Policy Inputs ————————→ **Policy Outputs** ————————→ **Policy Outcomes**

Policy Inputs	Policy Outputs	Policy Outcomes
Law, regulations, budget financing: Clean Air Act; OEO Head Start Program OEO: '68 $330m & 473k students; '08 $6.9b & 900k students	Workload: changes in source pollutants; HS placements; accountable systems; teachers	Health improvements attributable to lead, SO2, particulate matter reductions; HS cognitive achievements, use of preventive HC, improvements in health and nutritional status

Figure 1.2 Measuring Policy Impact

enforcement strategies; the effects on crime rates of community policing program techniques; and the congestion effects of a new light-rail line project. The linkage between inputs and policy impacts is again illustrated in *Figure 1.2*.

a. Three Levels of Policy Analysis: Basic Input-Output Analysis

The notion of a policy system with inputs, outputs, and outcomes is basic to the first level of analysis: econometric and statistical (see *Figure 1.2* and *Figure 1.4*). This is the most basic level, and it attempts to find the basic "nuts and bolts" linkages between inputs and results. Variables selected are expressed in quantitative terms, such as amounts spent, workload and activities performed, and results measures such as passenger miles of bus service delivered per day. Linkages should be straightforward and explanations of variances should be made in rigorous quantitative and statistical terms. But as we shall see in *Chapter 2*, the linkages between macroeconomic and fiscal variables are often not known. Microeconomic and macroeconomic variables and measures can be employed to examine costing and pricing relationships and to measure the larger impacts on consumption, investment, demand, employment, and inflation. For urban transport, the linkages between variables could be described as follows: inputs of public spending produce X volume of passenger miles of bus service as outputs, which translates into Y hours of outcomes in time saved, Z hours of reduced congestion, B tons of reduced emissions, and C reductions in lung and health problems as outcomes. These are basic variables using well-known performance measures in the urban transit industry. But a particular mode of bus service, such as rapid transit (BRT), might not perform as well in India, Indonesia, or Jordan despite similar designs and equipment. That would require more in-depth analysis from the political economy approach (below) that would bring in larger, less directly quantifiable variables as: culture, political institutions, and financing methods (as opposed to straightforward budget spending).

In short, more empirical analysis is needed to flesh out the relationships between inputs and results in most sectoral policy areas. One technique used, which was originally created to assess the impact of fertilizers on potatoes and was later taken up by the medical profession, has gained traction in social policy analysis: randomized control trials (RCTs). By giving a new treatment to randomly chosen patients and not giving it to "control" patients, resulting differences can be measured and attributed to the treatment itself. People eligible for help are randomly assigned to treatment and control groups. The difference in outcomes between the two groups is used to assess the intervention's effectiveness. RCTs intended to optimize rule and improve policy designs have been used in such areas as the impact of international aid programs on poor people; of smaller classes on student performance; of charter schools on student performance; and of pre-school for low-income students. They not only help determine whether a policy works but can also help optimize rules and prevent badly designed policies from being used, e.g the notion that higher tax rates on top earners generate more revenues is often false even though the policy is politically popular in the U.S. and other countries.

RCTs have been used in advanced countries such as Scandinavia, France, and the U.S. for small-bore operational questions such as the impact of longer school days. In developing and transitional countries, they are used to evaluate more fundamental reforms, such as welfare systems in Bangladesh and political decentralization in Zambia. In the future, randomized experiments should be used more to assess major policy shifts, such as the impact of devolving greater management and budget authority to school officials, and to remove perverse incentives in health care, e.g. through the Affordable Care Act in the U.S. (*Economist*, 2015a: 18). Once empirical linkages at the most basic level are established, more elaborate controls can be added in for such variables as culture and institutions for a comprehensive political economy explanation. Then the difficult work of applications in different settings must be tackled. Are the findings valid at the operational level only and thus mostly transferable? Or, are these larger policy results findings that do not travel well from one context to another?

b. Political Economy Analysis

We turn to the second level of political economy analysis to explain differences in policy performance. Once policies are identified and defined, results will differ over time. It is important to measure and explain those differences in order to apply lessons elsewhere. Many countries have similar problems in health, education, and urban transport, and they need to know what works and what doesn't. Then they need to know whether it would be worth the financial and political costs of trying to adapt lessons, systems, and methods from contexts outside their system.

Our political economy approach targets the marginal changes in incentives that could produce better policy results. Scholars such as V.O. Key (1940) recognized that making policy and budget choices (e.g. between programs A versus B) required marginal analysis and noted that the process would not be entirely rational for institutional and political reasons. He advocated a mix of economic analysis to produce options and recommendations adjusted to "second best" solutions for political realities. In country contexts of political paralysis and factionalism, such as the U.S. and many European countries, systems muddle along and survive by producing what economists call second-best solutions to problems in such vital areas as health care, education, and fiscal policy. Thus, institutional rules and incentives are included in our explanatory framework (see *Figure 1.3*). Political science contributes valuable insights, for example, on the systematic constraints to compromise and effective policy decision-making; the constraints to policy implementation; comparative political systems behavior, especially the role of political cultures; the effects of election rules and systems on partisan governance; and the effects of political organizations or structures, e.g. federalist, confederation, centralized, and decentralized fiscal and political systems. Economics enhances these insights by zeroing in on the micro-incentives of institutions and individuals. This focus can yield unexpected insights that force analysts to rethink their assumptions and to sharpen their analyses. This helps us learn why people behave as they do and how policies can help best to improve the public welfare.

The framework suggests that improved policy performance across a wide range of sectors can be achieved by digesting the lessons from similarly successful policies in other countries. The lessons should be ground-tested with a review of processes, cultures, and institutions. This should be accompanied by review of analytic tools and economic methods used in successful examples or those that produced probable analytic deficiencies in failed policies.

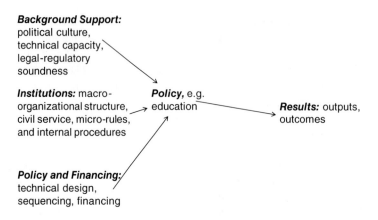

Background Support:
political culture,
technical capacity,
legal-regulatory
soundness

Institutions: macro-
organizational structure,
civil service, micro-rules,
and internal procedures

Policy, e.g.
education

Results: outputs,
outcomes

Policy and Financing:
technical design,
sequencing, financing

Figure 1.3 A Framework for International Political Economy

As is known, policies are often good for some people and bad for others. For instance, increasing minimum wages will raise the incomes of some low-wage workers. But it will also cause some small businesses to make smaller profits, some customers to pay more, and some workers to lose their jobs. Evaluating or analyzing the effects of such policies is the job of political economists. Traditional economics uses social welfare functions to try and find the policy design that maximizes the total utility of everyone in society. But unintended consequences, especially during policy implementation, often cause utility-maximizing policy designs to backfire (Mankiw, 2014: 4).

Needed then is humility by political economists in the use of their tools and advice since their values could be quite wrong. Worse still, their presumed opponents in policy debates may be right. The strengths and weaknesses of particular economic tools should be evident from our review of major sector or functional policies. For example, efforts to formulate successful fiscal policies to stimulate aggregate demand and maintain stabilization require solid forecasts of the effects of such variables as deficits, debts, and taxes on inflation, unemployment, and growth. Much depends on proper weighting of variables in forecasting models. Problem definition and macroeconomic simulation tools can be of use to calibrate such models and assist in the task of optimizing policy performance. For instance, to design urban transport policies based on best practices, it is important to properly use the tools of marginal analysis, price elasticity of demand, and measurement of opportunity costs. For design and implementation of urban transport infrastructure projects, the tools of capital financing, benefit–cost, and cost effectiveness analysis must be employed and their results in producing project rank-orders independently critiqued. Probable constraints to implementation that would drive up transaction costs and decrease actual benefit–cost ratios should also be reviewed before project approval. For projects justified on the basis of economic development, economic methods should be used to assess the impact of transport infrastructure on local and regional growth, i.e. to attribute growth outputs to resource inputs.

Further, in the energy sectors of many transitional and developed countries, subsidies should be monetized and analyzed as potential drivers of the perverse incentives that work against both conservation and the adequacy of demand and supply via generation, transmission, and distribution of each energy source. Subsidy monetization is often not done. In the environmental area, options for reducing externalities and encouraging greater production of this important public good need to be assessed in relation to costs to individuals and firms. In education, market competition in relation to student and teacher performance needs to be measured. Since most educational services are financed by more than one level of government, an important need is to demonstrate the alternate impacts of grant/transfer designs on local revenues and performance. In health care, economic methods should be applied to develop competitive markets with sufficient pools of paying customers to lower costs and finance state or national services. Finally, given the volatility of national financial sectors in the years 2008–2010, cost-effective regulations that can stimulate commercial lending but also reduce the systemic risk of using weak and opaque assets as collateral, such as toxic mortgages, should be developed and transferred based on lessons learned in particular countries and regions.

Using our political economy framework, defined problems and analytic techniques in each of the above policy areas would be filtered through the three sets of control variables. As indicated in *Figure 1.3*, the framework suggests that policy-makers face three constraints to implementing successful policies from three related directions: (1) background support, (2) institutions, and (3) policy design and financing. These constraints should be considered as hurdles which a country or regime must overcome to implement a successful policy.

1. Background Support

Political regimes are the ruling cluster of a country and determine indirectly or directly through background support which policies make the agenda and are implemented properly. The legitimacy of the ruling elite can be based on claims to superior performance or to popular mandates (sometimes both). The claim of performance is often based on its ability to maintain social order, promote economic growth, and ensure clean government through meritocratic advancement systems. The latter describes the Chinese Communist Party's claim to legitimacy and fits with its political culture (described below) that historically has relied on objective examinations for recruitment and advancement (*Economist,* 2015: 50). By contrast, other regimes, such as those in India and Indonesia, claim legitimacy on the basis of democratic accountability to popular mandate. Ruling clusters of both types can be bloated and strong in the sense of being uncontested for succession, e.g. one man, one vote, one time!

Regimes and states may not have the same ruling capacities, which can threaten national governance integrity. Strong regimes, in the sense of ruling continuity (e.g. held in place by the military), can coexist with weak states. Such states have minimal service coverage and are often unable to provide basic services or infrastructure to the rest of the nation. Officials in such states, e.g. Russia, China, and selected Latin American countries, largely serve the narrower state rather than the people. They are unaccountable and their policies, programs, and projects do not cover the nation—only specific regions or cities. Such representative vacuums allow non-state actors to govern, such as the Mafia in parts of Italy and Islamist groups in Egypt, Syria, Iraq, and elsewhere in the Middle East that provide social services. Regimes then direct the state and can determine whether governance will be effective. Referring to the three constraints noted above (regime support, institutions, and policy design), three countries ruled by regimes with similar policies (e.g. fiscal devolution which is a sub-type of fiscal policy) in the same region (e.g. East Asia) might respond effectively and similarly to the first two sets of constraints but differ on how they respond to the third set of constraints: policy technical design, sequencing of activities, and financing. Such conditions are not uncommon and allow comparison of similar country policy cases responding differently to technical sequencing challenges. Using our framework (*Figure 1.3*), measurable differences in policy performance (outputs and outcomes) among the three countries can then tentatively be attributed to differences in regime abilities to provide support, respond to cultural challenges, and design effective policy design and financing.

DIRECT REGIME SUPPORT

Regime support is often expressed through actions that strengthen or weaken the legal-regulatory framework through which it governs. Sufficient local technical capacity needs to exist to implement any new actions affecting regulations, laws, and management tools such as IT or economic analysis techniques. Of critical importance is whether the political culture is supportive. Opponents of policy lesson transfer often argue that these conditions must be immediately present for the policy lessons to succeed. Without top level support, local technical capacity, and a supportive culture, it is argued, the transfer of lessons and programs must fail. In fact, background support conditions are often variables rather than constants and can be provided by supporting public statements from the regime and effective legal action (e.g. authorization of laws and regulations). And as will be noted, significant operational components of policies, e.g. innovative financing techniques, can be transferred without the need for meeting all three conditions at the strategic level. That suggests many more opportunities for policy lesson transfer exist than had been recognized. Critics of policy lesson transfer on cultural and regime support grounds often ignore the immense possibilities of management systems and technical methods at the operational level offered by each policy sector.

As suggested, regime legitimacy matters. The design and success of economic policies both macro and micro depend in part on regime types. The classic work on regimes distinguished democratic from non-democratic types, classifying them as: authoritarian, totalitarian, post-totalitarian, and Sultanist (Linz and Stepan, 1996). Here we make a more modest attempt to link emerging contemporary regime types with their economic policies to solve core societal problems. For reasons of political history, regime types can change. For example, Brazil and Uruguay were closed bureaucratic-authoritarian regimes in the 1970s–1980s and supported corporatist economic policies. They are now vibrant market democracies and support broad initiatives in market economics.

Regime types clearly affect the design and implementation of macroeconomic policy. The regimes can be classified (as noted in *Table 1.1*) by economic agenda. An important litmus test of current regime economic agenda is how international markets treat the value of local financial instruments such as stocks and bonds. How particular regimes treat firms is clear to international investors through such actions as taxation, regulation, nationalizations, jailing of executives, and treatment of local investment partners. Lack of investment and capital flight contribute to poor economic growth and unemployment. Similarly, if sovereign bonds are treated as high risk, regimes must pay more in debt service from the annual budget which requires higher local taxes and/or cuts in local services and programs. Currently, for example, Russian stocks trade at a huge discount to much of the rest of the world. The average emerging market price-earnings ratio is 12.5; that of Russia is 5.2 or roughly a $340 billion loss due to what is called "discount for obnoxious governments" (DOG factor) (*Economist,* 2014d). The Iranian p/e is just 5.6 and the Argentinian p/e is 6.1. Argentinian 20-year bonds also yield 9.8 percent which is more than five percentage points above the yield on equivalent Mexican bonds. The average price-earnings stock ratio can be used as one indicator to compare regime governance quality and economic policies. Thus, bad governance driven by ruling cliques can cost money in international investment and confidence.

Table 1.1 Regime Types and Economic Agendas

Regime Type	Structure	Country Examples	Economic Policies
Market Democracy	Competing governmental and civil society institutions; values of pluralism, bargaining, and participation.	U.S., Commonwealth and EU, Brazil, Uruguay, Chile, Poland, Czech Republic, Mexico, India, South Korea	High value in markets and property rights but actual outcome of competition between technical and political interests.
Capitalist Autocracy	Party and tight cabal of rulers.	China, Indonesia, Malaysia, Hungary	High interest in market reform but outcome depends on struggle between party bureaucrats and technocrats.
Bureaucratic-Authoritarian	Corporatist representative organization with civil society participation; parliamentary coalitions co-exist with clientistic political system.	Nigeria, Pakistan, Greece, Turkey	Closed nature combined with weak state institutions means weak service coverage and high instability; interest in import substitution and tariffs to protect national economy.
Kleptocratic Autocracy	Tight control of society by cabal enforcing values of force, loyalty, and ethnicity and often puritanical faith.	Russia, Saudi Arabia, Iran	Nationalist economics often commodity-driven.
Populist	Great man or permanent party with demonstration elections only; informal governance by extreme nationalists, nativists, and crypto-communists.	Venezuela, North Korea, Egypt	Little or no interest in economics to improve efficiency or effectiveness of programs and services.

POLITICAL CULTURE

Opponents of policy lesson transfer also argue that particular political cultures are threats or constraints rather than opportunities to build on and change behavioral incentives. "Political culture" consists of those shared values and attitudes that affect institutional and policy decision-making (Inglehart, 1988). Another way of putting it is: "what determines how people behave when they are not being watched" or "the way things are done around here" (1988). Political cultures consist of the formal and informal rules of the institutional game for local survival. They are often far from clear to the outsider. They are a composite of beliefs and practices that affect policy design and/or implementation. They affect policy as like-minded communities of values that influence what rules should be made and how strictly they should be enforced. The effects of political culture on policy can be at the strategic or operations level.

For instance, bureaucratic rigidity and excess process is often considered an institutional problem to be remedied by re-engineering of process and state modernization. As is known, rigid centralization can maintain the hierarchy of rank through blind obedience to rules without producing efficiency of function. But the problem may be deeper at the political culture level. The Korean cultural legacy of hierarchy and deference to authority, for example, has been blamed for several air crashes (e.g. KAL 007, Asiana 214, and KA Cargo 8509) as cockpit officers deferred to the senior in command though instruments indicated clearly that the plane was erroneously off course (Halsey, 2013). The authoritarian cockpit problem can be transferred to other contexts such as: needed approvals for changes in policy course or budget implementation. One study found that authoritarian cultures varied among four Balkan states and this explained to a large extent the degree of permitted operational decentralization for local government budgetary management decisions (Guess, 2001).

Since political culture can operate at the strategic and operational levels, one should attempt to identify which level. At the strategic level, for example, a cultural stigma of "bankruptcy" (*Economist*, 2013b: 79) and debt (*schulde* implying sin and guilt in German) pervades Northern Europe in general and Germany in particular. The policy implication of this cultural feature is evident in rigid and complex bankruptcy-insolvency laws and tight fiscal and budget policies. More importantly, the German cultural aversion to debt drives its fear of taking on additional debts from southern European countries which they view as profligate and personally irresponsible. Even mortgages are considered a big risk in Northern European countries such as Switzerland and something to be avoided in favor of monthly rental payments. In addition, one should distinguish which "values and attitudes" are temporary versus enduring.

Political culture refers to the more enduring values. But suppose temporary values are mistaken for enduring? Throughout the Middle East and elsewhere, it can be seen that Islam is faced with an "invasive species of zealotry," or temporary values that pervert the dignity and meaning of the religion. Given the legal integration of state and religion in the largely klepto-autocratic political regimes of that region, religious values translate into state policy in countries such as Iran and Pakistan, enforced by puritanical Islamist militias which stunt growth and development (*Economist*, 2013c: 72). These more temporary values of religious nationalism can influence followers to take advantage of regimes that practice tolerant rationalism, e.g. the Dutch Netherlands. Mistaking permanent for temporary cultural values also causes policy problems elsewhere. For 25 years following Mikhail Gorbachev, the assumption by U.S. and Western policy-makers was that Russia shared their goals and values. But under Vladimir Putin, it is increasingly clear that "Russia does not pretend to be moving towards the West." (*Economist,* 2013d: 43). At the operational level, it is our contention that such temporary perversions or repressed values can be changed with new incentives to improve policy results. A more serious problem with the political culture concept is that it might be a consequence rather than cause. For example, in the area of racial values, it has been noted that the "self-destructive cultural norm" of blacks shunning high-performing black students in school, i.e. for "acting white," is almost non-existent in charter schools (*Economist*, 2013e: 11). This suggests that organizational structures and institutional incentives can override what appeared to be enduring values. The political culture variable needs to be applied rigorously.

The fact is that culturally reinforced systems are not easily changeable in the short run. For instance, a common cultural feature in many transitional and developing countries is centralized decision-making and popular distrust of frequently corrupt governments. Our perspective on political culture is that most behavior can be changed if the institutional incentives underpinning them are changed. Terms such as culture of poverty, culture of corruption, and cultural tendencies to self-destruction and violence are commonly used as if they were permanent features of national landscapes. But such events as persistent ethnic and religious violence are often institutionally determined and, therefore, can be remedied by changes in economic and behavioral incentives. For instance, Kyrgyz–Uzbek ethnic violence around Osh in Southern Kyrgyzstan has caused hundreds of rioting deaths over many decades.

But the causes of this ethnic hatred and violence are institutional: lopsided distribution of justice through the police and courts; high unemployment among Uzbeks; official obstacles against use of the Uzbek language; and organized crime (*Economist*, 2013f: 46). To the extent that these two ethnic groups have successful traits (e.g. impulse control or discipline, insecurity about attainment of standards, and belief in exceptionality) they can overwhelm the larger institutional forces in the political culture (Chua and Rubenfeld, 2014) and coexist.

The policy analytic trick is to distinguish those elements of the political culture which genuinely deter program results and can only be changed in the medium term from those that are distinctive but can be modified or built upon to facilitate program results in the short run. Some cultural practices are distinctive but may not affect implementation of, for instance, educational policy reform. These can only be changed in the long term, such as rote educational practices, nepotism in civil service hiring, and staff loyalties to groups/families in formal organizations. These are important and distinctive practices, but they may not be important to program implementation. More important for educational policy reform are those practices that directly affect central or local government systems and are changeable in the short term. For example, distrust of government (revenue collections), family-tribal loyalties (budgeting for development projects), and peremptory/arbitrary power over underlings (auditing) affect the implementation of educational reforms through new policy and management practices. In fact, persistent and repetitive administrative practices, such as generation of statistical reports (budget reports that are often unread) and centralized expenditure controls (to preserve hierarchical power within ministries), can be changed by modification of internal incentives. Statistical reporting can be converted into useful analysis for budgeting and auditing; passive line management can be turned into active program implementers by giving them targets and enforcing expenditure controls that already exist. In short, culture may be turned from a static obstacle to the dynamic foundation on which a decentralization policy reform can be built (Guess, 1992).

Culture and institutions are related. Focusing on the right institutional levers through changes in laws and regulations can change the cultural values, behavior, and policy results. For example, an important cause of the international banking crisis of 2008 was that bankers could place "asymmetric" bets (unequal relationships or parts) in which they pocketed the gains (i.e. derivatives) while shifting losses to taxpayers (i.e. receipt of bailouts). Since then, informational asymmetry has been reduced by introduction of higher capital standards and the separation of retail and investment banking (*Economist*, 2013g: 60). Regulatory changes that should reduce reckless decision-making can work on the banking culture, sustaining the fiscal position of banks and thereby preventing future crises and the need for public sector bailouts.

2. Institutions

Political economists focus on the institutional constraints and opportunities to achieving policy results. From this perspective (and ours in this book), institutional and economic inefficiencies are typically attributable to political sources. Institutions are the major constraints that weigh on ministers and officials when designing and implementing their preferred sectoral policies. Institutions are the formal and informal rules that establish the behavior of administration and are distinguished here from "organizations," which refer to the way government is structured (Peterson, 2015: 26). The emphasis just a few decades ago was on simply finding tried and tested policies to achieve intended results, bringing to mind such examples as the Washington Consensus of the 1980s (noted in the preface), to stabilize, privatize, and liberalize (*Economist*, 2013h: 72). In fact, one can identify a list of priority strategic and operational policies that have improved results around the world in sectoral areas such as public financial management, education, urban transport, and health care. But in most cases, the transferability of their lessons has been restricted by institutional contexts that profoundly affect policy design and implementation. Institutional obstacles are clear to field observers and must be recognized before any best practices are adopted. Nevertheless, the policies and their successful results in particular countries can be used as sound models and benchmarks. In short, comprehensive analysis to generate options and preferred solutions should include the institutional context before implementation to maximize results.

For example, crime in Central and Latin America has been a serious persistent problem for many decades. Honduras is the region's most violent country with the highest murder rate/capita in the world. Analysts focus attention on various causal factors such as demography (surge in uneducated young men), income inequality, criminal mafias and gangs linked to drugs, and the external demand for cocaine that strengthens the mafias. But none are as important as the institutional factors: weak rule of law—police, courts, prosecutors, and prisons. While the global rate for homicide convictions is 43 for every 100 murders, the Latin American rate is 20 (*Economist*, 2014c: 31). A focus on institutions can identify actionable causes and practical policy solutions that work elsewhere in the regions, such as in Colombia. Institutions and the economics of institutions, i.e. costs, operating rules, and management controls/discretion, are critical variables. While other factors are important, in most cases, it is the institutional systems that really cause and perpetuate such problems as regional crime here.

"Institutions" then are the formal norms, informal rules, and internal processes that shape organizational behavior. Examples include the NATO member commitment (or norm) of spending at least 2 percent of GDP on defense and modern equipment, and decision rules requiring consensus by its 28 members to take military action to enforce its Article 5 pillar: an attack on one member is an attack on all. When discussing appropriate policy frameworks, the critical sub-components are (a) legal and regulatory and (b) institutional, or local capacity to undertake technical tasks such as designing and implementing programs, projects, and services. It is thus important to narrow the "institutional" concept down, as it is otherwise too broad (Warner, 2013: 24). Unless narrowed, *institutions* could mean (and has been erroneously used) anything from inadequately enforced laws to lax administration and poor economic policies. That leads to ambiguous and potentially erroneous policy advice. A useful approach is to view institutions as the incentive structure for organizational and individual behavior in the form of rules and procedures. Whether formal or informal, these procedures are not neutral in their effects. In addition to the normative effects of rules and procedures through different layers of government and between ministries and departments, there are informal management disincentives that work against improving policy results. For instance, officials are often less interested in causal analyses and policy options to avoid future problems than in protecting themselves from legal prosecution now (Ignatius, 2013). In addition, bureaucratic departments and agencies have every incentive to increase rule complexity (e.g. via licensing and permitting procedures) and transaction costs (e.g. add more approval steps) (Niskanen, 1971; Downs, 1967). These perverse incentives weaken policy performance by breaking the chain of accountability between principals and agents (those highest in rank and responsibility versus those acting on the principal's behalf). The institutional solution is to try and reduce perverse incentives and to decrease information asymmetry, for instance, by using performance reporting and contracting to eliminate asymmetries in education between teachers, parents, and school administrators. Transfer of lessons on how to do this from other jurisdictions can and has improved policy results.

Two kinds of institutions generate incentives that affect policy implementation and the transfer of lessons from one setting to another: macro and micro. Macro-institutions include the constitutions and organic laws that set up national and sub-national governing rules. They set the framework for formulating policies and budgets and affect the course of policies implemented by the civil service. Macro-institutional frameworks do this through such actions as issuance of regulatory and judicial decrees; determination of whether the system will remain unitary or federalist; and, of course, establishing the degree to which the civil code or common law practices shall guide public policy and management decisions. In that these rules are rarely changed in the short run, their incentive effects must be gauged before policies are transferred. Many of these practices are seemingly immutable, baked into the local culture, and run counter to Western values central to devolution: transparency, accountability, due process, and majority participation in public decisions. Local parties and elite groups often oppose such Western "modern" institutional values as "imperialistic" and "imposed outsider" values to those that prevail locally. Unsurprisingly, debates over macro-institutional rules generate intense political conflict. In most countries, quid pro quos and bargains are made within relatively stable macro-rule frameworks. For instance, France has been making attempts at structural reforms of its labor and regulatory systems in order to gain leeway from the EU over its failure to reach the common budget deficit target of 3 percent (the French budget deficit was 3.8 percent in 2014). The point here is that form follows structure. If one wants to change incentives and wider policy results, the need is to change the way power is organized through such mechanisms as labor and regulatory systems. Official plans, public pronouncements, and cosmetic changes often through informational IT websites smack of "form." They do not drill down into the structures of real power that produce the incentives and disincentives.

At the micro level, institutions mean the formal and informal rules, the administrative management systems (e.g. personnel, budgeting, procurement) and incentive structures (e.g. tax codes, assignments of intergovernmental functions), that shape the behavior of organizations and individuals (North, 1990; Burki and Perry, 1998: 11). It is our contention that, often constraining effective policy implementation, such behaviors can be modified with the right incentives. For example, in Uganda, enforcing "readiness criteria" through performance agreements has encouraged and improved the reporting of health and education expenditures at the local level and produced a 60 percent increase in social expenditures reaching clients. It is not unusual that incremental changes in simple core reporting system rules can produce sustained modification of institutional practices. Cochrane (1983: 5) found paradoxically that some of the most authoritarian, centralized, and closed regimes guarding power jealously also promoted local government reform with reasonably effective management incentives (e.g. Nigeria and Pakistan).

An important lever for changing institutions, or linking macro- and micro-institutions for sustainable change, is to try and change the political culture (treating it properly as an independent variable that will in turn change institutional behavior). This is easier said than done at the macro level. For decades, the growing penetration of the Egyptian army into the state and economy has distorted the functioning of macro-institutions which has weakened both democracy-building and development efforts.

> Since the 1990s, more than half the regional governors have been drawn from the army. Meanwhile, buoyed by a privatization program, the officer corps captured large chunks of the economy. This provided post-retirement careers and financial security for them. Today tax holdings amount to a massive business empire. The officer corps generates income that bypasses public scrutiny and range from defense manufacturing to consumer goods. Army-owned firms dominate the markets for water, olive oil, cement, construction, hotels and petrol. Estimates of their size vary from 8 percent to as much as 40 percent of

GDP. Army families live in a parallel universe. They mainly live in separate military cities and go to shops, buy fuel at petrol stations and socialize in clubs run by the army. How sure can they be of hanging on to such privileges? The army relies on support from the civilians who are willing to govern alongside it in the "populist" regime. Without them, the impression of outright military rule would be overwhelming.

(*Economist*, 2013i: 39)

Such institutional distortions are similar in Pakistan and Turkey, but at least the latter has a long history of state and nation-building.

While macro-cultures are hard to change, at the micro- or operational level as noted, they can be changed more quickly. For example, conditional cash incentives programs in Brazil, Mexico, Peru, and other countries have changed family behavior and resulted in improved health care and school attendance for children. These incentives reduce micro-cultural constraints to behavior and improve social policy results. But changing internal institutional routines from the outside is difficult. Overseas aid projects last for years and accomplish often much less than planned. To achieve results, such projects have to involve a mix of: "refereeing, policing, coaching, incentivizing, arm-twisting and modeling" (Friedman, 2013). The problem is that outside influences on internal governance to sustain positive change require time (which aid donors cannot pay for) and more importantly that "the people themselves want to take charge of the process" (Friedman, 2013). The latter requires sound governing institutions which is often the problem in the first place!

3. Policy Design and Financing

The literature on the design of institutions indicates the importance of getting incentives right and taking into account cultural values (North, 1990: 137–138). But very little has been written on options for getting the technical sequence and financing options right for actual transfer of policy lessons. Successful international policy analysis and transfer of lessons across borders requires, in some cases, creating new institutions and building on existing practices with support from regimes and intermediary organizations. The design and financing issues are critical to success. It raises the questions of

1   Have designs been consistent with more successful policies in similar contexts?
2   How does the sequencing of policies in the target country compare with those in similar country contexts?
3   What financing methods were used, e.g. performance formula transfers, capital markets, budget financing?
4   What difference did the design, implementation sequence, and financing make to results?

Data problems exist in answering the third question in that often more than one policy or program step is being implemented in each stage and within each step. That leads to differences in the scope and intensity of activities. Even if data exists on the messy problem of multiple policy implementations, it would be hard to convert it into useful information for decision-making. That will affect design and therefore results. To provide fully reliable policy lessons, more precise data and applied research is required in these areas.

Regimes that effectively respond with top level support and appropriate institutional incentives by attempting to convert deeper problems into shorter-term issues are ready to follow the path of countries that achieved successful policy results. In the case of fiscal devolution policy, based on differences in technical sequencing and financing by the Philippines, Pakistan, and Indonesia, one study found that the Philippines had the most successful policy results and that lessons could be transferred and adopted by the other two regimes with high likelihood of successful influence (Guess, 2005). Following the Philippines, the other two regimes had to (1) rely on substantial international inputs for the development of their legal and regulatory frameworks, (2) use innovative capacity-building exercises and institutions, (3) provide incentives for monitoring-evaluation of the devolution program, (4) provide sufficient local fiscal autonomy, (5) increase efforts to streamline local government operations, and (6) replace input budgeting and legalistic management with systems driven by performance incentives and targets. In short, those comparable regimes following this sequence for their fiscal devolution policies were more likely to be successful than those which did not, illustrated by Pakistan and Indonesia at the time. Since 2005, the failure of the state and the onset of major security problems in Pakistan have eliminated the necessary background support for successful transfer of policy lessons to that country.

c. Comparative Analysis

Nearly 45 years ago, Holt and Turner (1970: 5) called for more cross-cultural research for theory-building. In this vein, Fred Riggs focused on comparison of "whole political systems" for this task, by which he meant government structures and their functions (1970: 80). But for purposes of public policy, Holt and Richardson (1970: 39) called for less macro-theory building and more emphasis on generation of middle-range propositions. While they meant bureaucracy and public administration, it was clear to them that cultural and institutional variables were needed to explain success and failure at the middle range in functional or sectoral policy areas. Our second level *political economy* framework focuses on explaining differences in policy results in order to generate transferable lessons. But comparable contexts are required for successful transfer and that is the job of the *comparative* framework or method. For, in the context of public financial management (or PFM), Allen et al. (2013: 4) note that:

> While countries can benefit from comparing their own PFM practices with those of their neighbors and peers, the simplistic transfer of legal frameworks or systems from one country to another without taking account of differing systems of governance and levels of capacity, is unlikely to yield positive results. In many countries, where the rule of law has not been fully established, informal rules of behavior are more important than formal laws and regulations in determining how well a new public finance law, say, or a fiscal rule will work in practice.

Thus, setting is important, and it is critical that comparable settings be targeted for lessons transfer. Not infrequently, results are compared in particular functional policy areas from incomparable contexts (Ashford, 1978: 82). The applicability of lessons drawn from such exercises is severely weakened by lack of a rigorous methodology. For example, Parkhurst et al. (2005) compared maternal care systems in four countries: South Africa, Russia, Uganda, and Bangladesh. Based on a review of system performances they proposed changes in the human resource structure and the mix of private-public service delivery. There were at least two methodological problems with this study. First, they concluded that country context determined the outputs and outcomes. But, it was not made clear which features of context explained target country system differences. Second, they found performance differences among the four country systems. But it was not made clear which contextual or institutional elements in the four countries accounted for the performance differences. In short, the researchers did not identify at the outset the similar features that made these maternal health delivery systems comparable.

For the third level of analysis, which seeks where and how to adapt policy lessons in different settings, we offer a simple comparative methodology. Applications should facilitate the transfer of systems, methods, and tools from one country, region, or city to another for particular policies. Called the *matched-case* method, it was skillfully employed by Xavier (1998) to compare public finance reforms in two Commonwealth countries: Australia and Malaysia. Using a two-step approach, he first searched for countries with similar institutional or governmental structures and reform programs. The countries there were similar in region (South Asia), size (population), governance (common law and parliamentary systems), and culture (Commonwealth). Second, he focused on explaining the differences in budget reform performance. Matching the cases first kept constant or controlled for other rival effects on budget reform policy. By this approach, differences in budget reform policy results were attributable with greater confidence to the immediate target: the actual PFM systems and policies and not the broader contextual features that would likely turn up if one had compared dissimilar contexts.

The matched-case approach might be termed *quasi-experimental policy evaluation.* That is, the Xavier method tried to ensure that the treatment and control groups were similar. That would mean that there is a greater likelihood that performance differences between two or more groups were being influenced by internal characteristics (e.g. program design) rather than external features. That is, the comparative method controls for rival explanations to explain budget reform. Xavier found that, in Malaysia, there were no formal or informal fiscal rules to act as incentives for budget reform. He concluded that lack of the right institutional incentives largely explained the performance differences. With greater confidence, he could then propose that Malaysia re-design its rules similar to Australia and the reform should work. The method allowed focus on the different ways of achieving budget reform and found that one didn't work as well. With similar cultural and institutional contexts established, policy-makers could change the rules with greater confidence than if the controls were not part of the methodology.

Application of Frameworks

For illustrative purposes, here we apply the three levels of analysis (*Figure 1.4*) to indicate how one or more of these variables can explain policy success or failure. They can be refined with more data and information on the relevance and operation of each variable to the important issue of primary/secondary level educational policy reform.

Many have noted that differences in the performance of educational policy reforms in the U.S. and Northern Europe versus Latin America can be explained by design of incentives and differences in response to the strong entrenched political power of teacher and school unions. Along with conditional cash transfers, education policy reform has occurred worldwide with many documented policy cases of measured results to explain and compare. Where reformers devolve authority to school administrations, provide conditional performance transfers (e.g. based on student scores, student progress, teacher performance, and classroom contact hours) for financing, enforce minimum performance norms, offer flexible teacher contracts with higher pay levels, and encourage competition from non-state schools (e.g. charter schools in the U.S. and academies in the UK), the results have been positive for students. It is also

1. Technical	**Determination** of empirical, statistical, and econometric relations between policy inputs, outputs, and outcomes (What is happening?)
2. Political Economy	**Explanation** of policy results using core variables of culture, institutions, incentives, regimes, financing, and political dynamics (How? Why?)
3. Comparative Method	**Applicability** of lessons to similar contexts (Where transferable?)

Figure 1.4 Analytic Stages and Frameworks

clear that reformers in many cases must mobilize support for student learning objectives to overcome the entrenched school union power that often obstructs reforms and maintains existing structures. These administrative and political structures often ignore both student and teacher performance and concentrate on the more routine input-driven workload of traditional grading and teacher tenure and promotion reviews. U.S. reforms at the city level demonstrate these trends, and also that where the incentives and political power exist, the reforms have been largely successful (e.g. New York and Washington, DC).

The third analytic stage or framework applies the comparative method to evaluate the applicability of lessons to other similar contexts. Here, similar educational policy changes have led to similar results in: Canada, Finland, and other European countries at the national and local levels. Macro-institutional reforms in greater devolution of fiscal and management authority to school levels and the availability of incentive-based financing have combined to improve student and school performance. Where these comparative policy ingredients are missing, e.g. many Latin American countries, the results have been disappointing. Chile has used them to achieve positive results; more recent changes in Mexico to implement the reform model and weaken union power over teacher activities have yielded positive performance results. Without these ingredients, successful transfer of choice, competition, and account-ability reforms from the mainly OECD countries cannot occur in particular Latin American countries suffering from enfeebled school systems.

Case 1.1 Culture and Institutions in British Health Care Policy

Source: *Economist*, 2013j: 61

The first thing Polish immigrants brought to Britain when the country opened its doors to Eastern European workers in 2004 was an admirable work ethic. Farm managers told stories about farm laborers picking cabbages at night, by the light of car headlamps. Then Polish delicatessens began to appear, selling herring and pierogi; then came Polish solicitors. But the Poles' most intriguing import, and the one that ought to cause native Britons to think hardest, is medical care.

Hard by the Hanger Lane gyratory, a busy eight-lane roundabout in west London is a quiet pioneer. The My Medyk clinic opened in 2008 and now has 30,000 patients on its rolls. The firm has opened a second branch in London and wants to open a third. Rivals are multiplying. Most of these private clinics contain dentists, general practitioners (GPs), pediatricians and gynecologists. They have pulled off the remarkable feat of selling medical care to working and middle class families who could get it for nothing.

The National Health Service (NHS) dominates British health care. Although private companies supply equipment, drugs and ancillary services and, increasingly carry out medical care under contract, patients rarely enter into commercial relationships with them. Private health care is sold as a luxury for the affluent and usually only covers hospital treatment, not primary care—that is visits to a doctor.

It is British primary care, however, that many Poles find wanting. Some prefer to see Polish-speaking doctors, although many who use primary clinics speak excellent English. More simply want better service than British GPs tend to provide, with their brief consultation and frustrating systems for booking appointments. And the immigrants are used to a different set-up. In Poland, as much as in continental Europe, GPs do not act as gatekeepers. Patients book appointments directly with specialists, who also perform procedures that would be classed as out-patient services in Britain.

"There was a gap in the market", explains Radek Przpys, manager of the Hanger Lane outfit. The clinics charge fixed fees, which are published on their websites, for consultations and treatments. This means that they rely on regular customers for revenue, and need to treat them well if they are to retain them. The clinics often invest in imaging and diagnostic equipment such as ultrasound scanners (a 3D pregnancy test cost L95 or $146). This is a booming business: more children in Britain are now born to Polish women than to women from any other foreign country.

The clinics hope to expand by offering major procedures at private hospitals in Poland. They also believe that they can convince Britons of ordinary means to pay for regular check-ups—something that is currently a lifestyle product aimed at the affluent. In short, they aim to improve British health care, doing to the medical market what Polish farm laborers did to England's fields. They may not succeed—but it is an attempt worth watching.

Questions

1   As discussed in this chapter, how, specifically, does political culture intervene between policy design and results?
2   How can state systems such as the NHS work through local institutions and culture to improve delivery of health care policy?
3   How can policy systems (such as health care) be designed to serve the multiple cultures which exist within most modern states?
4   Trace the two-way flow of lessons for managers and policy-makers from this case.

References

Allen, Richard, Richard Hemming, and Barry H. Potter (eds.) (2013) *The International Handbook of Public Financial Management* (New York: Palgrave Macmillan).

Ashford, Douglas E. (ed.) (1978) *Comparing Public Policies: New Concepts and Methods* (Beverly Hills, CA: Sage).

Burki, Shahid J. and Guillermo E. Perry (eds.) (1998) *Beyond the Washington Consensus: Institutions Matter* (Washington, DC: World Bank).

Chua, Amy and Jed Rubenfeld, "What Drives Success?" *New York Times*, January 26, 2014, pp. SR1, 6.

Cochrane, Glynn, "Policies for Strengthening Local Government in Developing Countries," World Bank staff working paper #582, 1983, World Bank, Washington, DC.

Downs, Anthony (1967) *An Economic Theory of Democracy* (New York: Harper and Row).

Economist (2013) "Conflict's Harvest," October 26, p. 45.

Economist (2013a) "Slipping," August 24, p. 37.

Economist (2013b) "The Euro Crisis: Debtor's Prison," October 26, p. 79.

Economist (2013c) "Stories of Zealotry," August 31, p. 72.

Economist (2013d) "Cold Climate," August 31, p. 43.

Economist (2013e) "Chasing the Dream," August 24, p. 11.

Economist (2013f) "Stubborn Facts on the Ground," April 20, p. 46.

Economist (2013g) "Training Day," June 22, p. 60.

Economist (2013h) "Going for Growth," July 13, p. 72.

Economist (2013i) "Ambitious Men in Uniform," August 3, p. 39.

Economist (2013j) "Another Kind of Health Tourism," June 8, p. 61.

Economist (2014) "Unbundling the Nation State," February 8, pp. 58–59.

Economist (2014a) "Waves of Problems," March 8, p. 76.

Economist (2014b) "The Opposite of Insurance," May 17, p. 71

Economist (2014c) "A Broken System," July 12, pp. 31–33.

Economist (2014d) "Trillion Dollar Boo-Boo," July 26, p. 57.

Economist (2014e) "You Kant Do That," September 13, pp. 60–61.

Economist (2015) "Unnatural Aristocrats," September 5, p. 50.

Economist (2015a) "Randomized Control Trials: In Praise of Human Guinea Pigs," December 12, p. 18.

Follett, Ken (2014) *Edge of Eternity* (London: Pan Books).

Friedman, Thomas L., "Foreign Policy by Whisper and Nudge," *New York Times*, August 23, 2013, p. D1.

Guess, George M., "Centralization of Expenditure Controls in Latin America," *Public Administration Quarterly*, 16, 3 (Fall 1992): 376–394.

Guess, George M., "Decentralization and Municipal Budgeting in Four Balkan States," *Journal of Public Budgeting, Accounting and Financial Management*, 13, 3 (September 2001): 397–436.

Guess, George M., "Comparative Decentralization Lessons from Pakistan, Indonesia and the Philippines," *Public Administration Review*, 65, 2 (March/April 2005): 217–231.

Halsey, Ashley, III, "Communications Comment Prompts Memories of 1999 Crash," *Washington Post*, July 9, 2013, p. A12.

Holt, Robert and John M. Richardson, "Competing Paradigms in Comparative Politics," in *The Methodology of Comparative Research*, Robert T. Holt and John E. Turner, eds., New York: The Free Press, 1970: 21–73.

Holt, Robert T. and John E. Turner (eds.) (1970) *The Methodology of Comparative Research* (New York: The Free Press).

Ignatius, David, "An Email Trail of Dysfunction," *Washington Post,* March 8, 2013, p. A23.

Inglehart, Ronald, "The Renaissance of Political Culture," *American Political Science Review*, 82, 4 (December 1988): 1203–1231.

Key, V. O., "The Lack of a Budgetary Theory," *American Political Science Review* (December 1940): 11–37.

Krasner, Steven D., "America Self-Contained," *The American Interest*, IX, 5 (May/June 2014): 41–44.

Linz, Juan J. and Alfred Stepan (1996) *Problems of Democratic Transition and Consolidation: America and Post-Communist Europe* (Baltimore: Johns Hopkins University Press).

Mankiw, N. Gregory, "When the Scientist Is Also a Philosopher," *New York Times*, March 23, 2014, p. 4.

Marmor, Theodore R. (2000) *The Politics of Medicare*, 2nd ed. (New York: Aldine de Gruyter).

Mikesell, John L. (2011) *Fiscal Administration, Analysis and Applications for the Public Sector*, 8th ed. (Boston: Wadsworth Cengage).

Niskanen, William A. (1971) *Bureaucracy and Representative Government* (Chicago: Aldine).

North, Douglas C. (1990) *Institutions, Institutional Change and Economic Performance* (New York: Cambridge University Press).

Parkhurst, J. O., Loveday Penn-Kekana, Duane Blaauw, Dina Balabanova, Kirill Danishevski, Syed Azizur Rahman, Virgil Onama, and Freddie Ssengooba, "Health Systems Factors Influencing Maternal Health Services: A Four-Country Comparison," *Health Policy*, 73, 2 (August 2005): 127–138.

Peterson, Stephen B. (2015) *Public Finance and Economic Growth in Developing Countries: Lessons from Ethiopia's Reforms* (New York: Routledge).

Pressman, Jeffrey L. and Aaron Wildavsky (1984) *Implementation*, 3rd ed. (Berkeley: University of California Press).

Ramirez-Djumena, Natalie, "Moving On Up," *Finance and Development*, 51, 4 (December 2014): 42–43.

Riggs, Fred W. "The Comparison of Whole Political Systems," in *The Methodology of Comparative Research*, Robert T. Holt and John E. Turner, eds., New York: The Free Press, 1970: 73–123.

Schiavo-Campo, Salvatore and David Tommasi (1999) *Managing Government Expenditure* (Manila: Asian Development Bank).

Strachota, Dennis (1994) *The Best of Government Budgeting: A Guide to Preparing Budget Documents* (Chicago: Government Finance Officers Association).

Sunstein, Cass R., "Making Government Logical," *New York Times*, September 9, 2015, p. 9.

Warner, Andrew, "The Elusive Revival," *Finance and Development*, 50, 3 (September 2013): 24.

Wright, Glen and Juraj Nemec (eds.) (2002) *Public Management in the Central and Eastern Transition: Concepts and Cases*, 33, 1: 20–21 (Bratislava: NISPAcee Press).

Xavier, J. A., "Budget Reform in Malaysia and Australia Compared," *Public Budgeting and Finance*, 18, 1 (March 1998): 99–118.

2   Macroeconomic and Fiscal Policies

Introduction

Fiscal policy is important for our purposes in that it provides financing for the other key sectors covered in this book. To the extent it cannot do that, in addition to contributing to weak economic growth, users of basic services and programs suffer. Macroeconomic instability at minimum results in unreliable service, program, and project delivery. At the strategic level, macroeconomic instabilities are evident in phenomena such as deflation, hyperinflation, deep recessions, high unemployment, low investment, greater poverty, and income inequality, all of which produce severe economic losses. The sources of instability are typically the large fiscal deficits and mostly public debts often derived from ill-designed fiscal policies. The annual budget deficit is termed the *public sector borrowing requirement* in Commonwealth countries. It correctly indicates the borrowing necessary to finance the excess of expenditures over revenues but provides no guidance on its sustainability given macroeconomic requirements over the medium term. For, deficits or not, sufficient public spending is needed to maintain aggregate demand in recessionary contexts where private consumption and investment are weak. There are limits beyond which the growth payoff from additional spending can be undone by the damage to consumption and investment done from additional (or poorly designed) taxation to maintain budgetary balance. Taxes have to be designed to minimize distortions to the economic incentives of firms, investors, and consumers. Beyond this limit, norms of tax policy design and fiscal discipline are violated, leading to unsustainable fiscal deficits and public debts.

This chapter explains some of the complex relationships between fiscal policy and macroeconomic aggregates such as inflation and unemployment. It provides examples of fiscal discipline problems and policy responses in particular countries. It notes the particular problem of trying to achieve growth in the context of severe structural constraints in countries such as Italy. The relation between fiscal policies and macroeconomic impact is complex, and country context usually determines the precise outcome. Nevertheless, much can be learned from comparative policy designs and their impacts for similar countries contexts in similar predicaments. As will be noted, much more needs to be learned at both the strategic policy and operational technical levels. Relationships between policy inputs, outputs, and outcomes are not straightforward and require further empirical refinement. The chapter also provides examples of fiscal management tools, such as budget formats, problem-definition methods, statistical analysis techniques, medium-term expenditure frameworks (MTEFs), and fiscal rules, which have been used to try and ensure that fiscal policies attain macroeconomic stability.

Central governments have three traditional functions: (1) macroeconomic stabilization, (2) efficiently allocating societal resources, and (3) altering the distribution of resources

(Musgrave, 1959). Strong, professional central governments, whose policy decisions affect the welfare of the entire nation, are absolutely necessary to perform these functions. Stable, predictable employment levels, lower inflation rates, accurate demand and growth estimates, and effective fiscal policies are needed by investors, consumers, and governments. Stabilization policy refers to the role of governments in maintaining employment, price stability, and economic growth through fiscal and monetary policy (Fisher, 2007: 25). Instability in any of these variables affects the others in largely predictable ways. For instance, weak consumer demand for goods and services, reluctance of banks to lend, and hesitance of investors to borrow for investments means slow economic growth. Failure of government to step in and increase purchases and investments, either through greater deficit spending or increasing tax revenues, will often perpetuate weak growth.

Governments around the world face these problems and dilemmas regularly. In the U.S., the major recent fiscal policy decision point was the Great Recession of 2007–2009 (Mikesell, 2014: 12). Decisions had to be made quickly at the central level by sector, intergovernmental level on transfers, grants, and subsidies, and at the subnational level on basic service delivery to respond to that crisis and prevent it from wider damage. Under normal circumstances, at the subnational level, revenue instability often caused by low collection rates and inadequate tax rates and bases can lead to unpredictable cutbacks in services, programs, and capital projects. At the national and subnational levels around the globe, cuts (and in some cases such as defense, additions) are made to programs covered in the following chapters, such as urban transport, health, and education without serious analyses of the costs and consequences. Such cutback decisions can temporarily stabilize the public finances but often weaken national growth and future tax collections that could stabilize finances more permanently. The predicament for many countries is that such cutbacks deal with macroeconomic problems but lead to major social and political instabilities.

Thus, this chapter will: (1) review the major sources of macroeconomic instability and suggest how they interact, (2) indicate the fiscal policy tools and analytic methods available and in use to deal with these instabilities, (3) review the structure and financing of policies by selected governments, (4) explain the differences in results from policy responses by referring to the frameworks in *Chapter 1*, (5) draw lessons for policy and operations management, and (6) present *Case 2.1: Slugovia Medium-Term Expenditure Framework* and other exercises for analysis.

Global Problems: Sources of Macroeconomic Instability

Macroeconomic stability depends directly or indirectly on governmental policies. Policies as noted in the first chapter are actions in the form of laws, regulations, and executive orders that authorize programs, projects, and services, and often require financing from one or more sources. Since the national budget is a reflection of what government does or does not do, fiscal policy should be the central focus of actions to improve employment, stimulate growth, minimize inflation, and control any subnational fiscal activities that would threaten macroeconomic stability. Fiscal policy (expenditure and revenue sub-policies) is a core measure and determinant of fiscal condition. The velocity of economic impact for tax cuts and increases on consumption and investment is very high; loan guarantees also work quickly to stimulate economic activity; expenditure increases (such as stimulus programs) work more slowly; and intergovernmental fiscal transfers can work almost immediately to stabilize incomes and employment. Often country adjustments to fix macroeconomic problems must be broader than only fiscal policy and may include structural issues such as public sector efficiency, private sector regulation of wages and prices, and labor markets as well. Fiscal condition is measured and monitored regularly by such organizations as the IMF, the World Bank, and NGOs such as the International Budget Program for fiscal transparency.

The need for other than purely fiscal measures is evident from the frequent spread between fiscal and broader country risk dimensions. For example, in slow-growth Japan (1.2 percent), the budget deficit is -8.1 percent of GDP, and its debt in 2013 was about 240 percent of GDP. Yet yields on Japanese bonds are low (10-year bond interest at 0.60 percent). For such reasons, credit rating agencies such as Moody's, Fitch, and Standard and Poor's measure broader fiscal conditions that include fiscal policies. The broader measures reflect international market investor judgments which, in this case, deem Japan a solid operation with minimal risk of debt service payment delay or default. Unemployment there is low at 3.6 percent and most of its debt is held by locals. The markets view India differently. High-growth India (6.0 percent) also has a relatively high fiscal deficit of -5.1 percent, relatively high debt of 67.6 percent, and high unemployment of 9.9 percent. Its sovereign bonds yield 7.73 percent, which indicates a much higher risk and high borrowing costs that could choke off future growth. And one would expect Chile, with a low budget deficit of -1.2 percent GDP, high growth, and small debt (11.4 percent of GDP), to have a high rating. In fact, it is investment grade but dependent on one commodity for much of its GDP (copper), which if international prices drop further could threaten growth and macroeconomic stability in the future. Thus, its bonds yield 5.5 percent, indicating acceptable risk instruments for which there are many buyers (*Economist*, 2013: 88).

Public Sector: Size and Efficiency

An ongoing debate in many countries is whether the size of government is too large or small as reflected, for instance, in deficits, debt, percentages of GDP expenditures, and over-regulation. The size-of-government debate is over-simplified and distractive for our purposes; the questions should be deepened to whether taxation, expenditure, monetary, and regulatory policies are smart (encourage the right incentives), and whether governments are strong enough to design and implement policies that achieve full national coverage. Governments have the full range of fiscal and monetary tools at their disposal: laws, regulations, executive orders, tax rates, bases and exemptions, interest rates, bank capital requirements, due diligence requirements for credit, direct budget expenditures, expenditure subsidies, intergovernmental fiscal transfers (or grants), loan guarantees, public investments, and temporary or permanent nationalizations. Each one of these policy tools can contribute to stimulation of growth, employment, and incomes. Distortions in their design, analysis, and implementation can occur from structural or "supply side" variables, such as inflexible labor markets buttressed by laws that favor powerful labor unions, subsidies for special industries and associations, and permanent benefits targeted to special interests such as the health sector, e.g. insurance, physicians, hospital, and retiree pressure groups. These "supply side" or structural problems can distort tax laws and expenditure patterns to favor their narrower interests often at national expense, resulting in unsustainable fiscal deficits and debt levels. They often require deregulation or at least smarter regulation efforts. Note again that the velocity of structural reforms is quite low while that of tax reforms is high. For that reason, structural reforms are considered medium- or longer-term policy options in most countries.

Unemployment and Poverty

Unemployment and low income are major sources of current instability in most parts of the world. This leads to more social and political unrest and exacerbates poverty problems. Unemployment occurs when one or more of the four sectors are not paying people to perform work: (a) the private sector, which is the main engine of goods and services production; (b) the public sector, including state enterprises (e.g. railroads, water-sewer, utilities, and banks) and majority state-owned private firms (such as hedge funds and construction firms, especially in China) which both sell goods and provide services; (c) the non-profit sector, which provides services but is financed by fees and contributions from the public and private sectors; and (d) the informal sector, which owes its existence to weak state and institutional coverage in the forms of perverse regulation of land and businesses and gaps in basic services (Singh et al., 2012: 52). Access to the formal sector in property rights protection, access to credit markets, and adequate labor standards is limited by weakness of state institutions to make and enforce rules throughout the entire country. Some countries have attempted to change the incentives that lead workers to stay in the informal sector. Mexico's recent tax reform proposal, for instance, includes a 10-year tax subsidy for companies that hire formal workers (*Economist*, 2015b: 30). A more cynical response by weak states is to capitalize on this defect by allowing their informal sector to employ or under-employ the many people needing jobs in the transitional and developing countries. The worst case is where state incapacity or unwillingness to provide national coverage of security and basic services creates a vacuum. Service coverage vacuums have spawned alternative service and security providers, such as vigilantes in Mexico, the Taliban in Pakistan, and mafias in Italy. In almost all cases, these alternative institutions compete for state legitimacy through illicit means such as corrupt and violent criminal extortion of populations. Failure of governments to budget sufficient funds for needed services and security often leads to the not uncommon international problem of failed states.

Failure to provide incentives to the private sector for hiring perpetuates the problem of financing the transfer-dependent poor from budgets and reduces employment chances for the less transfer-dependent who have some skills and plan to increase their self-sufficiency with jobs in the future. A major problem in Latin America, for example, is that 60 percent of the population lacks banking accounts (Demirguc-Kunt and Klapper, 2012: 42) and are therefore at the mercy of high-interest informal lenders; that 60 percent relies almost exclusively on inadequate social assistance payments for its sustenance. The severity of the unemployment problem as of early 2014 varies by region: in the European Union, the April 2014 average is 12 percent (Greece, 27.5 percent). Youth unemployment rates have reached 40 percent–50 percent in some countries such as Spain and 60 percent in Greece. Unemployment is also high in Central and Eastern Europe (around 10 percent), is lower in the U.S. (6.7 percent), but is much lower in Asian countries (only about 4 percent) (*Economist*, 2013: 88).

The causes of unemployment vary but are common to most regions. The three major ones are: (1) skills mismatched to jobs, (2) structural legal impediments, and (3) cultural practices. Schools in many countries are poorly funded with outdated curricula and schedules. Laws also favor full-time, often unionized labor, which locks in employers who suffer high personnel costs and find it hard to hire the right employees with the right skills or to fire those who do not perform. This is a major problem now in the EU. Laws also discourage youth from obtaining part-time work to learn new skills and to test out different jobs. Cultural practices such as caste quotas in India discourage members of particular castes (mostly the poorer classes) and women from obtaining employment (the unemployment rate there is about 10 percent).

Unemployment exacerbates poverty in removing income sources that reduce consumption. Reducing consumption or aggregate demand was considered by Keynes and modern economists as a problem constraining growth. Classical eighteenth-century economists viewed poverty as functional in providing cheap labor for growth and development. They identified savings as the constraint on growth, which meant that since the rich saved more than the poor, less poverty meant less growth. The modern and sensible view is that spending for health, education, and nutrition to help people break out of poverty will lead to greater consumption and growth (*Economist*, 2013a: 63). Programs such as conditional cash transfers (CCTs), e.g. Brazil's *Bolsa Familia*, that condition cash transfers on school attendance and health care vaccinations are based on the modern view that poverty needs to be eliminated and the poor should be converted to productive citizens, at least initially through a variety of public spending programs (see more on this in *Chapter 4*). The Brazilian transfers amount to 0.5 percent GDP annually and have lifted about 36 million Brazilians out of poverty. Moreover, unemployment benefits limited in duration and scope, unlike other economic stimuli, directly boost aggregate demand since they are mostly spent on consumer goods (*Economist*, 2014: 19).

Comparing social policy results requires common concepts and data before analytic methods can even be applied. The problem with international indices of poverty is that they exclude (or do not consistently include) the spending side which would raise consumption by the poor. Consumption is important since poverty is not simply the absence of money but also material well-being. In the U.S., for instance, an important question is how effective poverty spending has been in reducing rates and stabilizing the safety net. In 2011, the U.S. government spent $13,000 for every person below the $23,000 poverty line for a family of four. But the $588 billion (2012) aggregate figure for benefits understates overall related benefits for poor individuals provided by Medicare and Social Security, which also go to the non-poor. The point is that if public consumption spending is included, poverty rates will change. Including poverty-related consumption spending, the U.S. poverty rate of 15 percent would drop to 5 percent (Samuelson, 2014: A17).

Poverty in such countries as India dropped dramatically through public programs and growth. From 2004 to 2012, the poverty rate dropped from 37 percent to 22 percent. While GDP is normally used to measure living standards and poverty reduction, consumption may be a better measure. By this measure, poverty reduction has been dramatic from 2000–2013. By contrast, from 1980–2000, developing country growth was only 0.9 percent, and from 2000–2013, poverty grew to 4.3 percent. One study found that 66 percent of poverty reduction could be explained by economic growth and 33 percent by income inequality. Another study suggested that a 1-percent increase in incomes reduces poverty by 0.6 percent in the most unequal countries and by 4.3 percent in more equal ones (*Economist*, 2013b: 23). The remaining but soluble policy problem is the 1 billion poor in unequal countries that have persistently low consumption and have been beyond the reach of basic public services. In sub-Saharan Africa, average consumption for the poorest ($0.70/day) is about the same as 20 years ago.

The relation between poverty and income inequality is complex and to some extent context-dependent. That is, in some contexts income inequality may not be a constraint to poverty reduction. Societies that value merit, talent and work and provide commensurate rewards for them are probably going to remain unequal. Making the rich less so in these contexts through wealth redistribution programs may actually diminish growth without improving income equality, e.g. land reform policies which do not necessarily make the poor better off. In other contexts, wide income gaps actually constrain poverty reduction. The income gaps often reflect structural problems caused by skill deficiencies, growing levels of retirees, dearth of entry-level jobs for college graduates, and reduction of low-skill wages from global requirements for professionals in medicine, law, engineering, and media (Parker, 2014: A14). The structural problem often reflects wage and price inflexibility from poorly designed and intrusive regulation. While most governments spend substantial sums through such programs as conditional cash transfers and safety nets to reduce income gaps, this does not necessarily reduce income inequality—nor should it in most cases. Public policies can reduce income gaps through well-targeted programs with the right incentives. Health care and social assistance programs are two efforts that can contribute to income gap reduction by ensuring that most people work if jobs are available. But it is also clear that both income gaps and inequality are increased by extreme cuts to social safety net and unemployment programs. Countries with major successes in poverty-reduction, such as Brazil, Mexico, and China, provide lessons. Poverty reduction is possible with available comparative data, methods, and systems to identify, target, and distribute social assistance to the needy.

The relationship between income inequality and income growth is also complex. Some economists such as Thomas Piketty (2014) demonstrate that inequality is actually a constant in capitalist economies. Rates of returns to capital in rents, dividends, and profits have been about constant since the eighteenth century. Their study suggested that inequality is worsened by declining population growth and increasing technological innovations. They suggest that the drift toward oligarchy is an iron law of the free market system. The rich getting richer then is no mere throwaway line in the have-not lyric of resentment but a logical outcome of this system. Since this describes the context of the more advanced North American and European economies today, in order to mitigate inequality, they suggest that more redistributive tax and transfer policies will increasingly be needed in the future (*Economist*, 2014a: 60).

Growth and Demand

The U.S.-driven 2007–2009 worldwide recession was instructive because its effects have varied. In the U.S., collapse of the financial sector and property markets eliminated much of consumer savings and collateral, reducing their demand sharply for obvious reasons. Banking assets in money markets, mortgages, high-risk securitized instruments, and other receivables diminished in value and were unable to cover deposit liabilities (Dodd, 2012: 47). That meant that banks and other loan originators could not sell market-rate loans to either consumers or the private sector. So, investment levels dropped, decreasing the number of new jobs available and increasing unemployment—a vicious cycle. Beyond the U.S., growth was constrained in Europe and EU countries from mostly structural factors. For example, tax rates are still punitive in many countries. Italy has a 43 percent income tax rate and a 5 percent tax collection rate (meaning about 95 percent evade taxes). Hungary's flat rate 55 percent tax rate with no exemptions or deductions (meaning marginal and effective rates are the same) also impedes savings, investments, and legal tax-paying. Absence of efficient and vigorous revenue collection contributes to deficits and debts in these countries.

Inflation

Historically, increasing prices have been a major problem in Latin America and Europe, increasing poverty levels and trade deficits, while diminishing currency values, budgetary expenditure values, and growth. Currency values often change overnight, and state notes and bonds can be sold only at excessively high yields to compensate for risks. Continuing efforts by the IMF, international banks, and credit rating agencies to enforce fiscal transparency standards and to control fiscal deficits through tight conditions on loan repayment have produced stronger fiscal discipline and economic performance. In response, consumer price increases have been below 2 percent in the EU and U.S. for decades and few expect them to increase dramatically. Global sovereign bond yields, which are also predictors of short-term interest rates, are low: less than 2 percent in most countries. The major traditional fears that deficits and debt levels would crowd the private sector and lead to inflation have not materialized largely because firms and consumers have access to cheaper goods in global markets. If anything, low sovereign bond yields have also lowered corporate bond yields, meaning that their borrowing costs are low. Used for investment by corporations, these favorable conditions can at almost any time stimulate aggregate demand. Demand pull inflation (price increases from excess demand) has been held in check by recessionary fears and reactions to loss of savings in the last recession. Cost push inflation (price increases from excess costs of production) has been held down by lack of increases in major commodity prices such as food and fuel. Shale and natural gas production is serving as an alternative to dependence on oil consumption and is reducing that source of macroeconomic instability. With the exception of Central and Eastern Europe, there are few policy responses to inflation to be reported since it has not been a major recent problem. With sharper declines in most commodity prices from reduced Chinese growth in 2014–2015 and its corresponding demand from trading partners, the return of global inflation could be a problem in the next decade.

Subnational Governments

It is often argued that subnational governments in a federal system (also called federations) have limited effects on macroeconomic stability. Most countries in such systems have independent subnational units which in some cases have the authority to finance budgets with substantial own-source revenues and can borrow from banks or on capital markets, e.g. Canada, U.S., Australia, Poland, Mexico, China, and Germany. But states and municipalities have no independent monetary policies or central banks to influence prices and inter-state trade; there is thus no incentive for expansionary subnational fiscal policies since they would largely benefit other subnational jurisdictions. In addition, their aggregate fiscal position when in surplus assists national government financing of deficits and debts. Conversely, when there is a national recession, state and local authorities can increase spending or taxation to cover their deficit positions and to make up for loss of central grants (Fisher, 2007: 26). Fisher argues that the major role for subnational level governments is to allocate goods and services to make up for market failures (2007: 29). The chapters in this book cover sectoral activities (programs, services, and projects) that are planned, implemented, and financed by multiple levels of governments but often with subnational leadership and management.

A serious issue is the effect on consolidated fiscal positions of fiscal decentralization programs that devolve taxing, spending, and borrowing authority to subnational governments. In many transitional and developing countries, control over subnational expenditures, debts, and deficits can be difficult. In the 1980s, for example, Brazilian subnational governments borrowed with abandon from state banks, which seriously contributed to national macroeconomic instability. The well-known argument that fiscal decentralization increases efficiency by aligning the mixed preferences of citizens with governmental abilities to supply services applies mostly to advanced countries. In *Chapter 6* we provide additional discussion on how fiscal federalism can meet local needs by enhancing educational policy objectives. Transitional and unitary countries such as China and Russia have fewer preferences expressed through subnational governments (largely because governments are less responsive). The fear in unitary countries is high that subnational government can borrow and spend to the point of threatening overall stability. In such countries, the case for economic centralism is strong until institutional control mechanisms emerge (Bahl, 1995: 76). Countries with fiscal decentralization programs such as Pakistan, Indonesia, and the Philippines increased consolidated government expenditures by seconding substantial numbers of civil servants to subnational levels to fill gaps in their technical capacities. Rather than losing control over subnational finances, the decentralization programs unilaterally contributed to macroeconomic instability. In China, an ill-designed fiscal decentralization program that legally and formally forbids subnational borrowing but actually permits it in a variety of indirect ways, massive subnational government debts thus have been accumulated (up to 47 percent of GDP, *Economist,* 2015: 73) mainly in a form of contingent liabilities which are completely off-budget. Subnational debt finance is opaque and thus a serious fiduciary risk. In addition, issues of measuring the consolidated deficit remain and some argue that including subnational debts to banks for real estate developments and for city enterprise financing of infrastructure projects would greatly increase the reported level of fiscal deficit from 4 percent at present to about 6 percent–7 percent of GDP. It would also suggest that the subnational sector there is contributing to what many argue will be macroeconomic instability in the near future (Guess and Ma, 2015: 131).

National Fiscal Policies

Definitions

Fiscal and budget terminology cross-nationally is often confusing; even within countries, the same term can mean different things between levels of government. The UN Government Financial Statistics (GFS) system has attempted to develop common international nomenclature, classifications, and coverage of expenditure terms. The value of such efforts has been that institutions such as IMF and the World Bank have been able to set and enforce fiscal targets knowing that the country will measure revenues, expenditures, and other categories consistently. Thus, the deficits and fiscal positions of each country are measured with the same metrics and compared to GDP; exceptions are noted and qualified for each country. The most commonly used summary measure of *fiscal position* is the *cash deficit*: actual outlays less collected revenues plus external grants as measured in cash terms. Cash deficits are used because most governments consistently have them—not surpluses! In the UK, as noted, this is called the public sector borrowing requirement (PSBR). In the U.S., the Treasury uses this figure for financing, and the Office of Management and Budget (OMB), within the Executive Office of the President, uses it for managing cash flows throughout the year. The *primary balance* (deficit or surplus) is often applied to developing and transitional countries. In order to measure country adjustment efforts, such as for debt stabilization (which often requires a primary surplus), this measure subtracts out non-interest outlays and changes in exchange rates and interest rates (which are often beyond country control) from expenditures. Cash deficits are often converted into a primary surplus using this method, e.g. Greece was recently able to convert a -3.5 percent cash deficit into 2.9 percent GDP surplus.

For policy options and recommendations to be valid, they must be based on sound analyses and valid-reliable measurements. GFS efforts have helped in the measurement of budgetary classification and coverage. In the past, governments used budget gimmicks that could exclude many expenditures or include other revenues at will in order to reduce deficits artificially. As noted above, China is largely still able to do this with local government debts. Most budgets now are unified with separate accounts that can be consolidated to obtain the fiscal position in real time (i.e. via fiscal IT systems). For instance, the U.S. budget consists of four funds: total, federal funds, off-budget, and trust. These are used to distinguish spending and receipts that need to be kept separate for accounting purposes: *Total funds* include long-term capital expenditures and annual debt service to pay for them and other components of the debt. *Federal funds* categorize non-financial public enterprises such as Amtrak and the Postal Service to keep track of subsidies, revenues, and expenses. *Off-budget* expenditures include special pension and Social Security funds. *Trust funds* include the highway fund, which collects taxes to pay for highways and mass transit. The U.S. OMB publishes annual totals of loan guarantees (contingent liabilities for such items as student loans), monetized subsidies, and tax expenditures (revenue losses in the form of tax code exemptions and credits). Similar funding structures and publications accompany many country budgets to ensure fiscal transparency and to serve internal and post-audit functions.

Budgets are developed and approved according to charts of accounts consistent with GFS that allow analysts to make useful distinctions, e.g. mandatory versus discretionary spending (the U.S. budget consists of 62 percent mandatory spending mostly for entitlements and 31 percent discretionary spending for items like defense, environment, housing, and civil service). Budgets are also classified further to increase transparency into different formats. GFS describes the four common ones used around the world: object, function, organization, and program. All budget expenditures should be capable of being "cross-walked" across these categories, e.g. salary totals across all format categories; and environmental expenditures by objects, organizations, and programs.

Since the cash deficit is important to fiscal position, it is useful to distinguish the determinants of deficits that are internally and externally driven, e.g. urban transport and health needs and demand are internal, and defense and Social Security are driven by external overseas conflicts and involuntary demographics. That is, high fiscal deficit levels could be a serious direct contributor to inflation and unemployment. Or, they could be a symptom of crippled banks, deficient labor market structures such as high unit labor costs, and demographics such as declining fertility, which likely leads to fewer workers and reduced labor participation rates. For example, if "development" can be associated with low fertility and low mortality rates, continued high fertility rates can be associated with the high costs of increasing urbanization and population growth. These translate into social safety net, health, and spending on other needed services such as water-sewerage, schools, and urban transport investments. The "youth bulge" growth rates in most of middle Africa (between 5.0 percent–6.0 percent), which already has 78 percent of the total African population, will lead to more internally driven expenditures with continuing high pressures on fiscal deficits and debts (*Economist*, 2014f: 49). *Figure 2.1* indicates this interaction for the U.S. budget.

The most commonly used measure of *fiscal sustainability* is the *debt/GDP* ratio. Debts are the accumulated fiscal deficits carried forward. Excessively high debts suggest fiscal risks of debt service payments delays (arrears), defaults on principal amounts (e.g. Argentina in 2001 and 2012; Uruguay in 2002), or even repudiation of amounts owed (e.g. Argentina in 2004). It is important that measures and definitions be consistent for international comparison. *Publicly held debt* or consolidated gross public debt consists of accumulated budget deficits. In the U.S., debts from financial markets, including treasury bonds, are used to cover trust funds (e.g. Social Security) and to provide federal reserve financing. As noted in *Table 2.1*, U.S. debt by this measure was at its highest level during the financial crisis at 107.8 percent, running annual debt service payments to over 7.0 percent of total expenditures. Many consider the *net public debt* to be a better measure of creditworthiness since it subtracts governmental

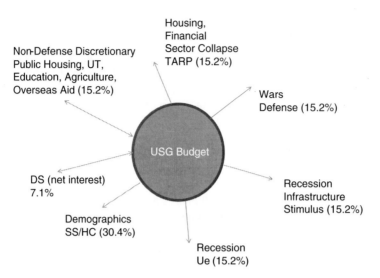

Figure 2.1 Internally v. Externally Driven Programs and U.S. Fiscal Deficits

asset values such as debts held by the public. By this measure, the U.S. debt would have been 73.3 percent of GDP. Such measures and figures raise the question of how much public debt is too much.

One answer is that it should be sustainable in relation to revenues and GDP. But policy-makers want to know if there is an absolute percent GDP figure that is too high. Reinhart and Rogoff once concluded that 90 percent was that figure until other researchers found they had produced skewed results. IMF suggested more recently that the trajectory of debt may be more important than its absolute level. This finding is based on studies indicating that rising public debt ratios are associated with slower growth than in those countries with falling public debt ratios—even if accrued borrowings are already high. In addition, rising private debt ratios also endanger growth (*Economist*, 2014e: 71). While the Portuguese public debt reached 130 percent of GDP in 2013, the loan to deposit ratio of private banks was 167 percent (*Economist*, 2014h: 75). As will be discussed further in *Chapter 5*, banks need to intermediate between borrowers and lenders. Depositors provide cash which become bank liabilities or payables that need to be paid back on demand. Borrowers, like firms, need funds to expand, but loans from banks cannot be so costly as to jeopardize depositors. A high loan/deposit ratio is an indicator of a weak financial position caused by private sector (not public) mismanagement and their high debt levels. The ratio reflects the need for external loans (e.g. from ECB) to cover major losses by the commercial banking system. For such reasons, fiscal policies need to be tailored to precise definitions of the problem—the link between deficits, debts, growth, and policy option results in comparative contexts.

The debt issue is also important in that the global trends are upward, which should pressure policy-makers to do something. How fast public debts increase will be a function of the external pressures noted plus the rates of economic growth and real interest rates (i.e. controlled for inflation). Doing nothing continues present trends and requires painful spending cuts or tax increases which may not be palatable if growth continues to be flat in many regions. The trends are: publicly held debt in the U.S. is growing four times faster than tax revenues and three times faster than countries which have undertaken austerity programs (e.g. UK, France, and Germany). Medicare and Social Security enrollees will grow from 44 million to 73 million by 2030, increasing those costs from 8.4 percent of GDP to 11.2 percent of GDP. This means with no policy changes, the U.S. debt would reach about 150 percent of GDP and debt service costs (from the current or operating budget), which would equal 11 percent–15 percent of total spending, crowding out even more discretionary programs.

In order to deal with the effects of deficits and debt, one must examine the cost drivers of each. Though the terms are often erroneously interchanged, *expenditures* are not equal to *costs*. Expenditures are measured in budgetary appropriations and reflect political pressures and procurement practices that may not purchase goods or services at least cost; costs refer to the consumption of goods and services reflecting market costs of production (Guess, 2015: 66). Cash expenditures are used to measure fiscal deficits in *Table 2.1*. For example, the U.S. spends about $2.7 trillion or 18 percent of GDP per year on health care, which has been growing at such a rate as to account for nearly all of GDP. They are the primary cause of long-term deficits. Though the rate of spending on health care has leveled off since late 2013, it is still driven to a large extent by inflated prices charged to Medicare/Medicaid and patients from hospitals, medical device makers, and physicians which often favor the most costly options (Rosenthal, 2013: 6A) (see *Chapter 4*). By contrast, expenditures are based on these unregulated and inflated costs. The distinction is important because about 30.4 percent of U.S. annual government spending is for health care, Social Security, and assistance entitlements. Expenditures are also increasing for new coverage applicants (Affordable Health Care Act) and deficits in pension funds must be covered at all levels of government from the current budget adding more pressure on the public finances. Still, the bulk of health care costs have increased from lack of strong institutional controls over prices and practices.

In the U.S., Medicare allows separate facility fees to be added where physician practices have been bought by hospitals. This means that laser eye surgery at a doctor's office, for instance, is almost twice as expensive as a procedure done at a hospital outpatient department. A simple site-neutral policy would save about $1 billion per year in health care costs and about $250 million per year in senior out-of-pocket costs (or expenditures). The power lies with the medical hospital lobby (American Health Association), which seeks to spread the high fixed costs of treatment in hospitals over patients. Cost-control institutions such as MedPAC have been largely unsuccessful in reducing these obvious cost inefficiencies. Another 45 percent of the debt consisted of carry-over annual spending on stimulus programs and aids to the financial sector to counter the devastating effects of the 2007–2009 recession. In the U.S., there are five main components of publicly held debt: (1) recessionary effects on receipts (roughly -$1 trillion in incomes) and spending (unemployment stabilizers); (2) bailouts to banks and the real sector (e.g. $1 trillion for TARP, some of which is now offset by more than $5 billion in profits from sale of company stock, e.g. AIG, GM); (3) debt carryover from before FY 2000 (about $3 trillion); (4) past and current wars ($3 trillion); and (5) entitlement costs from coverage of negative balances in funds (e.g. $35 billion for Social Security in 2011).

Since each country's debt composition will vary, it is important to tailor policy solutions to those particular problems. For instance, the Icelandic public debt is largely the product of governmental assumption of commercial bank losses (an implicit guarantee) to prevent collapse of the financial sector. In the U.S., many of the same expenditures took the form of guaranteed loans (contingent rather than direct liabilities) or stock purchases (effectively temporary nationalizations) that did not threaten the fiscal position or sustainability of the government. On the other hand, in most European and many Asian countries (with aging populations), larger debts are the product of growing pension and health care costs, roughly the same as in the U.S. These require application of one or more of the three policy options to be discussed below.

In macroeconomic terms, it is important to recognize that country debt is composed of government, household, and private sector obligations. The 2008 financial crisis was precipitated by private sector liabilities, mainly household mortgages and massive bank borrowing. Debts of financial companies often dwarfed the debts of governments, households, and non-financial or real firms. For example, in 2011 the Luxembourg financial sector had debts worth over 4,900 percent of GDP, Ireland 1,434 percent, and Britain 837 percent (*Economist*, 2013c: 74). Excessive debt from the financial sector is just as dangerous to economic stability as government debt. If financial firms make bad investments or over-borrow to buy more assets, this threatens their asset bases and they lose their ability to lend—which then constrains consumer spending and corporate investment. In response, consumers and the real (or industrial) sector de-leverage debts by spending less, defaulting, or selling assets cheap (ibid., 2013c: 74). All this moves an economy toward recession. Governments can respond with stimulus programs to compensate for these losses of spending, and they can also regulate the financial sector to ensure that excessive risks are avoided in the first place. For this reason, public sector regulation of the financial sector is critical to macroeconomic stability. Financial deregulation or efforts to weaken smart regulation are policies that sound plausible but are in fact fraught with peril.

Fiscal Policy Purposes

In the context of recent international recessionary and deflationary conditions, the objectives of macroeconomic policy should be to stimulate jobs and growth without threatening inflation or the current fiscal position by producing unsustainable debts for the future. The ECB and ultra-conservative constituencies in the U.S. Congress seem to have compressed fiscal policy into the narrow objective of cutting government spending and taxes in order to balance budgets and reduce future debt burdens. This is to confuse, in the words of Nate Silver, "noise" or politically distractive static from "signal" or the deeper truth of comprehensive fiscal policy solutions. Just as growth cannot be obtained by simple spending cuts in a recession where investment and consumers are not spending sufficiently, the market alone cannot be expected to provide health care or food stamps to non-elderly and poor Americans (Dionne, 2013: A17). Public spending and stimulus programs are often termed "demand side" since they target infrastructure, housing, and transport (railways, airports, ports, and roads) designed to increase demand for hiring workers, which in turn stimulate consumer demand, multiplying the effects through the economy. What this means is that the fiscal policy objective of reducing deficits has become the equivalent of overall macroeconomic policy (and vice versa).

There are two empirical problems with conflating macroeconomic and fiscal policy. Both relate to attribution of causation from statistical association data. That profoundly affects empirical analysis at the first and most basic level of our analytic framework (refer back to *Figure 1.4*). The variables here relate in complex, often non-linear patterns that are not always included as risks in policy recommendations to cut spending and change tax rates-bases. Since the macroeconomic forecast for GDP growth drives other calculations such as revenue and spending estimates, the econometric model used to calculate that growth is important. But GDP forecasts also depend on both measurement approach as well as the forecasting methodology. Nigeria, for example, recently doubled the size of its GDP by "rebasing" it with new surveys of industrial output reconciled with surveys of spending and income. It also updated its base year and will continue to do so every five years. The revised method shows that the level and structure of GDP are different: more booming factories and services and less reliance on oil and gas production (from 28 percent to 14 percent GDP in 2013) (*Economist*, 2014i: 71).

First, crude statistical associations exist between deficits, inflation, and unemployment that can lead to counterproductive policy recommendations. The orthodox thesis is that during normal times, deficits crowd the private sector from borrowing, which diminishes investment—decreasing employment and growth levels. So, deficit spending drives up interest rates, which can generate inflation. Decreasing deficits through austerity under these conditions should reduce capital costs and assist growth (Summers, 2013: A14). But at other "abnormal" times, such as the last decade, unemployment, aging populations, and lack of growth may be driving up deficits to cover needs and provide benefits through automatic counter-cyclical stabilizers. That is, the fiscal deficits by this perspective are symptoms of other internal and external problems that affect the macroeconomy to a greater extent than size of government or levels of expenditure.

Thus, the determinants of growth should be clarified for each country. This exercise will point to other factors that determine growth levels, especially "structural" or "supply side" constraints. These include the size of the informal economy (60 percent in Mexico, which itself is a reflection of the weakness of property rights and financial sector); lack of labor productivity (with an increase of 1.1 percent per year from 1981 to 2013, Chile grew 4.9 percent per year while Mexican productivity declined 0.7 percent per year and growth was only 2.4 percent per year in the same period) (*Economist*, 2013d: 38); ease of doing business (regulatory complexity); rigidity of labor laws (for hiring and firing); and loss of export markets (e.g. lower sales to the U.S. by Mexico from 2008 to 2009). In Japan, structural constraints take the form of: land laws limiting the size of farm plots, tariffs on rice and dairy products, boundless regulations, monopoly utilities, and labor market rigidities (*Economist*, 2013e: 25). As will be discussed further below, greater public spending under conditions of major structural constraints may be ineffective, can actually delay reform, and endanger medium-term growth. The Chinese 2009 stimulus, for instance, skewed the economy in favor of investment largely by state enterprises and lending by state banks to support unsustainable construction financed by high levels of local government debt (*Economist*, 2013f: 51). In short, the growth problem is a function of other variables in many cases, and spending cuts alone may well impede growth further (e.g. Mexican spending cuts in 2012 helped reduce growth to only 0.8 percent).

The link between deficits/debts and growth can go in either direction, depending on which problems are causing the deficits and debts (Guess and Koford, 1984). With strong statistical associations, for example, a deficits-cause-growth/inflation-problems vector or track suggests cuts in spending and reduction in taxation. The cause could be bloated government payrolls and high spending and taxation as percentages of total GDP. Analyses of government expenditures for efficiency and effectiveness, overall and by sector, can reveal where the cuts should be made. Analyses of revenue sources for efficiency (e.g. price elasticity of demand; volume of transactions; effects on locational decisions) and administrative effort for collections can indicate which sources should be modified, eliminated, or even expanded. Conversely, the growth-problems-cause-deficits vector suggests that lack of borrowing, business investment, consumer spending, and overall weak growth are driving up spending and reducing tax revenues. Automatic stabilizers might be one cause. More obvious candidates would be: financial sector collapse which reduces tax revenues; bank lending and investments; over-regulation of private sector firms; excessive labor protections for pensions and employment conditions; mismatch of educational supply in curriculum and program offerings versus student demand; growing needs in health care to ensure employment; and infrastructure investments to support private growth. If the macroeconomic problem is simplistically conflated to a fiscal problem, the risk of erroneous problem definition is high.

Over-obsession with fiscal discipline and budget deficits then can result in ignoring other important "deficits" in infrastructure, health care, and tax enforcement that could improve the overall fiscal position. More importantly, fiscal austerity policies applied to problems caused by other than public sector spending profligacy can worsen growth and unemployment— which would make fiscal deficits and debts worse. In Spain, Portugal, and Ireland, household and corporate debts were over 200 percent GDP before their sovereign debt crises. Fiscal austerity policies blindly applied in response made it harder to reduce private debts. An important lesson of the Euro crisis was to apply policies related to actual causes—not supposed causes such as public sector profligacy requiring draconian austerity measures (*Economist*, 2013g: 21).

Needed then are more refined analyses of causation between variables such as labor and business regulation and tax burden on investment decisions. Comparative micro-analyses by object of expenditure, e.g. public personnel costs, operations and maintenance (O&M) expenditures, and capital investment and sectoral expenditures (e.g. education, health) over a multi-year period can reveal how to program budget expenditures to stimulate growth. The medium-term expenditure framework (MTEF) used in many countries is a good tool for this purpose (see *Case 2.1* on p. 67). Planned spending can also be compared to projected deficits and taxation as percent GDP to other similar countries to develop better problem definitions. Failure to use such tools can produce political and economic disaster. Also, by applying the fiscal austerity policy solution from the first causal vector to the problem of low growth, in addition to continued unemployment and low growth, the risk might be "repressed deficits," such as deterioration of capital assets and poor overall health quality, that damage the long-term economic position (Summers, 2013a: A15). EU countries, for instance, facing austerity strictures from the "Stability and Growth Pact," which mandates 3 percent GDP deficit maximums, still face continued high unemployment (25.6 percent Spain; 10.4 percent France), growth rates of only 0.8 percent (France) and 1.8 percent (Germany), and growing popular opposition to these policies (Cody, 2013: A1).

The second problem with conflating macroeconomic and fiscal policy is that statistical associations that drive policy recommendations can be based on data errors. The Reinhart-Rogoff analysis indicating that exceeding a debt/GDP ratio of 90 percent would lead to stagnation in economic growth, for instance, was based on a coding error. That 2010 study had been used by austerity advocates in the EU, U.S., and elsewhere. The institutional flaw is that policy-makers often rely on single empirical studies or models without intuitive understanding of what drives them. While the Reinhart-Rogoff method was correct, the flawed use of data underscored the need to base policies on evidence from multiple studies using differing methodological approaches. Just as projects require multiple discount rates and assumptions of costs and benefits, macroeconomic studies require comparison of results beforehand (Summers, 2013b: A19). The related error is to rely on retrospective statistical analyses for firm conclusions. That study relied on data from 30 different countries, i.e. cultures, financial systems, political systems, growth experiences, assumed data regularity from past to future, and deduced a debt threshold level applicable universally. This country sample would violate our first requirement, noted in *Chapter 1*, that only similar countries and regions should be compared. One might note on the contrary that Japan, Germany, and Italy neared or exceeded the 90 percent threshold in 2013. But Japan has had slow growth for decades because of structural problems other than debt, e.g. a rigid labor market, educational system, and over-regulation of the private sector; Germany spends for investment to spur its future growth and has the burden of other EU country obligations to deal with; Italy's problems are also structural—over-regulation of labor and real and financial sectors. Put another way, under these conditions reducing their deficits and debts through greater austerity would be unlikely to improve growth or employment levels.

Another example of this policy conundrum is that between 2010 and 2014, Italy's public debt rose from 116 percent to 133 percent of GDP. But their budget deficit is only slightly higher than the EU mandated maximum of 3 percent GDP (3.3 percent). Italian public debt is growing because the economy is shrinking (GDP falling -4.0 percent in real terms over the same period). As indicated in *Question 2* on p. 72, in order to spur growth, the current Prime Minister Matteo Renzi cut taxes and would like to spend more. He knows that if he cuts capital spending, it likely would cause more economic contraction. But the EU austerity mandate is to maintain a path of deficit reduction even though the country already has a primary surplus and a deficit of only 3.3 percent. If the EU allowed Italy to spend more, it fears that other countries such as Spain and France would ask for the same treatment (*Economist*, 2014g: 53). The point is that it is the wrong policy applied to the wrong problem and will only constrain growth under these conditions. Meeting the EU 3 percent paper target is largely irrelevant to economic need and recovery.

Table 2.1 indicates size of government, deficits and debt levels, and major macroeconomic measures for major countries in multiple regions. In an attempt to define the core fiscal policy problems, several conclusions can be drawn from these data:

- First, a general inverse relation often exists between growth and unemployment. This is true in Europe, the U.S., Commonwealth, and Asian regional countries. The exception is Latin America with higher growth but higher unemployment levels.
- Second, a direct relation exists between fiscal deficits and debt levels. In the U.S., fiscal deficits have declined to 2.9 percent of GDP and the trajectory of public debt is dropping as growth and revenue collections increase. Both deficits and debt are relatively high in the UK and Europe, and both are low in Asia and Latin America. The exception in Europe is Eastern Europe, which retains its aversion to borrowing at both national and local levels.
- Third, there is a direct relation between size of government (percent GDP public taxation and spending) and levels of deficits and debt. They are high in the U.S. and Europe but low in Asia and Latin America. The exception is Japan; 95 percent of its debt is held by Japanese bondholders. Sizes of government and debts are high in Europe despite the fact that their debt composition lacks the large defense and wars components of the U.S. debt. The U.S. gross public debt figure is also inflated by inclusion of bonds in the pension plan, which other countries do not include. Exclusion of that component drops it to 73.3 percent of GDP—which is still high. Similar to Japan, 66 percent of the U.S. gross public debt is held by U.S. bondholders.
- Fourth, the general associations tend to support the James Buchanan thesis that institutionalized demand for big government programs persists and ratchets up fiscal risks. This is mistaken economic thinking but normal political thinking (Lane, 2013: A17). Buchanan foresaw persistent misallocation of resources through structural inefficiencies in the form of outmoded but politically untouchable government programs, e.g. U.S. persistent agricultural and later solar subsidies; EU and U.S. entitlement programs, many of which are regulated to needlessly drive up costs and waste scarce budget funds; Italian labor markets are full of wage and price inflexibilities; and the Japanese favor protectionism. This suggests that despite data problems noted in the Reinhart and Rogoff example (Summers, 2013b: A19) the persistence and upward trajectory of public debts means that they must be tackled efficiently and equitably.

Table 2.1 Macroeconomic Performance and Fiscal Policies

Country	Budget Balance % GDP (Economist, April 19, 2014)	Taxation % GDP (Heritage Foundation, 2011)	Spending % GDP (Heritage Foundation, 2011)	Debt % GDP (IMF, 2012)	Growth (Economist, April 19, 2014)	Unemployment (Economist, April 19, 2014)
U.S.	-2.9	26.9	38.9	107.8	2.8	6.7
Britain CW	-5.4	39.0	47.3	88.6	2.9	7.2
Australia CW	-1.9	30.8	34.3	27.0	2.7	5.8
Canada CW	-2.6	32.2	39.7	87.5	2.3	6.9
Germany EU	+0.5	40.6	43.7	83.0	1.8	6.7
France EU	-4.2	44.6	52.8	90.0	0.8	10.4
Italy EU	-3.3	42.6	48.8	126.3	0.5	13.0
Spain EU	-5.8	37.3	41.1	90.7	0.8	25.6
Netherlands EU	-3.0	39.8	45.9	68.2	0.9	8.8
Sweden EU	-2.0	45.8	52.5	37.1	2.5	8.5
Hungary EE	-3.0	39.1	49.2	74.0	2.1	8.6
Poland EE	-3.5	33.8	43.3	55.1	3.2	13.6
Turkey E	-2.7	32.5	23.4	37.7	2.2	10.1
India A	-5.1	17.7	27.2	67.6	6.0	9.9
China A	-2.2	12.4	20.8	22.2	7.3	4.1
South Korea A	+0.5	26.8	30.0	33.4	3.3	3.9
Pakistan A	-6.3	10.2	19.3	62.4	3.9	6.2
Japan A	-8.1	28.3	37.1	236.6	1.2	3.6
Thailand A	-2.3	17.0	17.7	44.2	2.5	0.9
Malaysia A	-4.1	15.5	26.3	53.0	5.1	3.3
Brazil LA	-4.0	34.4	41.0	64.0	1.8	5.1
Mexico LA	-3.7	29.7	23.7	43.0	3.0	4.7
Colombia LA	-0.9	23.0	26.5	32.1	4.7	10.7
Chile LA	-1.2	18.6	21.1	11.4	3.8	6.1

• Fifth, the data suggests differences in different regions with differing cultures, institutions, and structural features of government. In order to define the problem at hand and develop rules for policy-makers, it is important to follow Xavier's (1998) and Rodden's (2006) comparative methodologies and focus first on similar systems and specific fiscal problems within them. This can lead to context-specific institutional and macroeconomic policy financing lessons needed for improved results.

Analytic Tools and Methods

In any country, the budget process is the singular opportunity to match program, service, and project needs with scarce resources. The process should be more than numbers-crunching exercises and requires realistic planning and performance results analysis to be effective. Analysis is itself a process of measuring, comparing costs (including opportunity costs), benefits, and the consequences of budget choices. Analysis has been called forensic auditing and forensic accounting. In addition to measuring and comparing costs and consequences, analysis means making the numbers work to get something accomplished and finding out the technical and political rationale for a particular composition of expenditures (or tax rates and base definitions). Through the application of methods and tools, the analytic process aims to develop reasonable options for mayors and councils, finance directors and legislators. It is not research and should be done in-house and rapidly—some might call it action research.

1. Budget Formats

Policy-makers and managers need information on the strategic adequacy of expenditures, the consistency of budget composition with fiscal plans and priorities, and the efficiency and effectiveness of expenditures for projects, programs, and services. As is known, efficiency refers to doing things right (i.e. at least cost); effectiveness means doing the right things (e.g. appropriate steps to reform) (Peter Drucker cited in Peterson, 2015: 3). Of the four formats noted by GFS, the *object of expenditure*, *functional*, and *performance* formats, also noted in *Chapter 1*, are most useful for these purposes. For example, the object of expenditure or economic classification (*Figure 2.2*) reveals expenditure by standard line-items. This offers two opportunities: first, outlays for each item can be compared to those of similar countries, regions, or subnational governments to determine adequacy of expenditures. If country A spends 2 percent of GDP on operations and maintenance and country B spends 4 percent, analysts should want to know why.

Second, policy-makers also need to know the functional composition of expenditures. It could be the most funds are spent on the defense function or on the civil service salary line-item. Are these structural patterns justifiable in the context of macroeconomic stabilization objectives? Are they consistent with allocational efficiency? To answer such questions, analysts often face a dizzying array of line-items for hundreds of performance measures. The risks of particular items to macroeconomic stability and budget control should be evident. Other standard economic ratios and percentages can be used to convey the picture. For example, the budgetary costs of Indonesian fuel subsidies are 13.0 percent of revenues. The government will raise fuel prices 44 percent to control these costs and cover the poor withcompensatory cash handouts (*Economist*, 2013h: 46). Similarly, French pension, health, and social assistance spending amount to 32 percent of GDP (*Economist*, 2013i: 55). Even though the U.S. level of entitlement program spending amounts to only 18 percent of GDP, in both countries it constitutes a serious internal threat to budgetary discipline and fiscal deficits.

1. **Salaries:** These are usually the bulk of government expenditures; about 30 percent of the USG budget is allocated to civil service salaries.
2. **Employee Benefits:** This consists of social security, group insurance, and retirement benefits; a growing liability for all governments, e.g. 17 percent of the Illinois 2012 operating or current services budget; salaries and benefits amount to 83.3 percent of Milwaukee city expenses.
3. **Operating Expenses:** These are the running costs or operational procurements. Expenditures below a certain cash threshold and useful life are current; above that threshold they are capital expenditures. Montgomery County (Maryland), for example, uses $5,000 and one year (Montgomery County (MD) Office of Management and Budget, 2011: 1–3) as the cut-off point between operating expenses, such as printing, motor pool, travel, and office supplies from capital items, such as computer systems and police–fire trucks.
4. **Maintenance:** These are expenditures for minor maintenance of facilities such as roads, bridges, ports, airports, some of which may be partly financed by fees; the rest of O&M funds flow from general fund appropriations. In many state–local governments, O&M is contracted out to save budget funds, e.g. municipal refuse services and certain public transit routes. A useful measure of financial condition for this item is maintenance level/unit of asset.
5. **Subsidies:** These are often uncalculated amounts spent for special interest purposes, e.g. to attract local investments with roads, tax breaks, parking facilities surrounding such private projects as convention centers and stadiums. At the national level, fuel and electricity subsidies are critical but also typically uncalculated and unreported by finance offices. For local governments, calculating the value of expenditures for businesses or special interests and revenues foregone from abatements, tax exemptions, and other incentives is often difficult to do.
6. **Transfers:** These are grants to other units of government such as from county to city, city to school districts, or the federal to local levels, e.g. water facility grants from EPA.
7. **Arrears:** These are the total amounts plus interest costs of unpaid or late bills owed to suppliers for unpaid invoices, taxpayers for refunds, and in some cases state or local employees for salaries. Despite the fact that they can be used to finance deficits by reducing outlays artificially, they are rarely included in state or local budgets.
8. **Debt Service:** These are annual payments of principal and interest on bonded indebtedness for general obligation and other debt incurred by departments agencies by special or enterprise funds. Despite their GFOA award-winning budgets, it is difficult to determine total debt service/total operating expense ratios in either the Montgomery County or Milwaukee budgets because they are in round numbers rather than ratios or yearly trends. In exceptional cities, such as Ft. Collins (Colorado), debt service is cited (25.1 percent and compared with a baseline measure (>15 percent=high)) (Strachota, 1994: 83).
9. **Capital and Rehabilitation:** This consists of construction, replacement, and major maintenance of assets, such as sidewalks, roads, sewers, bridges, transit systems, airports, and seaports. Montgomery County uses a $5,000 and one-year useful life threshold, which is quite low. Milwaukee distinguishes types of infrastructure: $25,000 for new or replacement construction; $50,000 for durable equipment; $25,000 for renovation (City of Milwaukee Budget and Management Department, 2008: 4).

Figure 2.2 Object of Expenditure or Economic Classification

Thus, the remedy for the proliferation of objects of expenditure across many different budgets is to use a *functional* budget classification (*Figure 2.3*). Functions are groups of activities aimed at accomplishing a major service (Strachota, 1994: 164). The nine functions and many sub-functions of the U.S. budget relate budget authority, outlays, loan guarantees, and tax expenditures to national needs. Congressional budget resolutions actually target these needs (Mikesell, 2011: 284), and via *cross-walking* (inter-format reconciliation), every cent of functional expenditures can be translated into objects, programs, or organizations. Functions are independent of the government organizational structure (Schiavo-Campo and Tommasi, 1999: 70). Fourteen major ones are recognized in the UN Functional Classification of the

| ($000s) | Program Services | | Support Services | |
	In Hospital Care	Clinical Care	General & Administrative	Total
Salaries	$60,000	$13,700	$5,200	$78,900
Supplies	11,300	3,100	1,000	15,400
Rent	2,500	500	100	3,100
Other	2,500	200	100	2,800
Total	$76,300	$17,300	$6,400	$100,200

Figure 2.3 Functional and Object of Expenditure Budgets

Note: Functional budgets focus on the major functions performed by an organization. This format is often used to report to outsiders. Note the line-item or object of expenditure detail in column 1.

Functions of Government (COFOG). There are also 61 groups and 127 sub-groups (ibid., 1999: 70). For example, Social Service function includes the sub-group of Education and the sub-groups of Primary, Secondary, and Tertiary Education. Transparency and comprehensiveness are obtained by cross-walking expenditures objects across organizational units into combined functions.

The third format option is *performance or program*. It is critical that managers be able to estimate and track the costs, volumes, and results of services in order to know what improvements might be made and where cuts should be rationally focused if, for example, revenues collapse. Stockholm (Sweden) now uses its new "outcome-based health care" system to claim funds back from private health care providers if they do not meet performance criteria as agreed in their service contracts with the city (*Economist*, 2013j: 75). The opposite is also true. With sudden budget surpluses (on a cash basis) in states such as California, Connecticut, Utah, and Wisconsin, officials need to know how to sensibly reallocate funds (Nagourney, 2013: 1). Note the similarity between functions and programs. *Programs* are also groups of related activities performed by one or more organization (like functions). But the purpose of the program is to carry out the function (Strachota, 1994: 166). This gives the concept of a program budget an active meaning—it should allocate resources according to these programs and not simply objects of expenditure. But elected legislatures work from district constituent needs, and it is more feasible for them to use objects for allocation rather than programs. For this reason, most legislatures or parliaments approve budgets in line-items and often ignore efficiency and effectiveness information accompanying requests for the fiscal year. Note the high level of demand, workload, productivity, and effectiveness information provided in the social services department performance budget (*Figure 2.4*). In theory, all public funds should be allocated on the basis of such measures.

2. Problem Definition

In the context of fiscal policy and macroeconomic consequences, mis-specification of the problem can lead to application of the wrong remedy. Structural constraints are a problem that must be estimated to ensure that additional funds are not wasted on, for example, subsidies to over-regulated industries that do not contribute to growth. Weak problem definition can also lead to the wrong solution, e.g. protected Japanese construction firms with access to subsidies demanded and received $6.3 trillion over 1991–2008 to stimulate growth with infrastructure projects. This amount was larger than the total GDP and did not stimulate growth at all!

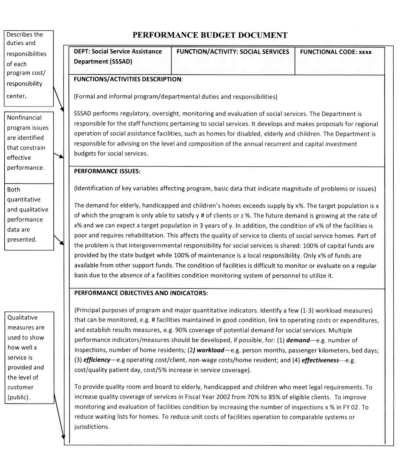

PERFORMANCE BUDGET DOCUMENT

Describes the duties and responsibilities of each program cost/responsibility center.

Nonfinancial program issues are identified that constrain effective performance.

Both quantitative and qualitative performance data are presented.

Qualitative measures are used to show how well a service is provided and the level of customer (public).

DEPT: Social Service Assistance Department (SSSAD)	FUNCTION/ACTIVITY: SOCIAL SERVICES	FUNCTIONAL CODE: xxxx

FUNCTIONS/ACTIVITIES DESCRIPTION:

(Formal and informal program/departmental duties and responsibilities)

SSSAD performs regulatory, oversight, monitoring and evaluation of social services. The Department is responsible for the staff functions pertaining to social services. It develops and makes proposals for regional operation of social assistance facilities, such as homes for disabled, elderly and children. The Department is responsible for advising on the level and composition of the annual recurrent and capital investment budgets for social services.

PERFORMANCE ISSUES:

(Identification of key variables affecting program, basic data that indicate magnitude of problems or issues)

The demand for elderly, handicapped and children's homes exceeds supply by x%. The target population is x of which the program is only able to satisfy y # of clients or z %. The future demand is growing at the rate of x% and we can expect a target population in 3 years of y. In addition, the condition of x% of the facilities is poor and requires rehabilitation. This affects the quality of service to clients of social service homes. Part of the problem is that intergovernmental responsibility for social services is shared: 100% of capital funds are provided by the state budget while 100% of maintenance is a local responsibility. Only x% of funds are available from other support funds. The condition of facilities is difficult to monitor or evaluate on a regular basis due to the absence of a facilities condition monitoring system of personnel to utilize it.

PERFORMANCE OBJECTIVES AND INDICATORS:

(Principal purposes of program and major quantitative indicators. Identify a few (1-3) workload measures that can be monitored, e.g. # facilities maintained in good condition, link to operating costs or expenditures, and establish results measures, e.g. 90% coverage of potential demand for social services. Multiple performance indicators/measures should be developed, if possible, for: (1) *demand*—e.g. number of inspections, number of home residents; (2) *workload*—e.g. person months, passenger kilometers, bed days; (3) *efficiency*—e.g operating cost/client, non-wage costs/home resident; and (4) *effectiveness*---e.g. cost/quality patient day, cost/5% increase in service coverage).

To provide quality room and board to elderly, handicapped and children who meet legal requirements. To increase quality coverage of services in Fiscal Year 2002 from 70% to 85% of eligible clients. To improve monitoring and evaluation of facilities condition by increasing the number of inspections x % in FY 02. To reduce waiting lists for homes. To reduce unit costs of facilities operation to comparable systems or jurisdictions.

FINANCING	PAST YEAR ACTUAL 2000–2001	PAST YEAR ADJ. BUDGET 2000–2001	CURRENT YEAR 2001–2002	PROPOSED 2002–2003
REQUIREMENTS:				
Personal Services	31,893,635	40,157,534	36,370,021	43,073,374
Non-personal Services	3,718,429	5,969,621	5,878,156	6,338,646
Interdepartmental Charges	148,733	330,542	307,536	513,186
Capital Outlay	6,844	0	0	0
Prior-year Encumbrances	6,694	2,011	98	0
TOTAL REQUIREMENTS	35,774,335	46,459,708		49,925,206
PERSONNEL QUOTA	30	23	23	25
RESOURCES:				
Fines, Forfeits, & Penalties	0	2,800,000		1,459,000
Rev from leases/rents	0	0	101	100
Revenues from Other Agencies	380,928	125,000	122,262	25,000
Charges For Current Services	0	0	295,143	310,000
Special Fund Revenues	17,371	1,000	34,387	200
Interfund Chgs for Svcs	857,261	1,442,182	1,684,847	1,177,220
Intragovt Fund Chgs for Svcs	0	0	9,897	373,323
General Fund	34,518,775	42,091,526	39,136,957	46,580,363
TOTAL RESOURCES:	35,774,335	46,459,708	42,555,811	49,925,206

Figure 2.4 Social Services Department Performance Budget

Note: This chart provides the operating details, financing requirements, and resources for the social services program, which is in part the responsibility of SSSAD. From the perspective of departmental program management, SSSAD could then be viewed as an organizational subunit or cost/responsibility center with three major sub-programs, i.e. (1) administration, (2) social services, and (3) capital investment.

(Zakaria, 2013: A19). As noted, imposition of fiscal austerity measures in the context of low growth and powerful structural constraints is likely to perpetuate low growth and high unemployment.

In general, a policy problem represents a set of "unrealized values, needs or opportunities, which, however identified, may be attained through public action" (Dunn, 2008: 72). A policy problem can also be viewed as a "system of external conditions that produce dissatisfaction among different segments of the community" (Dunn, 1981: 99). By these perspectives, a policy problem is an event that produces dissatisfaction beyond one or two individuals. People are upset. A single complaint about the slow response by police or fire services does not amount to a policy problem—though, collectively, more complaints would be symptomatic of a policy problem. This helps in the definition. But how do we know whether it is an *actionable* problem as opposed to something simply annoying? Here it may be useful to define a policy problem by analogy—like a public question that can be settled by evidence that all rival observers have no choice but to accept (e.g. congestion measured as road density and average speed of traffic that lead to x hours of time wasted and y gallons of fuel consumed which increases in measurable levels of NO_x or nitrogen oxide).

For messy, ill-structured problems like macroeconomic policy impacts under alternative conditions, application of the usual methodologies to define policy then suggest that more work is needed in measurement and analysis of assumptions and causes. Consistent with this purpose, Dunn (2008) offered multiple methods such as: brainstorming, classification analysis, review of assumptions, and additional measurement of costs and benefits including unintended consequences and causal analysis. These methods are useful but often lead back to the same issue of institutional constraint to sensible action during both the policy design and implementation phases (see *Figure 1.1*). Even structuring and defining a simple operational problem like city rat infestation leads into messiness. Suppose that the number of complaints in a community about stray dogs has been increasing annually. Suppose also that the number of impoundments has been decreasing at a similar rate. Based on this limited information, what would be the "animal control problem"? The problem could be subdivided into regulatory and investment sub-issues, i.e. the absence of regulation and/or public investment. Note that a "regulatory" definition focuses solutions on licensing, leashes, fines, and animal contraception (i.e. owner-controlled solutions). A "capital investment" definition would focus on the need for a larger and more accessible dog pound. Conservative anti-tax critics of defining the problem as lack of capital underinvestment might argue that a new pound would not necessarily eliminate strays (the real objective) and could threaten fiscal condition. They might argue that a new or larger pound might merely shift the costs to the non-dog-owning public for services required by improper behavior by dog owners. From their angle, a more appropriate solution would combine steeper fines, higher service charges or license fees for dog owners, and animal contraception (a regulatory package) (Lehan, 1984: 66–67). Since policy alternatives are ultimately traded in institutionalized settings (usually committees), *politics* will affect the ultimate ranking of a regulatory solution in relation to a capital investment (pound) solution. Strong preferences for capital construction solutions to complex policy problems are often driven by the political pressures of construction firms (such as in the Japanese example) that donate campaign money and often rely on the political benefits of leaving tangible results to local constituencies.

In short, a precise definition of the fiscal or policy problem is confounded by the reality that the same information can be interpreted differently. Different problem definitions derive from the fact that different constituencies or stakeholders are doing the defining. This in turn can lead to policies (and usually their rewards in form of earmarked expenditures) that disproportionately distribute costs and benefits among affected interest groups (Guess and Farnham, 2011: 33). In the case of economic policy, it should come as no surprise that structural solutions to growth problems face enormous political resistance from guilds, protected industries, and entrenched public bureaucracies. Those that conflate fiscal and austerity policies with improvements in growth face two problems of their own. One is the inability to establish clear empirical causation; second, an austerity solution is often ideologically driven by small government and anti-tax advocates who are unwilling and unable to name preferred and particular program, project, and service cuts. Actual cuts proposed remain at the abstract level of entitlements and health care for political cover and also gain from the general preference of most people to avoid fees and taxes while demanding more services. Most voting systems and parliamentary institutions allow these contradictions with economic policy to remain muddled.

3. Regressions and Simulations

To forecast the impacts of macroeconomic policy, causal analysis requires more refined regressions and simulations to devise solutions that apply in multiple contexts. The primary policy objective is to stimulate growth and reduce unemployment; the secondary objective is to improve fiscal positions with budgets that balance over the medium-term. The measurement need is for threshold indicators revealing that the wrong problem is being tackled, i.e. fiscal policy over financial sector reforms and austerity measures to improve public sector balance sheets instead of structural reforms. To date, it has been difficult to find similar country contexts where problems have been the same; policies applied have been different and growth-unemployment effects unambiguously attributable to those policies. Even for fiscal solutions, it has been difficult to find countries in economic crisis that have applied austerity measures (e.g. running primary balances) for more than five years to measure impacts. The comparative conditions and longitudinal data have not been favorable so far.

4. Medium-Term Expenditure Frameworks

We referred to the MTEF previously. Fiscal balances and performances have improved around the world from the use of medium-term expenditure frameworks. Designed to remedy the conservative defects of incremental budgeting, they are effectively multi-year capital planning formats, rolled forward each year, to improve fiscal planning and actual results for both capital and operating expenditures. Once institutionalized into country fiscal routines, they function as planning tools for rolling five-year periods with the intention of minimizing the gap between planned and approved budgets and actual spending, revenues, and results. Their origin is with Australian practice of the 1980s. In some form, they are now used in over 100 countries of Africa, Europe, Central Asia, the former Soviet Union, and Latin America. The World Bank has supported their diffusion globally in three forms: (1) medium-term fiscal frameworks (MTFFs), which are the most common form of MTEF; these are top-down and focus on planning and hard budget constraints to ensure fiscal discipline; (2) medium-term budget frameworks (MTBFs), which focus on minimizing the differences between multi-year budget plans and results (outturns); they are arrived at through a compromise top-down bottom-up process; and (3) medium-term performance frameworks (MTPFs), which focus on service and program performance and incentives to hold agency managers accountable for results (World Bank, 2012). MTPFs are the least common form of MTEF.

In MTEF countries, results are fed into annual hard budget constraints which anticipate downstream expenditure requirements against the constraint of economic growth and revenue receipts performances. Their narrow purpose is to keep fiscal deficits under control over the medium-term. MTEFs are reforms mostly commonly identified with Commonwealth budget preparation. A similar Canadian reform called "envelope budgeting" was implemented in the 1980s using a rolling five-year expenditure planning process that was updated each year. The purpose of an MTEF is to estimate budget requirements and revenues over a four-year period (budget year with an annual appropriation plus three more). If applied properly, the framework can ensure macroeconomic balance, permit allocation of funds to strategic priorities, and provide funding stability for line departments. Operating within typical MTEF rules, line departments estimate multi-year expenditures (mostly on a gross basis) based on guidelines provided by the finance department. In Australia, projections are based on assumptions for about 30 variables. The estimated budget is rolled forward each year and updated or reconciled with new estimates and a new hard budget constraint based on revised macroeconomic estimates for the next year (Petrei, 1998: 131).

The MTEF is designed to estimate downstream costs of major items like personnel, benefits, O&M for capital investments, and debt service and to forge a current budget constraint. Note that the framework relies on traditional object-of-expenditure budget data. To develop the "hard budget constraint," staff do not have to generate activity or program performance information. But staff must estimate multi-year expenditures and revenue requirements for each budget category. This ensures that expenditure decisions are made in the context of actual, multi-year program needs rather than simply global budgets. Annual budgeting results in unpredictable funding within and between years and leads to poor operational and service results. MTEFs in practice often help allocation decisions (allocational efficiency) if they are fully installed.

Figure 2.5 (Allen and Tommasi, 2001: 184) illustrates a four-year budget planning framework (CY + year plan). The framework requires linkage of current base estimates—the costs of current policies—with revenue and expenditure estimates over the planning period. Line agencies respond to calls issued by ministries of finance of MOFs to estimate current program and running costs, then add in nominal costs for new policy changes for the same period. The MOFs reduce these estimates in real terms to compensate for inflation by providing a rate for budget calculation. This means that available funding for delivery of services and programs will be less in real terms. Line agencies must budget for this deficiency accordingly by reducing staff, changing how services are delivered (e.g. more technology and less personnel), or charging separate fees. Thus, the MTEF is a framework for expenditure planning and annual reconciliation of new revenue figures with expenditure needs. The aim is to plan for future program needs and revenue contingencies. Proper use of the MTEF framework allows managers to reprogram savings in response to expenditure ceilings and to plan for hidden expenditures (e.g. O&M for capital maintenance). To date in the UK, not all expenditures are included in this process. About 50 percent of total expenditures are for entitlements, such as social security and health care. Because of the volatile nature of these expenditures, they are planned annually (Allen and Tommasi, 2001: 179). Nevertheless, the reconciliation feature makes the framework a unique combination of regulation (the hard budget constraint) and flexibility (rolling plans and reconciliation exercises).

Often, MTEFs are developed separately from capital budgets because of institutional structures and jurisdictional rules that defeat the purpose of comprehensive fiscal planning. This institutional defect is as true in Commonwealth countries as in the other regions. Limiting MTEF to current services budgeting calls into question the goal of programming all budget

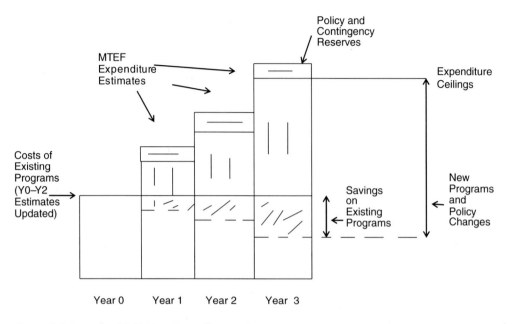

Figure 2.5 Preparing Multi-Year Expenditure Estimates

resources over a multi-year framework. International consultants and donors like exercises to develop MTEF frameworks. So, in many cases, MTEFs become trophy budgets (something like program budgets) that are not actually used except for display. Worse still, when implemented overseas either they are too narrowly focused as technical tools much like as activity-based costing (Shah, 2007: 128) as part of broader budget reform projects that include performance budgeting. The frequent result is that the MTEF budgeting framework is not used for real planning, allocation, or implementation. So, the more traditional South African MTEF works well—expenditures are estimated in current prices and the rolling three-year process links the problem of growing personnel costs with expenditure management constraints (Schiavo-Campo and Tommasi, 1999: 301). By contrast, the Mozambique MTEF does not work well. Budget staff there is unskilled and underpaid. Little confidence exists in the figures generated even for the annual budget in traditional object of expenditure format (ibid., 1999: 300). In this context, it is difficult to imagine why the South African MOF would push for a more extended rolling five-year framework—two years more than the current framework. As indicated by Harris et al. (2013: 147–149), two essential preconditions for MTEFs and MTBFs are credible and predictable annual budgets, and the capacity to forecast multi-year macroeconomic estimates (Cangiano et al., 2013). Every revenue and expenditure item is driven by some exogenous factor, e.g. income tax receipts are affected by household income and employment levels. It should be recognized by MOFs and country policy-makers that in many developing and transitional countries, these basic foundations are missing and can only be acquired by years of fiscal modernization. Nevertheless, the MTEF concept is sound and it is a popular reform around the world (Guess and LeLoup, 2010: 80).

   The World Bank's review of MTEF performance (2012) evaluated MTEF countries in 2000 versus 2010 on four criteria: (a) approved versus actual budget aggregates, (b) approved versus actual budget composition, (c) approved versus actual revenues, and (d) actual use of medium-term perspective in fiscal planning and budgeting. In most countries, implementation of MTEF systems takes more than five years until its processes can be fully institutionalized.

Question 1 on p. 69, the Slugovia case, provides an MTEF example using available information for a hypothetical country to develop a sensible fiscal plan within a 5 percent deficit hard-budget constraint by year four.

Structure and Financing of Policy Responses

Reducing Unemployment

Unemployment issues illustrate the importance of problem definition. Incomplete policy problem analysis or weak specification of the problem, as noted, can lead to the wrong solutions and wastage of political and financial capital. For example, efforts to reduce current high rates of youth unemployment in southern Europe (60 percent in Greece; 50 percent in Spain) have focused on importing the German model of apprenticeships and vocational training that have worked so well there. The EU is expanding its Erasmus Mundus educational exchange and apprenticeship programs, and the EIB is expanding programs for small business training. The EU is also developing a "youth guarantee" program to ensure apprenticeship and training for youth. But these efforts ignore the fact that when Germany was the "sick man" of Europe in 2005, its youth unemployment rate was 15 percent despite the availability of ample apprenticeship and training opportunities. The problem is that growth and economic recovery are needed to generate the demand for jobs. Increased demand for employees by firms is really what reduces youth unemployment in Europe and countries such as the U.S. Further focus is needed on removal of structural impediments, such as inflexible labor markets that favor permanent employment at the expense of temporary slots for the young. In response, Italy has reduced taxes on jobs for youth. Core structural items that can also constrain growth include labor market rules and regulations (often wage protection that increases costs of hiring and firing), government-owned enterprises (i.e. competition with the commercial sector), price controls (e.g. electricity, gas prices set below production costs), financial sector regulation (too weak versus too tight), social safety net (pensions and health), and public financial management (Abdel-Kader, 2013: 46–47). One should distinguish operational level public financial administration (PFA), e.g. compliance and control via improvements in budgeting, accounting, and planning systems, and financial management information technology from public financial management. (PFM) which refers to promotion of discretion to achieve public policy ends (Peterson, 2015: 3). Effective PFM then is based on establishment of sound PFA systems.

Structural reforms concentrate on improving aggregate supply side conditions. The aim with labor markets is to liberalize often rigid employment conditions to enable employers to discharge people in dying industries or poorly performing companies and to hire people in rising industries and firms more quickly and easily. Poor quality roads and infrastructure that impede growth in Brazil, for example, can be attributed largely to the perverse incentives of untenable labor laws that penalize employers severely for sacking employees and ensure paternalistic rules around working hours. For this reason, in many Brazilian boardrooms, employees are said to be a firm's greatest liability rather than their greatest asset!

Liberalized employment and pro-poor policies have worked well. More advanced countries such as Germany and Switzerland have used apprenticeship systems for years which track students toward jobs in particular industries and give them on the job training and credits.

State investments in apprenticeship programs generate skills but not necessarily jobs. Conditional cash transfer programs (see *Chapter 4*) which offer payment through targeted central government grants to the poorest families in return for meeting specific conditions such as attending school and receiving basic health care improve the workforce and encourage skill-taking. They have reduced poverty levels dramatically in Latin America (Mexico, Peru, Brazil, and Guatemala), but they cannot generate jobs either. Charter and private school alternatives to poor-quality public schools in many countries can also improve the workforce or labor supply. Public investments in infrastructure projects, such as tram lines for local economic development, lead to shorter-term skilled jobs for the duration of construction. After several years of operation, such projects normally generate investments in real estate from firms that locate near stations for ease of workforce commuting. While national governments may have financed them in part through capital transfers, concessionary low-interest loans, and loan guarantees, most of the investments are made by subnational governments for local economic development. In short, fiscal policies work indirectly if at all to reduce unemployment.

Stimulating Demand

The link between fiscal policy, demand stimulation, and growth is also indirect. The short- and medium-term effects on growth depend largely on the severity and timing of policies to produce primary surpluses. Running budget surpluses (i.e. subtracting out debt service and other adjustment efforts) will help reduce total cash deficits first, after which the policy can help reduce the accumulated deficits in the form of debts. The premise here is that if consumer demand and real-sector investment are low, to stimulate demand the government sector needs to step in according to the classic Keynesian formula. But it has been noted that the link between public sector investment and long-term growth is also indirect. In response to the 2007–2009 recession, public sectors mainly in the EU and U.S. stepped in to fill demand and investment gaps with short-term stimuli in multiple forms: temporary nationalizations, loan guarantees, loan capital, fiscal transfers to subnational governments to stabilize their employment levels, and public investments in capital rehabilitation and new facilities. The U.S. also moved to tighten lending standards, increase the adequacy of bank capital through such means as "stress tests," and implement smarter regulation to ensure the transparency and oversight of securitized instruments. When the U.S. policy response targeted the right problem and most of the main causes, the fiscal policy responses began to take effect about four years later. GDP growth increased 1.8 percent over 2012, tax receipts and increases in tax rates increased collections and reduced the deficit from about 7 percent to 5.4 percent of GDP—but the unemployment rate remained high at 6.7 percent. The responses in Latin America required minimal fiscal policy adjustment since their recession was caused less by any weaknesses in their banking and financial sectors (which are well-regulated for loan origination and minimum capital requirements) and more by trade gaps owing to reduced demand from their partners, largely the U.S. and EU countries.

Spain, for instance, attempted to reduce constraints to growth through structural or supply side reforms to expand exports, increase investment and stimulate consumer demand. Spanish policy-makers concluded that with individual and household consumption and investment diminished and levels of fiscal deficits and debts excessively high, fiscal austerity was first required. To do this, the Spanish government tackled civil service costs (375 jobs gone) and regional overspending which brought deficits down from -11 percent GDP in 2009 to only -7 percent in 2013. It continued to decrease to -5.8 percent in 2014. Spain then liberalized labor laws to make hiring and firing easier which has encouraged producers to relocate from other EU countries. The real economy picked up and unit labor costs also dropped (*Economist*, 2013k: 51). Unable to reverse consumption, investment, and governmental performance problems, it tried to liberalize its economy and stimulate imports instead. Nevertheless, unemployment remains high at 27 percent and exports cannot achieve much growth as two-thirds of them rely on demand from other weakened EU countries.

Often policy constraints act as a structural brake on growth by limiting both supply and demand. For example, the Japanese rice subsidy and import substitution policy is called *gentan*. Rice subsidies take the form of official protection of many small and inefficient farmers that by limiting the numbers of acres in production and selling yields at artificially high prices are aided by a 700 percent import tariff. Rice is considered a "sacred crop" for cultural and national security reasons. This allows local agricultural committees to keep out larger agri-business operations that would quickly apply economies of scale to production. Protection policy also keeps farmers out of the finance-banking system as they rely on credit from the giant Japanese Agriculture (JA) cooperative that stifles much of Japanese farming. The current Prime Minister Shinzo Abe is working to reform the *gentan* policy and let rice growers produce as much as they want. This would decrease prices and allow Japan to compete more effectively at home against imports. He is also seeking to replace the power of the local agricultural committees and the JA to determine rice supply and price by shifting crop zoning and participation decisions to local governments and financing to the banking system. Only through supply-side structural reforms such as these can the sector contribute to increasing the national rate of growth (*Economist*, 2013l: 46).

Controlling Inflation

Control of price inflation is the responsibility of central banks. Often independent of fiscal authorities in most countries (e.g. UK, U.S., and Chile), which are overtly political, they are able to affect short-term rates through a variety of tools (e.g. discount rates and reserve requirements) that can change the cost of borrowing from the banking system. The U.S. Federal Reserve, for example, manipulates the money supply and the terms under which credit is available. Lower borrowing rates can stimulate business and consumer borrowing quickly. It can also stimulate aggregate demand and growth quickly because its decisions do not have to flow through the delays of the political process that other stabilization tools must surmount (Mikesell, 2014: 13). But, in the current context of near-zero interest rates, traditional monetary tools have limited effect.

For this reason, central banks in Japan, the UK, and the U.S. Federal Reserve engaged in policies of "quantitative easing" (QE) to stimulate demand through artificially creating inflation. The idea was to buy bonds off the market (increasing their coupon rate or price) to lower yields or long-term interest rates—which should stimulate bank lending and lead to growth through more consumption and investment. This looser form of monetary policy purchases mortgage bonds and T-bills with newly printed money in order to stimulate the real estate market by keeping lending rates down. Since the property market has improved substantially, it can be said that as of late 2013 the effects of using this policy tool have been positive in these countries. Other countries such as Germany oppose QE because it blurs the distinction between fiscal and monetary policy in the EU where there is no equivalent to federal U.S. debt. Absent a federal or federation political structure, the EU is fragmented into 28 sovereign countries and the ECB does not represent one state. Given these structural constraints, according to the ECB, "purchasing a basket of sovereign bonds would pose immense economic, political and legal challenges" (*Economist*, 2014b: 57). All solutions create new problems. When QE is tapered or scaled back, the reverse consequences should occur: asset supplies should increase, bond prices would decrease, and yields would drop. For transitional countries, that means that foreign investments would likely diminish and weaken their currencies against the dollar. This has already happened in Turkey, South Africa, and India, which have all had to raise interest rates to defend their currencies from dropping in the wake of the 2014 U.S. Federal Reserve QE taper policy.

Stimulus through Monetary Policy

Monetary policy is considered the first line of defense for stabilization policy because (in contrast with expenditure policy changes as noted) it has flexibility and speed. But its effects can be perverse for fiscal policy in the short-run. In some countries facing political deadlock over fiscal policy solutions such as the U.S., incentives to compromise over a reasonable mix of tax increases and spending cuts are weakened by the reality that inflation often: increases sales tax receipts as consumers rush to avoid further price increases; increases income tax receipts as workers experience bracket-creep; and reduces deficits because debts and entitlements are paid off with deflated dollars. For this to work, the central bank (Federal Reserve) must keep rates lower than inflation, which it was still doing in late 2013. In the EU, inflation remains low (0.5 percent) and the ECB is contemplating quantitative easing (QE) policy. Like the successful QE policies of monetary stimulus in Japan, England, and the U.S., the central bank would create new money to buy assets including sovereign bonds in order to try and counter "lowflation" (*Economist,* 2014j: 61).

Controlling Subnational Finances

Subnational sources of macroeconomic instability often derive from perverse or misaligned incentives. Because fiscal roles and responsibilities have not been assigned properly, local decisions may increase contingent liabilities for the central government. Conversely, the center might encourage local officials to mobilize local revenue sources to reduce fiscal pressures on the center. For example, in China local officials and property speculators work together to buy property, build flats, and hold them off the market. The result is high land and rental prices, high vacancy rates, and scarce affordable housing. Local governments rode the bubble upwards with higher revenues. But the risk of debt default is high if the artificial price bubble collapses in the wake of reduced economic growth. In this case, the central government could end up with the obligation (*Economist,* 2013m: 43). Local ad valorem property taxes could reduce speculation and stimulate subnational development more transparently. Behind the local official-speculator nexus in China and elsewhere is the problem of corruption or rent-seeking. This institutional problem requires strong internal audits and prosecutorial units to take action. That, of course, points to a problem of political will in many countries. Still, in most other country cases of excessive subnational fiscal deficits and debts, institutional counter-measures and controls have been largely effective, e.g. local and state increases in sales and income taxes and fees, rules against borrowing beyond set percentages of past year revenues, and cutbacks in services. Increased pension liabilities often remain but can be controlled by reducing new employee benefits; using cash management through short-term borrowing to cover budget deficits; and providing incentives to private capital firms to finance public capital projects. Other means of reducing liabilities include strengthening oversight by state auditors and private credit rating agencies to monitor state and local fiscal behavior and to manage bankruptcy when required for the benefits of creditors and taxpayers. These counter-measures are common in federal systems and have served as effective damage control and early warning systems.

Targeting Fiscal Deficits-Debts

1. Problem Definition

Despite the complexity of fiscal problems, they need to be defined clearly so that they are actionable. That is, options derived from the definitions should lead to preferred policy solutions. Lack of growth and unemployment, for instance, are problems that are easily measured and tracked. In most countries, deficits and debts are also clearly defined and measured. Monetary policy actions are clear and measurable. Structural constraints are also measurable and clear: the potentially negative effects of trade restrictions on growth; of over-regulation on business investment and hiring; of tax burdens on consumption and investment; of subsidies and tax exemptions for guilds and other protected interests; and of income and employment effects from targeted public investments. The overall effects of discretionary fiscal policy on growth varies widely; Roberto Perotti found that public spending had less effect than in the previous 20 years and that it may have had more effect in larger than smaller countries (Perotti, 2007). He found that the effects of government borrowing on increasing demand might also be smaller than in the past. Some of this has to do with the openness of economies and increased access to international capital (*Economist*, 2002: 13). This means it may be harder to measure the independent impact of fiscal policies in response to the problem of how to stimulate growth.

In short, there is usually not one problem but a combination of problems that affect growth. A narrow problem definition can focus more on playing defense. Glen Hubbard, for instance, targets entitlement program cost and expenditure contributions to the debt, suggesting that the growing debt problem will ultimately threaten the financial condition of the U.S. government. By this narrow problem definition, structural deficits (those that do not vary with economic cycles) will force debt levels upwards and confront the government with insolvency. A broader, more active perspective, e.g. Lawrence Summers, contains more moving parts and suggests that the problem is how to get the economy growing (Davidson, 2013: 32). The latter definition takes account of the size of government variable, noting that growth was still high in the 1950s–1960s when top tax rates were highest (up to 90 percent). In the U.S., the recent contributor to growth reduction and increased deficits and debts was the financial sector meltdown and corresponding failure to provide more public investment stimulus; in the UK, the problem has been the bloated size of the state sector; in Greece, an oversized state sector, its leveraging of EU rules to acquire unsustainable debts, an over-regulated industry, and protected guilds, all of which constrained growth; in Spain, failure to control evident property bubbles led to financial sector meltdown which threatened public finances; over-regulation and guild protection also contribute to high unemployment; and in Ireland, assumption of commercial banking debt temporarily damaged the public finances (Baldacci and Gupta, 2009: 12). In all cases, simple reliance on austerity measures would have had predictably different effects: especially negative in the UK, Greece, and Spain. Given resumption of growth in some sectors of the U.S. and reduction of unemployment, austerity would not be as damaging.

2. Options

The difficulty of forecasting the effects of different policy options is sorting out how these measures affect each other and then affect growth. For example, some subsidies and public investments can contribute to growth (temporary real sector stimulus; e.g. energy subsidies with low prices) while others might stymy growth and add to the levels of deficit and debt (e.g. solar subsidies, poorly targeted light-rail projects) and others may have negative effects in the short-term and positive multipliers in the long-run (e.g. airports building ahead of demand). To try and deal with this issue, the IMF combined independent variables to develop a "fiscal multiplier." The multiplier forecast that in normal and boom times, public spending would work against growth; in recessionary times, it would increase growth. For example, in normal times, a 1.5 multiplier means that $1 increase spending would reduce GDP by $1.50; conversely, in a recession the multiplier would predict growth from stimulus spending. In growth periods, negative fiscal multipliers would raise growth, suggesting the need for counter-cyclical fiscal rules. But in recessions, austerity may reduce short-term deficits but hurt growth more which could raise deficits again later (*Economist*, 2012: 76). With interest rates near zero in 2014, most spending reductions led to hefty declines in national income. IMF also found from a study of 176 fiscal policy changes from 1978 to 2009 that cutting a country's budget deficit by 1 percent GDP reduced real output by 0.66 percent and increased unemployment by 0.33 percent (*Economist,* 2011: 79). Based on these multipliers, for the EU in 2014 with low growth, inflation, and high unemployment, more public investment by countries with fiscal space of their own or provided by the European Investment Bank was clearly needed to reduce unemployment and stimulate growth. There are then three sets of options for fiscal policies to improve growth:

A. TARGET AND REDUCE DEBT DRIVERS

This policy response requires attention to controlling the costs of the main debt drivers, which tend to be health care and pensions in OECD countries. Pension benefits have to be trimmed to cut unfunded liabilities that threaten national and subnational balance sheets. For example, the burden of fringe and pension benefits on future services is high in most U.S. states. It is estimated that about 60 percent of the revenues from the recent tax hike in California will simply ratify runaway health and pension costs and the massive unfunded promises in both areas. Fringe and pension burdens are crowding out all other state services (e.g. education) as well as infrastructure investments for which financing is badly needed to stimulate future growth. In wealthier countries such as Germany and the U.S. that have been obsessed with balancing budgets and achieving fiscal austerity, capital stock in such assets as roads and railways are depreciating faster than replacement. Institutional rules that protect insurers, hospitals, and other professional groups such as physicians tend to drive up costs. Parliaments, fearful of losses in election financing support, have mostly been reluctant to impose cost controls through such alternatives as payments boards.

Pension liabilities are a serious hidden cost contributing to government debts. U.S. subnational governments, for example, set aside an amount each year determined in part by the investment experience of their pension fund portfolios (e.g. T-bills, mutual funds, bonds, mortgage-backed securities, and equities). A problem is that gains from pension investments have been far below those assumed by governments. If the government assumes a higher return (often around 8 percent) than they will actually receive (around 2 percent), states and counties artificially limit both current contributions and future liabilities (*Economist,* 2008:

82). Overestimation of gains allowed by state and county accounting rules positively exaggerate financial conditions. The same kind of uncontrolled gimmickry allows national governments to reduce pension liabilities on paper to keep higher credit ratings. The problem with taking this option is that it reduces benefits for those who can least afford to lose them—which is far worse in recessions . . .

B. PERFORM BUDGET REVIEWS

This is the most sensible and effective approach to cutting public sector costs. Using outputs and outcomes formats such as for performance and program results as noted above, and MTEFs to ensure sustainable budgets, the tools can be applied to decrease costs/unit of services and programs and to increase outcomes and impacts on targeted clients, e.g. patients, transit riders, students, and permit-license applicants. The British government has long conducted annual Comprehensive Spending Reviews that review trends, set spending and service targets, measure service efficiency and effectiveness, and develop transparent Public Service Agreements. Similar to those in Canada, Australia, and New Zealand, the reviews analyze the costs and consequences of all public programs. In contrast with most national governments, these Commonwealth governments perform the annual reviews and implement the results, e.g. through performance transfers for the NHS to improve delivery incentives. In the U.S., efficiency reviews are conducted by subnational governments regularly—through performance audits and departmental budget analyses. In countries such as China, with massive governmental structures, bloated ministries, and largely inefficient and ineffective services, reviews are also conducted. But these are mostly formalities, often for political purposes that focus on streamlining operational processes. While that is a step forward, the reviews tend to leave structures intact (i.e. number of ministries and purposes) as well as the perverse incentives that increase amounts of spending no matter what processes or structures are recommended.

Of those countries that do perform regular budget reviews, they often exclude the opportunity costs of state property: the non-financial assets that may or may not be on balance sheets. Frequent use of cash accounting means no annual depreciation charges are added for the costs of capital. With no charge, there is no booked asset either. This underestimates the value of state holdings. It is estimated that state-owned property in OECD countries is equivalent to about 18 percent of general government gross public debt (*Economist,* 2014c: 18). Such countries as New Zealand, Britain, Canada, and France have all adopted accrual accounting methods which can reveal these opportunity costs. That may lead to either sales or privatization, leasing, or rationalization of ministry and departmental stewardship of assets. Privatization efforts have led to social unrest and intense local opposition, e.g. selling public forestry assets. Leasing is a better option because ownership remains in state hands and a steady stream of revenues can reduce annual deficits as opposed to one-off debt-reducing asset sales, e.g. public buildings in high-rent areas such as London and Paris. Finally, state management rationalization can be achieved by consolidating authority in one unit, e.g. UK Companies House, which accounts for holdings, calculates opportunity costs, and provides transparent recommendations of options on how to increase revenues from these holdings. For example, the New Zealand treasury imposes an annual capital (i.e. depreciation) charge on departments. This has encouraged sale or leasing of underutilized buildings.

The appropriate policy analytic technique then would be lease-sale, also called sale and leaseback, rather than lease-purchase. To assess the efficiency of selling versus leasing, one would use the present value of future lease payments versus the opportunity costs foregone from selling the asset. The latter could be calculated by using: property tax values for untaxed property and some combination of book value/market value of state stakes or shares in assets. To achieve this end, the International Federation of Accountants (IFAC) offers private-sector versions of public sector accounting rules and methodologies (*Economist*, 2014c: 21). (See *Chapter 3* for further discussion and examples of lease-purchasing methods.)

C. BUDGET CONSOLIDATION AND AUSTERITY PROGRAMS

To ensure that policy responses do not make problems worse, governments need to know the timing, composition, and effectiveness of austerity or budget consolidation programs. Despite the complexity of the problems and the relative simplicity of the policies (i.e. cutting programs), their probable impact must be assessed. Otherwise, fiscal austerity and consolidation policies could become a fiscal drag on economic growth. Unfortunately, to date the empirical results are conflicting and incomplete, mostly depending on assumptions, definitions, and degrees of actual implementation. Here, we offer more preliminary results for a group of countries that represent varying degrees of adjustment effort in response to growing deficit and debt trends in the context of recent economic problems from 2008 to present. The results are tendencies rather than statistical associations, suggesting that much more international comparative research is needed.

Adjustment and Austerity

The general theory is that deficit reduction will increase savings, stabilize currency, and increase growth. This will eventually reduce the debt/GDP ratio; debt and deficit reduction also will decrease debt service costs, which will save funds to cover current expenditure gaps. *Column 1* of *Table 2.2* measures austerity results by reduction in real expenditure growth. Spending reductions could be the product of tax receipts increases from greater growth and other cost reductions in service delivery, e.g. the rate of health care cost increases have declined in the U.S., which could also be due to tighter eligibility requirements and better equipment and drug purchasing. That is, the spending reductions may not have been caused by formal budget consolidation policies. In addition, austerity programs vary widely in three other areas:

First, they may be timed to kick in several years in the future, and they may be extremely severe or mild. The "troika" of IMF, ECB, and EC originally wanted a sharp consolidation of Grecian public finance because their deficits were viewed as *structural* and not *cyclical*. Once it was clear that output and employment were also dropping sharply, the IMF shifted and recommended a gradual fiscal consolidation, arguing that sharp consolidations would be inapplicable under conditions of financial sector-driven recessions. That would especially be true where public sector deficits and debts have been largely caused by absorption of financial and banking sector losses, e.g. Ireland.

Second, the size of the state matters. Some states with relatively low-spending percent GDP (e.g. India at 27.2 percent and Chile at 21.1 percent in *Column 2*) have less direct policy effect on growth than those with high-spending percent GDP (e.g. France, Germany, Italy, UK, and Greece). Next, austerity programs vary in composition, e.g. the UK program is 80 percent spending reduction and 20 percent tax increases; the U.S. program has been 50 percent defense and 50 percent non-defense, or about 90 percent spending cuts and 10 percent tax increases.

The size of the state also matters since an austerity assumption is that redundant state employees can be absorbed by the private sector, with minimal effect on short-term unemployment levels. That would not be possible in most large states because they produce most of the GDP (see *Column 2, Table 2.2*). In the short term, at least, austerity would therefore sap growth until any structural changes could kick in. That suggests that an austerity or budget consolidation response would be insufficient to deal with the larger problem of structural constraints on the private sector and could do more damage than good in the short term without these additional measures, e.g. Poland.

Third, austerity and consolidation programs vary by the degree of policy discretion. Rule-based approaches, for instance, largely correct for normal times—not financial sector-driven recessions. The benefits of rule-based approaches are that they: (1) contain pressures to overspend (often by increasing public awareness of problem), ensuring fiscal responsibility and debt sustainability, (2) bridge the transition to lower deficits, and (3) enhance the credibility of debt and deficit reduction plans: www.imf.org/external/datamapper/fiscalrules/map/map.htm.

Rule-based approaches typically provide for fixed ceilings but allow changes at the operational level through reprogramming and transfer of funds between and within programs. For instance, the U.S. across-the-board "sequester" in 2013 allowed transfer within the two defense and non-defense categories but not within them. The EU's Stability and Growth Pact requires a 3 percent deficit ceiling and 60 percent GDP debt limit but has no enforcement mechanism or vehicle to determine when exceptions should be allowed for "excessive" deficits. U.S. deficit reduction or elimination programs have a long history of laws, operating rules, and now automatic sequesters (provided for by the Graham Rudman Hollings law of 1985 and used in 1986, 1988, and 1990). This law provided for "emergency" exceptions to the balanced budget rule and "offset" rules which require increased spending to be matched with more revenue. A more formal and automatic approach has been the *Swiss Fiscal Error Correction Account.* This embeds deficits and surpluses over multiple fiscal years for medium-term budget control. So greater than projected deficits are debited to the accounting system and require payment later; conversely, greater surpluses are credited to the account. Through this mechanism, memory is embedded into the budget process. All budget rules suffer from the same defect of "process illusion." This is the notion that parliaments can write rules forcing themselves to make unpopular political choices. In the words of Samuelson, "They try to accomplish big political and social changes through technical, mechanical means that, by design, mystify the public. But once the consequences of these fiscal choices become clear, the politicians retreat. They circumvent, modify, ignore or weaken the rules" (Samuelson, 2014a).

Macroeconomi Results: Growth and Unemployment

The expectations for getting the policy right are that higher output or growth and employment in permanent jobs will be created and reduce unemployment. But there are at least three paradoxes here. First, growth depends on private investment in labor and capital to produce goods and services outputs. These depend on bank financing in most cases and that requires large banks with large balance sheets through such means as bond issuance. But many such loans inflate the financial sector without contributing to economic growth. This increases financial system risk that can result in collapse when innovative financing instruments such as collateralized debt obligations (CDOs) based on insufficient collateral suffer losses. Regulators have responded most recently by requiring banks to hold more capital (Basel 3; Dodd-Frank). But, paradoxically that could discourage them from more lending which will impede growth

(*Economist*, 2013n: 4). Second, according to Romer (2012), changes in fiscal policy can affect employment and output in the short term. But employment in many countries is in the informal sector (e.g. India, 85 percent of jobs) over which changes in bank lending rates may have less effect on many small shops than fewer large firms. Third, high public-sector costs and expenditures may paradoxically generate new support industries. An important determinant of future debt rates are health care costs. The U.S., for example, spends 17.9 percent GDP, which widens its deficits and debts. But at the local level, many private health care clusters and hubs have formed to process data and perform tasks related to new legislation at the national and local levels. Jobs in this sector are expected to grow 26 percent (2013–2020) and by 2020 will account for 14.2 percent of all workers (*Economist*, 2013o: 27). Should budget consolidation focus on cutting health care expenditures, this would also reduce employment and growth at the same time!

The data in *Table 2.2* indicate that in the seven countries (out of the 11 for which data is presented) with strong or moderately strong budget consolidation/austerity efforts, growth has been low or negative over the approximately six-year period: 2008–2013. One could argue that in the medium term, eventually such austerity programs might produce positive growth results, e.g. Poland after the transition of the early 1990s. But there, budget consolidation was part of a much larger strategy of "shock therapy" that aimed to remove the structural constraints as well as trim the size of the state. That was implemented and successfully removed both those constraints and reduced the deficit (now -3.5 percent of GDP). While growth slowed later to only 0.7 percent in 2013, it picked up a year later to 3.2 percent. But unemployment remains high at 13.6 percent, suggesting strongly that other intervening variables are at work.

Business Environment or Structural Context

The main contextual variables are the rule of law and levels of corruption. In many transitional and developing countries, these elements are missing and cannot be changed in the short term. Budget consolidation expects shorter term results in growth and employment, which means that firms must be able to generate profits in country. To stimulate growth and employment directly, firms must be able to manage their workforces and navigate the thickets of local bureaucratic rules to produce, sell, and export. Put another way, corruption, weak laws, and instability are more or less constants that have to be absorbed and circumvented if possible by cunning managers, e.g. bribes, alternate energy sources such as generators, private security forces, and so on. But if they ultimately interfere with direct production and generation of profits, the structural or supply-side constraints can become severe.

An important institutional constraint in many countries is that the financial sector consists of state banks which lend to state firms. The relation between banking and fiscal policies will be covered further in *Chapter 5*. Wasteful lending to favored firms and their unproductive spending weakens growth prospects. In China, for instance, credit is channeled to the housing sector, fueling speculation, while private firms operate in markets from railways to telecommunications that are dominated by state-owned enterprises (SOEs). The example is important in that China boasts four of the world's ten biggest banks and the state owns most of the equity in them. To prevent commercial banks from taking away their large deposit bases, states limit the interest rates that can be paid on commercial deposits. This restricts individual savings and investment and forces them into shadow financial institutions and out of the formal banking system. In China as in many transitional and developing countries, the state directs the banks to lend while it decides how to allocate losses and when (*Economist*,

Table 2.2 Impact of Fiscal Adjustments on Macroeconomic Performance

Country	Adjustment Effort: Real Expenditure Growth 2010–2013 (IMF Fiscal Monitor, "Fiscal Adjustment in an Uncertain World," April 2013, Figure 2.6); Less Expenditure Growth, 2008–2009 (2010–2013)−(2008–2009)=	Spending % GDP (Heritage Foundation, 2011); Budgetary Balance (Economist, May 4, 2013)	Business Environment: Rigidity of Employment on Hiring and Firing: 1–10, Least–Most Rigid (Econstats and World Bank WDI, 2009)	Business Environment: Ease of Doing Business (Degree of Regulation) Index: 0–100, Most–Least Friendly (Econstats and World Bank WDI, 2011 and 2012) 2011	2012	Growth (World Bank) 2008–2012 v. Latest (Economist, April 19, 2014)	Unemployment, 2009–2014 (Economist, April 19, 2014)
U.S.	7.0-0.2 = 6.8 HIGH	38.9 -5.4	1.8	4	4	1.7 2.8 MOD	6.7
Britain CW	5.0-0.2 = 4.8 HIGH	47.3 -7.9	1.0	6	7	0.8 2.9 MOD	7.2
Germany EU	2.1-0.0 = 2.1 MOD	43.7 -0.3	4.2	18	20	3.0 1.8 LOW	6.7
France EU	0.2-(0.5) = -0.7 LOW	52.8 -4.0	5.2	32	34	1.7 0.8 LOW	10.4
Italy EU	0.1-(0.2) = -0.3 LOW	48.8 -3.1	3.8	71	73	0.4 0.5 LOW	13.0
Spain EU	6.0-(0.8) = 5.2 HIGH	41.1 -6.5	4.9	42	44	0.4 0.8 LOW	25.6
Ireland EU	6.9-(0.9) = 7.8 HIGH	42.0 -8.5	1.0	16	15	-2.0 2.1 LOW	11.8
Greece EU	4.0-(-9.0) = 13.0 HIGH	46.8 -5.3	5.0	89	78	-7.1 0.0	27.5
Portugal EU	-1.0-4.0 = 5.0 HIGH	46.1 -6.1	4.3	32	30	1.2 LOW	15.3
India A	6.0 = 6.0 NONE	27.2 -5/1	3.0	129	133	6.3 6.0 HIGH	9.9
Chile	8.0 = 8.0 NONE	21.1 +1.0	1.8	33	37	6.0 3.8 HIGH	6.1

2013: 88). Guided by targets and state orders, state enterprises should be viewed as powerful interest groups that allocate budgetary resources to favored state and private firms for state projects. They impede the growth and functioning of competitive markets that could allocate capital more efficiently. The current Japanese government of Shinzo Abe is attempting to stimulate growth through demand-side fiscal stimulus, supply-side structural reforms, and monetary easing. But removing supply-side constraints depends on the ability of each country to make fundamental reforms of political and economic institutions, i.e. converting empirical data into useful policy information and then acting on it.

A related structural constraint on the banking systems of many countries is the legal and regulatory framework that often favors state banks over commercial lenders and deposit-takers. When fiscal and financial policies require the banking system to adopt anti-inflationary measures and it fails, who is to blame? Courts in Brazil recently ruled, for instance, that banks took advantage of failed anti-inflation (stabilization) policies in the early 1980s that cost holders of inflation-linked savings accounts substantial amounts of money. The question then was whether banks that followed the law (policy) to protect the currency were still liable for depositor contractual losses. The legal and financial dilemma caused the former finance minister to state: as it is said, "in Brazil, even the past is unpredictable!" (*Economist*, 2014d: 70).

Data tendencies show that austerity effectiveness requires that structural constraints on firms be minimal. Where employment rigidity and the degree of regulation are high, the effect of strong or weak austerity programs will be diminished on growth or employment. Unemployment and low growth tend to continue in countries with poor business environments regardless of the severity of budget consolidation, e.g. France, Italy, Spain, Greece, and Portugal. This reflects structural factors that cannot be removed in the short term. Conversely, countries with supportive business environments, e.g. U.S. and UK, have had moderate growth and more reduction of unemployment, i.e. weak recoveries. This moderate growth seems to have reduced levels of fiscal deficits and debts as much as any consolidation policy efforts. One estimate is that a 1-percent increase in growth each year over the next ten years could set the U.S. debt/GDP on a sustainable trajectory without requiring cuts in any major programs such as Medicare or raising tax rates (Lowrey, 2013: 5).

Application of Analytic Frameworks

Here we provide two issue examples: (1) designing macroeconomic policies in response to fiscal shock amidst of impact complexity and (2) explaining regional differences in fiscal policy impacts. First, some sectoral policies may not be ready for second-level political economy and third-level comparative treatment (refer back to *Figure 1.4*) because so little is known. Basic data and information on the impacts of differing policy designs in particular contexts is so weak that it is almost useless to try and derive refined lessons. The relation between international fiscal policies and economic impacts remains complex and is determined largely by country context. An almost clinical opportunity to compare the macroeconomic effects of fiscal policies arose in 2010. Researchers tried to examine the negative effects on aggregate demand of fiscal stimuli policies in the wake of the global economic crisis of 2008–2010 (a severe fiscal shock).

The challenges in tackling this issue reveal both the complexity of fiscal sector problems as well as the lack of previous applied comparative efforts at the country policy level. Dethier (2010), for example, performed an early literature review and identified similar income countries which of course did not mean similar cultures and institutions. He examined seven middle income countries, including Turkey, Russia, and Brazil. While the institutional, political, and cultural contexts were widely dissimilar, this important first effort in applied research identified the policy similarities, i.e. the composition of policies in public investments, fiscal transfers, and tax cuts and measured their effects on capital, labor, and/or consumption. Japan, for example, stressed consumption transfers; India tax cuts on consumption; Saudi Arabia public investment; China public investment in education, infrastructure, and telecommunications. The contexts and policy packages varied widely. Given these differences, how could one recommend tested policies that revealed the effect of such policies on growth resumption and releasing bottlenecks to growth? What levers should an individual policy-maker recommend be pulled or pushed and in what order? Recent efforts were made by the IMF using member country data and information to try to answer similar questions as: What was the composition of fiscal stimulus packages leading to the greatest fiscal multipliers? Under what conditions were fiscal consolidation and deficit/debt reduction efforts made? How effective have these fiscal policies been as counter-cyclical tools? (Cottarelli et al., 2014). Unfortunately, chapter analyses eschewed case studies or comparative country analyses and relied more on aggregate fiscal and economic data.

Design of macroeconomic policies in response to a severe fiscal shock is clearly a problem of action research. Policy-makers during the 2008–2010 crisis period were largely flying blind in a global financial attack and needed applied advice on comparable design and implementation experiences elsewhere. None really existed at the basic data/information level on different technical policy designs controlled for institutional and cultural context. For this reason, future research must begin at the ground level, examining technical policy designs and results in different countries. It should then proceed, as we suggest, to refinement by controlling for culture, political context, and institutions. Dethier (2010) developed and applied fiscal multipliers to estimate the effects of these different technical policies. The literature notes that a critical intervening variable between fiscal policies and growth is the labor market (incomes). This adds a structural element that cannot be changed in the short run by policy and affects some countries more than others.

Moreover, agreement on the importance of macroeconomic fundamentals in different contexts is still missing. For example, Pescatori et al. (2014: 39) examined a 34-country sample from 1875 to 2011 and found no simple threshold above which debt ratios severely undermined medium-term growth prospects. That suggests support for the conclusion that tight austerity policies designed to reduce debts below the previously accepted threshold of 90 percent can further diminish economic growth and performance. The intervening labor market variable might be less important than previously thought. In short, even at the technical level, major conceptual and practical problems need to be solved before policies can be compared and macroeconomic impacts traced clearly. Dethier (2010) did note that the literature points to different stimulus packages having different and often mixed effects in different contexts. International fiscal policy research is still at this aggregate stage and needs to proceed to country and regional levels. The problems revealed by the global fiscal shock is that much more comparative work needs to be done to provide policy-makers with the tested tools they need to apply in the next crisis. As noted in the preface, it may be more feasible to focus on one element of monetary policy (e.g. QE) to see where it has been effective in comparison with those countries in the same region that have not implemented the same policy. This allows for comparison of common policy measures in similar cultural and institutional contexts, producing much more applicable lessons.

Second, it is known that differences in the results of fiscal austerity policies exist between Central and Eastern Europe and Latin America that have puzzled fiscal experts. Latin

America had a lengthy history of high fiscal deficits and public indebtedness, especially during the 1970s–1980s. Efforts to impose fiscal discipline were resisted by powerful local groups and the economies were plagued by inflation, unemployment, and lack of growth. By contrast, Central and Eastern European countries such as Poland after the transition period in the early 1990s adopted tight fiscal policies and were reluctant to contract debt. The result was increased foreign investment, growth, low unemployment, and low inflation. To round out the picture, major Latin American countries engaged in fiscal reforms in the 1990s also and increased transparency, and reduced deficits (1 percent–2 percent of GDP in most cases with Chile regularly running surpluses). In almost every aspect of fiscal reform, Latin American best performers came to match those of Central and Eastern Europe. Thus, the first-level framework is useful here in evaluating the statistical and econometric relationships between the inputs, outputs, and outcomes of policy. That allows one to move to the questions of how did these relationships happen and what lessons might be transferable to other regions?

Variables in the second-level political economy framework would stress (1) growing regime support, (2) changed incentives in the political culture that modified practices such as internal audit and treasury management and that integrate financial management systems at the operational level, and (3) increased technical capacities in local policy institutions provided in part by international donors such as Inter-American Development Bank and World Bank. Changes in the background culture, provision of top-level support, and improved institutional incentives then might explain how and why Latin American fiscal austerity practices became more like the austere Central and Eastern Europe. The latter had suffered through decades of austerity under the Soviet system and was therefore able to endure a few years more in exchange for what turned out to be very successful policy results.

The second-level political economy framework then generates lessons on policy design. It tries to explain results using the core variables of culture, institutions, political regimes, and organizations. The analytic questions raised are: what features of these regions do the variables explain and do they lead to predictions on whether fiscal austerity will be designed and implemented effectively? First, regime support is often assured unless a robust media mobilizes support against spending cuts and/or tax-fee increases. In France, good analyses produced by local policy institutions, e.g. MOF and international organizations such as IMF, revealed that the 3 percent EU target might be too stringent under current low-growth conditions. For this reason, the regime let the target slip to 3.8 percent of GDP to allow for more public investment in order to stimulate demand (since consumption and private investment were not taking up the slack). The regime also promised structural supply-side reforms of labor markets and regulatory burdens to stimulate demand, thereby generating more tax revenues and lowering deficits. The regime used these policy arguments as the basis for obtaining temporary waivers from the 3 percent target (a political deal). Partisan support for austerity reflected this divided policy state. The 3 percent rule ran up against local politics as well as policy analyses. Second, the political culture will affect the result. Political cultures can translate into (a) capacities to defer gratification, (b) institutional resilience to follow through on policy implementation, and (c) the ability to resist short-term impulses contrary to sound economic theory and best empirical practices.

The German political culture, for example, facilitated maintenance of low wages (acquiescence by unions in wage increases below inflation and productivity for the past decade), amounting to an internal devaluation to make exports more competitive. Foregone spending power also contributed to large trade surpluses. Needed then were wage increases and more public investment to tackle slow growth (*Economist*, 2014d: 49). German political culture defers gratification, operates within a resilient set of policy institutions that achieve policy performance intended by the regime, and includes a lively media that reflects both partisan and national interests. Central and Eastern Europe also have many of these cultural qualities, which explains the success of fiscal austerity policies; Latin America for many decades did not. Their political culture could not defer gratification; regimes opted for short-term populist fixes to curry political favor (e.g. Venezuela for the past decade) and institutions could not follow through on policy plans. Parliaments and political parties opposed empirically driven policies that worked elsewhere in Latin America (e.g. Chile). But over time, advice, experimentation, and positive results spread the demonstrated benefits of fiscal austerity policies to other countries with similar results, e.g. Mexico, Peru, and Brazil.

The Asian region also demonstrates these cultural features. Consistent with the matched-case comparative approach described in *Chapter 1*, it can be predicted that austerity/consolidation policies could be enacted in most countries, e.g. India, China, Japan, and South Korea. However, it cannot be said that these features of the political culture favoring sound austerity policies exist in the African region. There appears to be less capacity to defer gratification; the policy institutions despite technical and professional qualifications (e.g. Kenya, Liberia, and Ghana) are overridden by weak and highly politicized ministries, parliaments, and partisan inputs that block needed policy results (e.g. Nigeria). In the African region, culture and institutional weaknesses, such as lack of trust in government and widespread corruption or lack of internal controls and audit systems, have inhibited efforts to instill fiscal discipline. Because Asian institutions and cultures are similar to those of Central and Eastern Europe and the newly modified cultures of Latin America, lessons could be largely interchangeable between all three at especially the operational level. One piece of evidence for this is that GFMIS systems operate effectively in all three regions to register transactions and provide information from which to control public expenditures. Consistent with our contention that operational systems such as GFMIS can be transferred successfully in spite of institutional and cultural differences, these systems also work effectively in many African countries (Dener et al., 2011: 143).

Conclusions

The general conclusion from our chapter is that much more empirical research is required into optimal fiscal policies for economic growth under differing conditions. Specifically, we can draw five narrower conclusions or lessons from *Tables 2.1* and *2.2*:

1   *Problem Definition and Response*: Fiscal policies in the form of taxation and spending adjustments and efforts to meet deficit and debt targets have narrower purposes. They are designed to improve the fiscal position and ensure fiscal sustainability. If it is expected that fiscal policies alone, in the form of austerity or stimuli programs, can remedy structural problems and problems in other sectors such as finance and banking, that is a much taller order. Growth and employment improvements may result from fiscal policy changes in the short run, but the policies must be more sophisticated and multi-faceted to remedy macroeconomic problems.

2   *Budget and Policy Analysis*: Across-the-board cuts or additions are likely to waste funds and increase the inefficiency and ineffectiveness of policy, program, or project results. For this reason, budget analysis tools such as MTEF, use of performance and functional formats, and statistical analysis to measure linkages between resource commitments and

outputs and outcomes are necessary. Often MTEF reforms remain at the broad line-item level, e.g. wages or capital spending, without drilling down into actual allocations and trade-offs that would be evident through marginal analysis. In order to refine fiscal policies (e.g. taxation versus expenditure composition), adjust timing (early versus later years), and target sectors and items such as subsidies, analysis needs to be performed regularly. Commonwealth systems engage in Annual Spending Reviews, and U.S. state and local governments typically analyze costs and consequences of fiscal adjustments. These may be performed by in-house budget analyst offices in the executive and legislative branches as well as internal and external audit institutions. Analyses with different results based on different assumptions from multiple sources, including NGO fiscal monitoring efforts, are useful in narrowing down problems and solutions.

Sound analysis avoids the problem of lump-sum, across-the-board cuts to achieve "phantom balances" that simply materialize later in infrastructure and service deterioration that will require greater expenditures later (usually several elections away). Lack of marginal analysis means that austerity cuts often lead perversely to greater unintended deficits and downstream debts.

3   *Size and Strength of State*: This question is often answered ideologically apart from the marginal analyses that could pinpoint its actual state strengths and weaknesses. Larger states may be required to plan and implement policies across the country either directly or through subnational governments driven by targeted matching and conditional grants. But large states producing most of the GDP, e.g. Greece or France, often have small private sectors incapable of absorbing the unemployed that suffer from austerity cuts to make states more efficient. State modernization analyses are required here to target ministries, departments, functions, and structures that may be politically appropriate but inefficient from a fiscal and economic performance perspective. Conversely, states that are too small will be unable to deliver policy implementation results and lack capacities to regulate needed industries and sectors, e.g. the Indian central state (27.2 percent GDP spending), which is largely inefficient, versus Chile, whose state is far more efficient (21.1 percent GDP spending).

4   *Structural Constraints*: If more employment and growth are the intended results, consumers and firms must save, invest, and produce. Many countries over-regulate private sectors, which can include informal taxes and extortion in the form of arbitrary regulations and payments to enforcers. Over-regulation facilitates corruption in public finance (e.g. multi-stage budget approvals for purchasing) as well as commercial enterprises (e.g. customs bribery). Regulations are often used to protect guilds, unions, and monopoly industries and ensure access to subsidies, tax breaks, and other leakages from the treasury that harm fiscal balances and service results. Such structural constraints are critical intervening variables between fiscal policies and the macroeconomic results. Where such constraints are severe (e.g. Spain) a purely fiscal austerity policy approach will have few direct effects on macroeconomic results and probably will damage growth and employment in the short run (*Economist*, 2013m: 57). Other structural constraints exist in the form of financial and banking sector over-regulation and poor oversight that prevent them from contributing to macroeconomic objectives. While outside the narrower parameters of fiscal policies (refer to *Chapter 5*), these sectors can constitute serious constraints to growth and employment. The failure of Spanish and Italian banks to lend to small and medium enterprises at reasonable rates still constrains job creation even though in some countries such as the U.S. and France, SMEs employ 50 percent–60 percent of all workers. While high-debt public sectors (90.7 percent in Spain and 126.3 percent in

Italy) crowd private borrowing to some extent and keep lending rates higher, a more important influence is the refusal of ECB to lower bank borrowing costs in the European region costs through policies such as buying SME loans directly from both banks and non-bank lenders (*Economist*, 2012a: 16).

5   *Transfer of Best Practices*: Given cultural and political constraints in the field, fiscal policy reforms in budget and taxation transfer slowly if at all. Budget and PFM reforms proceed in "fits and starts" and must be "scaled down to what is possible within the local context" (Allen et al., 2013: 5). Tax transparency norms, such as the OECD Tax Transparency Initiative, suffer from perverse international bureaucratic incentives to achieve a short-term least common denominator. International organizations promoting tax transparency across borders paradoxically demand effective standards transfer but settle for weak norms to preserve their own legitimacy in brokering international agreements at the strategic level. This leads to emphasis on incremental policy change (Eccleston and Woodward, 2013). Despite these practices, significant policy reforms can be achieved at the project level through aid programs that connect with local, regional, and national policy officials that demand changes in systems, and better analytic tools and practices. It should not be surprising then if PFM reforms in taxation or budgeting proceed incrementally given their complexity.

Cases and Exercises

Case 2.1 Slugovia Medium-Term Expenditure Framework

Based on the following 13 assumptions and using the data provided, answer the four questions below:

Background: Slugovia is a country of 2.6 million that combines services and light industry with farming of wheat/grains, beets, and corn. The unemployment rate is 15 percent; the foreclosure rate from the financial sector crisis was 25 percent and many homes are still abandoned in the city. Last year, its budget deficit was 10 percent of total expenditures and its long-term debt from pensions and loans is unsustainable at about 95 percent of GDP. Vacancy rates are high at about 30 percent and retail sales have been dropping over the past three years. Most importantly, the ratio of public assistance households per 1,000 households is about 30 percent. Revenues depend on income tax receipts, sales taxes, charges (customs and fees), and international grants. The Sluggish population has been declining, suggesting that this is a relatively poor country with a shrinking tax base. Its GDP is based mostly on tourism, agricultural exports (coffee and bananas), and some electronic industry assembly plants. The GDP growth will only be 0.5 percent over last year. The local currency is the Slug, which is pegged to the dollar at 1 SLG = $1.

1   The Slugovian economy is the same as its social services sector. The local budget provides 90 percent of the resources for social services, which are the responsibility of the Department of Social Assistance. Public expenditures from this department consist mainly of (1) cash benefits to eligible beneficiaries (social assistance payments) and (2) social services investments, mainly in elderly, handicapped, and children's homes, which include salaries and maintenance. Both kinds of social service

expenditures are driven by available revenues (largely from the farming sector—which itself is subsidized) and loans. Social services capital investments are also financed by a matching grant or transfer from the state or federal governments. The state department of finance pays 50 percent of the approved amount for social services and the local governments match this amount at 50 percent.

2   Poor or delayed maintenance results in premature need for rehabilitation and reduces economic value of the homes to social services users. This is caused by: poor fiscal planning at the national level, poorly designed grant formulae, and lack of local contributions to finance social services investments. Capital financing grants contain perverse incentives which discourage use of recurrent funds for O&M while encouraging premature replacement of facilities. At the same time, the department does not budget for or advocate funding for maintenance resulting in continued repair of facilities that should have been replaced. (There is some evidence of this here.)

3   Cancellation of projects after signed contracts results in a 10 percent penalty for the City. Project delays or cancellations after appraisal but before contract signature cause economic health losses to clients of existing facilities.

4   Each year, projects are being started, nearing completion, and being maintained and rehabilitated after completion. Rehabilitation takes place every four years (which explains the big jump in rehabilitation in year $P + 3$). Rehabilitation costs 50 percent of facility replacement.

5   Budget subsidies support employment in agriculture, soft loans to small and medium-sized enterprises, health care, and water sector industries. Subsidy cuts would lead to short-term increases in unemployment that would require increased social assistance transfers from the city.

6   Recurrent implications of new starts have not been calculated, resulting in exceeded deficit targets by year $P + 2$.

7   Despite projections of declining revenues, and eventual cuts in both subsidies and new starts, the fiscal plan calls for overall increases in recurrent and capital spending to stimulate growth. This could affect the stability of actual Slugovian allocations for social services and assistance payments.

8   The wages and O&M proportions of the budget in year P will approximate those of the Slugovian Fiscal Plan. The Plan quite accurately assumes that in the face of declining revenues, recurrent expenditures will remain roughly constant while capital expenditures will decline. The multi-year plan increases both recurrent and capital expenditures and this evolves into a serious fiscal crisis by year $P + 4$.

9   Wages are frozen for three years. Assuming inflation increases at 2 percent per year, wages are not meeting cost of living increases. This pressure leads to a planned wage increase in the fifth year. The multi-year fiscal plan ignores the revenue constraint in the interest of generating a crisis.

10   Because of increasing new starts up to year 5, debt service to external lenders (i.e. banks and bondholders) increases.

11   Slugovia will seek a $10-million loan guarantee to finance infrastructure in the social assistance sector.

12   The Slugovian budget is consolidated or unified (current and capital combined). The deficit target of 5 percent is as a proportion of total consolidated expenditures.

13   Because of the recession and slow projected GDP growth, the Government's MOF has undertaken a fiscal stimulus program. This program will consist of capital investments in homeless shelters, nursing and children's homes of 5 billion SLGs/ year starting in year P + 1. The program objectives are to (1) respond to projected increases in demand and (2) stimulate construction to provide income and employment. The projected investments should be added to the current forecast (which indicates a drop in new starts and near completion capital expenditures by year P + 4). Thus, the government of Slugovia (GOS) will be implementing both a budget consolidation policy (austerity to achieve the 5 percent deficit) and a fiscal stimulus program at the same time.

1. Define the problem(s). What are the dimensions of the evolving Slugovia fiscal crisis?

a   *Calculate* total recurrent deficits, total capital expenditures, the budget deficit, the primary balance, and their percentages of total expenditures.
b   *Decide* the proportion of expenditure-revenue causation for growing deficits. Focus on particular expenditure items that should be increased, decreased, or modified and do the same with revenue sources.

2. Analyze revenue and expenditure sources and uses and make adjustments accordingly to meet at consolidated 5 percent fiscal deficit target by year P + 4.

a   *Recommend* changes to revenue sources and any expenditure item that will change the forecasted trends, and justify their feasibility, i.e. expenditure fiscal and user needs implications, revenue yields, regressivity, etc. Consistent with the notion of a "hard budget constraint," these changes should ensure that Slugovia fiscal performance meets a 5 percent deficit target for the CY.
b   *Propose* any reasonable options that you think are necessary given the dimensions of the crisis. The options should lead to policy decisions that ensure current and medium-term fiscal sustainability and stability.

3. The GOS intends to implement a budget consolidation and stimulus program to encourage growth. Based on primary deficit figures, does the GOS have sufficient fiscal space to do this? What should be the composition of the stimulus program?

4. Design a rolling medium-term expenditure framework for Slugovia that could avoid future fiscal crises at the levels of (1) fiscal discipline and policy level, (2) functional allocation, and (3) operational efficiency and effectiveness. What data and information are missing to perform this task fully? What proxies or "action research" could produce sufficient information to justify decisions at all three levels?

SLUGOVIA MEDIUM-TERM EXPENDITURE PLAN

Year	P	P + 1	P + 2	P + 3	P + 4
REVENUES Billion $	150	180	170	160	140
Income Tax	106.5	127.8	120.7	113.6	99.4
Sales Tax	24.0	28.8	27.2	25.6	22.4
Grants	12.0	14.4	13.6	12.8	11.2
Charges	7.5	9.0	8.5	8.0	7.0
Recurrent Expenditures					
Salaries and Fringe Benefits	80	85	85	85	90
Transfers (social services/benefits)	15	15	20	25	25
Subsidies (functional or sectoral)	15	20	15	10	10
Debt Service	5	10	15	25	25
Operations-Maintenance	10	15	15	25	30
TOTAL RECURRENT					
Capital Expenditures					
New Starts	10	10	10	10	5
Near Completions	15	20	35	10	5
Rehabilitations	5	10	5	40	55
TOTAL CAPITAL					
CONSOLIDATED TOTAL					
Deficit					
Deficit Target (% Total Expenditure)	5	5	5	5	5
Deficit (% Total Expenditure)					
Primary Balance (Revenues less Expenditures less Debt Service)					

Case 2.2 Italy's Shrinking Economy

Source: *Economist*, 2014k: 24

On August 6, Matteo Renzi's government's statisticians disclosed that Italy was back in recession. Preliminary estimates suggested that GDP fell by 0.2% in the second quarter of 2014 after a drop of 0.2% in the first quarter.

This was the worst blow to the prime minister since coming to office in February. No one expected such a dismal performance. Forecast ranged from 0.1% to -0.1%. If the estimate is confirmed, it will mean second-quarter growth is weaker than at any time since 2000.

The finance minister, Pier Carlo Padoan, put a brave face on the numbers by pointing to an encouraging increase in industrial production in June. But the reversal of Italy's fortunes will have a profoundly demoralizing effect on a nation that had thought the worst was over. It could adversely influence decisions on investment, employment and consumption.

News that the economy is shrinking leaves a huge dent in the credibility of the government's overall strategy. On entering office, Mr. Renzi took a gamble—that the economy would recover without the need for much structural reform, enabling him to get on with what he judged to be the important business of institutional change. When the GDP figures came out, the prime minister was closeted with Silvio Berlusconi, the leader of Italy's second biggest opposition party, trying to agree on a new electoral law, the second phase in their ambitious plan for a more effective and stable form of government.

Mr. Renzi's main ploy for boosting growth has been a $107 (80 Euros) monthly tax break for lower-paid workers. That too had a political flavor because it helped the prime minister silence the left wing of his party and win an impressive victory in the European elections in May. But this week the head of the shopkeeper's association said the tax break's impact on domestic consumption had been "almost invisible."

Other growth initiatives are on the runway, notably legislation to restart building projects. But, unlike liberalization, privatization and labor-market reform, infrastructure projects need money for take-off. Even before this week's GDP shock, the government was struggling to find the resources it needed. On August 4 it withdrew plans to bring forward the retirement of school and university teachers after the treasury objected that there was not enough cash to pay for them. The government's spending plans for the rest of 2014 are based on the assumption of 0.8% growth by year's end, and that now looks as likely as summer snowfall in Sicily.

If Italy is to respect its euro-zone budget reduction commitments without yet more tax increases, deep spending cuts will be needed (15b–20b Euros by most reckonings). There is plenty of waste and extravagance to be tackled. But unless the government acts quickly to free up markets and encourage rationalization and efficiency, there is a risk that the cuts will simply subdue demand further, accelerating the downward spiral in which the economy is trapped.

Questions

1   What is the probable relation between further fiscal austerity and growth? Design a simple simulation to develop options for taxing and spending. What additional data would you need?

2   What structural features may explain weak growth here? Did the prime minister consider these structures as part of "institutions" needing change? Why or why not?

3   What other comparative fiscal policy performances could you recommend to Mr. Renzi as examples of successful responses, stimulating growth under similar conditions?

Case 2.3 Institutions and Culture in the Canadian Public Budgeting System

Source: Francis, 2014

Governance models have always been designed to meet specific and unique social and political objectives. The result has been many forms of government capable of good government and many forms of democratic government capable of democracy. Americans aimed to eliminate monarchy from their lives and keep government prerogatives in check at all times. The British objective was to keep a watchful eye on taxation and royal spending. The Swiss wrote a constitution in 1848 that smoothed over their religious divisions following a brief civil war between Protestants and Catholics; the result is a highly non-transparent but collegial system. The Germans bolstered their system following the hijacking of the Weimar republic by the Nazis; in it, coalitions are built for four-year tenures, there can be no snap elections, and the President's powers are weak. All these systems of democracy are distinct and they all work reasonably well.

To illustrate the differences, here is what Washington would look like in a Westminster scenario. The House of Representatives would be in charge of taxation and spending. The Senate would provide consent on laws, and could make recommendations about budgets but not veto them. The President would be head of state, elected by the Electoral College, and would be given important "reserve powers" designed to guarantee political stability. Each party member would have to vote party line, and toe the line.

Budgets are more than just accounting exercises. They are critical tools for organizations to plan and manage operations. Government budgets inform the public about taxes, forecasts, and the cost of policy initiatives. They reveal the state of the nation and provide critical guidance to voters and the markets. They are, therefore, important political documents in a democratic governance system.

Parliamentary and presidential systems require approval of a budget every year. But a Prime Minister who fails to gain approval for a budget is removed from office while a President and Congress that fail can simply kick the can down the road by approving stopgap measures to keep operations going. Unfortunately, this perpetuates disagreements and accepts indecisiveness. It is why the last budget approved in Washington dates back to fiscal year 2010.

If the U.S. were a publicly listed corporation, with the CEO, with the management and executives at war over budgets, it would have long since been de-listed from stock exchanges. But governments don't get de-listed; their creditworthiness get downgraded. So in 2011 Washington's internecine warfare caused a rating drop from AAA to AA+, and Standard and Poor's issued the following statement: "The downgrade reflects our view that the effectiveness, stability and predictability of American policymaking and political institutions have weakened at a time of ongoing fiscal and economic challenges."

Now, parliamentary systems do not guarantee better judgment, nor do politicians faithfully ascribe to fiscal rectitude. But they can expeditiously respond to crises or public groundswells. In 1992, Canada's debt rating was downgraded from AAA to AA+ after a downturn and years of profligacy. Markets, business, the public and media criticized the government privately and publicly. The Liberal government immediately reversed course for its February budget and announced cost-cutting measures, downsizing government departments and raising taxes to fix the fiscal challenges. They retained majority control and were able to impose austerity measures for several years until budgets were balanced. By 2002, the credit rating was restored to AAA.

The budget process is sacrosanct in Westminster parliaments. In Canada, the Minister of Finance publicly announces his budget in February or March, and the budget is usually approved within days. In Canada, there have been only three "no confidence" votes in parliament leading to resignations and snap elections in 50 years, and there has never been a government shutdown. Under Canada's constitution, the Governor-General allocates funds to keep the lights on during election periods when no budget is in place. This removes from the political fray a decision that could jeopardize the nation's fiscal health or survival.

By contrast, the American budget process is impracticable. The President submits his budget in February, and then House and Senate Budget Committees hold separate hearings. Their determinations and revisions are tabled in their respective houses and, if approved, are sent to a House-Senate Conference that attempts to reconcile and resolve disagreements. All this is to be completed within weeks, but needless to say never has been.

The latest hostilities erupted after the Republicans gained control of the House of Representatives in the 2010 midterm elections. Since then, they have fought the Democrat-controlled Senate and the President over the budget page by page and paragraph by paragraph. They have attempted to tie unrelated issues to their approvals, such as defunding the affordable Health Care Act, shutting down the government, or even threatening to let the Treasury default by refusing to raise the debt ceiling, notwithstanding the fact that since 1983 the debt ceiling has been routinely raised 15 times. By December, the public had run out of patience and public opinion polls plummeted to a historic low of a 12% approval rating of Congress. This led lawmakers in January to sign another allocation deal, but a comprehensive deal still eluded them, and another debt-ceiling ultimatum loomed.

Even well short of such dramatic innovations, the U.S. budget process could be simplified and expedited by referring the President's budget request directly for 60 days to a joint Congressional Super Committee of 12 legislators, similar to the Joint Select Committee on Deficit Reduction struck in August 2011. Membership would consist of six from the House and six from the Senate, with an equal representation of Democrats and Republicans. They would consult, review, and finalize a revised budget for a simple up-or-down vote, without amendment, in both Houses—just as the vote on BRAC and fast-track trade authority have worked in years past. If rejected, the previous year's budget would remain effective. This process could be repeated until successful. While draconian, some mechanism is clearly needed to stop the destructive partisan gaming that has been going on now for far too long.

Most urgently, debt ceiling brinkmanship must cease. One way to stop it is to agree to index the ceiling to GDP growth and require approval only if debt levels exceeded growth. Without this, obstructionists can flirt with default, as happened in 2011. This procedure is equivalent to letting toddlers play with matches to the point of immolating the entire global economy. The inherent danger underscores the need for immediate debt ceiling reform in the national and global interest.

Indexation and other reforms, but related and otherwise, would bring the U.S. political system incrementally closer to what works in Canada. A merger with Canada would do the trick tomorrow morning if it could be done, but such a radical maneuver would require the reincarnation of risk-taking and radical Founding Fathers on both sides of the current U.S.-Canadian border

Questions

1   Why have technical-legal-regulatory proposals to reform the U.S. budget process not worked well before?
2   What cultural and institutional obstacles exist to importing the Canadian budgetary and parliamentary government systems to the U.S.?
3   Francis mentions "some mechanism" to stop "destructive partisan gaming" in the U.S. What role does the U.S. electoral system play in perpetuating institutional and partisan gridlock and governmental ineffectiveness? Is electoral reform the mechanism?

Case 2.4 Japanese Public Debt and Economic Growth

Source: *Economist*, 2015a: 37–38

When, in November, Shinzo Abe postponed a second planned increase of Japan's consumption (sales) tax it was the right thing to do: after all, the first in April 2014, had knocked an already fragile economy. But with Japan running a far looser fiscal policy than any other rich country—the budget deficit is 6.9% of GDP—the prime minister needed at the same time to promise a credible longer-term plan for lowering the country's mountain of public debt, which stands at 246% of GDP and rising. The government has laid out two scenarios for the national debt. The gloomier one envisages that Mr. Abe's efforts to revive the economy will fall short, with average growth of just 1% a year, and that Japan will barely escape from the deflationary trap in which it has been caught for years. If so, the country would miss by a mile the 2020 target that politicians promised in 2010 of bringing the primary budget into surplus (i.e., before interest payments are taken into account).

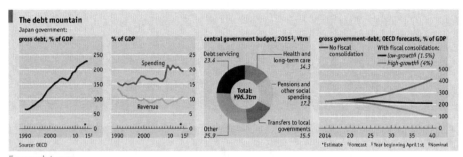

Economist.com

Under alternate optimistic "revitalization" assumptions of 2% inflation and 2% growth, the government predicts a flood of tax revenues, alleviating the need for big cuts to spending or for tax increases beyond the second rise in the consumption tax from 8% to 10% (postponed from this year to April 2017). Yet even so Japan would fall short of the promise to bring the primary budget into surplus by 2020: it would still be 1.6% of GDP in deficit.

The national debt, despite its gargantuan size, is not an immediate risk to financial stability. Nine-tenths of the debt is held domestically, so the government-bond market is not at the mercy of jittery foreigners. What is more, the Bank of Japan's huge program of quantitative easing has brought bond yields down to record lows. However, the government cannot keep those yields at rock bottom unless it remains credible, and the central bank will at some point want to end quantitative easing. As it is, the cost of servicing the national debt consumes nearly a quarter of the budget—more than pensions or health care. The cost would shoot up were bond yields to climb.

The government thinks that recent economic news justifies its optimism. After a period of slow growth, GDP expanded at an annualized rate of 3.9% in the first three months of the year, as inventories increased and businesses boosted investment in the hope of higher consumption. But such growth will be hard if not impossible to sustain. Not least, the government's prediction for productivity growth seems unrealistic. It posits that between 2016 and 2020 the growth in Japan's total factor productivity, that is, the efficiency with which labor and capital are used, will leap from 1% a year to 2.2%, the level that prevailed during the go-go 1980s.

Questions

1 Define the following concepts: fiscal consolidation, gross public debt, total factor productivity, fiscal deficit, structural reform, debt service, and quantitative easing. How are they used in this case?
2 What linkages are assumed in the Japanese fiscal plan between public debt, growth, and fiscal consolidation?
3 What are the assumptions behind the scenarios (particularly in the revenue area) in the strategy to lower the public debt? Are they realistic?
4 Distinguish high and low political risk spending cuts. Which are Mr. Abe likely to push for?

References

Abdel-Kader, Khaled, "What Are Structural Policies?" *Finance and Development*, 50, 1 (March 2013): 46–47.

Allen, Richard and David Tommasi (2001) *Managing Public Expenditure: A Reference Book for Transitional Countries* (Paris: OECD).

Allen, Richard, Richard Hemming, and Barry H. Potter (eds.) (2013) *The International Handbook of Public Financial Management* (New York: Palgrave Macmillan).

Bahl, Roy, "Comparative Federalism: Trends and Issues in the US, China and Russia," in *Macroeconomic Management and Fiscal Decentralization*, Jayanta Roy, ed., Washington, DC, World Bank, 1995: 73–103.

Baldacci, Emanuele and Sanjeev Gupta, "Fiscal Expansions: What Works," *Finance and Development*, 46, 4 (December 2009): 12–15.

Cangiano, Marco, Teresa Curristine, and Michael Lazare (eds.) (2013) *Public Financial Management and Its Emerging Architecture* (Washington, DC: IMF).

City of Milwaukee Budget and Management Department (2008), Plan and Budget Summary 2008.

Cody, Edward, "Austerity and Debts," *Washington Post*, April 30, 2013, p. AI.

Cottarelli, Carlo, Philip Gerson, and Abdelhak Senhadji (eds.) (2014) *Post-Crisis Fiscal Policy* (Cambridge, MA: MIT Press).

Davidson, Adam, "Boom, Bust or What?" *New York Times Magazine*, May 5, 2013, p. 32.

Demirguc-Kunt, Asli and Lenora Klapper, "Access to Banking Services," *Finance and Development*, 49, 3 (September 2012): 42–52.

Dener, Cem, Joanna Watkins, and William Dorotinsky (2011) *Financial Management Information Systems: 25 Years of World Bank Experience on What Works and What Doesn't* (Washington, DC: World Bank).

Dethier, Jean-Jacques (2010) "Measuring the Effectiveness of Fiscal Policy in Stimulating Economic Activity in Developing Countries: A Survey of the Literature" (Washington, DC: World Bank).

Dionne, E. J., "The Noise Around Obamacare," *Washington Post,* November 4, 2013, p. A17.

Dodd, Randall, "What Are Money Markets?" *Finance and Development*, 49, 2 (June 2012): 46–47.

Dunn, William N. (1981) *Public Policy Analysis: An Introduction* (Englewood Cliffs, NJ: Prentice Hall).

Dunn, William N. (2008) *Public Policy Analysis: An Introduction*, 4th ed. (Englewood Cliffs, NJ: Pearson Prentice Hall).

Eccleston, Richard and Richard Woodward, "Pathologies in International Policy Transfer: The Case of OECD Tax Transparency Initiative," *Journal of Comparative Policy Analysis*, November 2013: 10–19.

Economist (2002) "Weapons of Mass Distraction; Survey of World Economy," September 28, p. 13.

Economist (2008) "The Cracks Are Showing," June 28, p. 82.

Economist (2011) "Cut or Loose," July 16, p. 79.

Economist (2012) "No Short Cuts," October 27, p. 76.

Economist (2012a) "Mend the Money Machine," May 4, p. 16.

Economist (2013) "Economic and Financial Indicators," May 4, p. 88.

Economist (2013a) "Penury Portrait," July 27, p. 63.

Economist (2013b) "Not Always with Us," June 1, p. 23.

Economist (2013c) "Schools Brief: The Dangers of Debt," September 14, p. 74.

Economist (2013d) "Reality Blues," May 25, p. 38.

Economist (2013e) "Japan and Abenomics," May 18, p. 25.

Economist (2013f) "Walking the Talk," May 18, p. 51.

Economist (2013g) "Europe's Other Debt Crisis," October 20, p. 21.

Economist (2013h) "Unpriming the Pump," June 22, p. 46.

Economist (2013i) "Must We Work Harder?" June 22, p. 55.

Economist (2013j) "Schumpeter: A Hospital Case," May 18, p. 75.

Economist (2013k) "On Being Propped Up," May 25, p. 51.

Economist (2013l) "The Thicket of Reform," November 16, p. 46.

Economist (2013m) "Cat and Mouse," May 4, p. 57.

Economist (2013n) "Special Report on International Banking," May 11, p. 4.

Economist (2013o) "The Health Paradox," May 11, p. 27.

Economist (2014) "Long Time Gone," January 20, p. 19.

Economist (2014a) "All Men Are Created Unequal," January 4, p. 60.

Economist (2014b) "The ECB: No Palatable Choices," January 4, p. 57.

Economist (2014c) "Setting Out the Store," January 11, pp. 18–21.

Economist (2014d) "The Past Is Epilogue," February 8, p. 49.

Economist (2014e) "Breaking the Threshold," March 1, p. 71.

Economist (2014f) "The Dividend Is Delayed," March 8, p. 49.

Economist (2014g) "Reform in Italy: Gambler in a Rush," March 22, pp. 53–54.

Economist (2014h) "Portugal's Bail Out: Last Call," March 22, p. 75.

Economist (2014i) "Step Change," April 12, p. 71.

Economist (2014j) "Losing the Plot," July 17, pp. 61–62.

Economist (2014k) "Italy's Shrinking Economy," August 7, p. 24.

Economist (2015) "Local Government Debt in China: Swapping Spree," March 14, pp. 73–74.

Economist (2015a) "Hoping for Growth," June 20, pp. 37–38.

Economist (2015b) "Mexico's Economy: Shopping Therapy," November 7, pp. 29–30.

Fisher, Ronald C. (2007) *State and Local Public Finance*, 3rd ed. (Mason, OH: Thomson South-Western).

Francis, Diane, "Canada to the Rescue!" *The American Interest*, X, 1 (Autumn 2014): 54–61.

Guess, George M. (2015) *Government Budgeting: A Practical Guidebook* (Albany: State University of New York Press).

Guess, George M. and Kenneth Koford, "Inflation and the Federal Budget Deficit: Or Blaming Economic Problems on a Statistical Mirage," *Policy Sciences*, 17, 4 (1984): 385–402.

Guess, George M. and Lance T. LeLoup (2010) *Comparative Public Budgeting: Global Perspectives on Taxing and Spending* (Albany: State University of New York Press).

Guess, George M. and Paul G. Farnham (2011) *Cases in Public Policy Analysis*, 3rd ed. (and 2000, 2nd ed.) (Washington, DC: Georgetown University Press).

Guess, George M. and Jun Ma, "The Risks of Chinese Subnational Local Debt for Public Financial Management," *Public Administration and Development*, 35 (2015): 128–139.

Harris, Jason, Richard Hughes, Gosta Ljungman, and Carla Sateriale (2013) "Medium-Term Budget Frameworks in Advanced Economies," in *Public Financial Management and Its Emerging Architecture*, Marco Cangiano, Teresa Curristine, and Michael Lazare, eds., Washington, DC: IMF, 2013: 147–149.

Lane, Charles, "Austerity and Keynes Can Coexist," *Washington Post*, May 21, 2013, p. A17.

Lehan, Edward A. (1984) *Budgetmaking: A Workbook of Public Budgeting Theory and Practice* (New York: St. Martin's Press).

Lowrey, Annie, "The Politics of Low Growth," *New York Times*, January 13, 2013, p. 5.

Mikesell, John L. (2014) *Fiscal Administration, Analysis and Applications for the Public Sector,* 9th ed. (and 2011, 8th ed.) (Boston: Wadsworth Cengage).

Montgomery County (MD) Office of Management and Budget (2011) FY 12 Approved Operating Budget and FY 12–17 Public Services Program, Rockville, MD.

Musgrave, Richard A. (1959) *The Theory of Public Finance* (New York: McGraw-Hill).

Nagourney, Adam, "California Faces a New Quandary: Too Much Money," *New York Times*, May 26, 2013, p. 1.

Parker, Kathleen, "Language Inequality," *Washington Post*, January 8, 2014, p. A14.

Perotti, Roberto, "Fiscal Policy in Developing Countries: A Framework and Some Questions," Policy Research Paper 4365, 2007, World Bank, Washington, DC.

Pescatori, Andrea, Damiano Sandri, and John Simon, "No Magic Threshold," *Finance and Development*, 51, 2 (June 2014): 39–42.

Peterson, Stephen B. (2015) *Public Finance and Economic Growth in Developing Countries: Lessons from Ethiopia's Reforms* (New York: Routledge).

Petrei, Humberto (1998) *Budget and Control: Reforming the Public Sector in Latin America* (Washington, DC: Inter-American Development Bank).

Piketty, Thomas (2014) *Capital in the 21st Century* (New York: Belknap Press).

Rodden, Jonathan A. (2006) *Hamilton's Paradox: The Promise and Perils of Fiscal Federalism* (New York: Cambridge University Press).

Romer, Christina, "Fiscal Policy in Crises: Lessons and Policy Implications," 2012, University of California Department of Economics Working Paper, Berkeley.

Rosenthal, Elisabeth, "Same Quality of Care, Bigger Bill," *Denver Post*, June 2, 2013, p. 6A.

Samuelson, Robert J. (2014) "How We Won and Lost the War on Poverty," *Washington Post*, January 13, p. A17.

Samuelson, Robert J. (2014a) "Budgeting by Prayer," *Washington Post,* July 27, p. A14.

Schiavo-Campo, Salvatore and David Tommasi (1999) *Managing Government Expenditure* (Manila: Asian Development Bank).

Shah, Anwar (ed.) (2007) *Local Budgeting* (Washington, DC: World Bank).

Singh, Anoop, Sonali Jain-Chandra, and Adil Mohommad, "Out of the Shadows," *Finance and Development*, 49, 2 (June 2012): 52–54.

Strachota, Dennis (1994) *The Best of Government Budgeting: A Guide to Preparing Budget Documents* (Chicago: Government Finance Officers Association GFOA).

Summers, Lawrence (2013) "Beyond Austerity Slogans," *Washington Post*, June 3, p. A14.

Summers, Lawrence (2013a) "America's Many Deficits," *Washington Post*, January 25, p. A15.

Summers, Lawrence (2013b) "Lessons in Reinhart-Rogoff Error," *Washington Post*, June 6, p. A19.

World Bank, "Beyond the Annual Budget: Review of Global Experience with MTEFs," March 27, 2012, World Bank, Washington, DC.

Xavier, J. A. "Budget Reform in Malaysia and Australia Compared," *Public Budgeting and Finance*, 18, 1 (March 1998): 99–118.

Zakaria, Fareed, "Reform Isn't a Dirty Word," *Washington Post*, May 21, 2013, p. A19.

3 Urban Transport and Public Infrastructure

Introduction

Though returns to infrastructure investment remain controversial and debatable, that major urban mobility needs exist around the globe are not. Some doubt the causality for new investments such as whether a new road causes growth and employment or whether growth stimulates demand for them. Either way, the link between infrastructure and growth has been repeatedly demonstrated through comparative international research. Despite this evidence, the Latin American region invests only half (less than 2 percent GDP) of what is needed, under currently optimal conditions of relatively low public debt (regional average of 42 percent GDP) and low borrowing costs. This missed economic development opportunity perpetuates major bottlenecks to trade, investment, and growth in the rail, road, and urban transport sub-sectors. In countries like India, infrastructure also remains a major obstacle to growth. Roads, railways, and ports are all deficient. For the future, infrastructure investment must also include broadband and mobile phone coverage. Because service and knowledge industries are concentrated in and around cities in most countries, urban policies will increasingly matter for stimulation of economic growth in income and employment opportunities. Urban public transport is and will remain a large and necessary component of those policies.

The policy constraint for countries that have failed to take advantage of the demonstrable infrastructure-growth link is largely institutional. Lack of legitimate capital improvement planning (CIP) systems allows uneconomic, often socially useless projects to be approved for the benefit of corrupt contractors and other powerful political interests. This has been true with Chinese mega-projects in railways and airports as well as poorly designed projects in Latin America (e.g. the Lima metro). The CIP processes are leaky and permit access by those who lobby for other projects and different methods of financing. Many of these are political projects that have not been formally appraised; using private-public partnerships (PPPs) as risk partners adds complexity to project approval and implementation over traditional turnkey projects (where the contractor has full responsibility for project completion). Attempts to control these institutional weaknesses with more regulations often make matters worse: the "Philip II" problem of Latin American "control freakery" creates labyrinthine procurement and environmental procedures that end up causing more delays and pressures for end runs of the process that result in even more corrupt side payments. Thus, the institutional problem almost regardless of culture or region produces both costly unneeded projects and badly implemented but often needed projects. In this context, unlinked to actual results, the level of public investment can either be very high and clearly sufficient to meet needs (e.g. China) or very low and insufficient (e.g. Latin America).

This chapter will attempt to accomplish six objectives. First, it outlines three policy contexts of use for comparative lessons. Second, it describes four major urban transport problems: (a) fragmented organizational responsibility structures; (b) weak capital planning systems; (c) lack of system financing; and (d) weak accountability and low citizen participation. Third, it provides examples of successful and not so successful policy responses to these problems. Fourth, in *Annex I*, the chapter provides basic tools for capital investment planning and analysis: fiscal decentralization review; project analysis; costing/pricing of transport services; and budgeting and financing review techniques. Fifth, it offers applications of the frameworks and potential lessons learned; finally, it provides cases and exercises for practice.

I. Overview and Context

By 2020, more than half the world's population will live in cities (Worldwatch Institute, 2013, www.worldwatch.org/taxonomy/term/101). This has led to crises of public access and mobility, increased congestion, and pollution in many cities. With increasing urbanization, frequent deterioration of municipal infrastructure, and increasing costs of transport services, the movement of people within cities is increasingly costly and more difficult. The attempt to move people between and within cities may be the most visible and important policy or program of all that are covered in this book. Frustrated Santiago (Chile) bus passengers, stranded by abysmal bus service, for instance, commandeered two buses going in different directions and took them home (*Economist,* 2007: 52)! More recently, bus fare hikes in Sao Paolo (Brazil) sparked mass protests against the lackluster public transit system as well as waste and corruption in other municipal services (*Economist*, 2013; Fabiola and Moura, 2013: A1). Through public transport, which is a basic municipal or state service, citizens often express frustrated demands for more public policy accountability in countries around the world. Unlike rising food and housing prices, which of course add to mass frustration, bus fares (and taxes which in Brazil at 36 percent of GDP are rich-country rates) are under government control. Raising them even marginally affects mainly the poor and serves as a catalyst for protests and flashpoint for the creation of broader mass movements. The Sao Paolo protests of 2013 spread quickly to 12 other Brazilian cities and the capital Brasilia before mayors wisely cancelled the fare increases. National and subnational governments often combine resources to provide mobility and access for their increasingly urbanized populations. It is not an exaggeration to say that socioeconomic development depends on the efficacy of urban transport—to move people to jobs, schools, hospitals; for police and fire to respond to emergencies; and for the operation and maintenance of related services such as electricity, water-sewer, and sanitation.

In spite of this importance, land-use patterns and urban transport systems are rarely well linked or managed in most cities of the world. Even successful urban transport systems seem to deteriorate over time from underfinancing and mismanagement, suggesting that institutionalization of policy lessons has not occurred. European and North American cities are acquiring many Third World transport features, including poor planning, underfunding, clogged roads, and air quality problems caused by trucks and cars. Conversely, many Third World cities have come up with innovative solutions to increase mobility and access for both the poor and middle classes. European and North American systems have also developed innovative responses to urban transport policy problems (Guess, 2008: 2). It is important that these lessons be identified and transferred where possible to improve policy results and systems performance.

In order to identify transferable lessons and methods, it is important to focus on the transport mode. Lessons and methods for airports, ports, freight rail, roads, commuter rail, light rail, bus rapid transit, bus, and metro systems will mostly differ—as much between them as between other programs and services such as housing or education. They will differ in institutional and financing rules. The allocation of operational management and service financing authority and responsibility varies widely among cities and they affect policy results. Systems may be dependent upon central government transfers both for capital and operating subsidies. Given locally weak tax bases, subnational officials may not be able to finance needed services or maintenance. That means that transit managers might not be able to finance their own infrastructure or set their own fares. Thus, as in many policy areas, institutional rules and processes are critical to urban transport performance.

Much is made of the U.S. obsession with private automobiles. And, it is nothing less than an obsession. With exception of a few cities such as New York and Chicago, most trips almost have to be made by car. Distances in spreading low density metropolitan areas are great and public transit (mostly buses in places such as Houston and Los Angeles) is slow and difficult for shopping and other daily requirements. In 1990, the annual automobile passenger kilometer/capita in the U.S. was 16,045 versus only 6,602 in Europe (Hemily, 2004: 16). Less known is that the same automobile obsession is spreading throughout the rest of the world, including even cities with excellent mass public transit systems such as Budapest. Because cars are cheap, convenient, and often necessary to get to work and shop in most cities, urban public transit usage has decreased. Cars and unlicensed taxis (called *informales* in Lima because they are part of the informal sector discussed in the previous chapter) serve much of the public. But they do not constitute what is meant by "public transportation."

This chapter focuses on "public transportation" as a sub-sector of urban transport. In addition to rail-bus services provided directly by governmental authorities, this means regular/continuous service provided to the public by licensed taxis, jitneys, paratransit, vanpool, and similar vehicles under contract to a public agency (APTA, 2006). Based on this definition, private cars and mini-buses operating without public license or contract would be excluded from the definition. Public transportation ridership has grown 23 percent in the U.S. since 1995 (APTA, 2006). But even where public transit ridership has grown dramatically, e.g. Washington Metro, the total number of urban trips taken by public transit is still very small, perhaps no more than 5 percent–10 percent of all of them. Thus, the situation in the U.S. is similar to that of Germany, where 90 percent of the trips are taken by private vehicle despite the fact that 86 percent of the population live within ten minutes of a public transit stop (Toerkel, 2007). The figures are even more extreme for the U.S. outside selected major public transit markets like New York City, San Francisco, Boston, Washington, and Chicago. In medium-sized U.S. cities, most of the trips are taken by private vehicles. Given these facts, if the goal is to increase the "competitiveness" of public transportation with the private automobile, the most sensible policy is to regulate auto usage more tightly in urban areas, and increase the efficiency (unit cost) and effectiveness (quality, coverage, and responsiveness) of transit service.

It is now known that better inter-modal linkages (i.e. integration) through service planning and scheduling can generate ridership and lure passengers from cars. Riders anywhere do not like to wait outside for buses and trams in the elements and will try and avoid this option as best they can. But they can be coaxed back into public transit by convenient service. For example, the four-line Santiago (Chile) subway links all stations with fast, efficient service to a metropolitan area of 6.1 million people. This is the only subway system in the world that operates without subsidies, primarily because of high ridership and high operating efficiency (Guess, 2005: 5). However, it is largely a middle-class system and does not connect to the chaotic mesh of routes in greater Santiago operated by the private bus systems that serve the poor. The service regulatory framework is dysfunctional and frustrates passengers (*Economist*,

2007: 52). By contrast, the Manila (Philippines) light rail system is not linked to the bus system which overall carries only 10 percent of the people in the metropolitan area. Urban congestion in the area is massive and the poor are not served by its badly planned public transportation services (Guess, 2005: 5).

In a geopolitical sense, one can distinguish three kinds of urban transport or transit policy context, each with its own set of service management challenges. In the CEE/FSU (or Central European-Former Soviet Union region), pre-transition transit service delivery under state socialism was relatively simple. Residence and workplace locations were planned with direct linkage by multi-modes of transit based on city size (e.g. large cities like Budapest had all of them; medium-sized cities like Skopje, Macedonia, had buses and trolley-buses; small towns like Jalal-abad, Kyrgyzstan, had only buses). Funding was not a problem as physical service norms were funded based on the numbers of service miles managers decided. Demand figures were simply assumed to meet supply. There was little intra-urban migration. Capital for rolling stock and facilities was allocated on the basis of the material plan, which had little to do in many cases with passenger comfort and everything to do with on-time delivery of workers to factories. In the sense of setting objectives and providing incentives for staff to achieve them within fiscal constraints, there was little to "manage" in this kind of system. After the transition around 1991, demand for private autos increased as the new middle classes escaped from the trappings of the old system represented by rusty old Russian subway cars and rickety trams built locally. In EE/FSU countries, such as Armenia, private mini-buses moved in to provide daily mobility for the majority without cars that had to commute. Semi-public transit vehicles like mini-buses still have the potential to make the traditional public transit systems and structures irrelevant (like cell phones did to state phone companies). Indicating the need for a new cultural mindset, instead of responding to new demands, many officials in FSU transit agencies (operating from old state socialist command and control premises) still imagine that private buses can be banned or at least regulated out of existence. Since there was no tradition of autonomous management of services in this centralized and authoritarian context, transport officials now lack the skills to organize transit in order to respond to demand from actual customers. There was simply no tradition of soliciting, listening, or responding to customer or rider feedback.

In transitional/developing regions such as Latin America and Asia, rapid urbanization generated demands among the new middle classes for automobiles as status symbols and evidence of their recent independence from the lower classes. The ruling classes had their drivers and the poor were left to get around in aging Bluebird school buses. Urban underclass entrepreneurs responded by creation of informal mobility, such as through *peseros*, jitneys, and mini-vans that filled in the vacuum between poor public transportation systems and those with private cars. Sound service management was needed but could make little difference without sufficient capital and operating funds. Property rights were unclear for land and assets, and the financial sector had been unable to finance the emergence of a larger educated middle class that would demand more cars. Thus, even in cities such as Santiago with good subway networks serving the middle classes, the urban underclass majority still has to engage in ad hoc tactics to get around and to work.

In this second context, one should add the fast-developing transitional countries of Asia. China and South Korea are spending enormous sums on transport infrastructure as stimuli to regional and national development. Subways, high-altitude railways, pipelines, transmission lines, major roads, airports, and ports investments are all proceeding ahead at a rapid pace. The aim is less user satisfaction than creation of demand for investment and exports, which have been the central parts of their development models to the rest of the world. Given the tendency of local opposition to some infrastructure projects, projects of national importance (often termed "security") are given priority over urban transport. They are easier to approve in the centralized, top-down political institutions of this region, whether in India or China, and they promise positive development benefits where urban transport usually requires budget subsidies. This command and control advantage for authoritarian non-technical party-controlled governments is seen in countries such as China, where a huge new middle class is becoming increasingly frustrated with its powerlessness over issues such as education, health care, the environment, and property rights (*Economist*, 2014b: 16). These are part of the political regime contexts (described in *Chapter 1*) which must be considered before international comparisons can be made to transfer policy lessons.

In the third context, Europe and North America, the original public transportation systems of the nineteenth century were replaced by private operators that served cities and inner suburbs. Later on, driven by banking and financial sector housing loans for the middle classes and institutional thirst for profits, physical development spread to the suburbs and beyond. The private auto replaced public transit around the cities but the latter remained important for commuting to work from the outer suburbs (inter-urban rail, buses, trams, and subways). As public transit ridership declined, service quality followed suit in many cities and autos replaced commuter transit as well. The average number of trips by transit in the U.S. versus Europe is telling. In 1990, the percentage of total passenger kilometers taking transit was only 3.1 percent in the U.S. versus 22.6 percent in Europe. For urban rail, the U.S. percentage was 32.0 percent compared to 77.3 percent in Europe (Hemily, 2004: 16). These are familiar statistics. But if trends in transit passenger kilometers in the largest cities of North America are now compared with those of Europe and examined, the trend would be convergence—higher transit usage in big-city North America and growing use of automobiles by Europeans. These are the difficult conditions faced by public transportation managers and policy-makers in both Europe and North America.

II. Major Policy Problems

As noted in the first chapter, rough contextual equivalence must exist for comparative lessons to mean anything to mangers or policy-makers. Comparing Hungarian and British transport policies might have some meaning at the strategic level (both being in the EU). But at the operations level, such comparisons would be overbroad unless limited to mode (e.g. city bus financing) and financing method (e.g. the specifics of formula grants). Comparing large-city urban transport systems is useful because there are at least five descriptive similarities. First, such cities typically have special status in countries and are granted important degrees of fiscal and political authority, e.g. Budapest (Voszka, 2003: 278). Second, urban transport is governed locally by a multiplicity of organizational structures that fragment authority across the metropolitan region, e.g. Washington, DC's Tri-State Oversight Committee that tries to govern the Metro system. Such governance arrangements are somewhat responsive to small geographic units but unable to provide accountability, coordination, and sufficient financing area-wide. Third, cities offer a mixture of modes, including bus, bus rapid transit, light and heavy rail, jitneys, and commuter rail and bus. Fourth, systems must respond to a common demographic commuter pattern from suburban and ex-urban areas. Fifth, cities are segregated by class if not race geographically, which is important for pricing and modal offerings.

Given these similarities, one can draw valid lessons from city successes and failures in responding to the four major mobility and access problems (Guess, 2008: 3).

1. *Fragmented Organizational Responsibility Structures*

There are two related sub-issues here: (a) governance structure, and (b) fiscal and management authority.

a. *Structure*

In most cities, land use patterns and urban transport are not integrated. Decisions on highest and best use of private property are articulated through a host of smaller government units with limited jurisdiction and authority over metropolitan regions. These fragmented subnational units may share part of the burden of managing, delivering, and financing urban transit. This means that bus, heavy rail, and inter-urban rail may be the responsibility of one or more type of organization in more than one local jurisdiction. At the same time, geographic financial responsibilities for transit can range from complete (downtown areas) to none (areas served by inter-urban rail). For example, the many cities served by the four inter-urban HEV commuter rail lines in the Budapest area receive all the mobility benefits but pay none of the service or station maintenance costs.

Public transit delivery organizations may be operationally separate and coordinate periodically at regional and local planning meetings. At the same time, public transit jurisdictions overlap with road, water-sewer, broadband/IT, and electric utility organizations. These organizational complexities make effective transit service delivery extremely difficult in most cities; under such conditions, the wonder is that such systems function at all! Governance of urban transport may be assigned to varieties of organizational types: city or state enterprises, city or county departments, holding companies, non-governmental organizations, and/or private firms. The policy question is which institutional and structural type works best for urban transit? What is the appropriate legal and regulatory framework and what should be the structure of governance of transit in a metropolitan region to maximize efficiency and effectiveness? Local structural variables such as council-manager governments or non-partisan elections affect economic policy (Svara, 2005: 501). One should be able to point to different models with empirical evidence that they work best under specific conditions. But international policy research on governance and urban transport results has been minimal.

b. *Authority*

As cities grow and require transport for mobility, decisions are made at higher levels (national or provincial) to assign revenue generation and expenditure management authority for transit systems. They may be poorly assigned initially, or assigned properly and not revisited once the city grows beyond the capacities of the original assignments. As noted in the discussion of fiscal decentralization issues in the previous chapter (and below), revenue authority assignments often do not match or cover transit expenditure responsibilities. Shared expenditure and coordination responsibilities have to be financed in most metropolitan areas by multiple sources of finance from different levels of government. Assignments of local transit financial authority can range from: minimal (i.e. no borrowing authority and little authority to set tax rates or to define local tax bases) to full (complete fiscal autonomy, authority to share portions of certain taxes, such as income, and expenditure controls subject to credit ratings and audit requirements). In short, authority is poorly assigned and allows cities to fragment authority further. This prevents accountability and efficiency. Forcing cities to share financing and management responsibilities dilutes the vertical command structure for the region—area-wide decisions are not made. Conversely, the shared authority problem allows excessive influence by powerful transport interest groups like unions which short-circuit and compromise both board and management accountability and direct system responsiveness to riders.

2. Weak Capital Planning Systems

Like city planning in general, urban transport planning is a favorite professional pastime. Large or small, practically every city in the world has a transport and land use plan on display. The plans are typically based on estimated service needs and often include options to control and balance competing urban forces that can distort the quality of life. Transport plans work to balance future needs of residential and workplace trips, environmental protection, and economic growth. According to a multi-year planning calendar, planners plan and citizens comment, forcing new rounds of plan revision, public notice, and comment. Approved plans roll forward and are revised based on changed growth patterns, some of which may have been unanticipated. Often large projects, such as convention centers, are granted variances from existing plans which create new mobility problems. Such projects often require new transport infrastructure which changes land use and trip patterns. And once established, land-use patterns determine the demand for future urban trips (World Bank, 2006a: 59). Especially where new transport infrastructure is unavailable to support new investments, political influence supporting unplanned investments can weaken existing plans and distort local land markets. Sometimes transit plans underestimate urban growth and demand. In such cases, strict regulations on growth can stifle development around metro stations (e.g. Calcutta) while weak rules ignore harmful growth in other parts of the city. For example, Lima's (Peru) dependence on cars and buses has brought traffic to a near standstill in this metropolis of 8.3 million people. While other cities in the region such as Santiago, Quito, and Bogota have pursued new planning paths with light rail (LRT), dedicated lane bus ways (BRT), and subways, Lima's congestion and air pollution grow worse. Urban transport planning and financing failures in Lima are allowing competitor cities to seize its business, investment, and economic growth opportunities. In the U.S., a similarly weak urban transport planning situation may allow Charlotte (North Carolina) with its expanding LRT system to seize business opportunities from Atlanta (Crawford, 2007).

Other planning options to control auto use and encourage transit have included going to the source—enforcement of parking lot regulations to control air pollution. In the U.S., efforts to control parking lot construction in order to limit urban air pollution were authorized by the 1974 Transportation and Land Use Amendments to the Clean Air Act. The rapid and intense reaction to these rules by the powerful construction industry and parking lot firms by 1982 resulted in a twin political attack on the Amendments by Congress (which gutted the provisions) and political appointees in the Environmental Protection Agency (EPA) (which delayed enforcement). It should be no surprise then that in most cities of the world, transit master plans have not succeeded in controlling overall urban growth or in ensuring efficient use of land use and urban transport (World Bank, 2006b: 60).

Capital planning weaknesses are reflected in shortages of trained people in the public sector to design, evaluate, and supervise complex engineering projects. In Latin American countries such as Brazil and Mexico, that is in part the result of the investment drought in the 1980s and the zeal with which planning was thrown out with the dirty bathwater of statist development (*Economist*, 2014a: 34). Weak transit capital planning negatively affects policy results in two ways.

First, if plans are to be implemented, there must be a portfolio of appraised projects approved by the city's capital planning process. This is typically called the capital improvement program or CIP (see *Annex I*). Formal infrastructure project appraisal (which is almost synonymous with the term "urban transit"), usually by a firm of consulting engineers, can be as high as 5 percent of total project costs. Appraisal costs are not covered by external donors such as central or provincial/state governments (only since 2006 has the U.S. Federal Transit Administration (FTA) provided funds for local "alternatives analysis" for fixed guide way investment projects). Since local governments often lack the funds to appraise planned projects (few of which may be approved anyway), there is typically a small or non-existent portfolio of projects on the shelf. The lack of a project pipeline is important in that often appraised projects are rejected or halted for extraneous reasons and officials need high-priority substitute projects. If there are none, this opens the door to political projects that further distort existing transit and land use plans. It might also be said that in Central and Eastern Europe and the former Soviet Union, "appraisal" means review in narrow financial and engineering terms. Appraisal reports are practically all numbers with hardly a word about such items as the assumptions and premises of demand and cost estimates, the definitions of costs/benefits, and why some costs or benefits have been included and not others. The economic and social impacts of a do-nothing option are rarely examined. This means that formal benefits estimation is either politicized or flawed by weak methodology. Lack of formal appraisal of costs-benefits means that wider externality issues (*negative* such as environmental and congestion costs, and *positive* on mobility for the poor under class) are ignored. They are often left out of discussions on project approval and ranking in the context of available budget funds. In short, the transit capital project evaluation process in many places is deeply flawed. For national level fiscal programs to stimulate economic growth and for local economic development objectives, a portfolio of appraised transport infrastructure projects must be ready for implementation. In addition to the political subjectivity issue, often a rigorous methodology to link capital spending with its expected impact on economic benefits may be missing. In fact, the linkage between public investment and economic development itself is imprecise and needs to be refined. Estimated benefits for job creation, income generation, and treasury revenue collections for capital projects focused directly on economic development are often exaggerated. The Johns Hopkins University Science City in Montgomery County, Maryland, is a good example. Instead of a $31-million annual boost to revenue collections, independent recalculations have come up with a required expenditure of $38,000 per job created for county taxpayers (Spivak, 2010).

How can benefits be estimated more accurately? What information should be included in definitions of costs and benefits? For instance, clearly project impact on local school enrollments and running costs should be subtracted from estimated benefits unless there is excess school capacity. But by how much? The purpose of national or local economic stimuli programs that often center on transport infrastructure is to counter the effects of shrinking output, demand, and asset price declines. These are caused by crises, such as the 2008 global downturn and banking/financial sector collapse (Baldacci and Gupta, 2009: 35). Of the $862 billion to be spent over 10 years for economic stimulus via the American Recovery and Reinvestment Act (ARRA), $525 billion or 61 percent was allocated to infrastructure. The bulk of this was transport infrastructure. In G-20 countries, about 50 percent of stimulus funds were allocated to infrastructure and the rest for social safety nets/state aid and tax cuts. The 61 percent figure for ARRA is high for wealthier G-20 countries which spent only about 20 percent of their stimulus funds on investment (Baldacci and Gupta, 2009: 15). Employment and income effects for infrastructure generally can be assessed through examination of contracts and the expected multiplier effects of lump-sum and matching grants to states (especially for stabilization of education and health staff). The CBO estimated that the beneficial impact of all direct spending, direct assistance to individuals, health and education spending through grants and contracts was about 1.7 million jobs created between March and September 2009 (CRFB, 2010). But it was not possible to rigorously distinguish asset creation from salary support. Stimulus spending impacts both variables—the first in the long term, the latter in the shorter term. It is therefore critical that stimulus program funds be targeted to achieve maximum developmental impact. In that many projects and programs supported by ARRA were not new starts, it was difficult to distinguish the developmental effects of ARRA funds and those contributed by other federal, state, local and in some cases private funding sources.

Second, lack of strong capital planning processes short-circuit the annual sequence of needs assessment, project appraisal, project review, and financing. This institutional weakness paves the way for political projects, i.e. unneeded projects that breach weak planning systems through back-door and top-down political pressures. As noted, capital improvement planning (CIP) processes are often absent in OECD, transitional, and developing countries (Guess and Todor, 2005). As described in *Annex I*, transit master planning should proceed from technical estimates of needs translated into projects designed to meet those needs. As indicated, often there are insufficiently appraised projects to fulfill plans if funding becomes available or other projects are dropped from the queue. More important are large capital transit projects that overwhelm plans, due largely to central government financing rules. In some cases, projects such as "heavy rail" or metros are appraised and put in the local queue because generous co-funding (up to 80 percent in the U.S. has been available for eligible projects) is available from the central government (e.g. the U.S. Federal Transit Administration or EU regional development funds). In other cases, such as Budapest's M4 line, project "appraisal" and approval took place before financial feasibility was worked out. After several years of construction, the City still hoped the EU would pay for 60 percent of capital costs (*Budapest Sun*, 2007)! These examples suggest that in many cases, transit capital planning has been driven less by realistic solutions than by financial availability. The additional danger is that dependence on cheap capital financing can lead to under-maintenance of capital investments (reducing current expenditures and pressures to cut spending to meet deficit targets) as transit authorities simply allow rolling stock and other capital equipment to wear down. The official mentality becomes replace rather than repair which is wasteful in any country.

Until about 1990, a good example of this powerful financial pressure on project planning was the U.S. grants system (i.e. fiscal transfers) for urban transport. With 80 percent funding availability from the U.S. national level, pressure was immense to select and justify more expensive heavy rail projects as the preferred local option instead of others (e.g. LRT or BRT). This left the other 20 percent to be covered by local bank loans, revenue bonds (U.S.), or creation of special tax assessment districts along the path of the rail beneficiaries. With deep local capital markets in the U.S., this was not hard to arrange. With few legal constraints on U.S. local borrowing authority, the way was open to build major projects that often did not meet estimated ridership targets, did not reduce overall urban congestion, and constituted major urban eyesores, e.g. Miami Metrorail. That was a 22.5-mile mostly elevated rail line that cost over $1 billion (in the mid-1980s) to construct and still carries only 62,300 riders on an average 19-hour service day. The 80 percent funding rule for this and similar projects provided a means of artificially lowering opportunity costs since earmarked funds could not be used for other local transit projects. Even with generous funding available to encourage capital intensive solutions to mobility problems (and often less than rigorous review of appraisal assumptions and methods), some transit authorities still had difficulty meeting the rate of return criteria for acceptable projects ("acceptable" but which often distorted the real master plan or approved CIP portfolio!). In regions with such generous funding rules, predictably there would be intense urban competition for transfers. In Hungary, for example, because rolling stock is more expensive, unit costs are higher and revenues are lower, which lowers estimated rates of project return. Since Hungary must compete with other EU countries for a limited amount of regional "cohesion/convergence" and structural funds to finance urban transit projects, they remain at a disadvantage (Szucs, 2007).

3. Lack of System Financing

In countries with decentralized finances, urban transit is a big item in many city budgets. For example, transit current expenditures absorbed about 10 percent of the Metro-Miami budget in 2006. Much of the annual debt service covered repayment of loans for transit capital financing. In smaller cities, the proportions of total expenditures for transit can be much higher. In Budapest, even with national financing of capital investments (i.e. rolling stock, buses, rehabilitation, facilities) via soft loans, the "city holding company" (BKV) responsible for public transportation operations still absorbs about 17 percent of the city budget (Voszka, 2003: 277). For this reason, operating funds need to be targeted and spent properly to achieve the highest value for money. In response to new passenger demands and commercial opportunities, operating assistance for transit has changed. In many countries, the poor, elderly, and handicapped receive discounted fares and para-transit on demand, financed largely by national-level (federal) operating assistance. In Latin America, the poor ride free or via special pass with subsidy vouchers (Guess, 2005: 5). Contracting-out particular bus routes through competitive licenses and franchises can save substantial funds from city budgets and, if monitored properly, can ensure equal or greater levels of service than before. Systems in Atlanta and Washington have done this effectively, leveraging private contractors and neighboring county transit systems (e.g. Cobb County, Georgia; Montgomery County, Maryland) to generate more riders for them on a cost-sharing basis. Budapest's BKV transit company has contracted out operation of three bus routes, conditional on vehicle performance standards and payment of annual fees (*Budapest Sun*, 2004). Effective urban transport service requires both well-maintained capital investment and coverage of current expenses for salaried employees and other running costs.

This means that urban transit service requires two kinds of expenditures: current services or operations (for salaries, maintenance, and debt service) and capital investment or infrastructure (for rehabilitation and replacement). It is critical for transparent budgeting, accounting, and reporting to keep entries into these expense categories separate to prevent hiding of operating deficits as capital investments. In principle, public transit is delivered through "profit centers" that charge fees for service. In many cities, transit or public transportation is called a "proprietary service" since it is a business-like activity in which users pay all or part of the costs of providing the service. Transit authorities could in principle be required to cover full costs (direct plus share of indirect) or marginal costs (market costs associated with the last unit of service) if fares were high enough and costs behaved properly. In theory, capital usage and replacement costs could also be included (depreciation) and covered by transit system revenues (e.g. farebox fees, fiscal transfers, advertising, space rentals, and earmarked urban congestion charges as in London). Costs of public transportation service are objectively measurable, and outputs/outcomes are quantifiable. The major *output* is measured by passenger miles of service. *Outcomes*, such as reduced congestion, health costs, and air pollution, are not hard to quantify but nearly impossible to attribute to urban transit alone. Some "wiggle room" is possible between major rehabilitation and minor maintenance activity costs. But not much . . . Differing levels of maintenance can be precisely classified and audited after the fiscal year has ended to prevent any accounting classification games.

In the public transit field, laws and regulations are regularly modified to accommodate practical necessity and to make transactions transparent in order to control abuses. For example, the U.S. Urbanized Area Formula of the Federal Public Transportation Act of 1982 provided for merger of capital and operating assistance under certain conditions. A perverse incentive of financing a high proportion of capital with central grants is to encourage local government recipients to skimp on maintenance and replace the asset prematurely. It also encourages local transit authorities to distort urban plans and let them be driven by funding availability rather than least cost solutions to their needs. Thus, local transit authorities (all over the world) often acquire capital assets and allow them to deteriorate in order to save current funds for salaries and other current needs. To try and reduce the effect of this perverse incentive, the U.S. Act provided that eligible capital expenses include: investment as well as rehabilitation and preventive maintenance (APTA, 2006). Strict accounting for current and capital items allows more transparent estimates of real service costs for purposes of setting prices and calculating transfers. Pricing in most cities is "subsidy" (below marginal or full cost) because break-even is very difficult for this service. In transitional and poor Third World countries, riders cannot pay high fares and there is political pressure to keep them low (or free as in Recife, Brazil). This is because demand is price inelastic—fares can increase without much loss of demand because riders are dependent on public transit. But, as noted, raising public transit fares is a high-risk decision. Leaders know that gouging riders with high prices can cause instant labor strikes and rioting in countries places like Brazil, Argentina, and Panama that can threaten their governments.

To ensure efficient and effective services, public transit in many jurisdictions is now assessed by "profitability criteria," such as unit costs of service, farebox cost recovery ratios, and passenger miles of bus or rail operations. But, "profit" alone cannot provide an adequate bottom line for such public service organizations as public transit or health care that operate with the goal of providing a public benefit. It is also critical that transit services use their sources of revenue effectively to achieve the goal of quality service. Reserve funds for service contingencies can be budgeted and surpluses can be generated along particular routes that can subsidize less profitable lines (i.e. a cross-subsidy). These kinds of fiscal targeting decisions require capable personnel, sound financial management, and sustainable financing. It is well-known that public transit service delivery is costly given maintenance and operations expenses (often the product of bloated staffs) which cannot be fully covered by fares and which require increasing subsidies to forestall worsening service.

A common measure of profitability for government and non-profit organizations is the *operating margin* or operating revenue less operating expenses (Finkler et al., 2001: 483). The operating expenses of most public transit agencies exceed operating revenues by a wide margin. It can almost be said that public transit is "intrinsically unprofitable" because farebox revenues rarely cover more than 50 percent of salaries, maintenance, operating costs, and supplies. One would expect higher volumes of service to decrease the average cost/passenger—as more passengers share the fixed costs. In fact, this happens. But transit service is still unprofitable because as service increases, total fixed investment costs increase at a proportionately greater rate (see *Figure 3.5*). This increases average total costs and requires a policy response, e.g. outsourcing service or imposing higher fares. Transit authorities have found that by leveraging private capital (e.g. BOTs) and outsourcing (i.e. private firms for a regional service and/or particular routes), the fixed costs of public transit can be reduced.

Successful outsourcing to private suppliers depends on how well marginal costs of existing public services are estimated, whether outsourcing will eliminate many of the existing fixed costs (e.g. rolling stock and facilities), and how well the contractor will be monitored by the transit authority. In any case, such innovative policy options can often save the city transit authority funds. In 1990, the average transit operating cost farebox recovery ratio in the U.S. was only 35 percent compared to 54 percent in Europe (Hemily, 2004: 16).

A major fare increase in response to higher fixed costs is not socially feasible in most cities. Rider fares cannot be set at "full marginal cost" because it would produce high fares inducing more people to use automobiles (which in most countries do not pay full social costs) and therefore result in further inefficiency. Bird (2001: 173) notes that setting user charges to cover financial accounting costs (e.g. wages, rent, and operations) is easier than for coverage of economic costs (opportunity plus social or congestion costs). The latter are hard to measure and therefore hard to use as the basis for efficient prices. Thus, pricing rules for public transit usually have to be "second-best" (Bahl and Linn, 1992: 260). That means that transit subsidies are calculated on "earnings" from second-best pricing. On the annual income statement for a transit authority or city transit enterprise, one arrives at the "earnings" before subsidy by subtracting revenues from operations costs, depreciation, and administration (USDOT, 1985: 119). In the U.S., operating subsidies from the federal government are limited to 50 percent of operations (earnings before subsidy) and the average farebox coverage ratio of operations costs is only about 35 percent–40 percent.

Thus, because of the "natural monopoly" nature of the service (discussed below), most urban transit service cannot be "profitable." Nor is it likely that, without explicit or implicit public subsidies, a private company could make money from delivering transit services that would fully cover access and mobility needs of the urban poor and middle classes in most large cities. But, city companies or non-profit enterprises can break-even if subsidized up to reasonable levels such as 35 percent subject to hard budget constraints on operating costs (particularly staff size and salaries).

Selection of performance measures is another problem. Traditional transit operating subsidies in many transitional and developing countries (e.g. Hungary) are based on vehicle miles, which ignore the fact that on many routes vehicles are nearly empty. The Hungarian state railway (MAV) found that on 28 of its rural routes, consisting of 368 daily trains, averaged ridership was only 21 people (Eddy, 2006)! Like many public transit and passenger rail systems, its subsidy from the central government has been based only on kilometers of train operations. More modern performance incentive systems reward positive trends in "passenger kilometers" (Voska, 2003: 291) or "passenger miles" as the basis for allocating operating subsidies. This "benchmarking" or performance measurement allows national grantors (e.g. MOFs and/or Ministries of Transport) to monitor performance and to hold transit systems accountable for effective service delivery targets (i.e. greater coverage of the urban population). Many U.S. states (e.g. New York, California, and Pennsylvania) require transit system performance reporting as conditions for receiving financial assistance. They use U.S. FTA Section 15 performance measures such as operating cost/passenger mile and vehicle service hour/employee (Fielding, 1987: 82). As noted, modern public transit authorities operate hybrid core public systems supplemented by private contractors for particular routes on which they are also responsible for performance reporting. As supplements to general grants or traditional equalization transfers, the preferred mechanism for transit financing in many countries is becoming the performance transfer or grant.

Naïve but often politically necessary to ensure project approvals, assumptions are often made in transit operations that planned financing is usually available and expenditures will occur as planned. Often neither is true. Because of rigidities in budget processes and weaknesses in revenue collection systems, revenues and subsidies are not received on time. When emergencies or unplanned disasters occur, transit service requirements increase (e.g. Hurricane Katrina and demands on New Orleans transit services) (Lynch et al., 2008: 369). Even where budget rules are flexible enough to facilitate unforeseen expenditures, temporary shortfalls still occur. This is where cash management comes in—ensuring that sufficient cash is available to meet planned obligations. In the U.S., local transit systems typically rely on commercial banks which (for a fee) provide such services as farebox collections/counting, deposit handling, fiscal agent, bond trustee, investment counseling, term loans, payroll, and sales outlet/lockbox services for pre-paid transit pass programs (USDOT, 1985: 109). For revenue shortfalls of less than a year, transit agencies can borrow from banks by issuing promissory notes or contracting short-term loans to bridge the financing gap between expenditure obligations and the arrival of grants/subsidies (ibid., 1985: 125), e.g. revenue anticipation notes (RANs). In the FSU/CEE and other regions where banking relations are not as well developed, local transit enterprises often finance shortfalls with arrears that have to be paid back later with penalties (Chu and Hemming, 1991: 56).

4. Weak Accountability and Low Citizen Participation

Citizen participation is particularly needed to keep public transportation service responsive. Without active and critical public pressure, transit officials often lose touch with the many citizens whose daily lives depend on this service. They can become distant, arrogant, and dismissive of citizen needs. Citizens, in their view, deserve only what they get and they are lucky to have what they have. How else explain Budapest's rickety and unheated trams, some of which have been in service for 30 years? Citizen participation is a necessary part of the policy machinery for good transit service. It is the feedback loop in the policy delivery system (refer back to *Figure 1.1*). Real service improvements in any policy area (e.g. education, health, sanitation) rarely occur until consumers and stakeholders demand more from their systems (i.e. schools, hospitals, waste removal).

Public transportation programs offer a good example of the distinction between *government* and *governance* participation. Citizens attempt to influence the government of transit when they hold accountable those with formal authority and police power to plan and execute service activities. With transit districts, governing boards, city committees, and transit authorities, the link between jurisdictions and public management is clear. Nevertheless, public transit also provides an example of the "fragmented and disarticulated state" (Frederickson, 1999: 702; cited in Bingham et al., 2005: 548). This means that informal governance techniques (by and on those without formal government authority) must be applied to improve service results. As indicated above, the gap between the services of individual transit providers and the needs of metropolitan users is wide in many cities. It also suggests that informal groups and organizations must fill the representational gap. Use of networking, power-sharing, quasi-judicial and quasi-legislative processes of interdependence are means to the end of influencing local and metropolitan transit governance. Relevant tools for transit governance analysis include principal-agent theory, transaction cost analysis, and leadership theory (Bingham et al., 2005: 548). The most intense "transit watchers" are likely to be from networks of informal citizen groups and those seeking power-sharing over service planning and execution with formal transit authorities.

III. Policy Responses

Countries have responded in differing ways to these common urban transport problems. Some have been successful and others not. While empirical research has been limited on explaining results, it should be evident in most cases that the problems were institutional and financial and could be remedied with better information and professional judgment. That is, the problems were and are "actionable."

1. Policy Responses to Fragmented Governance and Mismatched Authority–Responsibility

Structure

Toronto and Miami, for example, govern transit through metropolitan federation structures. The 29 municipalities in the Miami structure contribute proportionate revenues for top-tier (area wide) and bottom-tier (local) services. Metro-Dade Transit is a department of this government. The revenues are supplemented by proprietary service fees and federal-state grants (transfers), and general fund appropriations from the Miami-Dade budget. But metropolitan Miami is a low-density area of 5.4 million people, and the federation lacks authority to impose area wide road or gas charges to reduce incentives for driving (Guess, 2008: 4). This results in underfunded transit services that carry a very small percentage of local commuters or local trips.

Similarly, Toronto created a two-tier federation structure in 1953 that served as a model for Miami's 1957 model. With 5.3 million people, Toronto's structure has the power to tax, plan, and finance capital investment. This enabled Toronto to build the second largest subway in North America (400 million riders per year) despite being the most dependent on farebox revenues (Bourne, 2001: 33). Unfortunately, by the 1970s, the city grew outwards (reducing population density) and the metropolitan jurisdiction did not grow with it. The Ontario (provincial) government created four new two-tiered public entities for the Toronto region surrounding the original metro area. This introduced fragmented governance and variability in the regulation of urban development for the area. In short, lacking applicable lessons on building sustainable organizational responsibility structures, a provincial higher-level decision wiped out much of the governance capacity gained from the original integrated federation structure.

Other cities have attempted to merge transit beneficiary boundaries with governmental jurisdictions by creating special public transport districts with authority to raise revenues. This should provide correspondence between revenue authority and expenditure responsibilities. The authority–responsibility mismatch has been reflected in revenue and expenditure assignments or "perverse regulation" (World Bank, 2005: 43). To avoid this problem, Portland (Oregon) created a regional transit agency for the metropolitan area that overlapped three counties (Tri-County Metropolitan Transit District or Tri-Met). That provided a dedicated source of revenue (as in Atlanta with its Metropolitan Atlanta Rapid Transit Authority or MARTA) for a district composed of three counties that share sales-tax earmarked obligations for the transit system. This structural solution enabled Portland to plan and manage transit services effectively for its system of light rail lines, trolley-buses, and buses for a large metropolitan area (Adler and Edner, 1990: 93). The estimated population of the Portland area is now about 2 million. Similarly, Barcelona (Spain) created a metropolitan transport authority in 1997 to integrate the fragmented services provided by local, regional, and central levels of government for the area (Borja, 2001: 22).

Authority

In the diverse market contexts described above, the question is how transit authorities (whatever their organizational forms) can plan and manage services more efficiently and effectively. What new programs and methods could be used to improve service? One can divide the systems internationally across a spectrum ranging from traditional state-subsidized Weberian bureaucracies to modern performance-driven management systems. The former tend to be in the remaining protected state environments of the FSU (Central Asia and hangover regimes such as Ukraine, Belarus, and Moldova). As noted, even newer EU members such as Hungary deliver transit services via traditional monopoly state structures (called "companies" but which are effectively city enterprises). There is little interest in service quality or performance among transit authority officials. Their incentives are to protect existing services and regulate away competitors. For example, in many FSU countries as noted, private mini-buses are in danger of making the old public transit systems and structures irrelevant. Instead of responding creatively to customer demands for access and mobility, the response from many FSU transit agencies (operating from state socialist old command and control premises) as noted has been to try and ban private mini-buses. In North America, "paratransit" (demand-responsive or dial-a-ride service via cars, vans, or small buses) is a major mode of public transportation with over 5,900 out of 6,000 transit agencies providing this innovative and alternative service (APTA, 2006). Banning it would be considered risky for local governments because it has developed a large and diffuse political constituency. Such civil society constituencies of activist transit riders do not yet exist in most of the former CEE/FSU countries.

There are well-tested methods from such regions as Latin America of innovative transit service delivery using: performance concession contracts, fiscal incentives for private transit franchising, and joint route scheduling (e.g. San Jose, Costa Rica, and Recife, Brazil). But for reasons of institutional jealousy and/or ignorance, they are often overlooked by officials from "traditional, top-down" monopoly, or separated systems (e.g. Santiago). This raises the perennial question of why evidently transferable policy lessons are ignored from one transit system to another. As noted, choking on air pollution from autos and trucks and facing mobility paralysis, Lima (Peru) still has no master plan or budget for transit other than for existing bus lines that simply share the clogged roads. Since more buses in heavy traffic do not reduce congestion, the question is why models from the region were not adopted 10–15 years ago when others went into service (e.g. articulated buses on exclusive roads or busways in Quito and Guayaquil (Ecuador), Curitiba (Brazil), Bogota (Colombia), and successful metros (e.g. Santiago and Caracas)). Latin America was the world pioneer in developing exclusive busways. In cities like Curitiba, they operate with up to 20,000 passenger/hour capacities effectively and at appropriate cost (Flora, 2001: 389). In Recife (Brazil), with 3.5 million inhabitants, the two elevated metro lines pass through the poorer areas of the city and provide them fare-free access to their jobs. In contrast with Western perspectives of public transit as a potentially profitable market service, Recife local officials consider the mass transit system to be part of its social services. Rail stations on the *Metrorec* system serve as centers of primary health (e.g. inoculations) and literacy (e.g. distribution of simple reading materials such as comic books). So, why has there been little transfer of successful lessons across close borders in the same relatively homogeneous region? One theory is that despite local autonomy, the Lima municipal government has been too weak (regardless of party in power) to enforce a unified solution for the metropolitan area. In Lima, special interests such as taxis and mini-buses have been powerful opponents of effective mass transit. This is plausible but even with the best implemented plans, at this point solutions lie years in the future at the cost of continuing health and economic losses. Although cultures may differ, tested transit delivery methods that work in a variety of contexts can often be transferred and serve as incentive frameworks to adapt local cultures to them.

It can be argued that the more innovatively managed and financed transit systems operate in decentralized countries with high degrees of urban local autonomy (e.g. Latin America, North America, and Europe). In these regions, for example, transit systems can be found that conform some or all of the institutional tenets of New Public Management. Moynihan (citing Schick) summarizes five core NPM ideas: (1) managers have clear goals, (2) managers have flexibility to use resources, (3) managers have operational authority, (4) managers focus on outputs and outcomes, and (5) managers are held accountable for resource use and results (2006: 79). To this list, for effective transit system management, accountability for financial transparency should be added, especially for operating and capital subsidies. To a large extent, the best U.S. local transit delivery systems have evolved consistently with NPM core ideas. There are about 1,500 local bus systems that also include other transit modes such as light rail (29) and heavy rail or metro (14) (APTA, 2006). While many of these systems are governed by city enterprises or responsible city departments, they manage public and private transit vehicles on publicly approved routes. Norms and regulations are centralized but they are (mostly) not the old top-down bureaucracies. Feedback and criticism to managers and governing boards from unions, passengers, the media, and NGO transit watchdogs is constant. Citizen's transit watchdog and riders associations attend service planning and budgeting hearings and make their voices known, e.g. in Washington, DC: www.metroopensdoors.com, and www.cfpt.org (Atlanta Citizens for Progressive Transit).

Bad transit service can and has been the nemesis of many mayors and powerful local officials. This is true in as diverse locales as Santiago (poor bus coordination), Budapest (new Siemens trams purchased that initially did not function as expected), and New York City (crime, filth, and homelessness previously associated with subways). Keeping the transit vehicles rolling on time and in good condition is viewed by many mayors as politically vital to their careers. As a political and fiscal safeguard, many U.S. urban transit systems operate subject to restraining policy rules (or spendthrift controls). For example, in exchange for a dedicated source of annual funding (a share of sales and use tax revenue), the Metropolitan Atlanta Rapid Transit Authority (MARTA) must recover 35 percent of last year's expenses via passenger fees and other revenues (e.g. advertising) or move immediately to raise fees, cut service, or downsize staff. This provides a hard budget constraint and ensures fiscal rectitude. While all agencies operate with subsidy fees (they cover only a portion of costs classified as marginal, full, or incremental), the restraining rule forces transit managers to think constantly about cost recovery or publicly bear the consequences. A maximum of 50 percent operating assistance is provided by the federal government (FTA) to all transit systems. In exchange, the "Section 15" system requires all transit agencies annually report service and financial statistics. These are used by the FTA to prevent greater than 50 percent operating subsidies and to allocate them as rewards for better transit operators (e.g. greater on time-performance, more passenger miles, and reduced operating cost/passenger mile). Thus, transit system management is to some extent incentive driven, financially transparent, and performance targeted. Other than in North America and the UK, there is little evidence that NPM thinking has so far permeated the management of public transit agencies to improve service results.

2. Policy Response to Weak Capital Planning Systems: Implement 12 Needed CIP Steps

CIPs are needed by jurisdictions for planning and analysis of proposed projects, ranking them according to transparent criteria, matching them against available budget funds, and financing them as part of an overall portfolio of projects that is the capital plan. This is a short- and medium-term plan that can be rolled forward each year as the fiscal and needs situations change. As indicated in *Annex I*, there are 12 basic steps or ingredients of CIPs. Those jurisdictions that attempt to institutionalize this legal, regulatory, and planning framework have more successful infrastructure programs than those that do not. Many in OECD as well as developing and transitional countries do not have effective CIPs despite the almost universal acceptance of this as a valuable policy tool.

3. Policy Response to Lack of System Financing

In most countries, transportation infrastructure is financed by capital grants supplemented by loans and designated taxes. In the U.S., dedicated portions of local taxes (e.g. sales) ensure repayment of bonded debt. There, the issues revolve around generating local political support for dedicated sources of funding, followed by the equally contentious matter of allocating projects consistent with the needs of jurisdictions that contribute the tax revenues. In Atlanta, this translated recently into a debate about extending the one-cent earmarked sales tax to year 2047 to maintain and expand the MARTA subway-bus system. That would serve additional residents far north of the city that have been engulfed by auto traffic congestion (Donsky, 2007).

But fees and taxes (including tax-sharing) cover only debt paybacks (debt service) and in reality finance by themselves only a small portion of total transit infrastructure needs. The bulk of funds come eventually from loans, loan guarantees, and grants. For instance, in the EU area, most of the regional cohesion and structural fund grants and loans have been and will be allocated to roads (53 percent) and railways (30 percent) (2007–2013). Only about 10 percent of the funds are available to finance urban public transit infrastructure projects (Stefanova, 2007). The EU bank known as European Investment Bank is owned by all 28 countries and considers itself a "non-profit bank." While EIB loans will cover 50 percent of total project costs and have lower interest rates than commercial banks, only about 5 percent of their loans are for urban public transport projects (Aymerich, 2007) such as station complexes, tramways, subway rolling stock, buses, and trolley-buses. Because of creditworthiness concerns, capital transit financing in pre-accession countries, such as Albania or Macedonia, still relies mostly on national transfers. Despite this constraint, local government transit enterprises in pre-accession countries, which had for many years been banned from borrowing, often contracted "vendor credit" to finance small capital equipment needs on a rolling "pay-as-you-go" basis. Each six-month-term loan would be paid off from current appropriations and rolled over for another six months. This worked in the sense that the assets were gained locally, except that the local government had to pay very high interest rates. It did give municipalities (that technically were not supposed to) experience in contracting and paying back loans, which became useful in developing successful local capital markets later (e.g. Romania, Bulgaria, and Croatia that are now in the EU). Nevertheless, in most of the FSU/CEE region and Third World regions such as Latin America, transit capital finance remains centralized in central government grants or low-interest loans provided to local public transport authorities. To improve capital financing in the FSU/CEE area, national transfers need to be based on system performance and management incentives for sound project planning and implementation.

Local government capital markets also need to be deepened and borrowing authority expanded along with fiscal controls.

To bridge the large gap between public transportation infrastructure financing needs and available resources from public budgets, regulatory frameworks in both the EU and the U.S. have encouraged "innovative" capital financing. In the EU, public-private partnerships (PPPs) are widely used. PPPs are privately financed infrastructure projects executed through contracts (often concessions) issued to private firms for the provision of public services (World Bank, 2005: 145). The private firm sells the service to the public or to third parties with public loan guarantees (ibid., 2005: 136). Private concessions in countries such as Brazil with decent credit ratings can bring generous yields of 10 percent of higher. Thus, private infrastructure firms gain from working with stable governments. Governments gain in that PPPs are used to generate budget savings and promote capital investment (which in Brazil is only 2 percent of GDP) (*Economist*, 2007a).

The way this works is that a private infrastructure firm pays project construction costs up front. Because PPPs operate on the margins of EU reporting requirements (World Bank, 2005: 137), accounts are not kept on an accrual basis. This means that government deficit and debt figures do not increase. The "availability payments" (which would be normal budget expenditures under an accrual system) to the provider do not entail accounting liabilities under Maastricht criteria and ESA95. The PPP remains off-budget and is not captured in most cases as even a contingent liability (ibid., 2005: 145). This is also the case for many U.S. states. The Virginia Public-Private Transportation Act of 1995 attracted private-sector investment to "jump-start" expensive transit capital projects, such as the Metrorail extension to Dulles Airport in Washington ($4 billion estimated cost). The Act provides for a "cloak of secrecy" that largely prevents public penetration of the contractual aspects of projects. This makes it difficult to evaluate financial risks, such as cost overruns (e.g. change orders) and scheduling delays. It also raises significant issues of secrecy, accountability, conflict of interest, and failure to protect the public trust. By contrast, similar contracts are published as part of the fiscal accounts in Argentina, Chile, Brazil, and Peru (World Bank, 2005: 145). Because of the use of questionable accounting rules and appraisal techniques for assessment of fiscal risk, EU PPPs tend to mask significant economic and fiscal risk exposure for national governments. Despite these problems, EU fiscal institutions tend to favor PPP financing when traditional public investment and financing would often be cheaper (ibid., 2005: 142).

This largely risk-free accounting treatment of PPPs under ESA95 is similar to that of "innovative" but off-budget financing of transit infrastructure projects in the U.S. The major difference has been the scale—U.S. local transit financing techniques cover only about 20 percent of total project costs while in the EU they can finance 50 percent or more—meaning much higher and less transparent risk exposure in EU countries. The bulk of transit capital financing in the U.S. is via formula-based capital transfers to local transit authorities. As noted, this provides up to 80 percent financing, and local authorities must co-finance the rest with one or more revenue sources. Much of the local share has been debt in various forms. The simplest and most transparent mechanism is with revenue or general obligation bonds, issued on the basis of transparent market creditworthiness and rating criteria. Earlier innovative techniques used before the advent of PPPs were: (1) leasing, (2) tax increment financing, and (3) "turnkey" or BOT contracts, which have all been called "non-debt" techniques. For instance, lease-finance is tax-code driven in the U.S. as it takes advantage of transit authority capability to borrow at tax-exempt rates and transfer tax benefits to "lessors" (private investors) that lease transit assets (e.g. rail cars) from public entities and take accelerated depreciation benefits (Guess, 1991: 27). That is, capital leases have been used to allow lessor investors to take depreciation tax benefits and deductions for rail cars that are then shared with the public "lessee" (transit agency) through lower lease payments. Capital leasing costs may be below those for issuing long-term debt. Local authority leases contain "non-appropriation" clauses which mean the obligations are conditional and therefore not debt, which must be unconditional (Vogt and Cole, 1983: 67). Through such legal fictions as "conditional debt" and calling purchase payments as "rent" (similar to PPP fictions noted), local authorities avoid classifying leases as debt or including them as contingent liabilities.

In addition to the financial issues in using private capital for urban transport, legal issues constrain investors. This is important since ownership of world railways is 87 percent public sector. While airlines use leasing and private capital to acquire airplanes, it is much harder for rail transport. That is because investors have little security over their rolling stock assets. They cannot repossess the capital goods across borders. They are often procured by state authorities with widely different specifications such as track gauges that make repossession difficult. A new codicil to the Cape Town Convention that governs airplane assets is being added to create a centralized system of serial numbers. This will reduce investor risks and costs for private investors and could lead to new investments in regions such as Latin America and Asia where railways are needed and private cash is almost entirely absent from this sector (*Economist*, 2015: 71).

Betterment or tax-increment financing districts are often used to finance local shares of transit capital projects as well. These are special tax districts that draw on beneficiaries (i.e. businesses) to finance part of the system. They are used in FSU/CEE countries by local authorities for such investments as lighting and street improvements. Metro-Miami (Florida) used this incremental tax method (above regular ad valorem rates) to pay for 15 Westinghouse Metromover cars, charging transit district business beneficiaries on the basis of net leasable square footage. The estimated revenue covered repayment of a portion of the debt service for the vehicles and a portion of the capital costs (Guess, 1991: 21, 45). A variant of betterment districts is to use sale of "air rights" above public transport facilities such as roads and metro stations to finance the infrastructure projects. Developers purchase the rights and achieve the policy objective of "transit-oriented development" and the state keeps the revenues. An important issue is whether this amounts to unfair competitive advantages to air rights purchasers where gluts of private office space exist (Jackman, 2013: B1). Air rights sales could also generate the excessive congestion around these facilities that they were built to remedy in the first place. Finally, transit authorities have used variants of vendor credit or supplier finance in the form of build-operate-transfer (BOT) with "turnkey" contracts in which the project is transferred to the vendor after completion. These have been popular with capital projects ranging from the Eurotunnel between France and the UK to U.S. sewerage treatment plants (Guess, 1991: 43). Finding private financing for BOT contracts has not been difficult since investors view transit as an essential service like electricity and water, and public guarantees (even implicit) are enough to reduce any risk of default.

4. Policy Response to Lack of Accountability Requirements

The exercise of citizen voice on public transit service (whether through its governmental institutions or its governance processes) is not sufficient by itself to remedy the other four issues noted above: financing, governance systems, service management, and planning. There are two reasons for this. On the transit authority side, officials are often threatened by citizen groups that want to see all the financial and service figures every day and to have a larger role in the planning of existing and new services. Often, citizen advisory boards are hand-picked precisely because they lack professional transit experience and are less likely to cause trouble (e.g. Montgomery County, Maryland). Officials know that the normal problems of political apathy affecting voter turnout do not afflict transit rider groups. They are organized (often based on riders of one scheduled commuter bus line), active, aggressive, and vocal on this single-issue. Single-issue advocates are the most feared by officials because they tend to be intense, direct, and zealous in their cause. Despite these important incentives for participation, the main requirement is that both the transit authority and the local governments have the authority to impose jurisdictional taxes and vary public transit fares. According to Kamenikova (2006), where that revenue authority is missing, there are few incentives to participate—local officials cannot really be held accountable. But for public transit in most countries, officials often can be held accountable. Vocal transit service complaints are considered non-political and often allowable even by the most authoritarian regimes. On the citizen side, groups are often single-issue (e.g. new line or route, more service, lower fares) on matters that affect the most vocal members. In this context, transit officials become overwhelmed by demands against limited service budgets and the need to finance legal minimum amounts of operations through fares. Citizen groups that represent all transit riders are needed but often do not exist in metropolitan areas. As noted, groups such as the Atlanta Citizens for Progressive Transit have been successful since they represent most riders.

Thus, an important issue is how to structure the relationship between the community served and transit management to ensure effective results. As noted by Wulkin (1990: 25), the local public transit operator is one of the few public services that come into contact on a daily basis with their customers or constituents. Transit managers are often the single focal point for complaints or inquiries. Yet, much of his/her capacity to manage the system depends on the transit governing board—its ability to define its role, delegate authority, and provide clear policy for the manager (ibid., 1990: 26). Wulkin examined which types of transit boards performed these functions best: appointed (*trustees*) by managers or the city, or elected (*delegates* whose authority is derived from their constituents). He found that efficacy of board types depends a lot on the modal-complexity of service and geo-political area served. More importantly, hybrid boards have developed where members are appointed by elected local officials. Unfortunately, the issue of transit system structure and governance has not been more recently examined in detail, especially its relation to service performance. More than 20 years ago, Perry and Babitsky (1986) compared the performance of urban bus transit in the U.S. of five types of ownership/management structure and found that privately owned/operated systems produced more output/dollar and generated more revenues than other types of governance structures. Clearly, more research needs to be done on the relationship between types of transit governance and service performance.

Participation issues are different in new transitional and developing countries. As noted, public reactions to bad transit service in developing countries are often swift and violent. There are few official channels of participation for effective inputs into the policy process and citizens must often take to the streets. In the transitional countries of FSU/CEE, citizens have a long tradition of enforced passivity on services. Most kept their heads down and endured the quite awful conditions of buses, trams, and subways out of fear of official retribution by the state security apparatus. Complaints were frowned on and in some countries, such as Albania under Enver Hoxja, could earn one a free trip for several years to an "exile village." In the post-transition period, political consciousness of the power of solidarity to change policies has grown. Citizens are taking a much more active role in protesting all kinds of government activities from election results to service delivery. Some questions for researchers then would be: What is the level of public participation in transit decision-making in these transitional political contexts? What are the institutional mechanisms for this, such as transit riders' associations? Do they exist and which are most effective in particular kinds of cases such as pricing policy, service delivery, and facility condition? At what stage of the policy process are citizens permitted to intervene and how far into the process can they exert influence? Comments on draft budgets/laws/plans? Comments on final versions? Comments during transit board deliberations? What is the most effective form of citizen transit participation?

A substantial amount of research has been performed on general citizen participation in budgeting in the FSU. For example, the International Center for Human Development (ICHD) of Armenia found that budget participation could be increased through the mechanism of a town hall meeting in which diverse citizen groups deliberated on the spending for city capital investment projects. They found that making connections between citizen participation, specific projects, and annual budgeting encouraged citizens in small Armenian towns to pay more taxes. As effective participation increased (because the project budget option they selected was implemented), so did ownership in the project and willingness to pay taxes for it and other local projects (ICHD, 2006).

The same logic could work for effective citizen voice on transit projects and willingness to pay higher fares. For example, the "Transit Watch" survey or inventory tool can provide transit rider associations and other stakeholder groups with an analytic means to examine the state of financial and service performance. The effectiveness of this and other similar tools to improve system performance needs to be examined in future urban public transportation research.

IV. Tools

1. Fiscal Decentralization Analysis

Fiscal federalism in education policy is discussed further in *Chapter 6*. Here, two criteria or tools are important for stimulating optimal urban transport service. They are: (1) *assignments* of revenue and expenditure authority to achieve maximum fiscal autonomy within a framework of strong internal audit and control, and (2) *transfers* that provide sufficient funding and incentives to use funds to maximize transport efficiency and effectiveness.

a. Assignments

As indicated in *Figure 3.1*, decisions here should be based on consistency with *correspondence* or efficiency (to minimize externalities) and *subsidiarity* or devolution and local fiscal autonomy (optimal responsiveness level). Delivery of subnational transit services requires devolution of expenditure, tax authority, and management discretion to use the funds properly. Adjustments are often required for structural problems to increase efficiency. For example, *externalities* (e.g. accrual of benefits to non-residents) often occur which may require expansion of local authority or transfer of some autonomy to a regional or metropolitan government. In most cases, regional inequities exist that may require authority to differentiate fares and taxes. Adjustments might also be required to remedy *diseconomies of scale.* Often local tax authorities are unable to register and collect taxes from non-residents for regional or metropolitan services such as transport that exceed beneficiary district boundaries. In such cases, tax administration should be moved to a higher level of government to take advantage of scale economies.

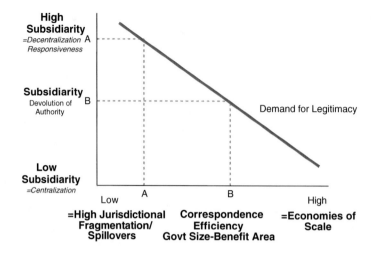

Figure 3.1 Dynamics of Intergovernmental Systems Design

Most governments follow established principles in assigning expenditure responsibility. Two important ones are: (1) assignment to governments whose jurisdiction most closely approximates the geographic area of benefits area provided by the function, i.e. urban transport, and (2) public goods and services should be provided by the government that can best realize economies of scale in production, i.e. reduction of unit costs. For any good or service, increasing the amount of service may result in decreasing, increasing, or constant unit costs (Ebel and Vaillancourt, 2007: 79). The cost impact is an empirical question. As will be noted below, urban transport faces the "natural monopoly" problem where more service often costs more and leads to increased unit costs. With some exceptions, this largely restricts delivery of this program to public monopolies.

b. Transfers

Vertical transfers flow largely from higher to lower levels of government (though tax revenues can be transferred upwards in the other direction). In the UK, central transfers provide 80 percent of local financing; local councils have limited tax bases and there are few elected mayors (e.g. London and Bristol). The over-centralized system puts municipalities at the mercy of Westminster central transfers which are often reduced to meet macro-fiscal targets. In the U.S., 75 percent of federal grants are for programs such as transport, social assistance, and education; 66 percent of the entire federal budget is for individual transfers—called entitlements for health, retirement, and welfare. Many U.S. government agencies merely pass through the funds via transfers to state and local governments. For example, transfers are 99 percent of the Education Department's budget but provide only 8 percent of total education funding. The other 92 percent of education financing is provided by own-source funds from state or local governments. This illustrates the feature that in most countries transfers facilitate cost-sharing for programs and services like urban transport. Vertical and horizontal transfers can equalize differences in tax base within cities, states, and countries and hold the political system together. The purposes of vertical transfers are to provide sufficient local funding and autonomy to allocate the funds for maximum results. There are four main types of *transfers*.

1   *Unconditional*: This assigns the highest degree of fiscal autonomy to local units. It may be formula-based (e.g. population density) or non-formula. Block grants to specific functions as transport allow local managers to shift funds depending on statutory definitions to reprogram funds within transport programs, e.g. road, rail, bus, bridges. U.S. transit capital assistance was initially based on population which rewarded large cities.

2   *Conditional Non-matching*: This may be program or project specific, and the only condition for the lump-sum grant is that it be used for targeted purposes. Block grants fit this category as well. Performance grants linking incentives to program performance are used in many countries, e.g. to reduce operating costs/passenger mile by encouraging managers to cut staff costs and economize on operations. Property tax incentive grants are used in Kosovo. The MOF sets a normative target for each municipality then sets the current year grant based on past year tax collections. Governments that exceed targets receive the full grant; those that miss the target but improve revenue collections over the past year baseline receive whatever percentage of the grant they achieved; those that fall short receive nothing (Peteri and Vaillancourt, 2007: 29).

3   *Conditional Matching*: These are lump-sum grants where the recipient must match up to a specified minimum. It maximizes local use of funds by reducing the tax price and encouraging recipients to contribute stakes to the program. The current U.S. Federal Transit Administration "New Starts" cost effectiveness process for capital transit projects awards more points for greater local financial contributions, i.e. no longer is there a set 90 percent–10 percent or 75 percent–25 percent cost share formula—the recipient is encouraged to finance as much of the project as possible. The purpose of this type of grant is to promote fiscal discipline and allocational/technical efficiencies for transit, and to incentivize local management discretion. If permitted by labor union agreements, the grants may be combined with "new" public management reforms that increase discretion to shift funds flexibly and to meet service performance targets.

4   *Equalization Transfers*: These are grants designed to recognize objectively measured variations in expenditure needs (i.e. workload factors such as number of riders, average commuting times, severe operating conditions such as ice, and amount of congestion) as well as unequal distribution of revenue bases (i.e. poverty levels) (Ebel and Peteri, 2007: 121). In many countries, they are often allocated on the basis of average revenue per capita. Equalization formulae are used for transport within some U.S. states and across provinces from the central government, e.g. Switzerland and Canada. A transfer "union" effectively means equalization transfers. In many OECD countries, the primary intergovernmental fiscal aim is to *equalize* subnational government capacity to provide a standard set of services given regional differences in costs, revenue bases, and revenue generation efforts. Germany uses a lump-sum grant for this purpose that actually punishes *lander*, which raise more revenues. So, perversely, Bavaria and Hesse lander are rewarded, and Berlin, which collects more, is penalized. The EU is a small transfer union with a budget of only 1 percent of EU GDP. By contrast, the U.S. budget spends 38.9 percent of GDP.

2. Project Analysis

Consistent with what is needed for an effective CIP described in *Annex I,* we offer three principles or criteria for project analysis:

1   The most important foundation for selecting an appropriate transport project is the definition of benefits and certainty that all costs have been included. Too often benefits are exaggerated and costs are excluded, making the project appear more cost beneficial.
2   To try and guard against narrow use of cost–benefit analyses, multiple methods of appraisal should be used, including net present value (NPV) and internal rate of return (IRR).
3   Data and operating premises for implementation of the project need to be justified in consultants' appraisal reports. Urban transport agencies need in-house expertise to challenge both data and assumptions. Hiring additional consultants often ends up in expensive confusion.

3. Costing and Pricing of Transit Services

Beyond taxes, such as the property tax, and central government transfers, the major sources of revenues for most subnational governments are fees and charges often levied by fiscal monopolies. Governments charge *fees* for activities requiring licenses such as business, hunting, and driving; they impose service *charges* where there are enforceable charge barriers such as student tuition, road tollgates, transit fareboxes, and water meters; and they generate funds from their utilities through the sale, for instance, of liquor, operation of lotteries, and water supply (Mikesell, 2014: 553). Of total own-source revenues, U.S. states collect about 29 percent from charges, fees, and monopoly operations, and localities about 33 percent (ibid., 2014: 540). By comparison, own-source local revenues in the federal systems of Germany are 35 percent, in Canada about 39 percent, and in the UK (unitary system) only 20 percent.

Officials need to know how and why to set prices for three types of services. With prices set, they are in a better position to estimate service volumes and to devise formulae for grants to cover services and programs to lower tiers of government, e.g. state-city and county-city. First, there are *public goods* such as planning, zoning, and law enforcement, where it is difficult to identify consumers (Neels and Caggiano, 1996: 173–174). These should be paid for out of the general fund, funded by taxation; no additional charges are usually levied.

Second, there are *private goods* where it is more feasible for public provision. Some services are naturally loss-making and more efficiently delivered by single public monopoly organizations than multiple competing private firms. These are called *natural monopolies* and the state or locality regulates them to provide optimal services and reasonable charges. Public transit, water and sewerage, and construction of public facilities are examples of natural monopoly service delivery. Technology has changed the status of this classification, allowing private firms to offer services at reasonable prices to customers in the public interest, e.g. road maintenance, sanitation services, animal control, public transit routes, and private concessions to build, operate, and maintain public capital facilities such as jails and highways. Localities also provide concessions to private firms to offer their services inside libraries, schools, and hospitals (e.g. food services and copying).

Finally, there are *merit goods* such as treatment of communicable diseases and social services that can be provided by non-profit organizations (Neels and Caggiano, 1996: 173–174). These include elderly and handicapped transport services. The city contracts with non-profits to perform services that it can now regulate on the basis of performance and cost-effectiveness. While regulation and standards remain with the public sector, delivery is the responsibility of the non-profit or private firm that bids successfully for the public service contract.

Prices for the second and third type of service vary by type and purpose. Officials set them to try and balance cost efficiency, revenue generation, and value to the consumer. Localities should attempt to recover the full cost of providing services to consumers (ibid., 1996: 174). Failure to receive full cost recovery means that the jurisdiction is subsidizing the activity. For revenue analysis and fiscal transparency, it is critical to identify subsidy prices. Such leakages may be for a public purpose, but it is critical that the finance departments be able to monetize or measure them to ensure that they are targeted (e.g. often food and fuel subsidies are not), and to recommend sound pricing policies based on this information. There are four main types of pricing strategies:

1   *Direct Cost Pricing:* Localities set prices to yield revenues sufficient to costs and no more than that. The idea is that non-profit entities like governments should not profit off the public. What are costs? As noted in the previous chapter, *costs* are not *expenditures* or budget outlays. Expenditures are measured by budget appropriations and reflect political pressures (such as union labor rules) and procurement practices that may not purchase goods and services at market prices or least cost. Costs refer to the use and consumption of goods and services or to the market costs of production. For instance, the costs of health care are typically far less than public expenditures for them. Initially, they can be divided into direct and indirect. Direct costs include all the core costs associated with a particular service (ibid., 1996: 178). For the city transit agency, the *direct costs* would include salaries, travel, maintenance, and supplies. *Indirect costs* are for overhead support and include administration. Dividing the direct costs by the number of riders served produces the average direct costs per rider. This would allow efficiency comparisons with other services in similar cities.

2   *Full Cost Pricing:* Full costs reflect market-based costs or the sum of direct and indirect costs. As indicated, the latter are support costs, such as administration and overhead, charged to the activity. Indirect costs are often apportioned on the basis of a predetermined rate based on such factors as: time spent supporting the activity (e.g. processing invoices, payment of staff, and common use of copier, fax, and phones). Income-generating activities such as local public utilities will often charge full costs to consumers plus a mark-up to provide returns to bondholders that pay for their capital improvements.

3   *Cost–Volume Pricing:* As the quantity of service increases, such as more passenger miles of bus service, costs will change in varying proportions. *Figure 3.2* indicates that costs behave unevenly with volume of service output. In the figure, note that *fixed costs* such as salaries (in the short term), capital, rent, and maintenance will not change up to a certain threshold. As supervisors are added to cover additional volume and output, the costs become *semi-fixed*. *Variable costs*, such as fuel, number of trips, and salaries (to serve increased ridership in the long term) will vary by volume. But with greater output, some of the costs have a fixed component, e.g. utility bills based partly on demand. These are *semi-variable* costs. Knowing cost–volume relationships allows more nuanced pricing to ensure that efficiencies are maintained. This type of pricing is especially useful for comparing service delivery costs with private contractors. Analysis of cost–volume relations may indicate that private contractors (e.g. private bus line operators) can charge the same price but be able to reduce their fixed or variable costs. By achieving the service level desired by the city, this can provide considerable budgetary savings.

   Because of *economies of scale*, average costs per unit typically decrease with greater volume of output. Unit costs normally decrease with increasing output. As more productivity is squeezed out of existing fixed assets, transit organizations experience this at lower levels of service as ridership and the number of rides increases. At higher outputs, however, the transit authority must rehabilitate buses, replace them, or add more rolling

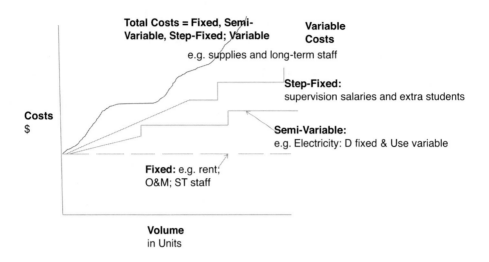

Figure 3.2 Types of Unit Costs

stock to accommodate more passengers. Additional staff is also required to cover higher workloads, meaning that indirect support costs also must increase. Average total costs no longer can guide pricing since they are both increasing at different rates with volume. Full-cost pricing to cover all costs would now be prohibitive to users. This is because demand for many services is sensitive to price. As indicated below in *Figure 3.3*, if the service is price sensitive, it is said to be *elastic*. Increasing the price too high will reduce ridership and encourage alternate means of mobility such as automobile use for middle class riders, causing greater congestion and air pollution. But poorer transit-dependent riders will suffer from the regressivity of a higher fare; they must pay the higher fares anyway to maintain access to jobs and other family needs.

Focusing on average or unit costs and their relationship to fixed-variable costs is not enough to set prices for some services. Marginal cost pricing is a better way to link cost–volume in the context of scarce resources and limited possibilities to recover full costs. *Marginal cost* is the cost of the last unit of service provided. For comprehensive cost analysis, marginal costs should be compared with *average costs* (total costs per number of units) for such local decisions as *outsourcing*. Unit cost behavior does not capture the change in fixed and variable costs with greater output. As noted, economies of scale at greater volumes should lower unit costs. Average costs, for example, might dictate outsourcing a service. But from a marginal cost perspective, it may save revenue to perform a task in-house, such as educating extra students. Marginal costs are often the same as variable costs over a specific volume range. When volume increases, some variable costs become fixed, e.g. salaries and wages which were a short-term variable cost now become fixed in the longer term. Where school capacity exists and the question is whether to add extra students, the marginal cost of each of them would be equal to variable costs up to a point. When more fixed costs must be incurred to accommodate them (e.g. buses, rail cars, classrooms, teachers, doctors), the marginal cost of extra riders, students, or patients will now be the sum of fixed and variable costs. Up to that point, no strains on capacity are required and the marginal costs are low, i.e. only the variable costs (e.g. light, heat, desk space) need be considered. If fixed costs change then, the marginal and variable costs will be different (Finkler, 2010: 134–135).

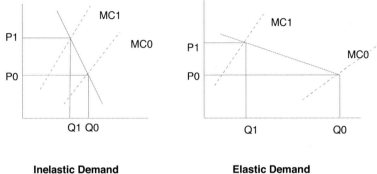

Inelastic Demand
(often poor and bus-dependent
riders: can't change modes!)

Elastic Demand
(often middle class rail & commuter
bus riders: shift to cars!)

Figure 3.3 Price Elasticity of Demand

Cost relationships vary by type of transport service. The marginal cost of additional riders, for example, is often below full or even direct costs. So, pricing to cover full or direct costs would be inefficient and likely reduce ridership. Public transit programs or services are considered ripe for *natural monopoly* delivery. Since it would be inefficient to require duplication of investments to deliver one type of service for multiple jurisdictions within the same metropolitan region, the service needs to be delivered by one monopoly. It cannot be a private monopoly because costs of required service will be greater than revenues. Given that the bulk of urban transport services are delivered by public natural monopolies, full-cost pricing would lead to an even higher subsidy requirement or reduction in service levels. The problems with using average or full-cost pricing for natural monopolies is indicated in *Figure 3.4* below. Cost-based pricing, and particularly marginal cost pricing, allows officials to recognize the maximum point at which all costs cannot meet demand. At this point, higher prices would reduce ridership, and some combination of alternative means such as greater subsidies, contracting out, negotiations with unions, and service reductions would be necessary. Continuously decreasing average costs imply that marginal cost pricing will result in more losses and a compensating operating subsidy will be needed (Hemming, 1991: 79).

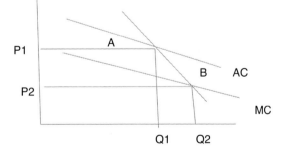

Figure 3.4 Natural Monopoly

Natural monopoly used to prevent duplication of investments in public transport, water-sewer type industries. But increasing *returns to scale*, @P2/Q2 means natural monopoly cannot generate enough $ to cover AC (TC/#units = AC). At P2/Q2 delivery should be efficient (P=MC). But cost/unit > revenue/unit. Q1 too low to generate break-even revenue. At P2, can generate normal ROR but Q required is inefficient. Context requires regulated monopoly + subsidy prices + other revenues.

4   *Income-Based Pricing*: Here, officials consider both cost and revenue to set prices. For many services, marginal cost pricing, as noted, results in subsidy levels below both average and even direct costs. Low-cost housing is *subsidy priced* below both marginal and full cost for social policy reasons. *Penalty prices*, by contrast, to dissuade harmful activities such as pollution and smoking are charged above full- and marginal-cost levels. As indicated below, below a break-even point, prices are subsidy and above that point they can generate surpluses.

In fact, most public services do not cover operating costs even with sensible pricing. As noted, public transit fares typically cover no more than 35 percent–50 percent of operating costs. On the other hand, cities do provide many services where certain patrons are willing to pay more and a reasonable attempt through pricing should be made to cover a greater percentage of total operating costs. Cities, of course, cannot simply gouge the public for use of parks where there are few alternatives. The goal would be to set a price to minimize losses (subsidies) rather than make a profit for these kinds of facilities. For other facilities and services such as transit, parking garages, swimming pools, and libraries, officials recognize the availability of private alternatives, e.g. bookstores and automobiles. Nevertheless, the alternatives are not free and in many cases cities can charge full costs and include mark-ups to generate a profit. In other cases, such as rush-hour transit, cities can use discriminatory pricing to charge higher peak fares. This generates funding to pay for increased maintenance of operating more buses and encourages those who could take buses during off-peak hours to do so and reduce congestion.

4. Financing Urban Transport Services

An important financing issue for urban transport is how to decide whether it is cheaper to make or deliver services in-house versus buying or contracting out for them. There are three simple methods that are employed for make–buy decisions:

1   *Marginal Analysis* or out-of-pocket analysis for change in service volume. This method is useful for determining when fixed costs will increase to a point at which it is wiser to find a contractor that will perform the service (e.g. transit service and more rolling stock and rehabilitation costs to accommodate more riders). Since average or unit costs relate inversely and directly to volume (e.g. decreasing with more volume), subnational governments should use marginal, not average, costs as the basis for pricing performance contracts where fixed and variable costs do not change in linear fashion with volume, i.e. most services.
2   *Break-Even Analysis* is used to calculate subsidies (or losses) for activities with revenue potential, e.g. urban transport lines, public pools, conferences, community feeding programs, recreation services, and charter schools. For these activities, policy analysts typically have the basic parameters: total costs (fixed and variable), total revenues, and all they need is the break-even volume. These figures are similar to those used for calculation of *operating ratios* (costs per dollar earned) in the private sector. This works for the many public sector fee-financed activities that generate profits or losses. Suppose the Bucharest City Municipal Orchestra incurs $1 million fixed costs per year. The variable costs for each person attending one of the orchestra's performances have been estimated at only $2. The average charge for a ticket to attend a performance is $60. How many tickets must it sell each year to break even? See *Figure 3.5*.

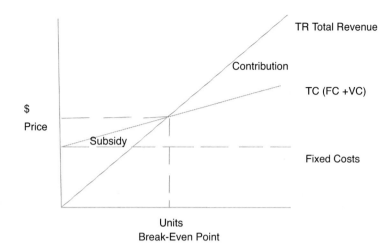

Figure 3.5 Break-Even and Subsidy Points

The formula for break-even volume (BEV) is:

BEV = Fixed Costs / Price or Revenue—Variable Costs

	Fixed costs	-	$1,000,000	
	Variable costs	-	$2	per ticket
	Price	-	$60	per ticket

$$\text{Quantity of tickets sold to break even} = \frac{FC}{P-VC} = \frac{\$1{,}000{,}000}{\$60-2} = 17{,}241 \ tickets$$

Therefore, 17,241 tickets must be sold to break even.

Note: The actual calculation yields the result 17,241.379. However, it is important to round up, even though the fraction is less than one half. If we only sold 17,242 tickets, the orchestra would lose money because it would be below the break-even point.

Discussion: What if price falls, variable costs rise, etc.? What if we expect demand for only 16,000 tickets?

This indicates that the BEV is $17,241 tickets (Finkler, 2010: 164). Break-even analysis now enables Bucharest to examine strategies on how services might be improved. How can the orchestra reduce the break-even volume in case its sales and patronage drop? It can do some or all of the following:

1   Reduce fixed costs by hiring a cheaper or smaller orchestra (hard to do without affecting quality!) or finding cheaper symphony facilities (Finkler, 2010: 142). This is usually not possible. In such cases, it may be cheaper to outsource the management of the opera to a firm.
2   Find internal variable cost efficiencies (e.g. consolidate schools, use part-time staff, consolidate personnel positions) to reduce the variable costs/unit.

3   Increase prices—which will raise revenue in the short term but, if the opera is price elastic (i.e. perhaps with people watching opera on TV), this could reduce patronage and revenue.

4   Increase patronage or number of units of service by marketing.

3   *Flexible Budgeting* provides budget figures for different levels of activity such as public transit and hospital health care. This tool provides two new sources of decision-making information: (a) fiscal managers can now see the break-even point for an activity or service, and (b) it also reveals how fixed and variable costs are behaving because of changes in volume. For example, some variable costs vary proportionately with volume such as fuel and supplies; others vary step-variably with volume such as management and administration in the longer term. As suggested, fixed costs do not vary with volume over a particular range, e.g. fleet management and personnel in the short term. Eventually, some fixed costs will vary with volume. The key concept here is that the amount of resources consumed will vary with the level of workload actually attained (Finkler, 2010: 289). Flexible budgeting allows a different angle on break-even calculations for managers.

It is evident from *Table 3.1* that the break-even point is about 42,000 delivered meals. The major contributor to results is the cost of supplies or meals. For public transit, the units would be passenger miles instead of meals, and fuel and maintenance supplies. Revenues would be fares, appropriations from the city, fiscal transfers, and advertising. Using the flexible budgeting tool allows managers to focus on that cost in the short term and seek more revenues from donations and the city.

Finally, states and cities in the twenty-first century are beginning to use a new option for service delivery and finance—one that had been typically used for long-term capital investment financing rather than current services: *social impact bonds* or SIBs. They are in use in such countries as the UK (where the tool originated in 2010), cities such as New York City, and states such as Massachusetts and New York (*Economist*, 2013a: 71). There, SIBs are used to deliver and finance social services for problems such as drug abuse, inmate recidivism, homelessness, and elderly-handicapped transit services. Bonds are typically sold by the

Table 3.1 Meals for Homeless Flexible Budget

Meals Delivered	35,000	40,000	45,000
Revenue			
Donations	$105,000	$105,000	$105,000
City	52,500	60,000	67,500
Total Revenue	$157,500	$165,000	$172,500
Expenses			
Salaries	$46,000	$ 46,000	$ 46,000
Supplies	87,500	100,000	112,500
Rent	12,000	12,000	12,000
Other	6,000	6,000	6,000
Total Expenses	$151,500	$164,000	$176,500
Surplus/(Deficit)	$6,000	$1,000	$(4,000)

Source: Finkler: Financial Management for Public, Health, and Not-for-Profit Organizations, 3rd Ed. © Pearson Education 2010

public entity to cover projects that have shorter performance impact expectations. NGOs bid on the service project and promise to meet carefully defined performance targets, e.g. one SIB provides an annualized return of 13 percent if reoffending rates do not drop by at least 7.5 percent. The bond funds cover NGO (e.g. St. Mungo's, a London homeless charity) costs for periods longer than typical government contracts and this allows them the stability to perform more efficiently. Investors take equity risks in buying the SIB but exercise social responsibility. If the NGO meets the target, the investors win that purchase the bonds, such as individuals and firms like Goldman Sachs. If the NGO fails to meet the targets, investors lose. Investors can gain substantial returns on a typical SIB if the NGO achieves the targets in the time specified. The state or local government saves on service costs by selling SIBs to investors and having NGOs deliver them. Governmental resources consist of the performance measures and targets and monitoring and oversight of reporting of progress and results.

V. Application of Frameworks

Application of the technical, political economy, and comparative frameworks can be illustrated by the international urban transport system known as bus rapid transit or BRT. These are "surface subways" that combine the speed and capacity of LRT and metros with the simplicity, flexibility, and lower cost of bus systems. BRTs serve 166 cities worldwide with 55 alone in Latin America. The first one was in Curitiba, Brazil (1974), and there are now systems in many cities in of different regions such as Jakarta, Indonesia; Johannesburg, South Africa; and even an attempted implementation in Amman, Jordan. At the technical level, BRTs function as planned along fixed routes. The technical systems, rolling stock, and signaling are straight-forward as is the construction and maintenance during operations. Needed to build and operate BRT are basic systems of administrative management, contracting, and procurement, and CIPs to plan the projects properly. Where these basic elements are present, the systems work as planned and 27 million passengers ride them worldwide, including 17 million in Latin America.

Though the technical links are clear, the linkages between public investment and wider economic benefits and costs are not. Many BRT projects are justified to voters and officials on wider bases than mobility, i.e. induced investment, employment, and higher local incomes. But there is substantial variability in the economic impact of BRT and in system cost recovery. For example, Cleveland's BRT attracted $5.8 billion in investment along its 6.8-mile route. It was built in 2008 for about $50 million or one-third the cost of the Washington, DC, streetcar (LRT) (*Economist,* 2014: 36). Other BRTs such as Baltimore, have neither generated economic development nor fiscal sustainability. Why not? So far, the policy studies are not conclusive. Failure to generate economic benefits and cost recovery means subsidies from the budget and potentially higher local taxes. For these reasons, application of the political economy framework is needed to try and identify the most important determinants of economic impact and sustainable ridership.

Regime support is likely essential even though BRT are subnational urban projects. The local regime's support is needed to unify fragmented institutions and ministries with their competing and dysfunctional agendas that derail many capital projects, regardless of need or national priority. Regime support would be less necessary in federal systems where devolution of political and financial authority places responsibility on lower-tier officials. Legal and regulatory frameworks that support basic and innovative financing methods such as revenue bonds, PPPs, tax increment financing, and leasebacks are essential. Latin American financial systems have evolved along with political cultures that now demand more precision and transparency over the past several decades. For this reason, the majority of BRTs and passengers are still in this region. Institutional certainty and professionalism to plan routes are also essential. That means integration of land use plans with CIPs and route planning that includes feedback from citizens of differing ethnicities, religious sects, income levels, and commuting needs. Integration can occur through participatory budgeting systems (also initiated in Brazil) as well as the use of well-known conflict-resolution mechanisms. Still, the precise link between planning, public investments, economic development, and cost recovery is not well specified for differing urban contexts.

Once the lessons of individual systems performances are measured and analyzed, they can be compared for transferability to other regions. As noted, BRT systems have already been transferred to other regions such as North America, South Africa, and Asia successfully at the technical–operational level. It cannot be said that there is a basic system and routing plan that will lead to development and cost recovery because the 166 BRT cities are all quite different geographically, demographically, and jurisdictionally, e.g. metro governments, city managers, and authority deconcentrated from national level political institutions. Lack of a strong legal and regulatory framework and financial institutions in Jordan explains why the BRT there has had serious difficulty in becoming operational. At the strategic policy level, devolution of financial/political authority is essential, e.g. Brazil, Ecuador, Mexico; internal audit institutions must be strong to counter the powerful tendencies to corrupt the contracting and implementation processes normally associated with larger public capital projects. These too have been developed in Latin America to ensure implementation successes; they have not been in regions such as the Middle East or countries such as Jordan, which explains the lack of BRT success there. Outputs in the form of completed BRT systems that perform well operationally can be related to expenditure and resource inputs with confidence. But explanations of varying outcome performance in growth and development have not been empirically developed. More research on input-outcome linkages is required. Until that has been performed, transfer of lessons on input–output lessons at the operational level can be made with the confidence that most BRT systems have been constructed and run well.

VI. Conclusions

The following conclusions and lessons can be derived from applications of our frameworks to urban transport and infrastructure planning and implementation:

1   *Comparative Method:* To generate useful lessons, urban transport illustrates the importance of targeting similarities or like cases first. This is consistent with our basic comparative methodology described in *Chapter 1.* That is relatively easy to do: cities deliver most of the service; they can be distinguished by size and region. In addition, the modes are clear—rail, bus, BRT, LRT; the conditions affecting service costs and results are also clear, e.g. severe weather. Finally, cities deliver transit through a variety of clear governmental and non-governmental units and structures. Their authority to manage and borrow for capital acquisition is also clear and can be differentiated. In short, identifying similarities is relatively easy, and this allows for focusing on operations-level transit system management and policy-making variables that affect costs and service more clearly. Research performed on urban transport systems already provides important lessons for policy-makers in the same urban regions. Some of the organizational structure and regime-type lessons from the strategic level can be adapted and transferred to other regions if these contextual limitations are recognized. As noted under fiscal policy in

Chapter 2, it may be more important to see which technical options work and then proceed with the difficult work of trying to adapt them to the cultural, institutional, and political differences of the local context with step by step caution, e.g. lessons from North America for China, while practices from Latin America may be adapted in the Middle East or Asia, e.g. LRT and BRT planning, operations, and financing.

2   *Culture:* Urban transport systems are often "closed," technically designed, and managed activities. This means the chances of routines and repertoires being modified by local cultural practices and affecting results significantly are perhaps less than other programs in health and education. The importance also of comparing systems in particular regions means that culture would likely play even less of a role—it would affect all units about the same. One might conclude that culture is more important where cultures are widely different, e.g. Middle East and Europe. It might explain, for instance, why the Amman BRT project was cut in 2012 during construction over cost estimates and selection of a foreign (German) contractor—when costing had been done years earlier during the design, appraisal, and contracting phases. The particular feature of centralization of decisions to political allies out of the control of designated technical officials may be cultural or simply a feature of weak institutions—assigned roles not performed because of political or bureaucratic intrusions.

3   *Governmental Structures:* Much is made of organizational structure and legal processes. While these are important, participants often adapt to them or are able to circumvent them in non-systematic ways (e.g. political influence channels). Thus, the effect of government structures is hard to measure. For transit, use of differing structures such as city enterprises versus city departments has not been shown to make a substantial difference to design or system performance. For larger issues, such as the design of urban transport fiscal transfers, research might show systematic linkages between partisan voting district boundaries, parliamentary rules, and urban transport financing results.

4   *Institutions:* It has been shown repeatedly that the formal and informal rules that guide behavior are critical to most policy areas. These institutional features provide the incentives and disincentives that affect results. For example, the rules for financing and contracting are critical to transport project design and implementation and service performance. As noted, they constitute an important obstacle to implementation in the Latin American region.

5   *System Design and Implementation:* It is important that lessons from other system design and implementation be absorbed during the planning phases of transport projects. This is often not done for institutional reasons and because of turf–ego–power problems that prevent learning. For these reasons, the wrong LRT cars or BRT systems are procured; for such reasons, obvious implementation constraints are ignored and stakeholder analyses that could have been performed during appraisal are not (Guess and Farnham, 2011: 141–142). A novel idea by Pressman and Wildavsky (1984: 143–144) proposed making the implementation phase part of the policy design and formulation phase of the policy cycle (refer back to *Figure 1.1*). Focusing on those factors during policy design that could lead to delay, overruns and/or stoppage, they employed a "points of decision and clearance" framework for a health center. Such forward planning methods could easily be done for public transport projects as well.

VII. Cases and Exercises

1   Read *Case 3.1* on Toronto and answer the following questions: (1) Which changes in Toronto transport governance, i.e. structure and authority, should be recommended? (2) What financing options should Toronto pursue to finance and maintain a truly metropolitan

system? (3) What mix of urban transport modes would you suggest? (4) What questions would you ask on design and appraisal of projects by mode? (5) What information would be needed to answer them? (6) Where might these options and recommendations be applied? If not applicable at the strategic level, what are the operational lessons and where might they be applied?

Case 3.1 Transport Trouble in Toronto

Source: *Economist*, 2012: 41

Stand on the platform at St. Andrew subway station in the Toronto (Canada) city center and the city's problems are evident. The walls are grimy and sections of the vinyl paneling are missing. Renovations begun in 2009 are unfinished. Chronic underfunding of an over-burdened public transport network, and the council's lengthy wrangling over a new plan have created a shabby and truncated subway that is unfit for the world-class metropolis Toronto claims to be. Although several new LRT lines funded by Ontario's provincial government are being built, the lack of public transport means that more than 70 percent of Torontonians with jobs drive to work. They face longer journey times than commuters in car-obsessed Los Angeles.

In fact, Atlanta has the most time-consuming rush hour in the U.S. At the same time, Georgia spends less per head than any state except Tennessee and what it does spend goes mostly for maintenance rather than the expansion that is needed. Voters in 9 of 12 Georgia regions including Atlanta recently rejected a special purpose local-option sales tax that would allow transit beneficiary communities to tax themselves to pay for new expanded transport systems.

According to Richard Florida, a U.S. urban guru who moved to Toronto in 2007, the city is now "a more divided and contentious place, its once enviable social cohesion at risk because of a growing split pitting downtown against the suburbs." The province paved the way for political conflict in 1998 when it merged the city of Toronto with six surrounding municipalities. The effect was to set councilors like Mr. Rob Ford (who as former Mayor of Toronto was found guilty of conflict of interest for trying to raise $3,170 for his private football foundation—and ordered to leave office within 14 days by the Ontario Supreme Court) from sprawling suburbs where the car is essential, against inner-city politicians who wanted more public transportation and bicycle lanes. The lack of political parties means that the 45-member council struggles to reach agreement. Mayors have profile but little power, a source of Mr. Ford's frustration.

Canada's big cities (like Toronto) have insufficient revenue-raising powers. They must rely on the provinces and the federal government which makes their funding less predictable than own source revenues. Similar to German and U.S. cities, Canadian cities are dependent on state (provincial or lander) and national grants for much of their revenues: Germany (35.1 percent), U.S. (40.1 percent), and Canada (38.8 percent). This has led to some seemingly desperate wheezes by Canadian cities to get revenue: Toronto is competing to host a new casino and remote towns are striving to attract a nuclear waste dump. Urban transport is but one of many essential services that must be financed and implemented to keep local residents content.

2   *Table 3.2* contains economic data for two sewage treatment plants (A and B), each with a
     10-year life. Assume that: (1) construction and useful life are the same; (2) O&M costs
     are a proxy for depreciation expenses, which are a portion of the total value amortized
     over the life of the asset; (3) Use of a 10-percent (0.386) discount rate to develop B/C
     ratios as well for data on NPV (use the methodology indicated on *Table 3.6*); and (4)
     formal economic BCR and NPV criteria are being used.

     Answer these three questions:
     1   Which project would you select and why?
     2   What components of the cost and benefit streams contributed to the kinds of BCRs
          each project had?
     3   Analyzing the same two projects using a 3 percent (0.744) DR, would you still make
          the same choice? Why?

Table 3.2 Economic Analysis of Sewage Treatment Plants

Project	Year	Capital Costs	O&M Costs	Total Costs	Total Benefits
A	1	1000000		1000000	
	2	600000	50000	650000	200000
	3	400000	80000	480000	250000
	4		100000	100000	300000
	5		100000	100000	350000
	6		100000	100000	400000
	7		100000	100000	500000
	8		100000	100000	500000
	9		100000	100000	500000
	10		100000	100000	500000
Total		2000000	830000	2830000	3500000
B	1	1500000			
	2	1000000	100000	1100000	500000
	3		120000	120000	600000
	4		120000	120000	700000
	5		110000	110000	700000
	6		110000	110000	600000
	7		110000	110000	600000
	8		110000	110000	500000
	9		110000	110000	400000
	10		110000	110000	400000
Total		2500000	1000000	3500000	5000000

3   Using the weighted-score framework in *Table 3.3* for three decision criteria, develop
     scores and a rank-order for these three rail car alternatives.

Table 3.3 Rail Car Purchasing Options

Alternatives		Rail Car A		Rail Car B		Rail Car C	
Criteria	Weights	Score	Weighted Score	Score	Weighted Score	Score	Weighted Score
Cost	.60 (x)	5	= 3.0	8 x .6	= 4.8	5	3.0
Reliability	.80	6		2		2	
Speed	.30	5		4		8	
Total Weighted Score							

Source: Michel (2001:16) Exhibit 2–3

4   For pricing purposes, marginal costs are not equal to variable costs when (indicate all that apply) (Finkler, 2010: 159).

   a   The time frame for a decision is more than a year.
   b   There is excess capacity.
   c   There is a change in fixed costs.
   d   Some costs are outside an organizational unit making the decision.

5   The Bucharest Community Clinic had annual total costs of $2 million per year at a volume of 10,000 patients. The fixed costs for the year were $1 million.

   a   What are the total variable costs for the year?
   b   What would the total costs be if the volume increased by 10 percent? (Finkler, 2010: 161).

6   The Bucharest Subway has 40,000 passengers every day. However, they are fairly price sensitive. If the current price of $2.00 were to increase to $2.50, it is likely that there would be only 30,000 passengers each day. On the other hand, if the price were to drop to $1.50, the ridership would increase to 50,000. The variable costs are only $0.08 per passenger. The fixed costs of operating the subway are $70,000 per day. How many passengers are needed each day to break even at the current $2.00 price?
       Using the template below in *Table 3.4*, prepare a flexible budget for the subway system at prices of $1.50, $2.00, and $2.50. Considering only the financial implications, what should be done and why? How can you reconcile the results of the flexible budget with the results of the break-even calculation (Finkler, 2010: 164–165)?

Table 3.4 Bucharest Subway Flexible Budget

Flexible budget			
Price	$1.50	$2.00	$2.50
Volume per day	50,000	40,000	30,000
Revenue per day			
Less fixed cost	$70,000	$70,000	$70,000
Less variable cost $.08 volume			
Surplus			

Annex I: Twelve Steps for a Capital Improvement Program (CIP)

1   *Determine Organizational Responsibility Structures:* Each governmental unit must designate a lead organization with sufficient authority to coordinate the 12 steps (Guess and Todor, 2005). Lack of a lead organization allows political projects from elected officials to be placed in the queue or inter-departmental squabbling to weaken the overall capital program. The lead organization should have authority to execute three functions:

   a   *Maintain Control:* Ensuring that only projects from operating departments that meet standards will be considered for the capital plan and budget; it must prevent systematic breaches, such as for political projects.

   b   *Ensure Accountability*: The lead organization designs and enforces a vertical command structure and at the same time provides clear feedback and access channels for line departments, citizens, and civil society through such mechanisms as participatory budgeting from community stakeholders.

   c   *Permit Implementation Flexibility*: It should have the capability to monitor project progress directly as well as indirectly through departmental reporting requirements. It should provide rapid clearances for needed course corrections, changed strategic priorities, funding shortfalls, and required new investments.

Changes in structure and authority often have to be made. For example, because of project cost overruns and excessive design changes, the City of Milwaukee centralized lead authority in its Department of Public Works for facility design and construction; the Budget and Management Division (BMD) was charged with the function of ensuring project monitoring, reporting, and accountability. Milwaukee decentralized expenditure authority for each project to the departments (City of Milwaukee, 2003a: 5). This reorganization tackled the common problem of a split between authority and responsibility in capital programs that drive up costs and often produce shoddy construction.

2   *Establish Capital Improvements Policies:* These are advisory rules that establish parameters for local fiscal decisions at the *strategic* and *operations* levels. They should remedy real or anticipated problems. For example, a city might be approaching its legal borrowing limit. Its formal policy response could be indicated in the budget as: "we will convert debt to cash via use of tax-levy financing. Borrowing will not be permitted for recurrent capital projects, e.g. alleys, traffic control, street lighting, underground conduits, sidewalks."

3   *Develop a Realistic Capital Calendar and Budget Request Forms:* Subnational governments can improve the calendar and forms by:

   a   *Improvements in Timing:* This ensures that capital programming will end before operating cycle begins; the lead organization must ensure that this happens;

   b   *Increasing Citizen Inputs:* Providing clear dates to enable critical feedback from citizens' groups on urban transport project plans; there should be channels for citizen group initiation of their own projects;

   c   *Reducing Departmental Reporting Burdens*: To increase incentives for better project management, forms should allow comprehensive justifications that include alternative analyses with use of annexes and supplemental data if necessary. As an incentive, make-work reporting requirements should be periodically pruned and replaced with faster approvals for departmental transfer and reprogramming requests; regular progress reports on spending, changes, and physical results; this is harder to do in civil code contexts that are rule-driven versus common law contexts where management at least in theory has more discretion and less fear of being prosecuted for making judgmental errors;

d   **Controlling the Planning Process**: Maintain control of the calendar to prevent insertion of projects after specified dates; breaches may threaten CIP affordability and city debt sustainability; and

e   **Integration of Budget Planning**: The lead organization should ensure that the current and capital budgets are planned together.

4   **Assess Capital Needs**: The CIP should be based on an objective assessment of facilities condition, especially rolling stock, stations, escalators, elevators, and safety-signaling equipment. The subnational government should have advance information on whether to repair, replace, or abandon facilities due to wear and tear or scheduled rehabilitation and evidence that the asset is at the end of its useful life. Needed are three sources of information:

a   **Facilities Condition Database**: This is an updated technical inventory of age and condition of all facilities, e.g. a technical survey or engineering specifications indicate that bridge X should be replaced in five years, rail car Y in seven years. Milwaukee, for example, began in 2000 using a computerized Pavement Management Administration (PMA) Database. This is a data-driven computer model that measures the condition of the city street system through a Pavement Quality Index (PQI). Each street category has a minimum PQI standard below which it must be reconstructed. The model is also used to predict pavement quality and is being adapted to other kinds of infrastructure (e.g. alleys) for inclusion in the city's six-year paving programs (City of Milwaukee, 2003: 193–194); using its facilities condition database, Washington, DC Metro (WMATA) knows that 75 percent of its escalators are 25 or more years old. WMATA now uses performance measures for preventive maintenance, has instituted shifts of priority evening inspections, and requires more hours of inspections.

b   **Citizen Survey Database**: This is an updated survey of citizen views based on complaints and service interruption. The city will contract with an NGO or firm to design and administer the survey and to report data to the city for review and decision-making. For example, increasing user complaints may lead to replacing bridge X in two years rather than five.

c   **Policy Foundation**: Based on state or local capital policies, the preferred option might be to preserve a facility rather than repair or replace. Reconstruction would then follow preservationist guidelines, e.g. for a historic station or metro rail line such as the 1896 Millennium (M1) Line in Budapest (the oldest line in continental Europe).

5   **Analyze Financial Capacity**: The finance department should analyze the ability of its jurisdiction to generate taxes and other revenues from its own sources to carry out its functions (Johnson and Roswick, 1991: 17). Measures should be examined to assess the financial condition (Berne and Schramm, 1986) and the risk of nonpayment of borrowed funds. Subnational jurisdictions are required to disclose basic fiscal data for ratings from major rating agencies, such as Fitch and Moody's. With increasing fiscal stress of subnational government caused by recessions and reduction in central transfers, finance departments often fail to disclose their risks and liabilities. Often they engage in fraudulent disclosure of "material events" that would affect financial condition, e.g. a large uneconomic

incinerator project in Harrisburg (Pennsylvania) that prevented reasonable investors in bonds to make informed choices. Acting in the wake of subnational bankruptcies, the U.S. Securities and Exchange Commission (SEC) now fines city officials or issues cease-and-desist orders to force accountability to the public (El Boghdady, 2013).

Some variables and sample measures that should be examined by finance departments are:

a   ***Demographics****:* The percentage of working population and its median age; personal income immigration and outmigration rates; poverty or public assistance households per 1,000 households.

b   ***Economics****:* Unemployment rate; plant closings; vacancy rates; retail sales; valuation of business property; business acres developed; property value; and residential development.

c   ***Finances****:* Debt/capita, revenue/capita, intergovernmental revenues/gross operating revenues; revenue shortfalls/net operating revenues; fringe benefit expenditures/total salaries and wages; general fund operating deficit/net operating revenues; long-term debt/assessed valuation; overlapping long-term debt/assessed valuation; and unfunded pension plan vested benefits/assessed valuation.

d   ***Management****:* This refers to the quality of the city's management and can be measured by indicators such as uncollected property taxes; personnel turnover rates; overall tax collection rates; budgets presented and approved according to the calendar; and successful management of debt-financed projects.

6   ***Prepare the Project Request***: The two steps here are: (1) *project analysis*: problem definition, alternatives analysis, measurement of benefits and costs; and (2) *formal evaluation* or application of appraisal techniques to the project proposals.

1   Project Analysis
   • **Problem Definition**: The project must respond directly to an actionable problem. Problems should have an empirical basis, e.g. rate of rat complaints per capita in New York City. In some cases such as dog bites, fragmented databases and regulatory structures may prevent accurate recording of strays and rabies infections. In such cases, the problem cannot really be formulated or diagnosed unless valid information is found (Guess and Farnham, 2011: 29). Failure to define the problem(s) properly can result in spending for the wrong solution, i.e. a more expensive capital project (e.g. dog pound or metro line versus LRT or BRT) when a proper response might be better regulation (e.g. of dogs or vehicular traffic which would be a current services expense).
      Internal control and audit systems should penetrate capital planning to ensure that conflicts of interest are avoided in problem definition, e.g. a consulting engineer defining the "urban transport" problem as absence of a metro system.
   • **Alternatives Analysis**: A formal alternatives analysis would compare impacts and benefits of respective alternatives, including no action at all—it should lead to a preferred alternative. In the case of animal control, for example, alternatives could include: new pound, licensing drives, animal census, leash law, steep fines, and sterilization services (Lehan, 1984: 27). The request should include data and information on rejected alternatives, e.g. light rail option reduces travel time by 5 percent and generates 10 percent more ridership and 15 percent more revenue than better traffic management, more buses, or bus rapid transit for

corridor X. Since many state and city functions are contracted out and others might be, make–buy and break-even analyses are useful analytic methods which will be discussed further below.

- **Estimate Financial Benefits**: These are primary monetary benefits, such as lives saved, trash cans collected, user/rider time saved, and vehicles serviced, that can be compared to costs to determine the most cost-effective solution or project (Michel, 2001: 78). They are not official facts, like costs and are measured on the basis of definitions, and are estimated by different forecasting techniques using data of varying validity and reliability. Such benefits as time saved from transit options are measured by surveys. Parking garage asset values are measurable by market values; other assets such as swimming pools or parks are measurable by consumer surpluses. That is, the benefits themselves are easily measurable, but their trajectories are not.

Such benefits as jobs and investments created from projects must be forecast from models using comparative data. Demand must be formally estimated to produce an estimate of total benefits. To obtain monetary benefits, the number of users must be multiplied by the fees. The users and the fees must be estimated by explicit modes, e.g. trip generation, gravity; or controlled experiment. In such cases as local economic development projects, this is not easy since the project is an intervening variable between other policies and public and private investments and the benefit expected, i.e. more jobs, incomes, and private investments.

How do we know if a proposed investment project or program is cost effective? For example, McKinsey Global Institute (MGI) estimates the worldwide burden of obesity to be 2.8 percent of global GDP roughly equivalent to that of smoking or war. MGI estimates the benefits of weight management and anti-obesity measures to be about $25 billion per year. Yet, Britain spends less than $1 billion on such programs. Programs would then be cost-effective if productivity gains and health care savings outweighed their cost over the lifetime of the target population (*Economist*, 2014c: 55). Another example from the health sector (see *Chapter 4*) would be the following. The average yearly cost of implementing the most cost-effective interventions for the prevention and control of cardiovascular diseases (produced as air pollution increases the particulates that penetrate the lungs) in all developing economies is estimated at $8 billion per year. However, the expected return on such as policy investment—a 10 percent reduction in the mortality rate from coronary artery disease and stroke—would reduce economic losses in low and middle income countries by about $25 billion per year (WEF, 2011).

It is important for finance departments to identify and control the use of *creeping benefits*. Benefits are often elastic and can easily be inflatable by facile assumptions, faulty methods, or exaggerated multipliers. For example, the estimated number of jobs from a pipeline (e.g. the U.S. Keystone XL pipeline for shale oil that was finally rejected on environmental grounds in late 2015) should be broken down into: number of people, years of employment, temporary versus permanent employees, and direct versus indirect (more health workers and teachers), which then need to be compared to the fiscal costs of the project to local services. The same critical perspective on elastic benefits should be applied to projects such as convention centers, rail ridership, stadium attendance, and the developmental impact of flood control canals. In some cases, benefits are double-counted to increase the benefit–cost ratio and increase the project ranking in the queue for funding. Counting the primary benefit, trucker time saved by a new highway project along with increased trucker firm profits and more gas sales, illustrates the problem—profits are mainly a function of time saved and gas sales may occur beyond state limits (Mikesell, 2014: 329).

It was noted earlier that considerable uncertainty exists even without resorting to gimmickry or politics in estimation of transit project benefits on economic development. For example, light rail transit (LRT) or tram investments have taken place in 29 U.S. cities. Built in response to increasing traffic congestion, gas prices, and the lure of economic development around stations, some systems have been in place for 30 years or more (e.g. Portland) while others have been built in the last five years (e.g. Charlotte) (*Economist*, 2006: 40). Light rail is a good target for benefits estimation because of its measurable impact around lines and stations. U.S. urban transport policy uses the concept of "transit-oriented development" (TOD), or the level of economic activity can be attributed to LRT systems. Those transit projects that can empirically demonstrate more TOD around stations receive higher scores and are considered more cost-effective for purposes of federal capital grants. Light rail lines are planned at street level through business districts from suburbs and try to produce sufficient ridership to cover enough of operating costs to meet cost-effective criteria (35 percent–60 percent). The lines are not planned to break even. Rather, they are intended to generate trips from commuters, shoppers, sports/events fans, and tourists, which translate into income and employment opportunities around stations. Since some city systems such as Portland (Oregon) offer free rides in central business districts to promote increased usage, it would be a mistake to assess the cost-effectiveness of such LRTs on the narrow basis of farebox coverage ratios.

Applying the comparative method described in *Chapter 1*, LRT systems are similar in that have about the same unit costs for rolling stock and signaling/control and station costs are about the same. Unit personnel costs and numbers of required employees for construction and later operations should be similar. LRT systems are also designed to move suburban populations to and from city routes (as opposed to older inner-city street car systems such as San Francisco, Boston, and Philadelphia). LRT systems will vary in: (a) ridership demand and service supply (frequency/headway); (b) size of systems (number of lines, length, and number of cars); (c) governing structures (city department, state authority, and/or autonomous city enterprise); (d) route alignment (where population growth and economic activity shift negatively during planning, the lines constructed may no longer be consistent with actual urban development patterns—this happened with the San Francisco BART heavy rail planned in the 1950s and opened 15 years later, and Tyson's Corner in Washington, DC, which was not a major business center during planning of the metro system); and (e) age (potentially more time for riders and businesses to adjust to new travel opportunities offered by LRT routes).

Despite the policy importance of finding a standardized method for assessing project impact, little systematic research has been done. Some LRT systems may score low on cost coverage but high on local economic development (LED) impact. For instance, Portland's cost coverage is only 37 percent (2006) while

Dallas, is 35 percent. The latter is known to have a minimal LED effect on jobs or incomes. But with lower running costs and service frequency, it scores close to that of Portland which has had a high LED impact by all accounts. LRT systems such as Salt Lake City have scored high on cost coverage and economic development. Other systems such as Baltimore MTA have had both low LED and low farebox recovery rates (14 percent) (Maryland General Assembly, 2006). Some lines have been effective in generating permanent LED and others have not been. All LRT projects create short-term construction jobs. But only some create permanent business positions and incomes. Lacking one best method, the U.S. Federal Transit Authority uses multi-criteria cost-effectiveness ratings for projects. This will be described further below.

- **Estimate Project Costs**: Resource costs include construction and operations for the useful life of the asset. In addition to the fixed and variable costs noted previously, capital projects also require estimation of opportunity costs. Typically resources used for a public project could also be used for a private project that would generate tax revenues, e.g. land for a public park or parking garage. In such cases, the opportunity cost would be the market value. For these reasons, opportunity costs must be added to project costs for this value and compared with estimated benefits.

  While less measurable, an amount should be included for both unintended but likely costs and benefits of proposed projects, e.g. congestion around transit rail stations that also generate tax and fee revenues. It is important also to include real and nominal costs as well as maintenance as part of life-cycle budgeting, e.g. escalator and track maintenance for rail systems and high increases in costs due to inflation. By failure to include inflation and maintenance estimates, construction costs for the New Jersey rail tunnel increased from $5 billion to $10 billion in five years of project approvals and negotiations! Failure to include an amount in the request for these likely cost increases can and has reduced discounted cost totals, allowing contractors to low-ball their bids. This leads to expensive change orders and likely cost overruns during implementation.

2   Formal Evaluation

Now that costs and benefits have been identified and measured, they must be compared formally in the second phase of request preparation. This is critical for individual project appraisal as well as for ranking it against others in different sectors for possible funding through the capital budget. It is useful to recognize (*Figure 3.6*) that for formal evaluation, all capital projects have a similar cost and benefit profile—with heavy capital costs early on followed by tapering off to operating costs. Returns are non-existent or minimal the first few years and then increase rapidly (Lee and Johnson, 1998: 188). The differences in timing between costs and benefits over time require *discounting* to compare them for each year and over the life of the project. If total discounted benefits exceed total discounted costs, there is a positive net present value, and the capital expenditure is likely to be efficient (ibid., 1998: 189).

There are four formal economic rules that can be used for project evaluation:

1   *Undiscounted Payback*: Projects net results for smaller projects, aka the eyeball technique. This simply compares annual net benefits over a payback period. Canadian local governments use this method, which assumes implicit benefits! But the opportunity cost of present cash use foregone is ignored. This can be seen in the last column of *Table 3.5* for three water and sewer projects.

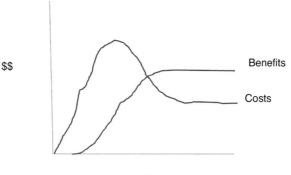

Time

Figure 3.6 Profile of Project Cost and Benefit Timing

Table 3.5 Undiscounted Payback Method

Project	Year	Capital Costs (A)	O&M Costs (B)	Total Costs (A+B)	General Benefits (D)	Net Benefits (E) (D-B)	Payback Years	Net Benefits/ Capital Outlay (E/A)	Undiscounted (B/C) (D/C)	Undiscounted Value of General Benefits – Cost (D-C)
1	1	10000	4000	14000	9000	5000				
	2		4000	14000	9000	5000				
	3									
	T	10000	8000	18000	18000	10000	2	1	1.0	0
2	1	3000	4000	7000	9000	5000				
	2	7000	4000	11000	7000	3000				
	3		3000	3000	10000	7000				
	T	10000	11000	21000	26000	15000	2.28	1.5	1.23	+5000
3	1	15000	6000	21000	11000	5000				
	2		4000	4000	10000	6000				
	3		4000	4000	16000	12000				
	T	15000	14000	29000	37000	23000	2.33	1.53	1.27	+8000

The undiscounted payback method ignores opportunity costs of capital. Use of discount rates compensate for the opportunity cost of present cash use foregone. Discount rates are weights attached to estimated costs and benefits for differences in their timing and the time value of money (TMV) in actual returns. Using the discount table, note how much more money is worth more today than in the future. For example, a promise of $100 in five years equals $78.35 at 5 percent. For a rational choice, we need to know the present *discounted* value of funds that someone plans to give us in X years—effectively reverse interest compounding (Finkler, 2010: 176). Discounting converts future value to *present value (PV)* of cash use, which decreases over time.

$$PV = \frac{FV\ (n)}{(1 + r)\ (n)}$$

PV for first year at 10 percent = 0.909

PV for 2 years at 10 percent = 0.826

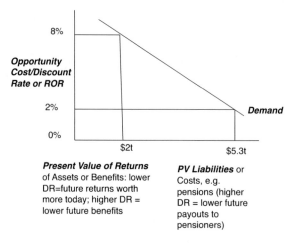

Figure 3.7 Relation between Discount Rates and Present Value

2   *Discounted Total B/C Ratio (PV)*: *Table 3.6* indicates the present value of net benefits for three projects using a 10-percent rate. To obtain the ratio for each project, one must discount each year and add them up. This is cost–benefit analysis (CBA) as described further in *Chapter 7*.

3   *Net Present Value (NPV)*: Often the purpose of the investment is to generate more revenue or additional financial support. Many public projects generate revenue, and one needs to know the present value of their cash inflows and outflows (Finkler, 2010: 193). The NPV is obtained by subtracting total discounted cash benefits from total discounted costs as indicated in the last column of *Table 3.6*. Investment efficiency using NPV would be where NPV is greater than $0 and the benefit–cost ratio is also greater than 1:

NPV efficiency = NPV > 0 and BCR > 1

Table 3.6 Discounted Benefit–Cost Ratio and Net Present Value

Project	Year	Total Costs (A) (Capital/ OM)	(X) DR 10% (B)	= Total Costs (AxB) = C	Total Benefits (D) Const + Life	(X) DR 10% (E)	= General Benefit (F) (DxE) = F	BCR-Discounted Total B/C (F/C) (Present Value of Net Benefits)	NPV (F-C)
1	1	14000	.909	12726	9000	.909	8181		
	2	4000	.826	3304	9000	.826	7434		
	3		.751			.751			
	T	18000		16030	18000		15615	15615/16030=.97	1.0
2	1	7000	.909	6363	9000	.909	8185		
	2	11000	.826	9096	7000	.826	5782		
	3	3000	.751	2253	10000	.751	7510		
	T	21000		17702	26000		21477	21473/17702=1.213	1.23
3	1	21000	.909	19089	11000	.909	9999		
	2	4000	.826	3304	10000	.826	8260		
	3	4000	.751	3004	16000	.751	12016		
	T	29000		25397 Discounted Costs	37000		23000 Discounted Benefits	30375/25397=1.197	1.27

4 *Internal Rate of Return (IRR or ROR):* Use of the IRR or ROR method combines break-even analysis, the ratio from B/C, and the cash behavior from NPV. It provides a more comprehensive perspective on projects than the other three tests. The NPV does not indicate the project's ROR, nor does it allow ranking of projects of different sizes. This is important for development of a CIP in that often a smaller project may be more profitable than larger ones with large NPVs.

Thus, the IRR is the rate at which B/C = 1 and NPV = 0. It is a method to incrementally arrive at break-even point for a project. A rule of thumb for analysis of IRR is that it should at least exceed the DR and break even. As noted, the discount rate selected is either on the basis of (1) the *opportunity cost of capital*, a market rate to compensate for bidding away capital from private sector, e.g. a city convention center versus a private redevelopment project, or (2) the *social rate of time preference*. This is a planner preference that considers future welfare, e.g. water purification systems may or may not break even, but they are essential to welfare. Use of this test allows for a lower discount rate, which would underestimate the value of current private consumption and favor large, long-term public projects by making later benefits more attractive. There is powerful pressure to use lower discount rates for public projects, e.g. the Miami Metrorail project used the UMTA (now FTA) required 7 percent rate for urban rail projects when the inflation rate or market cost of capital was more than 15 percent in the 1980s. This inflated benefits and diminished costs on paper and served as a justification for later approval and implementation (Guess, 1985: 580).

Table 3.7 indicates the effect of discount rates on benefit and cost calculation for a ten-year health investment project. Where is IRR? Note that it would be at a 7 percent discount rate (BCR equals 1) and $1.6 million (where NPV equals 0). What happens to the NPV of this local health care project as the discount rate increases? Why?

7 **Review the Project Request**: Prior to ranking the projects into a full CIP, the state or city must rely on a qualified institution to review the four elements indicated below for each project proposal. This is the lead organization referred to in *Step 1*. In Milwaukee, for instance, there is no one organization with CIP request review responsibility. As noted above, formal authority for preparation and approval of the capital budget is shared

Table 3.7 The Effects of Discount Rates on Health Project Efficiency Estimates

	0%	3%	5%	10%
Benefit (B) expenditures necessary to provide increased quality measured in treated patients (available drugs, proper tests, and functioning equipment)	$15,000,000	$10,448,000	$8,456,000	$5,442,000
Costs (C) in construction, site preparation and equipment	$7,500,000	$6,741,000	$6,409,000	$5,906,000
B/C	2.00	1.55	1.32	0.92
B-C (NPV)	$7,500,000	$3,707,000	$2,047,000	-$484,000

between line departments and two staff organization, beyond which the council and mayor provide approval decisions. In Montgomery County (Maryland), there also is no formal unit with singular review authority for capital requests at the staff level. More than likely, most states and cities rely on informal or semi-formal structures for the project review function. For example, Gallatin County (Montana) relies on review of annual departmental project requests from a citizen committee (CIPC). The County Administrator and Grants and Projects Coordinator advise this committee. These officials, along with the Finance Director and the Facilities and Procurement Manager pre-screen project applications for the committee. The same group of individuals and offices also manages the "Facilities Condition Inventory" as well as other smaller capital improvements. According to the County Administrator: "This system seems to be working" (Mather, 2013).

Overall, there needs to be a strategic responsibility center charged with coordinating the review process, which focuses on:

1   *Administrative Process:* Were requests backed by citizen needs surveys? Was there compliance with environmental impact statement requirements?
2   *Planning:* Were studies of fiscal service impacts and demographics used to determine the impact of this project on service cost requirements? Is the project consistent with physical land use and strategic plans? Would the project negatively affect other services, e.g. a parking garage on bus–rail revenues?
3   *Financial:* Does the proposal include all costs (direct and indirect), non-investment project alternatives, proper benefit and cost measures and data, impacts on tax rates, and downstream estimates of O&M costs?
4   *Engineering/Architectural*: Were other alternatives such as continued repairs or rehabilitation considered? Is the construction schedule realistic? Is the level of probable change orders included? Are there clearance points and potential legal bottlenecks that could clearly affect the implementation schedule? If so, what are the costs and liabilities for the city or state as well as the contractors?

8   ***Rank Project Proposals***: Needed now is a method that can organize project information and generate an approved rank-order of projects to be funded by the capital budget consistent with the CIP. Unfortunately, this is the most contentious part of CIP process! Tools, methods, models, and systems are needed to narrow the range of disagreement over technical issues, and many technical disagreements often turn on fundamental value differences. Policy-makers need tools that can anticipate public reaction, e.g. flashpoints on increased bus fares that can bring down governments altogether. They also need a solid decision framework and authority to provide them cover when tough decisions must be made that favor technical requirements over public opinion, i.e. public opinion is important, but so is safety, mobility access, and cost savings. This means that technical "facts" must be carefully critiqued and user–citizens surveys must be treated with respect but not as the final answer. Part of the analytic problem is that urban transport systems interact—isolated analysis of a rail line or bridge must almost certainly be flawed. Other transport systems will be affected and accordingly raise their costs and benefits. For example, analysis and debate of options on what to do about congestion at Heathrow Airport in London have continued for almost 20 years. The options of expanding the existing airport with more runways versus building new ones or adding to other regional hubs are well-known. Trade-offs, measurement, and comparison of sunk costs and new benefits have been compared and debated without final decision. They have turned on the cost, noise, and disruption of rival plans (*Economist,* 2013: 40). The institutional framework must force consideration of

all costs (opportunity costs to the economy and required new investment in transport infrastructure) compared to the full benefits to the region (mostly reduced noise to particular residents). Thus, to avoid paralysis by analysis, policy institutions need to prevent endless menus of options that inhibit rather than facilitate choice.

In short, there will be disagreement over both which tools are appropriate and which criteria should be used to assess rival policy and program proposals. One remedy for this problem is the *weighted score table* or *weighting and scoring model* illustrated by *Table 3.8*. Weighting and scoring models serve the overt purpose of structuring choices where stakeholders have multiple values and argue about multiple criteria (Lehan, 1984). Such models or tables are useful because criteria in most decisions are not of equal importance, which makes it difficult if not impossible to evaluate alternatives (Michel, 2001: 14).

These decision models are derived from methods used to select capital projects but can be applied to current expenditure programs and policies. Moreover, "investment" programs include not only physical assets such as buildings but human capital (health and education) as well as research and development. For example, health care requires medical personnel and testing and operating equipment as well as hospital and clinic facilities. This makes it difficult to distinguish relative rates of return for sub-components of particular policies. Beyond the methodological problem, in any case most policy-makers do not have access to quantitative economic studies on relative rates of return before allocating funds to programs (Posner et al., 1998: 17). For this practical reason, providing more criteria for decision making can increase the chances that a project will be transparent, acceptable, and ultimately effective. As noted, the weighting and scoring model uses multiple criteria that allow the ranking and trading of policy options based on stakeholder values. It can serve as a summary framework to structure choice once problems have been defined and analytic tools utilized to isolate potentially beneficial programs and policies.

Whatever method of project selection is used, it should incorporate elements of *soft* and intangible values (e.g. user occupancy as a proxy of need, health–safety effects, social benefits, health risk if deferred) and *hard*, quantitative criteria (e.g. ROR, BCR, economic worth, fiscal–economic impact, availability of grants and cost-sharing). There are many possibilities here and analysts should develop a system that utilizes the values from assessments (e.g. health clinic facility conditions) to produce a separate and overall summary score for decision making. The goal of such systems should not be to replace judgment or exclude political considerations. Rather, a ranking system is needed to make issues and trade-offs explicit.

For example, as indicated in *Table 3.8* using a combination of existing and recommended criteria, health project planners could assign scores of: 0, 1, or 2 for each category (Guess and Farnham, 2011: 359). The weighting and scoring model then produces rankings based on these combined scores (see *Table 3.9*).

To determine timing of implementation, the scores can be added and projects classified according to six categories of urgency (e.g. 14–16 equals urgent). For example, the World Bank uses an ascending scale of project rehabilitation (1–3) to program needed renovations: (1) minimal level, (2) increased level of services, and (3) higher level of services. These criteria appear in *Column 5* of *Table 3.8*. Since the interest is typically to bring health and education facilities up to minimal levels of service, a 2 should be assigned for "minimal" existing levels of service, a 1 for "increased levels," and a 0 for "higher levels" of service. The *Table 3.8* matrix could be used for ranking health or education projects.

Table 3.8 Sample Weighting and Scoring Matrix for Health Investment Projects

Capital Repair Project	Cost Sharing: or Available Funding 2-high/ 1 some/ 0 none	Benefits: or Forecasted Demand 2-high/ 1 some/ 0-low	Condition: 2-bad/ fair-1/ good-0	Need: 0-minimal/ 1-increased level/ 2-higher level of service 3-higher level of service	Location: 2-rural/ 1-semi-rural/ 0-urban	Investment: 4 new/replace/ 3 utility support/ 2 rehabilitate/ 1 complete construction	Cost: 3-less than 850,000 som/ 1-850-1 million/ 0- greater than 1 million	Occupancy: 2-75-100%/ 1-50-74%/ 0-less than 50%	Score
A									
B									
C									

There are four steps to developing a weighting and scoring model: *(1) Develop Strategic Decision Criteria (hard–soft)*—participants must develop a range of criteria based on probable impacts of capital project investments. These criteria will be hard fiscal and economic as well as soft social and environmental. *(2) Establish the Scoring Range* (e.g. 1–10), including preference ranges for each criteria to be applied to each project. This score will reflect the consistency with strategic decision criteria and the preference range. *(3) Calculate the Weighted Score* (e.g. 1–10). The score reflects the extent to which stakeholders believe the project meets the strategic decision criteria. And *(4) Rank the Projects* on basis of the total weighted score. This provides the cut-off point for funding in annual capital budget (which is for a multi-annual period). Note that the total project score and rank-order provide a transparent cutback or add-on point for later adjustment to changes in revenue availability and needs.

Table 3.9 provides an example of how to calculate a weighted score for three light rail (LRT) car purchase options using three decision criteria. The same type of framework could be used for the more complex problem noted above of Heathrow Airport option by adding additional criteria, e.g. citizen surveys, and disaggregating costs-benefits into such categories as: economic opportunity costs, transport investment costs for replacement airport, and congestion benefits. This would allow more transparency than if stakeholders employ aggregate benefit cost ratios.

Table 3.9 The Weighted Score Method Applied to a Rail Car Purchase

Decision Criteria	Rail Car Weight (of strategic criteria: cost, reliability, speed)	Score (project consistency with hard/soft decision criteria)	A Weighted Score	B	C
Cost	0.60 (x)	5 =	3.0	4.5	3.0
Reliability	0.50	6	4.8	1.6	1.6
Speed	0.30	5	1.5	1.2	2.4
Total Weighted Score			9.3	7.3	7.0
Ranking			1 (A)	2(B)	3(C)

9   ***Evaluate Financing Options and Conduct Affordability Analysis***: In budgeting as in other areas, necessity is the mother of invention. Deadlock at the federal level has generated extreme fiscal uncertainty on both tax rates as well as grant availability to states and cities. While it varies by program, states rely on about 30 percent of their revenue from U.S. government grants; cities and counties rely on about 36 percent of their revenue from state sources and 4 percent from the federal government. The effect of a blanket sequester (i.e. hard budget constraint), and going over the fiscal cliff has required innovation and reform from increasingly cash-strapped states and cities. For example, Indiana has turned to privatization to raise road-building funds; Chicago created a special trust fund to refurbish city facilities (*Economist,* 2013b: 13).

The three components of financial options analysis are:

- ***Affordability Analysis:*** The purpose of affordability analysis is to determine if the project poses unreasonable risks to the state or city public finances. The proposed project should be analyzed in relation to the debt structure. Two financial condition measures are useful here to determine debt sustainability with the project: (1) *debt service/operating revenues* and (2) *project debt/total debt.* This review should be conducted as part of prudent budgeting and financial management. Many cities have approved and implemented capital projects without doing so with disastrous results for financial condition. For example, in 2003, Harrisburg (Pennsylvania) borrowed $125 million on the capital markets to rebuild an incinerator that was expected to generate revenues from burning garbage in the city and surrounding counties. The failure of the project to meet expectations for a variety of reasons put the city $288 million in debt. It has been unable to meet its total debt service payments (including one for $68 million for the incinerator alone), was downgraded by the ratings agencies, and may be forced into bankruptcy (Cooper, 2010). Users now pay the highest trash fees in the U.S.! The failure was to assess the risk of failure for a project whose debt was disproportionally high in relation to total debt. It absorbed so much that little was left for other projects, and now Harrisburg must pay the price of a weak CIP process.
- ***Review of Capital Financing Policies:*** These are straightforward and should be consulted to ensure that debt is sustainable and that the state or city credit rating is not jeopardized by one or more new projects. Examples include: (1) the legal debt limit (e.g. 30 percent of past year operating revenues or operating budget expenditures) and the project proportion of that limit (e.g. 25 percent); (2) borrow only for assets that meet capital definition, e.g. minimum two-year life; $50,000 durable equipment; exceeds $25,000 for construction; (3) borrow only to finance capital assets (i.e. the "golden rule"); (4) ensure that current services are financed only with current revenues over a multi-year period; (5) balance current budgets, and finance the capital budget (this prevents future periods from bearing the costs of both current and past operating expenditures (Mikesell, 2011: 300)); and (6) no debt should be issued beyond the useful life of the asset, e.g. equipment (two years), financial management information systems (FMIS) (five years), and hospitals (15 years).
- ***Review of Financing Options***: most projects will be funded by multiple sources. For transparency, the Milwaukee 2003–2008 CIP is presented by function and funding source. Note that the "surface transportation" function is the largest item in the capital budget plan (27.5 percent):

o   Note that about 60 percent of planned capital investment for this city will be financed by debt (tax-levy supported) and enterprise funds (e.g. transit fares, water, and sewer fees). Capital transfers will finance only about 13 percent of the CIP. This financing pattern is typical of U.S. municipal capital financing.

o   For further transparency, CIPs should be disaggregated into projects and linked to revenue sources. But projects should be selected for the CIP on the basis of multiple criteria, only one of which should be funding availability. This prevents lower local priority projects with funding from driving the CIP rather than needs and efficiency concerns.

o   The two broad sets of capital financing options are: (1) pay-as-you-go from the recurrent budget, and (2) pay-as-you-use from debt term financing.

Table 3.10 Milwaukee 2003–2008 CIP by Function

Functional Area	2003 Adopted Budget	2004 Budget Plan	2005 Budget Plan	2006 Budget Plan	2007 Budget Plan	2008 Budget Plan	Total Six-Year Plan
URFACE TRANSPORTATION							
Streets	$46,450,135	$21,840,090	$25,144,000	$21,598,890	$25,128,000	$24,048,890	$164,210,005
Alleys	2,489,000	2,500,000	2,500,000	2,500,000	2,500,000	2,500,000	14,989,000
Bridges	9,737,000	10,400,000	4,495,000	5,280,000	3,950,000	8,750,000	42,612,000
Street Accessories	6,433,000	7,046,639	7,291,581	7,477,246	7,572,348	7,689,136	43,509,950
Sidewalks	2,300,000	2,300,000	2,300,000	2,300,000	2,300,000	2,300,000	13,800,000
Parking	1,661,000	1,395,000	1,240,000	1,555,000	1,625,000	850,000	8,326,000
ubtotal	**$69,070,135**	**$45,481,729**	**$42,970,581**	**$40,711,136**	**$43,075,348**	**$46,138,026**	**$287,446,955**
NVIRONMENT							
Sewer System	$23,159,000	$24,909,000	$24,909,000	$26,909,000	$28,073,000	$30,073,000	$158,032,000
Water System	14,900,000	15,070,000	15,496,400	15,482,388	16,078,247	16,309,271	93,336,306
Sanitation	1,354,000	800,000	800,000	1,200,000	1,000,000	1,000,000	6,154,000
Forestry	979,485	841,000	841,000	861,000	901,000	901,000	5,324,485
Environmental Remediation	641,400	2,085,000	996,900	777,200	858,100	892,400	6,251,000
ubtotal	**$41,033,885**	**$43,705,000**	**$43,043,300**	**$45,229,588**	**$46,910,347**	**$49,175,671**	**$269,097,791**
EALTH AND SAFETY							
Fire	$5,105,000	$5,395,000	$6,415,000	$4,525,000	$4,915,000	$3,375,000	29,730,000
Police	7,571,793	10,290,293	8,745,679	4,913,072	4,675,000	4,735,000	40,930,837
Public Health	1,129,700	1,128,900	1,038,500	1,077,200	1,020,600	1,032,000	6,426,900
ubtotal	**$13,806,493**	**$16,814,193**	**$16,199,179**	**$10,515,272**	**$10,610,600**	**$9,142,000**	**$77,087,737**
CONOMIC DEVELOPMENT							
TID	$14,000,000	$14,000,000	$14,500,000	$14,700,000	$14,700,000	$14,700,000	$86,600,000
Development District Funds	1,850,000	1,850,000	1,850,000	1,850,000	1,850,000	1,850,000	11,100,000
Business Improvement	1,000,000	1,000,000	1,000,000	1,000,000	1,000,000	1,000,000	6,000,000
Port of Milwaukee	2,000,000	3,175,000	2,700,000	3,450,000	2,400,000	6,275,000	20,000,000
ubtotal	**$18,850,000**	**$20,025,000**	**$20,050,000**	**$21,000,000**	**$19,950,000**	**$23,825,000**	**$123,700,000**
ULTURE AND RECREATION							
Libraries	$990,000	$3,815,000	$5,740,000	$4,635,000	$1,245,000	$675,000	$17,100,000
Recreational Facilities	530,000	689,200	717,000	663,000	694,500	667,500	3,961,200
Pabst and Art Fund	25,000	25,000	25,000	25,000	25,000	25,000	150,000
ubtotal	**$1,545,000**	**$4,529,200**	**$6,482,000**	**$5,323,000**	**$1,964,500**	**$1,367,500**	**$21,211,200**
ENERAL GOVERNMENT							
Maintenance and Remodeling	$22,124,820	$27,668,480	$15,621,600	$19,280,900	$15,106,400	$15,023,800	$114,826,000
Underground Conduits and Manholes	760,000	760,000	760,000	760,000	760,000	760,000	4,560,000
Communications and Control	626,000	645,000	664,000	684,000	704,000	725,000	4,048,000
Capital Equipment	4,968,000	5,662,400	6,246,800	6,831,200	7,415,600	8,000,000	39,124,000
Other Projects	1,000,000	2,390,000	8,165,000	9,300,000	12,500,000	12,500,000	45,855,000
ubtotal	**$29,478,820**	**$37,125,880**	**$31,457,400**	**$36,856,100**	**$36,486,000**	**$37,008,800**	**$208,413,000**
RANT AND AID	**$10,300,000**	**$10,300,000**	**$10,300,000**	**$10,300,000**	**$10,300,000**	**$10,300,000**	**$61,800,000**
RAND TOTAL	**$184,084,333**	**$177,981,002**	**$170,502,460**	**$169,935,096**	**$169,296,795**	**$176,956,997**	**$1,048,756,683**

Table 3.11 Milwaukee 2003–2008 CIP by Funding Source

Department	2003 Adopted Budget	2004 Budget Plan	2005 Budget Plan	2006 Budget Plan	2007 Budget Plan	2008 Budget Plan	Total Budget Plan
TOTAL CAPITAL IMPROVEMENTS PLAN	$184,084,333	$177,981,002	$170,502,460	$169,935,096	$169,296,795	$176,956,997	$1,048,756,683
LESS:							
Enterprise Funds (Parking, Water, Sewer)	36,261,000	37,965,000	38,236,400	40,537,388	41,203,247	42,659,271	236,862,306
Special Assessments	7,955,400	6,650,900	7,382,300	6,572,250	7,454,500	6,731,740	42,747,090
Cash Revenues	9,600,000	9,600,000	9,783,000	9,600,000	9,600,000	9,600,000	57,783,000
Tax Incremental Districts	14,000,000	14,000,000	14,500,000	14,700,000	14,700,000	14,700,000	86,600,000
Grant and Aid	40,694,950	18,120,645	16,224,900	16,852,245	17,034,750	23,237,245	132,164,735
Infrastructure Cash Financed	12,177,510	12,701,141	14,588,581	13,740,246	14,886,848	13,997,636	82,091,962
As a Percent of Total Infrastructure Funding	91.04%	95.52%	100.00%	100.00%	100.00%	100.00%	
Compared to Percent Required by Resolution	91.04%	95.52%	100.00%	100.00%	100.00%	100.00%	
Infrastructure Debt Financed	1,198,490	595,698	0	0	0	0	1,794,188
REMAINING EXPENDITURES TO BE FINANCED	$62,196,983	$78,347,618	$69,787,279	$67,932,967	$64,417,450	$66,031,105	$408,713,402
Cash	3,410,293	3,917,381	3,489,364	3,396,648	3,220,873	3,301,555	20,736,114
Debt	58,786,690	74,430,237	66,297,915	64,536,319	61,196,578	62,729,550	387,977,288
SUMMARY OF FINANCING SOURCES							
Tax Levy Supported Debt	$59,985,180	$75,025,935	$66,297,915	$64,536,319	$61,196,578	$62,729,550	$389,771,476
Tax Incremental Districts	14,000,000	14,000,000	14,500,000	14,700,000	14,700,000	14,700,000	86,600,000
Special Assessments	7,955,400	6,650,900	7,382,300	6,572,250	7,454,500	6,731,740	42,747,090
Cash Revenues	9,600,000	9,600,000	9,783,000	9,600,000	9,600,000	9,600,000	57,783,000
Tax Levy	15,587,803	16,618,522	18,077,945	17,136,894	18,107,721	17,299,191	102,828,076
TOTAL CITY FUNDING	$107,128,383	$121,895,357	$116,041,160	$112,545,463	$111,058,798	$111,060,481	$679,729,642
Enterprise Funds (Parking, Water, Sewer)	36,261,000	37,965,000	38,236,400	40,537,388	41,203,247	42,659,271	236,862,306
Grant and Aid	40,694,950	18,120,645	16,852,245	16,852,245	17,034,750	23,237,245	132,164,735
TOTAL CAPITAL INVESTMENT	$184,084,333	$177,981,002	$170,502,460	$169,935,096	$169,296,795	$176,956,997	$1,048,756,683

Note: Totals may not sum due to rounding.

*Does not reflect a PDAF withdrawal of $5 million.

- *Pay-As-You-Go: Recurrent Budget*
  Depending on the type of project, such sources as:

1   *Earmarked taxes* can be used to link a capital needs (road maintenance and rehabilitation) to a logical funding source, such as fuel tax;
2   *Capital grants* from higher-level governments can serve as effectively a source of operating revenue for particular projects. These should be performance-based where possible, e.g. expenditures/mile, usage/facility;
3   *Own-source revenues* from sources such as: utility charges and transit fares, which partially cover subsidies and debt service payments;
4   *Reserves*: special funds, replacement funds, and retained earnings from utilities;
5   *Private finance*: lease–purchase (often a form of transferring investment tax credits/ depreciation to a supplier/lessor for lower "rent" payments); concessions; build–operate–transfer (BOTs), public-private partnerships (PPPs), and tolls from which to repay road debt. The state of Florida, for example, is using PPP financing for a tunnel; Texas and Virginia are using this method for roads (*Economist*, 2013c: 14). Denver has financed 70 of 122 miles of its light rail/commuter rail system by PPP. The city pays an annual fee to the private partner. The partner pools all sources of funds (e.g. fees, federal grants, state grants, its own funds) to build and operate the urban rail system. The fee paid by the state investor (Denver) is higher than annual operating subsidy, but the project is built more quickly and at lower cost than if the public sector planned and built it in-house. The state of Maryland is planning to use PPP for the "purple line" light rail system between two counties of Maryland near Washington, DC.

A potential problem with the PPP method, as with all capital financing, is that if governments do not maintain the assets, they deteriorate and require premature replacement, repeating the cycle over again. One solution is for the government to let maintenance contracts simultaneously with the PPP for capital. The problem with that solution is that the contracts have to be renewed each year during current budget negotiations, i.e. multi-year current services contracts cannot be financed via long-term methods. Another solution is to build maintenance in to the PPP agreement, effectively a BOM contract (Dannin and Cokorinos, 2012: 730).

Leases are used by state–local governments as an alternative to buying or procuring capital assets in order to overcome legal limitations on debt; provide financial flexibility in that no initial down payment may be required; and to compensate for equipment becoming obsolete (Finkler, 2010: 237). It is thus important to determine whether it is more efficient to lease or to buy. Capital leases resemble installment purchasing where the lessee (government) buys property from the lessor through installment payments over time. Interest payments on the capital lease are treated as debt and an asset on the government books. But from the legal perspective, it is exempt from debt ceilings through non-appropriation clauses, which mean that lease payments have to be appropriated annually (Mikesell, 2011: 661).

   Capital lease payments are treated similarly to principal and interest on mortgage payments. To determine financial obligation, it is necessary to find the present value (PV) of the payments to be made (Finkler, 2010: 235). Since lease payments are equal payments over different periods, the amount needed is the present value of an annuity (ibid., 2010: 236). As in pension and project cost and benefit calculations, the question is how much is the payment worth today. Once this is determined, the financial benefits of leasing or buying (similar also for make-versus-buy problems) can be determined.

- **Pay-As-You-Use: Debt Financing**
  As one indicator of the vehemence of the anti-debt movement that constrains both current and capital spending, in 2010, Colorado Amendment 61 would have prohibited all new borrowing unless paid by fees or current funds. If it had passed, the referendum would have prohibited all long- and short-term debt, capital leasing, and public enterprise borrowing. The implication is that all such assets should be acquired only by pay-as-you-go financing.

  Guaranteed Debt: This type has an unlimited claim on taxes and other revenues (Mikesell, 2011: 637) and is used for general tax-levy supported projects, mainly by school districts. The main forms are bank loans or general obligation (GO) bonds (tradable securities of 1+ year maturity with regular coupon interest), often supported by property taxes. This is full faith and credit (FFC) or guaranteed debt.

  2 *Short-Term Debt (one year or less):* smaller projects often use commercial paper and treasury bills that have claims on tax, bond, and even grant revenues (TANs, BANs, or RANs); these mechanisms are also used for cash-flow management problems to finance within-year shortfalls. As noted, for some cities such as Milwaukee interested in reducing their debt burden, current revenues may be used to finance "associated capital maintenance" such as alleys and sidewalks. But most short-term borrowing is for "bridge financing" to make up for cash flow shortages during the fiscal year (Axelrod, 1995: 243).

  3 *Non-Guaranteed Debt*: About 75 percent of state debt is this kind, which requires a higher interest rate than FFC debt. Used for self-supporting projects that generate their own revenues, such as transit lines and water-sewer systems, they are also issued by public authorities and enterprises to pay off bonds from bridges, power projects, and highways (Mikesell, 2011: 637).

  4 *Municipal Development Banks (MDBs):* These are used in some states to provide low-interest loans to more creditworthy local and county governments.

  5 *Beneficiary Assessments*: These include tax increment financing (TIFs), betterment districts for economic development, business improvements, and industrial parks. Tax increment or betterment districts are self-sustaining development districts to finance facilities with repayments from increases in property tax increments. Roughly 9 percent of the Milwaukee CIP is financed through TIDs or TIFs. They are considered self-sustaining and are funded through issuance of GO bonds. The issuer (Milwaukee) sets aside increments in property tax increases to retire the debt contracted by the city or special authority (City of Milwaukee, 2003a: 10).

  6 *Infrastructure Trusts*: Cities such as Chicago (CIT) have established these as conduits for multiple sources of funding for local infrastructure needs. Similar to MDBs, CIT provides bond financing collateral and capital grants. CITs enable the city to raise funds from foreigners, charities, and pension funds not interested in municipal bonds because they have little tax liability in the first place. It means that projects with lower CIP rankings but clear benefits can go ahead sooner. The assets remain in city hands and under city management, i.e. this is not privatization. Chicago is involved so far in $200 million of the $7 billion infrastructure investments planned for 2013–2016 (*Economist*, 2013c: 14).

7   *Supplier/Vendor Credit*: This option is used by cities with no or low credit ratings to obtain financing, e.g. bus manufacturers, equipment, and construction companies. The disadvantage is that the borrower must pay higher than market interest rates.

10–11   **Draft and Approve CIP and Budget Documents**: In these steps, the executive has the responsibility of drafting the CIP and matching it with the capital budget for the first year of the plan. The council, board of commissioners, or legislature then approves them. As indicated, the advantage of this system is that it is based on transparent criteria and weighted scores and matched against a budget that will only cover a small proportion of proposed projects. The legislative side must then provide a cut-off point. Should this not prove acceptable to either side, the opportunity exists to revise rankings based on revised criteria and scores. This allows stakeholders to be part of the process of matching capital needs to scarce resources in the most optimal way.

12   **Implementing the CIP and Capital Budget**: There are a number of systems that have been in use for many years to monitor and evaluate capital project implementation:

1   *M&E Systems*: State and local governments need to control physical and financial progress of capital projects in the CIP during implementation. Most governments have systems in place to perform these tasks.

2   *Current Expenses*: Governments must also ensure that once the construction phase is completed or rehabilitation finished, the O&M continues as current (not capital) expense.

3   *Internal Control and Audit*: Efficient implementation is important to ensure that "ghost projects" are not paid for, i.e. by the treasury for non-existent works. The best safeguards against this are the internal control and audit systems noted above.

4   *Inventory Controls:* It is also essential that the state or local purchasing system is capable of monitoring the linkage between invoices, purchase orders, deliveries, or actual activities inspections of inventory or works completed, and actual payments (Coe, 1989: 104–105). While the extensive use of FMIS of IFMS systems has strengthened this linkage, execution depends on local institutional will and capacity.

For example, the $112-millon train and bus hub in Silver Spring (Maryland) has been two years behind schedule and $80 million over budget. The project is finished but unusable. This is because of problems in (a) design structure (i.e. beams, girders, and slabs wound too tightly and contributing to cracks) and (b) inspection (i.e. poured concrete that failed compressive strength tests), which all slipped through the process because Montgomery County inspectors were not properly accredited and certified (Turque, 2013).

5   *Contracts Bidding System:* The remaining control leakage is that of the competitive bidding system, which has a large potential for corruption at state and local levels. Again, the best safeguard against this problem is the internal control and audit system.

References

Adler, Sy and Sheldon Edner, "Governing and Managing Multimodal Regional Transit Agencies in a Multicentric Era," in *Public Policy and Transit System Management*, George M. Guess, ed., Westport: Greenwood Press, 1990: 89–113.

APTA (American Public Transit Association) (2006) *APTA Public Transportation Fact Book* (Washington, DC: APTA). Available online at www.apta.com/research/stats.

Axelrod, Donald (1995) *Budgeting for Modern Government*, 2nd ed. (New York: St. Martin's Press).

Aymerich, Mario, "The Role of the European Investment Bank," presentation at the 2nd European Commission Technical Workshop: Urban Transport Financing Experiences from Different Cities, Szentendre, Hungary, March 6, 2007.

Bahl, Roy W. and Johannes F. Linn (1992) *Urban Public Finance in Developing Countries* (New York: Oxford University Press).

Baldacci, Emanuele and Sanjeev Gupta, "Fiscal Expansions: What Works," *Finance and Development*, 46, 4 (December 2009): 12–15.

Berne, Robert and Richard Schramm (1986) *The Financial Analysis of Governments* (Englewood Cliffs, NJ: Prentice Hall).

Bingham, Lisa, Tina Nabatchi, and Rosemary O'Leary, "The New Governance: Practices and Processes for Stakeholder and Citizen Participation in the Work of Government," *Public Administration Review*, 65, 5 (September/October 2005): 547–558.

Bird, Richard (2001) "User Charges in Local Government Finance," in *The Challenge of Urban Government: Policies and Practices*, Mila Freire and Richard Stren, eds., Washington, DC: World Bank Institute, 2001: 171–183.

Borja, Jordi, "The Metropolitan Project: The Management of Variable Geometry," in *The Challenge of Urban Government: Policies and Practices*, Mila Freire and Richard Stren, eds., Washington, DC: World Bank Institute, 2001: 19–27.

Bourne, Larry S., "Designing Metropolitan Region: The Lessons and Lost Opportunities of the Toronto Experience," in *The Challenge of Urban Government: Policies and Practices*, Mila Freire and Richard Stren, eds., Washington, DC: World Bank Institute, 2001: 27–47.

Budapest Sun, "BKV Begins Route Privatization," December 9–16, 2007, p. B5.

Chu, Ke-Young and Richard Hemming (eds.) (1991) *Public Expenditure Handbook: A Guide to Public Policy Issues in Developing Countries* (Washington, DC: International Monetary Fund).

City of Milwaukee, Budget and Management Department (2003) "Plan and Budget Summary 2003" (Milwaukee: Department of Administration, Budget and Management Division).

City of Milwaukee, Budget and Management Department (2003a) "2003–2008 Capital Improvements Plan" (Milwaukee: Department of Administration, Budget and Management Division).

Coe, Charles K. (1989) *Public Financial Management* (Englewood Cliffs, NJ: Prentice-Hall).

Cooper, Michael, "An Incinerator Becomes Harrisburg's Money Pit," *New York Times,* May 20, 2010, p. A4.

Crawford, Colin, "More Roads: Dead End for Atlanta Area," *Atlanta Journal-Constitution,* April 6, 2007, p. A13.

CRFB (Committee for a Responsible Federal Budget) (2010) "The Budget Outlook" (Washington, DC: CRFB).

Dannin, Ellen and Lee Cokorinos, "Infrastructure Privatization in the New Millennium," in *The Oxford Handbook of State and Local Government Finance*, Robert D. Ebel and John E. Petersen, eds., New York: Oxford University Press, 2012: 727–756.

Donsky, Paul, "Northside May Balk on MARTA Tax," *Atlanta Journal-Constitution*, April 4, 2007, p. B1.

Ebel, Robert D. and Gabor Peteri (eds.) (2007) *The Kosovo Decentralization Briefing Handbook* (Budapest: Local Government and Public Service Reform Initiative and Kosovo Foundation for Open Society).

Ebel, Robert D. and Francois Vaillancourt, "Intergovernmental Assignment of Expenditure Responsibility," in *The Kosovo Decentralization Briefing Handbook*, Robert D. Ebel and Gabor Peteri, eds., Budapest: Local Government and Public Service Reform Initiative and Kosovo Foundation for Open Society, 2007: 75–87.

Ebel, Robert D. and John E. Petersen (eds.) (2012) *The Oxford Handbook of State and Local Government Finance* (New York: Oxford University Press).

Economist (2006) "All Aboard!" September 2, p. 40.

Economist (2007) "Chile: Transport Heaven and Hell," February 17, p. 52.

Economist (2007a) "Brazil: Dreaming of Glory," April 14, pp. 1–16.

Economist (2012) "Model-T Ford Breaks Down," December 1, p. 41.

Economist (2013) "Taking to the Streets," June 22, pp. 40–41.

Economist (2013a) "The Multiplexed Metropolis," September 7, p. 71.

Economist (2013b) "Road Privatization," July 12.

Economist (2013c) "Privatization of Roads," August 10.

Economist (2014) "The $9t Sale," January 11, p. 36.

Economist (2014a) "The PPP Traffic Jam," May 17, p. 34.

Economist (2014b) "The Struggle for Hong Kong," September 6, p. 16.

Economist (2014c) "Heavy Weapons," November 22, p. 55.

Economist (2015) "Investing in Railways: On the Right Track," April 16, p. 71.

Eddy, Robert, *Budapest Sun*, April 15, 2006, p. 6.

El Boghdady, Dina, "SEC Files More Cases on Municipal Bonds," *Washington Post*, June 29, 2013, p. C1.

Fabiola, Anthony and Paula Moura, "The Summer of Middle Class Rage," *Washington Post*, June 29, 2013, p. A1.

Fielding, Gordon J. (1987) *Managing Public Transit Strategically* (San Francisco: Jossey-Bass).

Finkler, Steven A. (2010) *Financial Management for Public, Health and Not-for-Profit Organizations*, 3rd ed. (Upper Saddle River, NJ: Pearson Prentice Hall).

Finkler, Steven A., Robert M. Purtell, Thad D. Calabrese, and Daniel L. Smith (2001) *Financial Management for Public, Health and Not-for-Profit Organizations* (Upper Saddle River, NJ: Pearson Prentice Hall).

Flora, John, "Management of Traffic and the Urban Environment," in *The Challenge of Urban Government: Policies and Practices*, Mila Freire and Richard Stren, eds., Washington, DC: World Bank Institute, 2001: 383–395.

Frederickson, George H., "The Repositioning of American Public Administration," *PS: Political Science and Politics*, 32, 4 (1999): 701–711.

Guess, George M. (1985) "Role Conflict in Capital Project Implementation: The Case of Dade County Metrorail," *Public Administration Review*, 45, 5 (September/October 1985): 576–585.

Guess, George M. (1991) "Comparative Financing Techniques for Purchasing Urban Rail Cars" (Washington, DC: Urban Mass Transportation Administration GA-11–0021–91–1).

Guess, George M. (2005) "Transport and Justice: Problems and Lessons," Local Governance Brief (Budapest: Local Government and Public Service Reform Initiative of the Open Society Institute), 6 (Autumn 2005): 4–7.

Guess, George M. (ed.) (2008) *Managing and Financing Urban Public Transport Systems: An International Perspective* (Budapest: Local Government and Public Service Reform Initiative of the Open Society Institute).

Guess, George M. and Costel Todor (2005) "Capital Programming and Budgeting: Comparative Local Government Perspectives," in *Encyclopedia of Public Administration and Public Policy*, Jack Rabin, ed. (New York: Marcel Dekker (E-EPAP-120040385): 9).

Guess, George M. and Paul G. Farnham (2011) *Cases in Public Policy Analysis*, 3rd ed. (Washington, DC: Georgetown University Press).

Hemily, Brendon (2004) "Trends Affecting Public Transit's Effectiveness: A Review and Proposed Actions," (Washington, DC: American Public Transit Association).

Hemming, Richard, "Transfers to Public Enterprises," in *Public Expenditure Handbook: A Guide to Public Policy Issues in Developing Countries*, Ke-Young Chu and Richard Hemming, eds., Washington, DC: International Monetary Fund, 1991: 75–81.

ICHD (International Center for Human Development) (2006) "Citizen's Participation in Local Government Budget Policy Development: A Case Study on Involving Citizen's Voice into the Policy-Making Process" (Yerevan: ICHD; Budapest: Local Government and Public Service Reform Initiative).

Jackman, Tom, "Virginia Weighs Building Over Metro and I-66," *Washington Post*, July 6, 2013, p. B1.

Johnson, Freda and Diane L. Roswick, "Local Fiscal Capacity," in *Local Government Finance*, John E. Petersen and Dennis R. Strachota, eds., Chicago: GFOA, 1991: 14–32.

Kamenikova, Vera, "Principales Desafios de los Procesos de Descentralizacion Fiscal," in *Democracia, Descentralizacion y Reforma Fiscal en America Latina y Europa del Este*, Grupo Propuesta Ciudadiana (eds.), Lima: Grupo Propuesta Ciudadiana, 2006: 359–373.

Lee, Robert D. and Ronald W. Johnson (1998) *Public Budgeting Systems*, 6th ed. (Gaithersburg, MD: Aspen).

Lehan, Edward A. (1984) *Budgetmaking: A Workbook of Public Budgeting Theory and Practice* (New York: St. Martin's Press).

"LRT Financial Performance" (2006), Annapolis: Maryland General Assembly.

Lynch, Thomas D., Cynthia E. Lynch, and Peter L. Cruise, "Disaster Transit: The New Orleans Experience," in *Managing and Financing Urban Public Transport Systems: An International Perspective*, George M. Guess, ed., Budapest: Local Government and Public Service Reform Initiative of the Open Society Institute, 2008: 351–375.

Mather, Earl, email communication, 2013, Gallatin County, MT: Office of County Administrator.

Michel, Gregory R. (2001) *Decision Tools for Budgetary Analysis* (Chicago: GFOA).

Mikesell, John L. (2014) *Fiscal Administration, Analysis and Applications for the Public Sector*, 9th ed. (Boston: Wadsworth Cengage).

Moynihan, Donald P., "Managing for Results in State Governments: Evaluation for a Decade of Reform," *Public Administration Review*, 66, 1 (January/February 2006): 77–99.

Neels, Kevin and Michael Caggiano (1996) "Pricing Public Services," in *Budgeting: Formulation and Execution; Workbook* (2nd ed.)*; Data Sourcebook* (2nd ed.), Jack Rabin, Bartley W. Hildreth, and Gerald J. Miller (eds.), Athens, GA: Carl Vinson Institute of Government, 1996: 173–174.

Perry, James L. and Timlynn T. Babitsky, "Comparative Performance in Urban Bus Transit: Assessing Privatization Strategies," *Public Administration Review*, 46, 1 (January/February 1986): 57–66.

Peteri, Gabor and Francois Vaillancourt, "Local Government in Kosovo," in *The Kosovo Decentralization Briefing Handbook*, Robert D. Ebel and Gabor Peteri, eds., Budapest: Local Government and Public Service Reform Initiative and Kosovo Foundation for Open Society, 2007: 19–33.

Posner, Paul, Trina Lewis, and Hannah Laufe, "Budgeting for Capital," *Public Budgeting and Finance*, 18, 13 (1998): 11–24.

Pressman, Jeffrey L. and Aaron Wildavsky (1984) *Implementation*, 3rd ed. (Berkeley: University of California Press).

Spivak, John, "Overestimating of Economic Project Benefits," *Washington Post*, February 14, 2010, p. B10.

Stefanova, Anelia, "EU Cohesion Policy: Experiences and Urban Transport Priorities," presentation at the 2nd European Commission Technical Workshop: Urban Transport Financing Experiences from Different Cities, Szentendre, Hungary, March 6, 2007.

Svara, James H., "Exploring Structures and Institutions in City Government," *Public Administration Review*, 65, 4 (July/August 2005): 500–506.

Szucs, Lajos, "Transport and Cohesion Policy," presentation at the 2nd European Commission Technical Workshop: Urban Transport Financing: Experiences from Different Cities, Szentendre, Hungary, March 6, 2007.

Toerkel, Bernd, "Opening Remarks" at the 2nd European Commission Technical Workshop: Urban Transport Financing Experiences from Different Countries, Szentendre, Hungary, March 6, 2007.

Turque, Bill, "Concrete Tests Faulted," *Washington Post*, March 27, 2013, p. B1.

USDOT (U.S. Department of Transportation) (1985) *Financial Management for Transit: A Handbook* (Washington, DC: Urban Mass Transportation Administration).

Vogt, John A. and Lisa Cole (eds.) (1983) *A Guide to Municipal Leasing* (Chicago: Government Finance Officer's Association).

Voszka, Eva, "The Transformation of the Budapest Public Transport Company," in *The Budapest Model: A Liberal Urban Policy Experiment*, Katalin Pallai, ed., Budapest: Local Government and Public Service Reform Initiative of the Open Society Institute, 2003: 273–294.

WEF (World Economic Forum) (2011) "From Burden to 'Best Buys': Reducing the Economic Impact of Non-Communicable Diseases in Low and Middle Income Countries" (Geneva: WEF).

World Bank (2005) "Better Urban Services: Finding the Right Incentives" (Washington, DC: IBRD).

World Bank (2006a) "Current Issues in Fiscal Reform in Central Europe and the Baltic States 2005" (Washington, DC: IBRD).

World Bank (2006b) "Sustainable Transport: Priorities for Policy Reform" (Washington, DC: IBRD).

Worldwatch Institute, 2013. Available online at www.worldwatch.org/taxonomy/term/101.

Wulkin, Alan C., "Elected Versus Appointed Boards and Transit System Effectiveness," in *Public Policy and Transit System Management*, George M. Guess, ed., Westport: Greenwood Press, 1990: 25–39.

4   Health Care Policies

Introduction

Health outcomes are the fundamental test of government success in this policy area. Since good health is the most basic element of human welfare, wellness is both a test of public sector performance effectiveness and of health care policy design and implementation results. The complexity of determining health outcomes makes health care a difficult challenge for governments. Should the focus and funding be on preventive measures such as vaccinations, clean air and water, and related programs such as social assistance? Or is the problem medical intervention at the right time? Governments can make a clear difference here by sponsoring research to discover new treatments and provide access to curative care (Adolino and Blake, 2011: 234). They can also make a difference by designing smart programs that target improved health care outcomes with poverty-reduction efforts such as the conditional cash transfers found in many Latin American countries. Such operational-level programs that rely on properly aligned incentives have now spread to countries in most regions of the globe.

Three important issues for health care in industrialized, transitional, and developing countries are health outcomes, access to curative care, and cost control. We will discuss them below. Note that health care is an important example of the input, output, and outcome linkages described in the policy models from *Chapter 1*. From public and private expenditure and resource inputs, public expectations are that outputs in the form of effective delivery systems will produce outcomes in access or services coverage, cost-effective curative care, and efficiency or cost control. Where these expectations are not met, pressure for fundamental reform of health care systems and even the replacement of government regimes responsible for them is often intense.

Like urban public transport, the health care and social assistance policy functions are mostly financed by national governments and delivered by local level authorities and facilities at varying degrees of efficiency and cost-effectiveness. Health care is an amalgam of other related services such as water and sanitation, education, and nutrition as well as formal and informal institutions and cultural practices. For health policies and strategies, the notion that one size fits all is ill-founded because social structures, customs, political systems, economic capacities, and historical legacies vary so widely across countries. For example, in some cultural settings, it is unacceptable for females to be examined or treated by male physicians (Bloom, 2014: 10). As noted in the preface, cultural practices in places such as India that encourage defecation in public diminish the value and effectiveness of health programs to install sewerage infrastructure. Health care spending is often viewed as a burdensome consumption expenditure. In fact, it is an investment in productivity, income growth, and poverty reduction (Bloom, 2014: 6). Incomes and employment then depend on the quality of these health-related services. Predictably, systemic failures in access to health care and the quality of its delivery are often met with public outcry. It is also clear that design and delivery of health care affects levels of poverty and income distribution. Unlike urban public transport and infrastructure, optimal modes of service delivery and financing are not agreed upon and remain controversial. Also unlike services such as public transit, new challenges in the form of diseases and famines arise regularly to overwhelm many health care systems. The fact is that global poverty, hunger, and the lack of adequate health care all threaten the well-being of millions of the world's population, particularly those living in the underdeveloped countries.

The eradication of extreme global poverty and hunger by 2015 is the first of the eight United Nations Millennium Development Goals (MDGs). The World Bank has also pledged to devote its considerable financial resources and efforts to ending extreme poverty by 2030 and to shift the focus on economic growth designed to benefit the bottom half of the income distribution. While this seems like an enormous task—the World Bank estimates the level of extreme global poverty in the world, measured at a poverty line of $1.25 a day per person, at 1.4 billion people—much progress has been accomplished. Extreme poverty continues to be large, but it has been reduced by 700 million since 1990. In percentage terms, this represented a reduction of extreme poverty from 36 percent of the world's population in 1990 to less than 18 percent. In addition to poverty, MDGs attempt to stimulate improvements in global health. While it is impossible to rigorously estimate the contribution they have made to improvements, they seem to have focused attention of the international development community on health and sparked increased health spending especially in low-income countries (Bloom, 2014: 11).

A considerable amount has been accomplished through a variety of government programs designed to provide relief for these extreme conditions. Redistribution and health programs are established by governments to protect children, elderly, and disabled citizens and can also be used to assist the poor who are not earning a "living" wage. Even so, many of these policies benefit better-off citizens and may reduce governmental ability to alleviate these conditions. Social programs throughout the developed and developing countries provide both cash, in-kind, and/or conditional cash transfers to different population groups. Many countries redistribute income directly to poor households as social assistance and/or to the elderly through social pensions. In some countries, this income assistance is included with a guarantee of employment through the private sector or by government employment. In-kind programs include support for health care, food, housing, and jobs.

The one major social assistance program that operates as both cash and in-kind is government spending on health in countries throughout all regions of the world. It ranks at or near the top of all government expenditure responsibilities. The United Nations also lists among its eight Millennium Development Goals other health goals, including the reduction of child mortality, the improvement of maternal health, and the reduction of HIV/AIDS and other devastating diseases. In 2010, the World Health Organization (WHO) estimated about $6.5 trillion was spent on healthcare, amounting to over 10 percent of global GDP. Large expenditures are particularly true in the countries making up the developed world. Countries in North America and Europe account for nearly 75 percent of the world total. The size of these expenditures is growing in most countries. According to Coady et al. (2012), health care spending as a share of GDP has gone up six percentage points since 1970. They attribute more than two-thirds of that increase to increases in government spending on health care. They link this increase in health care spending to rising real income, increasing elderly population, advancing technology in the health care sector, and governmental health care policies and regulations. However, even with this general growth in spending, inter- and intra-country health care outcome inequalities remain significant. As with education, these outcome inequities reflect factors outside of the health care system and are difficult to remedy.

Health care is provided through several different mechanisms by government or by the private sector (either by "for profit" or "not for profit" medical establishments). It can be fully (or partially) financed by the government or through a medical insurance market (either financed privately or by government provided social insurance). The standard approach to the provision of health care in Europe is a high level of government involvement often providing universal care, meaning the provision of medical care of the option of medical coverage for all citizens. The United States remains the outlier among OECD countries. It is by far the largest personal and government spender on health care. However, aside from large government health care programs covering the poor (Medicaid) and the elderly (Medicare), most health care in the U.S. is generally provided through the private insurance market. This insurance coverage is coordinated by employers and offered as a tax-free benefit to employees. Although most of the OECD countries do not incorporate medical insurance plans into their coverage, a few European countries like Germany, Switzerland, and the Netherlands have interjected the insurance market in some of the health care decisions.

There are "market failure" justifications for government involvement in the production/ provision of health care for its citizens. Health care is also an important component of a large patchwork of social welfare or redistribution programs found across all countries. The types of programs and the extent of the assistance provided vary considerably across regions and countries. In addition to health care, these social welfare programs include income support, food provisions, child care, and housing assistance.

This chapter will: (1) discuss the different measures of extreme poverty, which is important in the determination of social assistance program eligibility, (2) review the various social assistance programs designed to address extreme poverty in the countries, (3) describe the various design issues that arise in the development of these programs, (4) outline the justification of the government's involvement in the provision of health care, (5) review the various health care financing policies, (6) explain the differences in results from a specific policy response to infectious disease outbreaks by referring to the analytic frameworks described in *Chapter 1*, and (7) draw lessons for policy and operations management using several cases to highlight these lessons.

Poverty Measurement

The identification of individuals in extreme poverty and potentially needing government assistance is a critical problem in both developed and developing countries. Hagenaars and de Vos (1988) propose three broad definitions of this relationship between the individual's (or family's) resources and adequate consumption:

1 Poverty is having less than an objectively defined, absolute minimum.
2 Poverty is having less than others in society.
3 Poverty is feeling you do not have enough to get along.

Each of these definitions has a common structure. They differ in either the way needs are determined and/or the way family resources are calculated. Each definition is described more fully below.

Poverty Is Having Less Than an Objectively Defined, Absolute Minimum.

As described by Hagenaars and de Vos (1988), the most common measure of poverty is to compare an individual's (or family's) income with some threshold level of income/ consumption. If this income threshold is a minimum level, it is referred to as the poverty income level. In developed countries, poverty might be defined as a situation where an individual's (or family's) resources (e.g. income) are less than the minimum amount necessary to consume some adequate bundle of goods (e.g. composed of food, clothing, and housing). In the developing world, this threshold income level may be arbitrary but involves an extreme measure. As mentioned in the introduction, the World Bank has defined the extreme poverty line as people living at or below $1.25 per person throughout the world. This level is associated with the basic subsistence level in a sample of underdeveloped countries and represents an average of poverty lines across those countries. An arbitrary determination of this level can obviously be controversial. In 2012, the Argentine government set a controversial poverty line equal to a monthly food bill of 688 pesos for a family of four, the equivalent of six pesos per person per day. While the government sees this level as sufficient for the daily diet, an independent study from the University of Buenos Aires calculates the minimum daily diet budget to be 24 pesos per day per person (*Economist*, 2012a). Once the poverty line has been established, the "head count" poverty rate is measured by the percentage of individuals/ families with incomes below this minimum amount.

As Hagenaars and de Vos point out, this measure creates problems of how to account for family size and composition. The determination of the poverty rate requires the appropriate measurements of available resources and the threshold minimum. However, it is important to note that the poverty line measure is somewhat arbitrary. Individuals on either side of the poverty line will have a shortage of resources. Increases or decreases in the line will not affect the amount of this deprivation. Once the poverty line is established, the question remains of who should receive government assistance, particularly in the usual situation in underdeveloped countries where government budgets are acutely inadequate to eliminate poverty or even extreme poverty entirely. One critical drawback of measuring poverty by calculating the number of individuals/families below a minimum income level is that it does not distinguish between families close to the line and those much farther away. If the ultimate goal is to reduce the incidence of poverty, then preference should be given to those individuals closest to the poverty line, so that the number of people/families in poverty are reduced. Alternatively, if the concern is on the "worst off" citizens/families, then the assistance should be directed to that group. However, in the situation of limited government budgets, there is no expectation of poverty reduction with this policy. One possible measure to take these differences into account is the "poverty gap," which is measured by the distance between the individual/ family's income and the established poverty line as a proportion of the poverty line. The square of this measure is the squared poverty gap index. The advantage of using the squared poverty gap measure is that it puts more weight on individuals/households who are farther away from the poverty line.

The standard poverty line measure generally only includes cash household income, excluding any in-kind benefits. Although this is the most common measure, Barrientos (2013) describes some of the problems, particularly in developing countries, associated with using cash income for this measure. He lists measurement errors from survey instruments, variability of income over time, and the general unavailability of goods and services makes the simple measure of income ineffective. Many others have pointed out the other potential drawback of this measure is the exclusion of in-kind benefits. In the developed countries with well-established and relatively generous social assistance programs, in-kind programs like medical and housing benefits represent an increase in resources.

Poverty levels and medical expenses are intimately related. Medical expenses represent an additional major expenditure category that affects the well-being of low-income individuals. For example, the current U.S. measure of family resources excludes the value of Medicare (health insurance for individuals aged 65 and older), Medicaid (health benefits for low-income individuals), and employer-provided health benefits. The measure also does not exclude out-of-pocket medical expenses (e.g. entire medical expenses, health insurance premiums, deductibles and co-payments, and uncovered medical procedures) even though these outlays reduce the family's consumption abilities. Although the consideration of these medical benefits and costs could potentially affect a family's poverty status, the treatment and measurement of medical care benefits are not as straightforward as food and housing in-kind benefits. There are three problems. First, medical benefits are not as interchangeable with money or fungible as food stamp benefits. Specifically, insurance coverage and/or free care do not free up income to use for other purposes. One peculiarity of simply adding medical benefits to family resources is that sicker people (e.g. disabled or the elderly) would appear to be better off than healthy ones. A second issue is that, unlike food and housing purchases, medical needs are generally lumpy—that is, during some years, medical care may not be needed or extra medical benefits cannot be used to finance extra consumption. A third problem is that it is difficult to measure out-of-pocket medical expenditures. Some medical insurance plans have low or no coverage on certain items (e.g. drugs, long-term care, and elective medical procedures) and it may be inappropriate to simply subtract out-of-pocket medical costs from and add health insurance premiums to family resources. People in poverty may not have access to health care and, therefore, have low out-of-pocket expenditures. Health insurance may encourage medical expenditures beyond the point where the value of the service is equal to the cost.

Poverty Is Having Less Than Others in Society.

Hagenaars and de Vos' (1988) second measure of poverty is also objectively determined and is based on the individual's or household's relative position in the income distribution or the ability to purchase and maintain or replace a market-basket of commodities containing goods that are commonly consumed by other individuals and families during that time period. One proposed relative measure based on income is that the poverty income threshold is some fixed percentage (e.g. 50 percent) of median income. The advantage of this consumption-based measure is it allows the consumption bundle to be updated to reflect changes in consumption patterns. For example, the bundle of durable goods might now most likely contain a computer and possibly other electronic equipment. However, as pointed out by Hagenaars and de Vos (1988), this particular relative measure of poverty is weak because the choice of consumption goods to include in the threshold measure is arbitrary. Moreover, it does not take into account the fact that families at early stages in the life-cycle (e.g. young singles and couples) would be less likely to own all of these durables and, as a result, would be more likely to be classified as impoverished.

Poverty Is Feeling You Do Not Have Enough to Get Along.

One drawback of the previous two poverty measures is their reliance on experts either to determine the income threshold or to choose the goods to include in the consumption bundle. In both cases, the poverty threshold is exogenous to the affected individuals and families.

However, families may be in the best position to evaluate their own relative position of well-being or standard-of-living. Hagenaars and de Vos' (1988) third definition of poverty thus allows self-evaluation of poverty status. Public opinion polls in the U.S. and other developed countries ask individuals how much income is "just sufficient" or "enough to make ends meet." Answers to these questions are then used to calculate a subjective minimum income level that is "just sufficient." Income is compared with this minimum income level to determine the poverty status. Measures of poverty based on the answers to these types of questions often (but not always) take into account the respondent's family size and own income.

Several subjective poverty measures have been developed in the U.S., Europe, and Canada based on different surveys. Poverty measures created from these surveys varied significantly across the different surveys. Threshold estimates for a family of four (two adults/two children) in 1992 dollars ranged from $32,530 (de Vos and Garner, 1991) to $12,160 (Colasanto et al., 1984). Moreover, the subjective income thresholds are substantially larger than the official needs-based income threshold. The threshold measure calculated by de Vos and Garner (1991) is 229 percent of the official U.S. income threshold for a family of four. Vaughan (1993) used answers from the Gallup Poll question "What is the smallest amount of money a family of four needs each week to get along in this community?" to calculate a subjective income threshold. He found that the subjective threshold was about 168 percent of the official U.S. income threshold. In more recent Gallup Polls, individuals were asked: "People who have income below a certain level can be considered poor. That level is called the 'poverty line.' What amount of weekly income would you use as a poverty line for a family of four in this community?" Based on the answers to this question, the subjective poverty-income threshold is consistently at least 115 percent of the official U.S. poverty line. An advantage of the subjective thresholds over the official poverty-income thresholds is that they appear to follow changes in income levels over time—rising during periods of economic expansions and falling during recessions.

Social Programs and Redistribution

As noted in *Chapter 2*, the standard outcome of a market economy can yield considerable income inequality and may include many citizens defined as living in poverty. The World Bank estimate of 1.4 billion people living at or below $1.25 per person is a measure of the extreme poverty throughout the world. There are significant differences in measured inequality between the developed and underdeveloped regions. Birdsall et al. (2011) show inequality (as measured by the Gini coefficient) is significantly greater in Latin American, Africa, and Asia than in OECD countries.

The general policy "solution" to the inequality found in these less developed countries is strong economic growth. Many argued that the growth sectors of the real economy (e.g. manufacturing) needed support through such policies as import-substitution industrialization (ISI) programs as the private market did not seem to correct inequality. Indeed, Birdsall et al. (2011) show this large inequality can be found even in those less developed countries with a relatively high per capita income. As programs failed to generate sufficient economic growth or as the economic growth failed to lift a large segment of the population facing extreme poverty, there were renewed calls for public policies to provide relief and strengthen the social safety net. Although this inequality might not be classified as a "market failure," it often is considered unacceptable by policy-makers or citizens.

There are two primary and potentially conflicting objectives with social assistance programs which could lead to significant trade-offs. Barrientos (2013) lists the objectives to reduce poverty and "vulnerability." Poverty is measurable and, in the extreme, it requires immediate attention and can be largely addressed through either cash or in-kind transfers. Cash transfers could potentially lead to bad incentives causing recipients to rely on the government assistance rather than private sector actions. The more complicated concept of vulnerability (which is more difficult to measure) is represented by the potential or probability of being in poverty in the future. Immediate cash provisions are not designed to address this vulnerability. Instead, assistance for vulnerability is more long-term and may involve the provision of nutrition, medical care, education, and asset accumulation/protection.

Barrientos (2013) explains that the theoretically optimal redistribution in a country will "reflect social preferences with regard to aversion to poverty, as defined in the understanding of poverty present in the minds of policymakers." This aversion could mean a desire for a reduction in the numbers of people in poverty, which leads to transfers to the "least poor," those closest to the poverty line, or it could mean a desire to close the poverty gap, which leads to transfers to the "poorest poor," those the furthest from the poverty line. Another possibility is a hybrid social transfer program, combining these two goals in a single program.

Although many forms of social safety net intervention are possible, there are several reasons why they may ultimately be ineffective or not as effective as necessary or expected. Coady (2008) lists some of these reasons. Large program administrative costs, corruption, and basic government inefficiencies will significantly reduce the amount of program aid. Coady describes the "short-term" nature of safety net programs that focus benefits on reducing current poverty without expanding the "long-term" programs that would encourage the level of economic growth necessary to reduce or eliminate future extreme poverty. In fact, some of the factors that make these programs unpopular are because of the disincentives created by these short-term programs which may reduce labor supply, savings, and income.

The primary justification for government involvement in social welfare is due to benefit associated with the redistribution of resources necessary to reduce the extreme poverty levels that exist in these countries. As noted, programs can provide two general types of assistance—cash transfers and/or in-kind. Often the social welfare "patchwork" of programs contains both types. It is straightforward to show that consumers will generally prefer cash transfers over equivalently valued in-kind benefits. However, governments may want to take on goals that can best be accomplished with in-kind programs.

Government social programs have operated in both developed and underdeveloped countries to provide some relief for these extreme poverty conditions. These programs are motivated by the individual citizen's sense of duty to assist. Of course, that sense of duty could lead to particular types of social assistance programs. Government programs are typically a mixture of cash transfers, in-kind programs, and/or a combination of these programs already described as "conditional cash transfers." Ideally, these social assistance programs would be just one of several interventions used to reduce poverty. Permanent reductions in poverty require economic growth sufficient to provide economic opportunities.

Social Assistance Program Design Issues

All types of government social assistance programs must address a basic set of design issues. Barrientos (2013) discusses three: classification, productive capacity, and incentives. First, "classification" requires an accurate identification of eligible assistance recipients or program inefficiencies will result. Two types of errors are possible and should be minimized. Type I errors occur if the program selection excludes eligible program recipients (error of exclusion or "under coverage"). Type II errors occur if the program selection includes ineligible program recipients (error of inclusion or "leakage"). These types of errors will decrease program effectiveness and increase program cost and they should be minimized. Unfortunately, as is well known in basic statistics, reduction of one error type will lead to an increase in the other type. For example, efforts to increase recipient coverage perhaps by being less "targeting" and minimizing Type I errors will certainly increase the numbers of ineligible recipients and thereby increase Type II errors. In addition, these errors, particularly type II leakage errors, might also decrease the taxpayer's support for these assistance programs.

Various methods of recipient identification have been used, including means testing of programs. However any self-reporting mechanism requires "honest" reporting. This is relatively easy within a developed country with a formal labor market, where employers and government can record earned income and taxes owed. The task of recipient identification could be given to officials at the local community level where government officials are closer to the recipients and the information is expected to be more accurate. Programs could be centered on groups with typically higher rates of poverty and in-kind programs could set up distribution centers where "queuing" is required so that ineligible recipients with higher opportunity costs are discouraged from this deception. Many countries have programs providing assistance to the elderly and children, age categories that are more easily identified with common government documents. Identification by category will require an additional step to determine the poverty status. Programs could be designed to motivate eligible recipients to self-select or, better yet, ineligible individuals to not participate in the program. One method is to require some form of obligation, for example, a work requirement, that provides a salary below the private sector.

Second, when assistance is given based on an individual's income level, there may be incentives for the individual to adjust their earnings adversely or reduce "productive capacity." One way to protect against this reduction is to build in work requirements, once again providing a salary below that found in the private sector to discourage higher-ability individuals. In order to make sure productive capacity is not reduced, the requirement must be greater than the recipient would have taken on without the benefit. Other types of conditions of assistance can also be required consumption of productive inputs, including services like schooling for the children and family health maintenance. These activities obviously contribute to the productive capacity. Once again, in order to be effective, the program must require a level of these activities beyond what the individual/family would have purchased without the assistance.

The third program design issue is the impact of benefits on "work incentives." Some programs, particularly in the developed countries, have a large tax rate on labor income as a result of program assistance—some programs reduce income by a dollar with a dollar of program assistance (the actual relationship is a dollar of earned income lowers the program benefit available to the recipient). The design of incentives has a strong impact on the individual's decision to work. Barrientos (2013) points out that program benefits in the developing countries are generally "fixed level" and therefore do not get reduced with earned income. In addition, the informal nature of some of the work (i.e. the large size of the informal economy) in the developing countries reduces the exposure to these high tax rates.

Examples of Social Assistance Programs

Social assistance programs worldwide are of three basic types: pure income transfer programs, in-kind assistance programs, and "conditional" income transfer programs. As described above, the basic design issues of classification, productive capacity, and work incentives must be addressed for each program type. Barrientos (2013) describes the tremendous growth of these programs in the developing countries and he provides several examples, including the *Diabao* program in China which grew by 20 million recipients between 1999 and 2002 and the Child Support Grant program in South Africa which reached 9 million recipients by 2009 after its start in 1998. Birdsall et al. (2011) describe the countries of Latin America as among the most unequal in the world, and this inequality has also been persistent. However, improvements in the provision of universal education have helped to reduce this inequality. Although recently created large scale income transfer and in-kind assistance programs in Argentina, Brazil, Mexico, Peru, and Uruguay have contributed to the significant improvements in income inequality in the region, the reductions are small relative to the countries in Western Europe, given the universality and the larger budgets devoted to income assistance in these countries. In addition, a critical design issue distinction is how the programs are targeted. In those countries where the program focus is on individuals/families in extreme poverty, poverty has been reduced. According to Lustig et al. (2012), Argentina has had the most success in reducing extreme poverty. It provides cash transfers to nearly all (about 90 percent) of its poor. Brazil and Uruguay have also seen recent reductions in poverty and inequality with these programs. However, compared to Argentina, Brazil spends the most but its cash transfers reach only about 70 percent of its extreme poor and, as a result, is not as successful in overall poverty reduction. Lustig et al. (2014) point out that Argentina's success may ultimately be undone by its lack of fiscal stability. Mexico spends considerably less than Argentina and its primary program, *Oportunidades,* combines conditional cash transfers with education and health care requirements. Consequently, a large percentage of the extreme poor do not receive assistance. This program is described more fully below.

Income Transfer Programs

Cash or income transfer programs that provide some minimum level of individual/family income are used extensively in the OECD countries, but are relatively new in the developing countries. Birdsall et al. (2011) credit these transfer programs, in part, for recent improvements in the distribution of income in Latin American countries, particularly Argentina, Brazil, and Uruguay. Barrientos (2013) lists the Kalomo Pilot Social Transfer scheme in Zambia and the Old Persons and Child Support Grant programs in South Africa as examples of these pure income transfer programs.

As described in the next section, economic theory suggests the poor are theoretically better off with pure income transfers than with in-kind transfers. Although this might be true, the generally negative views of income transfers made their use less likely, particularly in developing countries. Hanlon et al. (2010) list the use of cash transfers as a critically important way to reduce poverty and to satisfy the Universal Declaration of Human Rights guarantee of an adequate standard of living for all. They also see cash transfers as providing the poor a means of empowerment to be able to make appropriate consumption decisions, without the concerns associated with extreme need. They also believe cash transfers are directly tied to improving the status of women in these countries, by reducing their need to find alternative (often involving illicit behavior) activities to earn money. Finally, they see cash transfers as a means for redistributing revenues gained from oil and mineral deposits found in the country, allowing all citizens to benefit from the natural resources found in many underdeveloped countries.

International development organizations (e.g. World Bank and International Monetary Fund) frequently tie aid to the implementation of policies designed to improve economic growth and development of the private sector. In retrospect, the growth in poverty in many countries receiving this aid indicates the ineffectiveness of a pure economic growth to reduce poverty levels. It is the case that many of the poor in developing and transitional countries work in the informal sector outside of the market and do not benefit much from any improved economic growth. In addition, one view in developing countries, as well as many developed countries, is that unconditional cash transfers are wasteful and ultimately unproductive. The primary concern focuses on the perceived disincentives associated with such programs. Hanlon et al. (2010) disagree and note the propensity to consume for poor people is higher than for the rich and that these cash transfers are used to purchase local goods rather than the more expensive imports. Furthermore, they also believe that the poor will use of these funds to make productive investments in work and trade. Finally, they note a big difference between these programs in developed countries which are based on formal labor markets—unemployment insurance is an example of a large government anti-poverty program but private pensions are formal and labor market-based. Informal labor markets will not have these same types of programs available.

Income can be transferred to specific individuals and groups or it can be universally provided across the general population. Programs can designate particular needy individuals or groups as eligible beneficiaries. For example, many countries provide benefits to the very young and/or the very old in the population who are not otherwise able to support themselves through employment. Hanlon et al. (2010) note the factors behind taxpayer support for those types of programs. Citizens were young once and plan to be old in the future. It is this possibility of need or the ability to relate to the helplessness of the young and old which make these programs less controversial. Still, Hanlon et al. (2010) make it clear that these programs of specific transfers are insufficient to eliminate poverty in a developing country. That is, there will be limits to the amount of inequality reduction as a result of such targeted programs. For example, generous pensions may be given to individuals who otherwise benefited from employment and are, as a result, relatively well off.

One of the newer ideas in countries from both the developed and undeveloped regions is a universal cash benefit provided to all citizens. While Hanlon et al. (2010) propose a universal cash transfer to the poor in the underdeveloped countries, calls for universal support are not limited to developing countries. For example, a recent referendum in Switzerland called for a universal basic income scheme to provide $2,800 per month to all Swiss citizens (Lowrey, 2013).

In-Kind Assistance Programs

Governments may desire a more direct approach to social assistance and often take on a paternalistic role to provide a minimum amount of critical goods such as food, housing, education, and medical care (e.g. the Affordable Health Care Act of 2010 or "Obamacare" in the U.S.). The direct approach may put governments in the position of providing goods rather than simple income support. For example, Coady (2008) describes three common methods used to provide food support—food subsidies, rationed food, and food stamps. As he explains, food subsidies were commonly used in the 1960s and 1970s in many underdeveloped countries, but large increases in worldwide food prices and the general program inefficiencies, as measured by the inadequate program benefit targeting and price manipulations, made many of them too expensive to maintain. Ineffective recipient targeting led to program changes specifically applying subsidies to goods consumed by the poor (or the weakest targeting approach), putting food rationing operations in areas with the greatest concentration of poverty, and/or issuing food stamps based on income level (which is the strongest targeting approach). A drawback of universal food subsidies, even those on specific goods, is the potential lack of program progressivity. The identification of these goods is often imprecise and, as a result, there is considerable leakage to non-poor individuals which increases program inefficiency. Coady (2008) lists possible methods of identifying the appropriate recipient population. These include the provision of foods in poorer areas at inconvenient times and requiring queuing, which plays on the higher opportunity costs of the more well off citizens. Other programs incorporate means tests and/or ration cards. Several countries, including Bangladesh, Sri Lanka, Tunisia, and some countries in Latin America have switched from universal food provision to a more targeted food provision program.

The provision of in-kind assistance can be less efficient than cash transfers. Suppose the government wants to make sure its citizens have an adequate amount of food, housing, and health care? The government could accomplish this by either providing the consumer with the good directly as an in-kind transfer or give the consumer cash to be able to purchase the good. Both types of assistance will give the consumer more resources and a greater ability to consume more goods of all kinds. It is the case, however, that $1 of cash may not be valued as equivalent to $1 of in-kind assistance. If the consumer is given cash, then this will directly increase his/her ability to consume more of any good, including the good the government wants to give. If the in-kind assistance forces the consumer to consume more of the good than he/she would have otherwise wanted to purchase (and the consumer is prohibited from reselling the good) relative to the cash transfer, then this type of in-kind assistance makes the consumer worse off relative to the cash assistance. The relative value of these two types of assistance depends on the consumer's desired level of consumption.

Even though recipients may prefer cash assistance to in-kind transfers, there may be incentive-based reasons that justify their use. The visibility of some in-kind benefits may discourage consumers who are not eligible to receive them to deceive in order to obtain the benefits (for the same visibility factor, otherwise eligible recipients may also be discouraged from obtaining these in-kind benefits). Until recently, there was a preference toward in-kind assistance over cash transfers. The prevailing view in many countries was that poverty is the result of laziness and a lack of will power. Consequently, cash assistance was viewed by many in these countries as a way to promote bad habits.

Conditional Cash Transfer Programs

A relatively new type of social assistance program, as noted, combines the cash transfer with in-kind support by making the receipt of cash assistance conditional on meeting certain health and/or education requirements. The programs typically incorporate various targeting schemes to identify the appropriate recipients. In addition, this conditional support provides funds in exchange for the recipient's agreement to purchase certain items or to carry out certain investments in activities such as education, health, and/or food. As such, while the government does not necessarily provide the goods in-kind, they represent a hybrid of income transfer and in-kind assistance programs. Focusing on nutrition, education, and health, the program goal is to alleviate long-term extreme poverty rather than just providing shorter term relief. These programs have been developed relatively recently, primarily in Latin America but also in Mozambique and Turkey. After Mexico initiated its program in 1997, several countries in Latin America— Brazil, Colombia, Honduras, Jamaica, and Nicaragua—also adopted conditional cash transfer programs. The primary difference between these programs and the other types of social safety programs is that while cash transfers are used, like income transfer programs, the cash is expected to be used for specific purposes. In exchange for mandatory use of public services such as health care and education, the recipient is expected to purchase the cash goods in the regular market. For example, Colombia provides school subsidies and Honduras awards education vouchers to poor households to increase the education of children living in poverty. Grants are also provided in many of these countries to improve the health and health education of the poor citizens.

Mexico's conditional cash transfer program, *PROGRESA,* replaced their existing safety net programs that were largely ineffective in reducing extreme poverty. Initial program benefits went to families living in extreme poverty from the rural areas of Mexico. In order to receive cash assistance, recipient families were required to provide proof of 85 percent school attendance of their young children (through primary and middle school grades) and regular health center visits. Total benefits were based on school attendance and health center visits and were capped at less than $100 per month. The success of this program at the rural level led to an extension of the program, *Oportunidades*, into the urban areas of the country. The federal program managed to bypass the state and local governments, which reduced the possibility for the local corruption sometimes found in social safety net programs. As described in Lora (2007), the federal program was distinct in its ability to target poor communities, identify families in those communities, and award funds to the most appropriate beneficiaries. In addition, the program was subject to review by outside evaluators. That kept the program "honest" and prevented it from being used as an election tool for the incumbent government. Overall, according to Coady (2008), the program successfully targeted recipients with nearly 90 percent of the cash benefits going to the families in the bottom 20 percent of national income. Proof of program success was evident in the improvements in basic health and education measures. Coady noted that preventive health care improved as did access to nutrition information and supplements. Common adult and childhood health measures also improved. Among these measures, the incidence of childhood illness decreased and childhood height increased. In addition, education measures improved—increased enrollments, particularly in secondary schools. Overall, many improvements occurred in the rural areas of Mexico. It is interesting to note that the positive results and widespread popularity of this program led directly to improved household credit and investments in private enterprises, with obvious long-term anti-poverty gains.

Lora (2007) describes how the other programs in the region adopted the basic design features of the *PROGRESA* program. Each of the programs carefully identified eligible families in extreme poverty and attached measurable outcomes to recipient behavioral change based on transfer outlays such as school enrollment and health center visits. Honduras replaced an unconditional income transfer program with *PRAF II*, a conditional cash transfer program targeting family education, health, and nutrition improvements. Colombia replaced an ineffective set of assistance programs with a conditional cash transfer program designed for the poorest families in both the country's urban and rural areas. Program incentives were given to participants in order to improve education, health, and nutrition. The *PETI* program in Brazil required recipient families to enroll their children in schools so that they would not be subject to labor market exploitation and to attend health centers for pregnant mothers and young children. As Coady (2008) describes, the Nicaragua *RPS* program also linked cash benefits to primary school attendance and household visits to health centers. Targeting for program eligibility was linked to an index based on municipality characteristics such as family size, literacy rates, and access to potable water and latrines. Similar to the results in the other countries, significant measurable health and education improvements resulted and were persistent. The Bangladesh *FFE* conditional program has seen significant health and education improvements for families in extreme poverty since it was established in 1993.

Why Does Government Provide Health Care?

One of the largest government in-kind social assistance programs in developed and underdeveloped countries is for health care. In that sense, health care consists of multiple policies and related programs. While a consumer's decision to get inoculations against various communicable diseases is an example of an externality associated with an individual's decision to get health care, the primary benefits from this decision to seek health care are primarily private. In theory, the private market through a well-functioning price system is capable of providing medical service to consumers. However, the economic justification for governmental involvement in the health care market is twofold. One is that there may be market imperfections associated with the provision of health care which require government intervention through direct provision or health insurance to address. The second justification through direct provision of in-kind benefits or cash transfers is to correct for income inequalities that may cause consumers to be unable to afford adequate health care. Governments intervene to provide socially desirable levels of health provision as unregulated markets find it hard to do that because of (1) the spillover effects of infectious diseases and (2) the opportunistic behavior of private health providers who use their superior information and perceived status to exploit consumers by advising them to undertake unnecessary and costly procedures (Bloom, 2014: 10). Beyond the economic rationale, as noted, lies the core fact that health is the most basic element of human welfare which places a social obligation on governments to provide the essentials of public health. This is to protect both individuals and the public at large from diseases, and epidemics that often contaminate whole populations. In this broader sense, the state obligation is fulfilling an obligation to provide essential health along with other basics as housing and food as a human right.

The first economic justification is derived from imperfections in the healthcare market. Perfectly competitive market conditions require many suppliers and full information. These conditions lead to a competitive market outcome of price equal to the marginal cost of production. Referring back to *Chapter 3*, *Figure 3.4* indicates the problems in organizing services and pricing them in uncompetitive markets requiring, for urban transport at least, a natural monopoly solution. However, many health care providers, particularly medical specialists, operate in market conditions that cannot be characterized as "competitive." The provision of health care can vary by the extent of the coverage. As described below, most countries outside of the U.S. provide universal health coverage either through insurance-type programs or by providing health care directly, through government-run medical establishments, by operating insurance-type programs and regulating prices paid to providers for services, or by subsidizing consumers. Federal government run insurance plans in the U.S. have generally been focused on individual categories of the population. Medicare, the primary program providing health care to the elderly in the U.S., sets reimbursement fees for doctors and other health care providers. Medicaid health coverage, financed partly by the state governments, covers individuals classified as "poor." The biggest disadvantage of this more "piecemeal" approach is that universal healthcare coverage is not achieved.

The recent Obamacare (ACA) legislation in the U.S. was designed to fix that lack of universality and market imperfection through an incentive-based system financed in part by employer mandates. In addition to providing a source of user/patient finance, the mandates, as will be described, are also to prevent free-riding in the newly created health market. Several forms of asymmetric information in the health care market present the most important sources of market failure/imperfections. Arrow's work (1963) was the first major examination of these information asymmetries in the functional policy area of health care. Even with the introduction of scores of medical governmental websites providing general information on diseases and treatments as well as specific information on individual doctors in developed countries particularly the U.S. (some websites legitimate and others not), consumers of healthcare are better informed but continue to be at an informational disadvantage relative to healthcare professionals. This is particularly true in underdeveloped countries where doctors and other medical professionals are scarce or even non-existent. In technical terms, consumers face "information asymmetry." Doctors possess the critical information necessary to diagnose the medical problem and to assess the benefits associated with the various treatment options. Additional asymmetries arise as consumers often must select doctors based on limited information. "Word of mouth" recommendations by other consumers of health care are not always reliable, as medical conditions differ and expectations for care vary across different consumers. In addition, since treatments will differ based on the specific doctor or patient, consumers will generally not possess the knowledge of the doctor's specific skills in diagnosis and/or treatment. The inability of consumers to know with certainty the timing of and/or even the need for medical care creates another possibility for market failure. The primary uncertainty involves future medical care expenses, which creates demand for some type of medical insurance.

Another motive for the government's involvement in the health care market is to perform its "redistributive" function where inequalities in access to basic services exist. Tobin (1970) argued that services like health care (and education) should not be conditioned on the individual's income level and justified government intervention as "specific egalitarianism." Although the recent debates over "Obamacare" in the U.S. have focused on providing health care to low income citizens, this concern for the poor in the U.S. is not new. Congressional support for the passage of the U.S. Medicare program in 1963 was due to the fact that nearly half of the elderly population at that time had no health insurance and many of these individuals had low income and/or wealth to draw on in the event of large medical expenses. As described below, the health care financing redistributes in two important ways. The first way is the most straightforward—low income individuals might receive free, government-provided health care or at most pay a heavily subsidized amount. Either approach could be accomplished through the direct government provision of health care directly or by subsidizing health care through means-tested premium discounts. The second redistribution is from healthy individuals to the less healthy. For example, the financing of the Social Health Insurance programs in many OECD countries and the U.S. Medicare program is by taxes paid on wage income. Generally this funding arrangement represents a redistribution of funds from the younger, relatively healthy working population to the older, less healthy population.

How Does Government Finance Health Care?

There are several problems that need to be addressed when considering the provision of health care in a country. The primary objective of many government health care systems in the OECD as well as other countries is to provide universal coverage across all citizens. This universality is most easily achieved through central government intervention, either through a governmental system of direct public healthcare provision or through the creation of private sector provision (e.g. coordinated with medical insurance plans) combined with government mandates requiring all citizens to participate. Universal coverage has benefits beyond it being socially responsible—health care being an important "right" of a country's citizens along with food and housing. Universal coverage allows for health care providers to spread the risk. Healthy people will be low-end users of health care and will ultimately subsidize the high-end, more sick users of health care expenditures. This should help keep the government's health care expenditures under control and strengthen the overall health market.

The financing structure of the health care system is a critical aspect of the broadening health care coverage. Health care in most countries is financed through a combination of government programs via taxes and direct private expenditures. This type of mixed financing can limit the ability to achieve universality, which requires a system where the benefits are independent of the financial contribution, meaning the contributions are by "ability to pay." A greater reliance on "ability to pay" requires a larger (perhaps 100 percent) contribution from the government. Private expenditures are represented by private health insurance, any payments for government provided health care, and for non-insured health care. The shares of public and private expenditures in health care vary considerably across developed countries. The U.S. has by far the greatest private health insurance percentage and the smallest public percentage (even after the Affordable Care Act or "Obamacare"). Other OECD countries also have significant private insurance markets—e.g. Australia, France, and Germany—but far smaller than in the U.S. One of the ways private insurance is used is as a supplement to existing government programs. These combinations are found in several OECD countries, with a major example being the various private plans associated with the U.S. Medicare program. The programs may also provide coverage for pharmaceuticals or for charges, such as co-payments, not otherwise covered by the government's health care plan. A large variation is present across non-OECD countries as well. With some exemptions, countries in Southeast Asia, Africa, and Latin America rely heavily on private health care coverage for their citizens. Titelman et al. (2014) note the most basic problem is the lack of fiscal resources available to generate tax revenues and the large informal and largely untaxed sectors found in many of these countries. Nevertheless, considerable progress toward universality has been made in several Latin American countries, such as Brazil and Cuba, to improve their health care systems. However, new tax policy and administration institutions will need to be developed that will not create incentives to evade taxes and to reduce the size of large informal labor markets. In addition, there is a general lack of coordination between the public and private health care sectors that can be found in the more developed countries. This lack of coordination creates great inefficiencies.

To expand briefly on the issue of informal economy, it is important because it represents about 17 percent of global GDP. Powerful disincentives to formalization exist in perverse public laws and regulations. Workers, smaller firms, and micro-entrepreneurs are driven to go underground by (1) social security infrastructure, such as mandatory payments, and (2) high tax burdens. For example, Italy's burden is 44 percent including direct and indirect taxes and social security contributions. The result is an informal sector of 20 percent of its GDP, and (3) rigid labor market regulations that make it hard to register businesses and hire/fire employees as product markets change. De Soto (1989) provided empirical evidence for the destructive effects on growth and equity of restrictive licensing on new businesses, bureaucratic red tape for services leading to corruption, and absence of clear land titles that prevent property use as collateral for bank credit in countries such as Peru and elsewhere. These institutional constraints prevent formalization and participation in the market economy and must be removed. Thus, how can incentives be changed to encourage conversion to formal status? In rural areas with poor services and infrastructure, there are fewer incentives to make the shift: the informal economy offers protective networks that substitute for the state with lower transaction costs and better efficiencies in reducing the impact of income shocks. Under such conditions there are few incentives to pay taxes on "undeclared work." In sub-Saharan Africa, 70 percent of the labor force is undeclared; 60 percent in Latin America; and 55 percent in

Asia and the post-Soviet economies. Informal economies also offer micro-entrepreneurs space to start up and experiment. If they become successful, such as moving from a corner kiosk to a small rented store, incentives to formalize increase (i.e. register and pay taxes) in order to have legal ownership, enforce contracts, and gain new access to credit for further expansion.

Better quality of government (less corrupt and bureaucratic process, better services, and needed infrastructure projects for basics such as health care and sanitation facilities) can also change incentives and induce formalization via greater willingness to pay taxes for actual service benefits. To provide incentives for formalization, public policies can: (1) reduce regulations, e.g. simplified licensing processes in Uganda and Mexico; (2) reduce tax burdens, e.g. Argentina, Peru, and Brazil have replaced their VATs, income taxes, and social security taxes with a single tax; and (3) reduce the amount of cash transactions, e.g. Italy has lowered the ceiling for cash payments from $15,000 to $1,200; Romania allows tax payments by bankcards, which increased its level of tax payments by card 34 percent in the first year of the reform (Dore, 2014: 49–53). Probably the best incentive to formalize economic behavior is to improve programs and services such as health care.

Informal labor markets and the lack of organized, well-functioning tax structures are much smaller problems in the developed countries. Many OECD countries, for instance, Switzerland in 1996, France in 2000, and Germany in 2009, have adopted universal health care coverage through financing using general tax revenues. These revenues have been used to contract systems of private and/or public providers of health care, involving doctors, drug programs, and other forms of health care. Some countries such as Britain refer to their core public health care institution as a National Health Service (NHS). The second type of program is through a network of taxes, typically on employment earnings, where all individuals are "mandated" to enroll. In the cases where individuals are unemployed or at a low income level, the state may provide the necessary fee payments through a subsidy to forgive the payment. This type of system is known as Social Health Insurance (SHI). Although they involve distinct operations and revenue sources, some countries employ a mixture of these two types. The use of private medical insurance, if used at all, represents a small part of health care coverage in most OECD countries, with, as mentioned above, the primary exception being the U.S. health care system.

NHS and SHI programs can be compared in two basic ways. The first is to determine the relative effectiveness on health and other outcomes as a result of these programs. The standard economic model of competition reveals benefits associated with lower competitive prices and greater "outcomes," measured by improved health outcomes. Since a standard characteristic of government provision is that either the government provides health care directly or that it will regulate prices, then "nonprice" or "quality" measures as a result of competition must be examined. One of those performance measures is waiting times for service. In their review of the literature examining waiting times, Stabile and Thomson (2013) found some evidence of reduced waiting times as a direct result of competitive forces, but there was also some mixed evidence on the quality impact. Some studies found an increase in death rates and length of stays in competitive hospitals, particularly between public and private hospitals, while other studies found decreases in death rates and hospital stay lengths.

The second comparison is by the relative equity and efficiency of the government taxes used to fund the program (i.e. the input design issue). The NHS or the equivalent programs employ general taxes and user fees, and the SHI programs employ some form of social insurance contributions usually collected from employees. General tax revenues used for NHS programs could come from several different sources, including income, value added, and/or general sales taxes. Standard public finance tools can be used to evaluate these taxes for equity and economic efficiency and will depend on which taxes are used. For example, income taxes can be progressive—that is, average taxes paid by consumers increase as incomes increase. On the other hand, value-added taxes and other consumption taxes may not be as progressive. However, when considering how the revenue is spent, the ultimate net progressivity will obviously depend on both the tax burden and the health care beneficiaries. The goals of this transfer (or conversion) of revenues into health care expenditures is to recognize the externalities associated with health care, to improve the health outcomes across all citizens, to promote the redistribution of health care toward the poor.

All general taxes used to fund NHS and the labor taxes used to fund SHI programs have potential negative effects on economic behavior (e.g. labor supply, savings, investment, and risk taking) and therefore are economically inefficient. Every tax increase creates income and substitution effects. While both these effects reduce the quantity demanded of the taxed good, they will work in opposite directions with income taxes. Taxes on income will obviously reduce income and this income effect causes people to reduce their leisure taking (considered a "normal" good) and work more. At the same time, because the wage has been reduced by this tax, the substitution effect means the opportunity of cost of leisure (defined by the rate of return to work hours) goes down and leisure becomes more attractive. It is this substitution effect causing individuals to work less as a result of taxes that creates the economic inefficiencies associated with taxes and raises the cost of taxation beyond the revenue collected. These offsetting effects mean the theoretical effect on labor supply is ambiguous. These two effects also work in opposite directions when considering an individual's decision to save and take on risk. An efficient tax system is defined by its ability to minimize the distortions on economic decisions. Of course, if different revenue sources are used, it is impossible to measure the exact equity and efficiency conditions associated with health care taxes.

As with all government activities, different expenditures compete for the budgetary allocation and, consequently, governments are unlikely to fully fund health care through general revenue. In many cases, general tax revenues are supplemented by private point of service contributions from the health care demanders. These contributions are a form of cost sharing with the public or private provider of health care. They can come in a variety of forms—co-payments (fixed amounts per doctor or health care establishment visit) and deductibles (amounts charged before health care payments are made by the program) are common in private insurance plans. User fees are standard in government-provided health care programs, but they have a bigger role in the lower-income countries. According to Schokkaert and Van de Voorde (2011), these contributions cover nearly 50 percent of total expenditures on health care in the low- and middle-income countries and about 15 percent in the high-income countries. They represent over 75 percent of health care expenditures in Myanmar, Guinea, Pakistan, Afghanistan, Georgia, and India.

User fees have two distinct roles in the health care market. The most obvious role is that they reduce the reliance on general tax revenues necessary to pay for expanded health care. However, they can also improve efficiency in the health care market as a form of prices used to allocate services across the citizens. Within a system of health insurance, user fees can have the effect of reducing moral hazard, making the market more efficient as consumers have to consider a partial price for service when they make health care decisions. As noted, health care insurance requires a broad risk pool and financing fee or tax if everyone in the pool or market is to benefit from quality coverage. Since medical care is like any good, attaching fees for this service could, without subsidies or conditions, reduce the demand for it, which will most adversely affect the poor that need both preventive and curative care. As Blomqvist (2011) indicates, the necessity of considering the administrative cost of user fees also means determining the optimal level of fees. There is considerable empirical evidence that wealthy citizens have a much higher willingness to pay for health care services, which indicates that even at modest fees, the poor could be "priced out" of health care. In short, it must be determined how sensitive or elastic health care demand is to user fee charges. Any increase in the user charge will increase revenue from those using the health care service but could also reduce revenues as citizens may stop using the health care.

If the demand for health care is not particularly responsive to price (demand is said to be price "inelastic"), then the demand for health care is relatively unaffected by these higher fees and user fee increases are expected to raise health care revenue. On the other hand, if demand for health care is responsive (price "elastic"), then revenues are expected to go down as usage goes down. Schokkaert and Van de Voorde (2011) review the empirical evidence measuring elasticity and find demand is responsive to price and user charges reduce the consumption of health care (and prescription drugs in the U.S.) in both high- and low-income countries. Indeed, there is some evidence that the elimination of user fees in 20 African countries would reduce the amount of health-related deaths by between 150,000 and 300,000. In order to target individuals in poverty, Schokkaert and Van de Voorde (2011) describe policies that are employed to lower user fees for the poor and/or chronically ill or to apply caps on these fees based on individual/family incomes. The disadvantages to these policies are that they involve considerable administrative oversight and since wealthy individuals can also be chronically ill, there will be some leakage. Gertler and Hammer (1997) review the many studies that have been carried out in Burkina Faso, Cote d'Ivoire, Ghana, Kenya, Indonesia, Mali, Nigeria, Pakistan, Peru, and the Philippines, and they conclude that demand for health care is generally inelastic overall but does vary based on income and age. Indeed, some of the studies indicate user fee increases cause a greater reduction in health care utilization by lower-income citizens and children. These are two groups who governments would generally want to support with health care expenditures. As might be expected, an additional finding using data from China and the U.S. is that the utilization of health care for severe illnesses is more price inelastic relative to regular care utilization.

User fees can be used to reallocate and promote spending priorities across particular health care activities. Since there is a price effect on the demand for health services, an increase in user fees for certain, less desirable, health programs will decrease demand as well as the required government general revenue subsidy. A corresponding decrease in user fees for the more desirable health programs should increase the utilization but will require greater government general revenue subsidies, which are now available from the other program. One limitation is that government revenues may be syphoned off to other government expenditures rather than as subsidies for other health activities.

Since they may have a negative effect on health care utilization, it is appropriate to determine the impact of an increase in user fees on health outcomes. Stabile and Thomson (2013) review some of this empirical evidence. As substitute goods, user fees instituted on prescription drugs in Canada caused citizens to switch from drug treatments to doctor services and emergency rooms, particularly low-income individuals. They report similar findings from studies carried out in the UK, Netherlands, France, Finland, Australia, and U.S.

The typical SHI is funded by a combination of contributions from employees and government expenditures to fund the unemployed and retired. Blomqvist (2011) notes that under a plan that is compulsory, as it would need to be under universal health care, these contributions are equivalent to taxes. Moreover, he observes that the practices in some countries (e.g. Japan) have different employee contribution rates by employer and creates an equity problem where taxes are different for similar citizens ("horizontal equity"). The added characteristic with SHI programs is the need to use general revenue sources to fund anyone who is not making employee contributions. An important category of these citizens is the elderly, who will experience larger than average health care expenditures. As such, any analysis of the equity and efficiency characteristics of these taxes is identical to the ones described with general taxes under NHI. There are certain advantages associated with SHI programs which help to fund universal coverage, particularly in developed countries. To best administer such a program of employment taxes requires a significant formal labor sector where record keeping and expertise related to more sophisticated administrative requirements would be manageable. In addition, employment in a more urban sector is also beneficial. These conditions are less likely in less developed countries. The same issues of payment for service rendered that were described in NHS programs are also present in SHI. The payments made by workers may not be sufficient for the full health care benefit package, so enrollees may be required to pay user fees at the point of service.

Provision of Health Care

The type of government provision of health care is an important aspect to consider under any type of program. There are two basic ways medical care can be provided. Public provision is characterized by governments directly providing health care services through governmental hospitals and clinics where the healthcare professionals are all public sector employees. Although these are not common in the developed countries, other less developed and emerging countries have such systems. Indonesia promised a "single-payer" government-provided health care system by the end of 2014, making it the largest such system in the world (*Economist*, 2012b). Alternatively, privately run hospitals and clinics (and the health care professionals) could be compensated by the government at "fee for service." The U.S. Medicare program operates under this type of system. These are the extreme types, and various hybrid systems also exist. Other factors create different market conditions as well, including the assignment of citizens to doctors. The possibility of market competition increases the likelihood for great efficiency.

As Blomqvist (2011) describes, these various payment mechanisms create different incentives for the hospitals and health care providers. When doctors are government employees and paid a straight salary, then there is no incentive to see a large number of patients, which will increase queuing and waiting times for service. Hospitals under a fixed governmental budget will have similar incentives and, as a result, generate greater waiting times for health care. Fee for service care will create greater incentives to see more patients and potentially provide more efficient health care with shorter queuing and waiting times to see doctors. Fees for health services, it should be noted, can also create perverse incentives by inducing staff to treat as many patients as possible with less attention to quality of care in order to be reimbursed by the insurance firm and or government programs. Blomqvist (2011) lists other limits to market competition in health care. One important characteristic of a competitive market is full information of all market participants, and one critical characteristic of the health care market is the presence of asymmetric information (discussed more fully below) with regards to diagnoses, potential treatments, and the payments for these services. Which mechanism is most efficient? On the one hand, productive or cost efficiency through the government setting of health care professionals' salaries and hospital budgets can potentially be achieved by keeping health care costs under control. On the other hand, allocative efficiency of medical care provision might best be achieved through a fee for service system which might encourage at least limited competition in the health care market.

Another approach to improving health resource allocation is the use of performance-based transfers from public budgets (often subnational governments). Similar to that used for education (described in *Chapter 6*), funding formulae are linked to subnational health needs. In Punjab province (Pakistan), for example, each provincial district (local government) automatically receives 70 percent of the base allocation. To claim the remaining 30 percent, the district must improve performance according to defined indicators, such as the proportion of babies delivered at a health facility or by a skilled birth attendant and the proportion of fully immunized children ages 18–30 months. This approach gives Punjab's districts an incentive to improve health outcomes (Fan and Gassman, 2014: 13). Other countries have successfully used the incentive approach to improve health services. For example, the national government of Rwanda conditions payments to subnational public and providers on the amounts and quality of services for HIV/AIDS patients and mothers. Payments are approved on the basis of independent and representative audits of performance reports. The Argentinian national government bases 60 percent of its health transfers to provinces on enrollment in the *Plan Nacer* to reduce newborn deaths and provide prenatal care. The other 40 percent of the transfer is based on improvements in health care coverage and outcomes. From 2004 to 2008, neonatal mortality decreased by 22 percent (Fan and Gassman, 2014: 14). Finally, the Indian national health insurance program (RSBY) provides incentives for each state to buy into the program. District-level private insurers are motivated to enroll as many people as they wish to maximize revenues. Beginning in 2007, the program now enrolls more than 100 million people with a relatively generous hospitalization package. Early results suggest that fewer people have been impoverished because of out-of-pocket health payments (Fan and Gassman, 2014: 14).

As described in the Indian example, competition has an important role in the individual's choice of health care plans. The private plans offered by the provincial agencies were on the basis of best-value premiums. Such plans can be offered within systems where health care is provided through private insurance. Plans with different benefits, co-pays, deductibles, and fees could be offered to the prospective health care consumer. These different plans could then compete for the citizen's adoption, as in Obamacare through competitive insurance exchanges and similarly designed institutions in Germany and Switzerland. This competition creates incentives for the health care professionals in each of these health care coverage plans to keep costs and fees down.

Application of Policy Analytic Frameworks: Public Sector Responses to Infectious Diseases in Poor Countries

At the first technical level, research and experience indicates that health systems have to choose between cost, coverage, and choice. The trade-offs are evident in the policy options produced and faced by decision-makers in OECD countries on a regular basis. In developing countries, most patients are poor, though wealthier strata can opt out and find private providers, often physicians moonlighting from public systems. The vast majority of poor face low service coverage and curative care quality. The socioeconomic cost to the government is usually high from high-cost drug imports and inefficient local systems design. This constrains coverage of the population for basic preventive and curative care services. Such relationships and results are well-known and empirically tested in widely different contexts. The design of effective health policies and operational delivery systems to serve poor countries profits from an extensive set of case studies and comparisons from around the world by international health organizations such as WHO, the World Bank, PAHO in Latin America, and the UN in general. In other words, the elements of effective systems are known as well as the consequences of not having them. Thus, when sudden outbreaks of infectious disease occur, such as the 2014 Ebola outbreak in three African countries, resources are scarce but effective responses are known.

In addition to the lack of universality of health care, there is perhaps a larger problem of insufficient medical resources (World Bank, 2004). Insufficiency becomes a particularly acute problem when countries face large public health disasters such as widespread infectious disease. There are countless examples of the occurrence of infectious disease in world history and governmental efforts to control epidemics or to eradicate the disease through its health care policies and implementing institutions. One finds clear distinctions across countries in the response effectiveness and impact on epidemics, which is usually based on income. The reality of many of these outbreaks and associated deaths and illnesses is that they are preventable with adequate level of common public health measures and medical responses. Unfortunately, these common preventive and curative care standards, availability of drugs, technologies, and trained personnel are more often inadequate in the developing countries. For example, diarrheal diseases are responsible for the more than two-thirds of childhood deaths in developing countries. However, simple hand washing with soap would reduce transmission of the disease and would significantly reduce the incidence of death. Unfortunately, because of the lack of a communication infrastructure in many developing countries, this public health information on good hygiene practices is not readily available, particularly in those areas (e.g. rural areas) where it could do the most good. Again, these problems are easily foreseeable and effective responses to them have been tested and applied in many contexts.

Weak responses are expected where health services lack basic resources as in many developing countries. Although some progress has been made to reach the three health goals in the United Nations Millennium Development Goals, Africa lags behind other developing regions in the maternal mortality rate, HIV/AIDS mortality rate, and life expectancy. The World Bank (2004) documents the inadequate levels of medical personnel in many African countries—for example, 3.4 physicians per 100,000 people in Burkina Faso, 6.9 physicians per 100,000 people in Zambia. This is compared to the developed country average of over 300 physicians per 100,000 people. Low pay and poor living conditions present more attractive opportunities outside of the African countries and create the conditions for the exodus of healthcare workers. The healthcare workers that remain are found in the urban areas and not in the rural areas where the public health needs are greater. Patients also engage in "medical tourism" by evacuating to neighboring countries in search of adequate health care. Libyans traveled to Tunisia for basic medical care and patients from Chad traveled to the Sudan for vaccinations. The Tunisian health care system is a magnet because its indicators, specifically no malaria and low rates of HIV/AIDS and maternal mortality, as well as a relatively long life expectancy, rank at the top of countries in North Africa. Great strides have taken place in a few African countries to achieve universality. About 90 percent of Tunisians are covered by health insurance plans funded by employee contributions and, for those who are not employed, government expenditures. This favorable medical structure is attributed to its history of French colonialism. Ethiopia also has made progress in reaching universal health care. The 85 percent health care coverage has improved infant mortality rates and reduced maternal mortality.

Shortages in medical personnel have been severely felt in the Ebola outbreak in the West African countries of Liberia, Guinea, Sierra Leone, and, to a lesser extent, Nigeria. Each of these countries had thousands of cases that were increasing at an alarming rate, resulting in high rates of death. To combat this outbreak, Liberia had 51 physicians for its entire population of 4.3 million. One result of this shortage in health care was that officials in Sierra Leone admitted "defeat" in fighting the progression of the outbreak and urged families to keep the infected people at home. In addition to the shortages of personnel and drugs, there was also a shortage of basic medical supplies like gloves and gowns. That meant that these countries experienced Ebola mortality rates two to three times higher than probably would have occurred in more developed countries. Indeed, even with the dire predictions, the World Health Organization cautioned policy-makers that the outbreak was being underreported—potentially three times higher incidence than that reported. The differential effect of these resource shortages has been observed with other outbreaks. When Marburg hemorrhagic fever (a disease related to Ebola) broke out in Germany and Yugoslavia in 1967, the health systems of those countries were able to keep the mortality rates low, even though the health systems had not completely recovered from the destruction of World War II (Boozary et al., 2014). The expectations were that the Ebola outbreak would be a major health concern in the developed countries but one that would be quite manageable within their basic health care structures. These expectations were correct.

But the impact of the outbreak extended beyond the individual toll of illness and death, as the economies of these regional African countries were dramatically affected by the outbreak. The agricultural sector was disrupted as the transportation and export of goods from these countries was restricted. The World Bank (2014) forecasted a human toll of nearly 1.5 million people infected and an economic loss of more than $32 billion.

The Ebola outbreak in the West African countries, as well as other infectious disease medical disasters, is an example of the strain created on the otherwise insufficient medical systems found in many underdeveloped countries. Although these systems are, in large part, the result of inadequate government resources that are part of competing budgetary demands, the weaknesses of the delivery systems are not the same in all countries. In fact, some have reformed their systems despite lack of resources.

At the second or political economy level, the political, cultural, and/or institutional sources of economic efficiency/effectiveness need to be identified and weighed in importance. The general question is why some poor countries in a particular region responded more effectively to such outbreaks than others? This is the second level of explanation. Assuming partly or fully dilapidated health care systems, was it political culture that constrained results? Were institutional incentives misaligned? Was lack of political regime support a problem? These explanations are needed before more money is allocated to health care systems to avoid wastage and more inefficiency.

As noted in the *Chapter 1* discussion of the case of British health care policies, the effective provision of health care is a function of institutional performance and the effects of political cultures. Though the 2014 Ebola outbreak started in Guinea, its epidemic was not as acute as in neighboring Liberia and Sierra Leone. What explains this? First, it might be noted that the medical infrastructure and access to basic health-related services such as clean water was much higher in Guinea: 83 percent access to water versus 11 percent in Liberia and 25 percent in Sierra Leone. In addition, the affected countries have received different levels of international assistance from former colonial overseers: France to Guinea, America to Liberia, and Britain to Sierra Leone. This support represented more than funding and was linked inextricably to laws and cultural practices in the health sectors of the respective more advanced country suppliers. Finally, weaknesses in state institutions, particularly in Sierra Leone, were illustrated by recurring strikes and the inability or unwillingness to pay health workers hazardous duty pay, prevent bribery from releasing infected bodies to relatives who wanted a traditional burial (more cultural effects), and controlling shortages of gloves that ended up on the black market instead of in clinics. These institutional weaknesses diminished the effectiveness of responses to the Ebola outbreak (*Economist*, 2014b: 50).

In general, poor countries have seen significant improvement in providing universal health care, even in the face of underdevelopment. Two factors have been important: (1) clear universal care mandates, and (2) decentralized system designs within overall structures of normative centralization. First, effective poor country health systems have clear government mandates to provide this health care to all of its citizens. Ghana is a good example of this. Like other African countries, it had a seriously high rate of maternal mortality in the early 2000s. In 2004, the country's government made a critical health policy decision to exempt women from delivery care costs in all health facilities. This effort was initially funded by the World Bank/IMF debt relief fund initiative, the Highly Indebted Poor Countries (HIPC). Eventually Ghana moved to a national health plan that paid for this care. Although there has been considerable improvement, many of Ghana's women continue to give birth outside of these health care centers and maternal deaths remain too high.

Second, delivery systems have been decentralized and accountable to local populations. Outside of Africa, Cuba is an example of a country with an excellent medical system even though its personal income levels are also low. Its low infant mortality rate ranks at the top end among all developing countries and it also compares favorably with many developed countries. The Cuban health system can be characterized by the provision of clear instructions to medical advisors, staff motivation, and, perhaps most important, constant monitoring and evaluations of the system. This has allowed the government to put an emphasis on placing doctors in rural areas, where there had been severe resource deficiencies. The government has established opportunities for public involvement and confidence in the system by providing health indicators and carrying out routine inspections of health facilities. Although Cuba has not faced a severe outbreak like the Ebola outbreak in West Africa, its tight healthcare structure makes it better able to sustain such a crisis. Thus, institutions must be properly designed with built-in political and fiscal incentives to deliver health care effectively. The central government role in such crises is to absorb international assistance and ensure that the proper lessons of international practice are being applied.

Thus, the third level of comparative analysis should be performed at the center, by national health ministries that allow them to apply lessons quickly of what might work and what would probably not. In the case of Ebola, the outbreak was in an African region, which permitted opportunities for an almost naturally controlled experiment. Similar conditions in all three countries allowed for focus on the local explanations for differences in health care system response to Ebola.

Pharmaceuticals

Another important aspect of medical care is the role of pharmaceutical drugs in basic treatment. Essential drugs are needed to produce the healthy people who can work and earn incomes in the economy. For this reason, they need to be available and affordably priced. The pricing of medications is part of our larger discussion of user fees. Significant government regulations affect the pharmaceutical industry because of the presence of asymmetric information, which is a major characteristic of health care. Most advanced country governments require companies to undertake rigorous and substantial clinical tests to determine drug efficacy. In addition to determining effectiveness, government regulations provide greater consumer confidence by limiting the ability of drug companies and medical professionals to overstate drug benefits and understand the risks. Although there are benefits associated with pharmaceutical regulations, they routinely slow the drug approval process and, as a result, possibly delay the distribution of much needed medication. Danzon (2011) warned against the possibility of increased recall of inadequately tested medications if such gatekeeping regulations were relaxed. The combination of asymmetric information and the relatively inelastic consumer demand for pharmaceuticals also affects pricing decisions and without proper regulation can lead to patient gouging. In addition, as noted by Danzon (2011), demand is even more inelastic in those countries where health insurance provides drug coverage or in those countries where governments provide drug price subsidies. As described above, the presence of various forms of user fees (e.g. co-pays) reinserts some price effects. Generic drugs, which will appear in many countries after the patent has expired and if the patented drug is profitable, also provide an opportunity to price compete. Of course, their success will be a function of the health care provider's willingness to prescribe them.

Drug costs constitute a large and growing proportion of health care cost in many underdeveloped countries—nearly 50 percent of health care costs in China and India (*Economist*, 2014a: 10). The research and development of new drugs in many countries benefit from the ability to be protected from competition by a government acquired patent. Because patents block entry of rival producers, the producer of the drug will have monopoly power and, as a result, charge a price greater than the cost of producing the good and certainly greater than a competitive market price. Of course, since research and development of these potentially life-saving drugs is critical, then the drug patents benefit both the industries and the patients. Drug companies could lessen the impact of these higher drug prices through such means as creating systems of "tiered pricing." Companies could charge different prices based on national income—e.g. higher prices to the U.S. and EU countries and lower prices to the underdeveloped countries in Africa. As explained in *Economist* (2014a: 10) (and in a second case that appears in this chapter, *Case 4.1*), pharmaceutical firms do increase their profits by using this type of discriminatory pricing as they charge higher prices to customers in higher income countries who have more inelastic demands for drugs. This allows the firms to expand their markets. The Swiss pharmaceutical company Roche has substantial experience with marketing lower-priced drugs in India and Egypt. But there are risks to "tiered pricing." As with all discriminatory pricing, profit maximization requires separating the groups of people who face different prices. If people can buy up the low-priced drugs in one country and then sell them in an alternative market in the high-priced countries, then the firm's profits will be negatively affected and patients in the first country cheated out of proper health treatment by corruption.

As described, some drug costs cannot be reduced until after the patents have expired. Developed country allowance of tiered pricing for firms (perhaps in exchange for continued patent protection) could push the issue down to poor countries. At the country level, local regulators would have to be able to control the resulting corruption. Drug pricing, particularly under the common national health insurance systems, must balance several considerations. If insurance creates prices that are too low, then consumers may be inclined to over-medicate (perhaps doctors will also be less price sensitive, as well). On the other hand, prices need to be high enough to encourage pharmaceutical companies to engage in research and development.

Medical Insurance

Consumers generally prefer constant levels of consumption over periods of high consumption and low consumption. When the future is uncertain, insurance is valuable to the consumer because it smooths out consumption. Consumers pay a premium to protect against the uncertainty of adverse outcomes. This action reduces consumption from relatively higher consumption levels (where there is lower marginal utility of consumption) to pay for protection to maintain consumption (with a higher marginal utility of consumption) in the event of adverse events. However, although consumers will maximize their expected utility levels by purchasing actuarially fair insurance, they will face a lower cost for medical care, which may introduce other market imperfections. This "moral hazard" problem arises under these conditions.

While there is an asymmetric information problem when the medical professionals know more than the consumer, it is also the case with insurance markets that the insured know more about their medical conditions than the insurers. Insurance companies will survive financially as long as they can insure individuals who have the lowest chance of an adverse outcome (low-risk). To pay for the high-risk, insurance prices will be set as the average between the high- and low-risk groups and, in the extreme condition, only customers who face the highest adverse outcome result will purchase insurance. The consequence of this "adverse selection" problem is that insurance companies will lose money under these conditions and will be forced to stop providing the insurance to consumers of both types. Because of the likely possibility of adverse selection, there is a need for a "risk pool" of insured and, as a result, employers are the primary providers of private health insurance in the U.S. Indeed, nearly 100 percent of large firms (more than 200 employees) provide some type of health insurance as an employee benefit. It is unlikely that employees choose their employer, particularly larger employers, based on their health status. As a result, employer provided health insurance naturally creates these health pools. An additional benefit of larger employer pools is that average administrative costs of the insurance fall with the size of the employee pool.

But the reliance on employer-provided health plans creates a large gap of health coverage with unemployed workers or those employed individuals who do not have an employer-sponsored plan (e.g. non full-time employment or the self-employed may not be eligible for the health care benefit). These individuals may decide not to purchase medical insurance coverage. One reason for this decision not to insure is that the cost of individual private medical insurance, depending on the level of the coverage, can be prohibitive. A second reason is that consumers believe they have a low probability of being sick enough to require medical care. This factor is particularly acute in the U.S., as many hospitals are required to provide emergency care, even if the consumer does not have medical insurance. This regulation creates a moral hazard problem, as consumers do not face the true cost of the trip to the hospital, therefore reducing the consumer's penalty for the decision not to self-insure. Given the informational asymmetries described above, individuals may not be assessing their risk accurately.

There are costs associated with the lack of individual health care coverage. One cost is due to the potential externality associated with communicable diseases that can be controlled through vaccines, pharmaceuticals, and/or other public health measures. There may be paternalistic and/or equity justifications for government provision of health care. One governmental solution is the direct provision or subsidization of universal health care. Alternatively, under a health insurance system, this could be accomplished through the imposition of an individual mandate requiring all consumers to have health insurance at a certain level of coverage (e.g. Obamacare). This policy creates large risk pools among groups of newly enrolled individuals which should lower the overall risk and allow the insurance companies to avoid the losses and encourage the provision of coverage.

Adverse selection does not necessarily involve a market failure. Because most consumers are risk adverse, they will opt to purchase insurance in the private market at a premium (a price higher than the actuarially fair premium). Alternatively, the insurer could provide policies at different prices (e.g. Obamacare) based on premiums, deductibles, co-payments, co-insurance, and coverage levels. It is expected that individuals will reveal their health riskiness, and therefore reduce the adverse selection, by their choice of health care policy. These coverage provisions describe the terms of the split between the insured and the insurance company's financial responsibilities and define the plan's generosity. Coverage can range from no patient responsibility for health care expenses to a requirement of partial for some to full payment (i.e. no insurance coverage) for other specific medical expenses. Of course, the purpose of medical insurance is to reduce the loss of income as a result of a medical event. The efficient level of health care is where the marginal benefit of the care is equal to the actual marginal cost. However, consumers of health care with insurance (or even government-provided health care) face at most a co-payment and/or deductible which by definition is a fraction of this marginal cost of medical care. Consequently, too much of the service will be demanded, relative to the economically efficient level. This represents a clear trade-off between the efficient use of medical care priced at the actual marginal cost and the protection against income loss (consumption smoothing) associated with the use of medical insurance. The insurance companies must also have a financial arrangement with the medical professionals regarding the reimbursement of expenses.

Conclusion

The incidence of extreme poverty in the world remains a serious problem, even though some progress has been made in some of the countries where inequities are the greatest. The established "remedy" for extreme poverty, economic growth, has not been the solution, and governments have stepped in to provide social safety nets consisting of a patchwork of programs, both cash and in-kind. All governments, particularly the governments of underdeveloped countries, have severe budget constraints that force critical choices regarding eligibility for assistance. There is some evidence of a *generation phase*, wherein there is high demand for health care among those suffering because of extreme poverty. Poverty, as noted, hits hardest those individuals who may not be able to benefit fully from this economic growth, e.g. the retired, young, disabled, and others with special needs. One of the largest of these government programs to deal with the unequal impact of growth is health care. In theory, all countries would attempt to eliminate poverty and/or provide universal health coverage and do so by minimizing the costs of production, delivery, and access to this assistance. This chapter described the difficulties faced by countries as to establish redistributive "ability to pay" tax systems as well as the incentives on the demanders and suppliers of these services that make the achievement of this goal quite impossible. While these goals may be present, the lack of a formal labor market and the insufficiency of resources make the development of a well-functioning redistributive tax systems unlikely. As a consequence, poverty will continue and the limited health coverage provided in most countries will rely more heavily on private contributions.

Various rules and regulations regarding program development and functioning ultimately affect the costs associated with all types of assistance. These rules are in place to attempt to control the costs associated with the provision of benefits and involve the identification of eligible participants, the transmission of benefits, and any required assessment measures. Failure to review and control health care cost increases caused by leakage increases the costs of the programs and further strains government budgets.

Cases and Exercises

1   Read *Case 4.1* on the Swiss proposal to give every citizen a monthly income and answer the questions following:

Case 4.1   Swiss Monthly Income Proposal

Source: Lowrey, 2013

This fall, a truck dumped eight million coins outside the Parliament building in Bern, one for every Swiss citizen. It was a publicity stunt for advocates of an audacious social policy that just might become reality in the tiny, rich country. Along with the coins, activists delivered 125,000 signatures — enough to trigger a Swiss public referendum, this time on providing a monthly income to every citizen, no strings attached. Every month, every Swiss person would receive a check from the government, no matter how rich or poor, how hardworking or lazy, how old or young. Poverty would disappear.

The proposal is, in part, the brainchild of a German-born artist named Enno Schmidt, a leader in the basic-income movement. Schmidt told me, "What would you do if you had that income? What if you were taking care of a child or an elderly person?" Schmidt said that the basic income would provide some dignity and security to the poor, especially Europe's underemployed and unemployed. It would also, he said, help unleash creativity and entrepreneurialism: Switzerland's workers would feel empowered to work the way they wanted to, rather than the way they had to just to get by. And it's not only in vogue in wealthy Switzerland. Beleaguered and debt-wracked Cyprus is weighing the implementation of basic incomes, too. They even are whispered about in the United States, where certain wonks on the libertarian right and liberal left have come to a strange convergence around the idea.

The case from the right is one of expediency and efficacy. Let's say that Congress decided to provide a basic income through the tax code or by expanding the Social Security program. Such a system might work better and be fairer than the current patchwork of programs, including welfare, food stamps and housing vouchers. Even better, conservatives think, such a program could significantly reduce the size of our federal bureaucracy. It could take the place of welfare, food stamps, housing vouchers and hundreds of other programs, all at once. The left is more concerned with the power of a minimum or basic income as an anti-poverty and pro-mobility tool. In the mid-1970s, the tiny Canadian town of Dauphin acted as guinea pig for a grand experiment in social policy called "Mincome." For a short period of time, all the residents of the town received a guaranteed minimum income. About 1,000 poor families got monthly checks to supplement their earnings. Evelyn Forget, a health economist at the University of Manitoba, has done some of the best research on the results. Some of her findings were obvious: Poverty disappeared. But others were more surprising: High-school completion rates went up; hospitalization rates went down. "If you have a social program like this, community values themselves start to change," Forget said.

---

a   Why might this type of guaranteed income be more economically efficient than the existing redistribution programs like welfare, food stamps, and housing vouchers?

b   What are some of the political economy barriers to the enactment of such a program in the U.S.?

2   Read *Case 4.2* on drug pricing in India and answer the questions following:

Case 4.2 Indian Pharmaceutical Drug Pricing

Source: *Economist*, 2014a: 10

Of all the goods and services traded in the market economy, pharmaceuticals are perhaps the most contentious. Innovation accounts for most of the cost of production, so the price of drugs is much higher than their cost of manufacture, making them unaffordable to many poor people. Firms protect the intellectual property that drugs represent and sue those who try to manufacture and sell patented drugs cheaply. For all these reasons, pharmaceutical companies are widely regarded as vampires who exploit the sick and ignore the sufferings of the poor. Arguments over drugs pricing are rising again. Activists are suing to block the patenting in India of a new Hepatitis C drug that has just been approved by American regulators. But the main battlefield is the Trans-Pacific Partnership (TPP), a proposed trade deal between countries in Asia and the Americas. The parties have yet to reach agreement, partly because of the drug-pricing question. Under the Trade Related Aspects of Intellectual Property Rights, a deal signed in 1994, governments can allow a generic drug maker to produce a patented medicine. America—home of most of the world's big pharma, whose consumers pay the world's highest prices for drugs and thus keep down prices for others—wants to use the TPP to restrict such compulsory licenses to infectious epidemics, while emerging-market countries want to make it harder for drug firms to win patents.

The resurgence of conflict over drug pricing is the result not of a sudden emergency, but of broad, long-term changes. Rich countries want to slash health costs. In emerging markets, people are living longer and getting rich-country diseases. This is boosting demand for drugs for cancer, diabetes, and other chronic ailments. In emerging markets, governments want to expand access to treatment, but drugs already account for a large share of health-care spending—44 percent and 43 percent in India and China respectively, compared with 12 percent in Britain and America. By varying their prices more— charging Americans and Britons more than Africans—firms can pep up their profits at the same time as expanding their markets, making both shareholders and the sick better off. Some companies are trying this. Roche, a Swiss company, has created new brands and packaging for lower-priced drugs in India and Egypt. But there are risks to so-called "tiered pricing," People may buy drugs in low-price countries and sell them at a profit in high-price ones.

---

a   Why does this type of discriminatory price increase the firm's profits?

b   What types of methods are used in other discriminatory pricing situations to separate out the two types of demanders?

c   Is there evidence that patents encourage new drug innovations?

3   Read *Case 4.3* on Asia's health care revolution and answer the questions following:

Case 4.3 Asia's Next Revolution: Health Care

Source: *Economist*, 2012b: 11–12

Thanks to years of spectacular growth, more people have been pulled from abject poverty in modern Asia than at any other time in history. But as they become more affluent, the region's citizens want more from their governments. Across the continent, pressure is growing for public pensions, national health insurance, unemployment benefits and other hallmarks of social protection. As a result, the world's most vibrant economies are shifting gear, away from simply building wealth towards building a welfare state. The speed and scale of this shift are mind-boggling. Last October Indonesia's government promised to provide all its citizens with health insurance by 2014. It is building the biggest "single-payer" national health scheme—where one government outfit collects the contributions and foots the bills—in the world. In just two years China has extended pension coverage to an additional 240m rural folk, far more than the total number of people covered by Social Security, America's public-pension system. A few years ago about 80 percent of people in rural China had no health insurance. Now virtually everyone does. In India some 40m households benefit from a government scheme to provide up to 100 days' work a year at the minimum wage, and the state has extended health insurance to some 110m poor people, more than double the number of uninsured in America.

The creation of Europe's welfare states took more than half a century. At a time when governments in the rich world are failing to redesign states to cope with ageing populations and gaping budget deficits, this could be another area where Asia leapfrogs the West. History offers many lessons for the Asians on what to avoid. Europe's welfare states began as basic safety nets. But over time they turned into cushions. That was partly because, after wars and the Depression, European societies made redistribution their priority, but also because the recipients of welfare spending became powerful interest groups. The eventual result, all too often, was economic sclerosis with an ever-bigger state. America has kept its safety net less generous, but has made mistakes in creating its entitlements system—including making unaffordable pension and health-care promises, and tying people's health insurance to their employment.

Asia's governments are acutely conscious of all this. They have little desire to replace traditions of hard work and thrift with a flabby welfare dependency. Asia also faces a number of peculiarly tricky problems. One is demography. Although a few countries, notably India, are relatively youthful, the region includes some of the world's most rapidly ageing populations. Today China has five workers for every old person. By 2035 the ratio will have fallen to two. In America, by contrast, the baby-boom generation meant that the Social Security system had five contributors per beneficiary in 1960, a quarter of a century after its introduction. It still has three workers for every retired person. Another problem is size, which makes welfare especially hard. The three giants—China, India and Indonesia—are vast places with huge regional income disparities within their borders. Building a welfare state in any one of them is a bit like creating a single welfare state across the European Union. Lastly, many Asian workers (in India it is about 90 percent) are in the "informal" economy, making it harder to verify their incomes or reach them with transfers.

a   What are the projections for the ratio of working citizens to social security beneficiaries in the U.S.? What are the other available funding options? What are the advantages/ disadvantages of these alternatives?

b   What are the advantages and disadvantages of Indonesia's "single payer" provision of health care rather than developing a health insurance framework?

References

Adolino, Jessica R. and Charles H. Blake (2011) *Comparing Public Policies: Issues and Choices in Industrialized Countries* (Washington, DC: CQ/Sage Press).

Arrow, Kenneth J., "Uncertainty and the Welfare Economics of Medical Care," *American Economic Review*, 53, 5 (December 1963): 941–973.

Barrientos, Armando (2013) *Social Assistance in Developing Countries* (Cambridge, UK: Cambridge University Press).

Birdsall, Nancy, Nora Lustig, and Darryl McLeod, "Declining Inequality in Latin America: Some Economics, Some Politics," Center for Global Development working paper #251, May 2011.

Blomqvist, Ake, "Public-Sector Health Care Financing," in *The Oxford Handbook of Health Economics*, Sherry Glied and Peter C. Smith, eds., Oxford: Oxford University Press, 2011: 257–284.

Bloom, David E., "The Shape of Global Health," *Finance and Development*, 51, 4 (December 2014): 6–11.

Boozary, Andrew S., Paul E. Farmer, and Ashish K. Jha, "The Ebola Outbreak, Fragile Health Systems, and Quality as a Cure," *The Journal of the American Medical Association* (November 12, 2014).

Coady, David, "Social Safety Nets," in *Public Expenditures, Growth, and Poverty: Lessons from Developing Countries*, Shenggen Fan, ed., Baltimore: The Johns Hopkins University Press, 2008: 147–183.

Coady, David, Bendict Clements, and Sanjeev Gupta, *The Economics of Public Health Care Reform in Advanced and Emerging Economies*, Washington, DC: International Monetary Fund, 2012.

Colasanto, Diane, Arie Kapteyn, and Jacques Van der Gaag, "Two Subjective Definitions of Poverty," *The Journal of Human Resources*, 19, 1 (Winter 1984): 127–138.

Danzon, Patricia M., "The Economics of the Biopharmaceutical Industry," in *The Oxford Handbook of Health Economics*, Sherry Glied and Peter C. Smith, eds., Oxford: Oxford University Press, 2011: 520–554.

De Soto, Hernando (1989) *The Other Path: The Invisible Revolution in the Third World* (New York: Harper Collins).

de Vos, Klaas and Thesia I. Garner, "An Evaluation of Subjective Poverty Definitions: Comparing Results from the U.S. and the Netherlands," *The Review of Income and Wealth*, 37, 3 (September 1991): 267–285.

Dore, Giovanna Maria Dora, "Shining a Light on the Shadow Economy," *The American Interest*, X, #3 (January/February 2014): 46–53.

Economist (2012a) "The Six-Peso Diet," September 8, p. 36.

Economist (2012b) "New Cradles to Graves," September 8, pp. 11–12.

Economist (2014a) "The New Drugs War: Pharmaceutical Pricing," January 4, p. 10.

Economist (2014b) "Exorcising the Deadly Fever," December 13, pp. 49–50.

Fan, Victoria and Amanda Gassman, "Going Local," *Finance and Development*, 51, 4 (December 2014): 12–15.

Gertler, Paul J. and Jeffrey S. Hammer, "Strategies for Pricing Publically Provided Health Services," World Bank working paper, March 1997, The World Bank, Policy Research Department, Washington, DC.

Hagenaars, Aldi and Klaas de Vos, "The Definition and Measurement of Poverty," *Journal of Human Resources*, 23, 2 (Spring 1988): 211–221.

Hanlon, Joseph, Armando Barrientos, and David Hulme (2010) *Just Give Money to the Poor* (Sterling, VA: Kumarian Press).

Lora, Eduardo, ed. (2007) *The State of State Reform in Latin America* (Washington, DC: Inter-American Development Bank).

Lowrey, Annie, "Switzerland's Proposal to Pay People for Being Alive," *New York Times Magazine*, November 17, 2013. Available online at www.nytimes.com/2013/11/17/magazine/switzerlands-proposal-to-pay-people-for-being-alive.html.

Lustig, Nora, George Gray-Molina, Sean Higgins, Miguel Jaramillo, Wilson Jimenez, Veronica Paz, Claudiney Pereira, Carola Pessino, John Scott, and Ernesto Yanez, "The Impact of Taxes and Social Spending on Inequality and Poverty in Argentina, Bolivia, Brazil, Mexico, and Peru: A Synthesis of Results," Commitment to Equity working paper, 2012 (New Orleans, LA: Tulane University; Washington, DC: Inter-American Dialogue).

Lustig, Nora, Carola Pessino, and John Scott, "The Impact of Taxes and Social Spending on Inequality and Poverty in Argentina, Bolivia, Brazil, Mexico, Peru, and Uruguay: Introduction to the Special Issue," *Public Finance Review*, 42, 3 (May 2014): 287–303.

Schokkaert, Erik and Carine Van de Voorde, "User Charges," in *The Oxford Handbook of Health Economics*, Sherry Glied and Peter C. Smith, eds., Oxford: Oxford University Press, 2011: 329–353.

Stabile, Mark and Sarah Thomson, "The Changing Role of Government in Financing Health Care: An International Perspective," NBER working paper #19439, September 2013, National Bureau of Economic Research, Cambridge, MA.

Titelman, Daniel, Oscar Cetrangolo, and Olga Lucia Acosta, "Universal Health Coverage in Latin American Countries: How to Improve Solidarity-Based Schemes," *The Lancet* (online), October 16, 2014. http://www.thelancet.com/journals/lancet/article/PIIS0140-6736%2814%2961780-3/fulltext

Tobin, James, "On Limiting the Domain of Inequality," *Journal of Law and Economics*, 13 (1970): 263–277.

Vaughan, Denton R., "Exploring the Use of the Public's Views to Set Income Poverty Thresholds and Adjust Them Over Time," *Social Security Bulletin,* 56, 2 (Summer 1993): 22–46.

World Bank (2004) *World Development Report 2004: Making Services Work for Poor People*, Chapter 8, Washington, DC: World Bank Group.

World Bank (2014) *The Economic Impact of the 2014 Ebola Epidemic: Short and Medium Term Estimates for West Africa,* Washington, DC: World Bank Group. Available online at http://documents.worldbank.org/curated/en/2014/10/20270083/economic-impact-2014-ebola-epidemic-short-medium-term-estimates-west-africa.

5 Financial Sector Policy

Introduction

A strong financial sector and an independent monetary policy are critical to increasing a country's economic growth and ensuring stabilization. The recent *Financial Development Report* (WEF, 2012) lists banking financial services, non-banking financial services, and financial markets as three of the "seven pillars of financial development." The report defines financial development as "the factors, policies, and institutions that lead to effective financial intermediation and markets, as well as deep and broad access to capital and financial services" and it summarizes the empirical studies linking financial development to economic growth. The World Bank (2014) also emphasizes the critical role played by a well-functioning financial market. In this book, the financial sector in the sense of rules and laws governing banking, finance, trade, and business is a critical component of the institutional context. To draw valid and relevant comparative lessons and to explain why sectoral policies work or not, the institutional contexts must be similar as noted in *Chapter 1*. The degree of institutional strength of financial sectors and the level of enforcement of their legal frameworks are thus critical to policy analysis at the second political economy level.

As discussed in *Chapter 2*, the relationship between public fiscal policy and the financial sector is or should be tight. Public policies at the strategic level must provide the proper legal and regulatory framework by: ensuring rule of law, enforcement of contracts, and macroeconomic risk management. It is this last requirement that broke down in 2008 when the financial system teetered on the brink of collapse and the biggest problem was lack of liquidity. At the operational level, banks were unable to finance themselves in the short-term debt markets and therefore unwilling to lend. That required massive interventions by central banks around the world to offer financial support. The crisis underscored the importance of proper governmental regulation of the financial sector.

The "central bank" plays a lead role in the financial sectors of most developed and underdeveloped/emerging market economies. It is generally charged with overseeing and regulating the country's commercial banking system. It is also the institution with the primary responsibility for carrying out the country's monetary policy. Note that the institutions responsible for fiscal policy (*Chapter 2*) and monetary policy in every country are separate and different: usually MOFs or treasuries for fiscal policies and central banks for monetary policies. Central banks know that the amount of money in the economy will determine the interest rates, which will then affect the amount of consumption and investment. As a result, the central bank is able to use various instruments to control the resources to affect the amount of money in the economy, which, in turn, affects the interest rate, the size of real resources, the rate of economic growth, the rate of inflation, and the value of the nation's currency. An important lesson of past financial crises, such as that in 1929, is that the financial and real economies move at different speeds. The market value of equities and household consumption behavior with new savings from cheap oil savings and lower produce prices are key variables in the financial economy. The underlying real economy of industries such as construction and housing firms is different. This means that central banking must be about more than interest rates. New "macro-prudential tools" such as raising capital, liquidity, and leverage requirements offer central banks more ways to curb excesses in equity markets and sectors with too much borrowing (*Economist*, 2015a: 26).

Governments and their central banks must decide on the appropriate interest rate goals in order to either defend their currencies (with higher interest rates) or reduce the risk of recession (with lower interest rates) but create inflationary pressures. Central bank independence from government control can vary by its ability to set monetary policy aggregates or its overall authority to determine its policy goals. As a consequence, the central bank's goals could be in direct conflict with the government regime's agenda. Before deciding on interest rate increases or decreases, central banks must delve into macroeconomic considerations. But unlike setting fiscal policy (described in *Chapter 2*), monetary policy is anticipatory, i.e. it will have a delayed impact on the economy. That means central bankers must be more forward-looking than even fiscal forecasters in ministries of finance and think tanks. Thus, measurement of current macroeconomic conditions and forecasts of the impact of new decisions are critical. Bankers will need to know unemployment rates and underlying labor force participation rates, as well as the core inflation (which excludes volatile energy and food commodity prices) in relation to bank inflation targets. With that arsenal of information, the bank can then estimate impacts on consumer spending; investment, which often links to business confidence; exports (e.g. possibly lower if rates are increased with corresponding upward pressure on the currency); and imports (i.e. cheaper if the currency value increases) (*Economist*, 2015d: 67). For example, central bankers may desire a reduction in inflation, which would require a reduced amount of aggregate demand, while government regimes may want to directly increase aggregate demand through higher spending and/or lower taxes, which will require debt to be purchased. With no independence, some country governments can require the central bank to "monetize" or purchase this government debt. Alternatively, central banks might be charged with doing the central government's "bidding."

This chapter: (1) describes the key characteristics of a country's financial structure; (2) examines the relationship between how the development of the financial structure aids the country's economic growth in the developing countries as well as critical public policy decisions that should be considered in these countries and in the developed countries; (3) describes the basic accounting structure of the assets, liabilities, and capital found in these banks since commercial banks are the primary institutions used to connect individual savers with businesses and individual investors in most countries; (4) presents models of financial crises in developed and developing countries; (5) reviews the evolution of central banks, primarily in the developed countries, and their relationships to the financial structure and its government economic and financial policies, and describes the central bank's balance sheet and monetary policy initiatives; and finally, (6) discusses the impact of central bank independence from government pressures to control macroeconomic outcomes, and stresses the importance of central bank transparency in achieving its goals and policies.

Financial Structure

The narrower purposes of the financial sector are to (1) process payments, (2) extend credit and capital to businesses to stimulate growth, (3) manage savings, and (4) deal with economic risks (*Economist*, 2015b: 69). The institutions which make up the financial structure in most every country are the most important sources of financial capital for investment opportunities for both individuals and businesses. The most common financial institutions include banks and similar bank-type institutions (e.g. credit unions), stock and bond markets, and insurance companies. Transaction costs vary for standard financial and business dealings. For example, small investors may be blocked out of common investment opportunities because certain investment categories might require a high minimum level of "buy in," which creates substantial transactions costs (e.g. commission charges). In addition, high transactions costs on all trades or investments combined with the small amounts of money available may restrict the individual's ability to protect against risk through portfolio diversification. Banks and other financial intermediaries in all countries play an important role in reducing these transaction costs by providing access for smaller investors to these markets. Reforms to the financial sectors of most countries focus on ensuring that credit from the banking system goes to the most dynamic firms, not simply those with political/family connections or state firms that often are loss-making and require public subsidies from the budget (i.e. fiscal policy paying for the financial sector).

As with other economic markets, differences in information critically determine the incentives and successes generated in financial market transactions. Asymmetric information in financial markets creates problems of adverse selection and moral hazard. Mishkin (2013) describes how adverse selection prior to the financial transaction may lead to loans being most actively pursued by individuals with the highest credit risks because they will be less likely to repay the loan. "Collateral" against the loan amount that would be sufficient to transfer back to the bank in the event of the borrower's default protects the lender, and it also makes it more likely for the better borrowers to be revealed. Financial information flows within societies are facilitated by networks which are based on interpersonal trust. Thus, informational exchanges (and the degree of asymmetry) are ultimately a function of local political cultures and institutions. A large source of asymmetric information occurs when financial transactions involve risky financial securities like stocks. The structure of a well-developed financial market adapts in response to these informational access problems. The standard microeconomic model of consumer choice of risky instruments involves the trade-off between risk and return. Returns from different types of investments are expected to be positively related to the amount of financial risk assumed by the consumer. *Figure 5.1* illustrates this direct relationship between expected return and risk with different broadly defined investment categories.

The presence of asymmetric information involving the potential investor's knowledge of the actual level of risk (i.e. whether a firm is good or bad) causes the investor to make suboptimal risk choices. As Mishkin (2013) describes, private firms in the developed countries (e.g. Standard and Poor's, Moody's, and other bond rating agencies) provide assessments of creditworthiness, specifically measured by the likelihood of default and the size of the potential losses, for the issued financial debt instruments (e.g. bonds) of single corporations and governments. The rating agencies use ratings designations such as AAA, AA, BBB, BB, with lower and/or fewer letters to classify security issues with greater degrees of risk. The agencies then add descriptive terms for relatively highly rated firms (e.g. AAA or BBB) such as "investment" grade and relatively lowly rated firms (e.g. BB and lower) as "speculative" grade. The ratings have now been attached to other more complicated financial instruments as

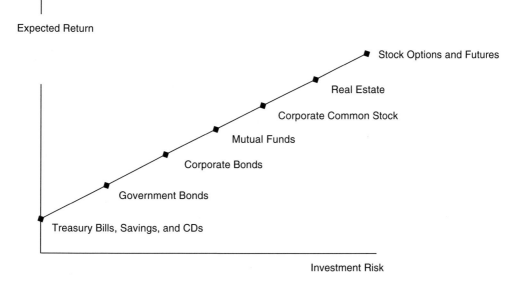

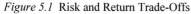

Figure 5.1 Risk and Return Trade-Offs

described below. Government agencies like the U.S. Securities and Exchange Commission and a variety of federal regulations also provide protection against misrepresentation by firms. However, even with this government intervention, consumers may not be fully informed about a particular investment and will need to assume some risk associated with this asymmetric information. Banks and other financial intermediaries can also work to provide accurate information to potential investors, since it is in the interest of all parties for this relationship—banks profit from being able to obtain funds from investors and offering this service makes them more attractive to individuals.

Mishkin (2013) explains the moral hazard problems created after the loan is made, as the consumers take on greater risks with borrowed money that may not ever be repaid. Banks loaning these funds will have every incentive to reduce this moral hazard. The financial market could adapt to this particular type of problem. Terms of loans could be written to provide some protection to the lender, including specific allowable expenses, required upkeep of the collateral, and routine income and expense reports and/or other reports useful for monitoring financial activities. However, even with potential safeguards, the nature of loans will continue to create moral hazard incentives for individuals to take on larger risks with outside financing. The borrower gets any gains beyond the fixed loan payment (based on the principal and interest of the loan) received by the lender.

There are also moral hazard problems associated with the separation between owners and managers of a company. This is a problem with the issuance of ownership corporate shares of the company through stocks. In the common situation where the company owners or the majority shareholders are not the company managers, then these managers will have different incentives, at least in the short term. The incentives may not include a profit maximization motivation and could even involve the diversion of company funds for the manager's personal use. This separation of ownership and management makes monitoring operations difficult if not impossible. Of course, eventually information will be provided as profits are reported and/or revelations are discovered about corporate malfeasance. Mishkin (2013) listed venture capital firms as one way financial intermediaries can be used to avoid the moral hazard problem. Venture capital financial firms receive an ownership share in new start-up businesses in return for financial capital. Owners will often gain membership on governing boards, closing the gap between owners and managers. However, as with any adverse selection, such information is not expected to be fully known, since the managers will have every incentive to hide it. So, anything that is revealed in standard ways may not provide full information to the investor.

Governments are often involved in a country's financial structure, ranging from fully government-owned banks and other financial intermediaries to a strict set of financial regulations and oversight. National development banks are a different type of financial institution created by the country's government for the purposes of economic development. They exist in all the world's regions and include the Brazilian Development Bank (BNDES), the China Development Bank, the Croatian Bank for Reconstruction and Development, and the Agricultural Development Bank of Ghana among many others. Government-owned and operated banks suffer from the same deficiencies found in most state-owned enterprises—the lack of a profit motive and/or the need to operate in a competitive marketplace. On the other hand, governments can and do intervene through formal regulations requiring firms to follow strict and consistent accounting principles. Because of their financial importance in business activities as well as their importance in all kinds of individual financial decisions, the financial structure is characterized by a heavy amount of government regulation. As described, consistent financial information is critical to an efficient financial market. Only to the extent that this information is unavailable, as in many underdeveloped countries, will this affect the country's ability to improve its economic growth.

Financial Development and Economic Growth

The strong relationship between a country's financial development and its economic growth is well established in the academic literature. A well-developed financial system improves the allocation of capital to the private sector and expands opportunities for firms to acquire external investment funds. Even though increased access to funds might be expected to increase income disparities between the rich and the poor in less developed countries, Mishkin's (2006) review of this literature finds no significant relationship between financial development and increased poverty. Indeed, he finds that a more developed financial system, as one would expect, gives the poor greater access to credit. Although these relationships are clearly established, local country conditions limit the ability of less developed countries to liberalize their financial systems. For instance, state-owned banks dominate the Chinese financial system and have prevented interest rate liberalization which will allow households to reap bigger incomes from their savings in bank deposits and other instruments. That will now change by regime decree allowing banks to publish benchmark deposit and lending rates and abide by them on actual loans and deposit accounts (*Economist*, 2015c: 69). Adverse selection and moral hazard problems which are inherent within any financial system are particularly present in developing and transitional countries such as China. But commercial markets and governmental institutions are not equipped to address them in the same way they can be addressed in developed countries. As described, an important method to address adverse selection is the availability of collateral, which can be private land or other asset ownership. But extremely high transaction costs in some underdeveloped countries create property right impediments. As a result, clear property ownership may not be established which diminishes any collateral value. For banks, this makes credit more risky and reduces its availability. Even when collateral is available, the weak and inefficient legal structures (i.e. absence of rule of law) make its use difficult.

A weak and inefficient legal structure further creates barriers in the application of loan conditions to reduce the problems associated with moral hazard. Mishkin (2006) explains the possibility of incentives for the judges to not enforce these conditions on certain preferred individuals, creating further difficulties. This is particularly true in the event of government-owned banks, common in many of the underdeveloped and transition countries. Without the private profit-making incentives, banks may be inclined to loan money to the government or other preferred borrowers, without seeking out the borrowers with the greatest opportunities for productive investments. Banking operations are described further in *Chapter 8*. As a result, in countries where state-owned banks are common, there is lower financial development, slower economic growth, or threat to continued growth as in China. Other policies that can reduce these problems, such as establishment of strong regulatory institutions and accounting requirements, are not generally present in underdeveloped countries, further limiting financial sector development. State efforts are required to put into place great transparency through regulations and regulatory oversight to develop a stronger financial structure.

Another example of this is the large amount of lending that has been done in Brazil for infrastructure investment that has not yielded results. The Lula government announced several infrastructure projects to improve access to ports for farming and mining interests as well as new railroad lines. These projects have either not been completed or are far over budget. There were additional concerns to get this work done before the World Cup and Olympics arrived to the country (*Economist*, 2013c). Of course, these same regime and/or current elites often benefit from government-owned banks and weak regulatory institutions. These powerful interests are not inclined to introduce the reforms necessary to increase financial development. The governments in some poorer countries do not desire an increase in transparency surrounding the relationship between them and the financial institutions. An argument that has been made is that China is the exception. While its financial structure is less developed than those in the OECD, the country has recently seen tremendous economic growth rates, about 7.2 percent in 2013. However, state banks there have suffered from the same problems that exist in other, less developed countries and the "financial repression" leads to financial instability (*Economist*, 2013a). Banks in China profited from double-digit growth for over a decade. But now they are barely breaking even. Savers there, as noted, now have other borrowing options than state banks (*Economist*, 2015c: 69). India also suffers from an inadequate financial regulatory system that could be beneficial if it tried to liberalize its financial markets. But even with those reforms, the small percentage of adults who have bank accounts—35 percent—makes the primarily informal economic and financial structure inadequate for loan processing or tax collection, where only 2.5 percent of the population pay taxes (*Economist*, 2013d). Even so, India has also seen strong economic growth at 6.0 percent in 2013.

Bank Structure

A bank's balance sheet contains its assets, liabilities, and capital, and for a bank to be in "balance" requires its assets to equal its liabilities plus capital. The bank's assets include cash reserves, deposits at other banks, debt instruments or securities (e.g. interest-bearing federal, state, and local bonds), and loans, which represents the bank's largest asset and largest source of the bank's profit. A typical bank balance sheet is illustrated in *Figure 5.2*. While little or no interest is earned on the bank's reserves, it is required to hold reserves equal to some percentage of bank deposits. Excess reserves beyond those required are also generally held by the bank as protection against unforeseen and/or extraordinary bank withdrawals and reduces the need for the bank to borrow (and pay interest) from external sources (e.g. from other banks or from the central bank) or sell assets to cover unforeseen bank withdrawals. The bank's liabilities include bank deposits (e.g. checking and savings deposits) and borrowings from the Federal Reserve System (the "Fed") and other banks. Fed loans to banks are called "discount loans." The interest rate is the "discount rate" and is one of the Fed's monetary policy instruments (discussed below). Banks frequently borrow excess reserves held by other banks and pay an interest rate known as the federal funds rate.

Bank capital represents the difference between bank assets and liabilities. Banks are the most important source of individual and business investment financing in most countries. Bank capital is earned as the bank, through what is called intermediation, links savers to borrowers and is earned by the difference between the interest paid to savers and the interest charged firms. Because of this relationship, the level and volatility of interest rates will affect the level of bank capital. Mishkin (2013) lists three determinants of the bank's decision to hold capital rather than putting these funds into income generating risky assets. First, as a measure of the bank's fiscal healthiness, bank capital protects it against potential failure. Adverse selection and moral hazard problems determine the overall level of bank riskiness

Assets (Receivables)	Liabilities (Payables)
A. *Core or Safe Capital:*	Deposits (from savers)
1. Cash (liquidity)	
2. Treasury Bonds (liquidity)	
3. Equity (owner investments)	
Return on Assets (ROI) = from investments and debts	
B. *Loans* (to borrowers):	
1. Property (mortgages)	
2. Business (commercial ventures and firms)	
3. Governments (purchases of bonds)	
4. State Enterprises (non-financial)	

Figure 5.2 Bank Balance Sheet

because they affect the bank's liabilities. A sufficient level of bank capital may be required to absorb losses from any bad loans. A second factor that must be considered when choosing the level of bank capital is that holding a greater amount of capital lowers the rate of return to bank equity holders. Finally, financial regulators require banks to hold a minimum amount of bank capital.

In recent times, various "off" bank balance sheet activities, those which do have a direct effect on the bank's balance sheet, have been created in the financial sector as additional sources of significant bank income and profits. Banks commonly sell loans to other banks or financial institutions and, in the U.S., the sale of mortgage loans with a relatively high interest is an attractive financial activity. Recent financial innovations have introduced a more "tarnished" instrument with the creation of structured finance or derivative securities that pool or bundle assets in a design intended to be less risky than the average asset in the pool, as assessed using the same scales by the various rating agencies described earlier.

Mortgage-backed securities are an example of these new financial instruments. More lenient lending policies were put into place to provide "subprime" home mortgage financing to individuals with less than perfect credit histories and with little personal savings available for a down payment. By the most common measures, these policies led to the historic home ownership rates in the U.S. and, as might be expected, housing prices increased considerably, eventually leading to a housing price "bubble." Adverse selection problems arose as borrowers were able to get relatively cheap credit to buy homes.

The financial industry created complicated debt instruments to fund these mortgages. U.S. government-sponsored agencies like Fannie Mae and Freddie Mac purchased subprime mortgages from banks and created structured securities with government guarantees. Bond-like securities represent a bundle of different individual mortgages with different principal and interest payments. This arrangement should in theory reduce the portfolio's risk, relative to a single mortgage, because each is a bundle of mortgages with different levels of risk. That would be particularly true when the asset value (e.g. houses) continued to rise and the default probabilities of the assets included in the portfolio were not highly correlated. Unfortunately, that was not the case with most of these financial instruments. As more "high-risk" borrowers obtained these subprime mortgages to buy homes with little or no equity, the loans faced significant default probabilities. The bursting of the housing price bubble started the downfall of these financial instruments. As housing prices fell, homeowners with small amounts of home equity found themselves with home values less than their mortgage (they were now "under water"). People walked away from their mortgages and defaulted on their loans, leading to a significant drop in the value of these mortgage-backed securities, which were assets on the balance sheets of many banks and other financial institutions.

Lenders were left with collateral that had dropped significantly in value, and bank capital was negatively affected by these events. Mishkin (2013) observes that while the new types of financial instruments start off the bank's balance sheet, if they decline in value and a default on the asset occurs, the bank must reacquire and return them to the balance sheet as an asset with reduced value. Bank capital suffered as a consequence. In an effort to protect their balance sheets, banks were forced to sell off assets and restrict the amount of lending to individuals and businesses, further weakening the economy. Some of these assets sales amounted to a "fire sale," with banks selling assets at lower than market values which also negatively affected the bank's balance sheet. This downturn was softened by then-President Bush's Troubled Asset Relief Program (or TARP), which purchased billions of dollars of subprime mortgage-backed assets. The openness of the U.S. capital markets also caused several non-banks which had invested in "toxic" mortgage-backed securities to also suffer from the downturn in U.S. housing prices.

What Creates Financial Crises in Developed Countries?

Financial crises create "substantial changes in credit volume and asset prices; severe disruptions in financial intermediation and the supply of external funding to various actors in the economy; large scale (firm, household, financial intermediaries, and sovereigns) balance sheet problems; and large scale government support" (Classens and Kose, 2013). Asymmetric information in the financial structure creates problems associated with adverse selection and moral hazard and contributes to the incidence of financial crises in both developed and underdeveloped countries. Mishkin (2013) describes the stages of events leading to financial crises. He lists asset price busts, like the tech stock bubble in the late 1990s and the housing price bubble in 2008, and/or general financial uncertainties as being the primary motivators of financial crises in developed countries. Sweden's financial collapse in the early 1990s is an example. Following a housing price bubble which burst after an increase in home loans, the Swedish GDP fell 5 percent and employment fell by 10 percent during the crisis. There was a run on the krona, and the Swedish central bank increased interest rates to 500 percent in an attempt to defend the currency. The crisis had irreparable damage, moving Sweden down from one of the highest income levels in Europe to below several EU countries.

Bubbles are often a creation of the changes in the financial structure which may influence a higher number of loans in order to purchase these financial assets and, therefore, a more risky loan portfolio. Obviously, the magnitude of any financial crises depends on the reaction of the public and the financial intermediaries. There could be bank runs or panics, where depositors rush to banks to withdraw their funds, which reduces the bank's assets and may result in bank failures. The financial costs to the lender associated with defaults and the resulting bank panics may be reduced if the government has instituted safety nets like the federal deposit insurance found in the U.S. But under more calm conditions, these remedial programs might perversely create additional incentives for the banks to make more high-risk loans.

What Creates Financial Crises in Underdeveloped and Emerging Market Countries?

There are several ways a fiscal crisis can affect an emerging market and/or an underdeveloped country. Some of these events resemble those that arise in financial crises in more developed countries. However, more severe problems can result because of the weakness in the financial sectors of the less developed countries, inadequate regulations, and a general lack of government infrastructure to reduce the impacts of these events. The Spanish Central Bank had imposed counter-cyclical reserve requirements that acted almost like automatic stabilizers. The policy impact was that higher reserve requirements kicked in during good economic periods that reduced the amount of funds available for the possibility of risky lending. During bad times, the extra reserves were to be used to protect the bank's financial health. Indeed, these extra funds helped Spain survive some of the 2008 turndown. However, Spain's extra reserves were insufficient to survive the more recent fiscal problems in the Eurozone. The latter problems were caused by regulatory weaknesses in Spain's financial markets that allowed exceptions created by banks that lobbied for relief from the credit restrictions that required extra reserves.

An important example of the economic risks created by weak and perverse regulation is Pakistan's huge informal economy where few pay taxes or have access to services, especially financial services. Small firms are kept small by lack of credit at reasonable rates. But they generate about 50 percent of GDP and 90 percent of non-governmental employment! Because many rely on informal lenders, the central bank does not really control the economy and has a hard time fighting inflation. Similarly, in India only 2.5 percent of the population pays taxes, meaning a huge informal sector. These institutional weaknesses present larger opportunities for adverse selection and moral hazard problems to develop. In addition, such countries are also more vulnerable to any crises originating in developed countries because of "globalization." Globalization opens up their economies to foreign goods, capital, direct investment, and even financial institutions. This openness has obvious benefits associated with increasing economic development in the developing country (Mishkin, 2008). One way is the increased competition for all goods when foreign goods enter into the country's market. Competition is expected to make the domestic producers more efficient and keep market prices lower. Of course, the competitive effect on prices will lower the firm's profits. In response, firms have to seek funding outside the small local financial sector in order to increase its investment and grow. That problem can provide firms with incentives to change their financial structure, improving their management and balance sheets, to accommodate any financial institutions that will offer them credit.

A second and more direct way globalization affects a country's financial structure is through the increase in foreign capital entering into the country. One example of this is "hot money," which is the flow of foreign money and/or capital (portfolio investments and bank loans) into a country that has a relatively high interest rate. Countries that generally experience this inflow of hot money funds are emerging market economies like India, Brazil, China, and Turkey. This inflow has been increasing with the lower interest rates in the developed countries like the U.S. A large inflow of this hot money can raise the monetary base and result in high inflation. Consequently, some countries have enacted measures designed to reduce or moderate this inflow, including Turkey's reduction of interest rates by the Turkish Central Bank, and capital controls and foreign debt quotas set by the Central Bank of China.

Of course, any increase in the supply of investment funds reduces the price of these funds (the interest rate) and should, depending on the elasticity of demand, increase the quantity demanded of investment funding, leading to higher economic growth. Mishkin (2006) noted that countries which opened up their markets to foreign capital saw increases in the average growth rates of investment as well as increases in average productivity (output per worker). He does note that the full effect of these benefits is mostly limited to countries with a sufficient level of financial development to protect against adverse selection, moral hazard problems, and financial mismanagement. One further cautionary note regarding the introduction of foreign capital is that any economic benefits are potentially threatened when the developed country economies are weakened and developing countries become exposed to this weakness. These problems will be exacerbated if financial institutions are not constrained by hard financial regulations and take on excess levels of risk. That describes the financial problems in developing and emerging market countries associated with the 2008 collapse of the subprime mortgage-backed securities market in the U.S., the effects of which spread worldwide.

An additional source of crisis is if the government pressures the banks to finance fiscal imbalances. That breaches the "firewall" between fiscal and monetary policy and ignores the distinction in national accounts between monetary and fiscal (budgetary and taxation) transactions. It contributes to the weakening of both types of policies to stabilize the economy. Powerful governmental and/or business interests may be in place in particular countries to prevent passage of tough regulations to limit this excessively intimate relationship between governments and the commercial banking system. Recent crises related to such policy and accounting breaches have been observed in Latin America and in Russia. Moreover, major currency crises can immediately occur for geopolitical reasons, such as the dramatic decline in the value of the Russian ruble after the Russian invasion of the Ukraine in March 2014.

Mishkin (2006, 2013) explains the impact of this behavior on the financial markets of particular transitional countries. As the central bank's balance sheet deteriorates as a result of financial mismanagement and/or the government's requests for capital to cover fiscal imbalances, currency speculators and investors may react by dumping the domestic currency, causing the value of the currency to plummet. As a result, the financial markets in these countries are affected adversely by a deterioration of central bank balance sheets. Any debts denominated in U.S. dollars or any other stable currency will become much more expensive now with deterioration of home currency value. Increases in inflation and interest rates typically follow, causing further deterioration of the bank's balance sheet as it now must pay higher rates to investors to induce external funding. The problems of adverse selection and moral hazard intensify as central banks acquire risky assets to stem the deterioration. This type of financial crisis creates great unease among the general population; because these financial markets are not well developed in such countries, financial safety nets like those that exist in the developed countries to protect the deposits of consumers against bank runs (e.g. the Federal Deposit Insurance Corporation (FDIC) in the U.S.) have not been created to bail out the balance sheets of commercial banks and put depositors at ease. A currency crisis in one country with weak separation of fiscal and monetary policies often leads to currency crises spreading to other countries, as speculators and investors become concerned that the problems plaguing one country are also present in others. This "contagion" in the financial markets is particularly pronounced in countries in closest proximity to the country where the events were initiated and where direct comparisons of the economies and financial sectors may be most germane.

The most recent currency crisis in Argentina is an example of the impact on the financial sector, the Argentinian economy, and a fear of contagion throughout Latin America (*New York Times*, 2014). China's weakened economy has reduced the demand for commodities in Argentina and throughout Latin America. Moreover, the strengthened developed country economies, particularly in the U.S., have caused money/capital to leave many developing country economies. Both of these effects have weakened the currencies in developing countries. Governments in Venezuela and Argentina, which have been identified as the most vulnerable, have responded by putting limits on the purchase of foreign currencies, in particular U.S. dollars. The Venezuelan government has even tried to restrict international travel in the fear of currency leaving the country.

The differences in the composition of the bank balance sheets and the organization of the financial sectors create large differences in the impact of financial crises on the financial markets. The impact is greater in developed country economies than that experienced in underdeveloped and emerging countries. In developed countries (e.g. OECD), debts are generally denominated in the home currency, so currency devaluations will not have as great an impact on bank balance sheets. Moreover, export industries benefit from these devaluations, as exports become cheaper as a result of the "cheaper" domestic currency. Government policies and regulations in the developed countries are also better able to protect the country's financial institutions from problems associated with adverse selection and moral hazard. Indeed, the transparency in these markets help all of the actors make the appropriate decisions and reduce the mismanagement and bad decisions regarding inappropriate lending and investing.

Central Banks

Central banks are found in many countries throughout the world, particularly as part of more advanced financial systems. While the U.S. central bank, the Federal Reserve System (the "Fed") turned 100 years old in 2013, Sweden's central bank opened in 1668 and the Bank of England opened in 1694 (Crowe and Meade, 2007). The European Central Bank (ECB) was more recently created in June 1998 to conduct monetary policy for the European Union. The importance of central banks and their basic functions cannot be overstated as they affect a country's economic growth and can possibly provide some protection against financial crises as a "lender of last resort" during economic downturns. Their role in financial markets is to control the country's money supply in an effort to affect interest rates and/or inflation. The tools generally available to central banks to carry out this duty involve the central bank's assets and liabilities, which will have a direct effect on interest rates. For example, the U.S. Fed balance sheet lists federal reserve notes ("currency"), commercial bank reserves (these were described earlier as either required reserves or as excess reserves to protect against bank asset/liability uncertainties), and other deposit holdings from government and international agencies. The Fed holds these reserves and then controls the market for overnight borrowing of excess reserves by other banks through purchase and sale of securities to target an interest rate charged for those short-term borrowings (the "federal funds rate"). By far, the largest percentage of Fed assets consists of "securities," including government treasury notes and bonds. A small but important part of these securities are repurchase agreements ("repos"), which are purchased under agreement that the purchase will be reversed (repurchased) on a specified future date, sometimes as early as the next day. The magnitude of the buying and selling of repos by the Fed at any point in time determines how much currency is injected into or taken out of the financial system. Loans to financial institutions (the so-called "discount window" and the interest rate charged on bank loans called the "discount rate") as a source of liquidity are another Fed asset and represent a small but important monetary policy instrument. Foreign exchange reserves and gold are a small percentage of Fed assets. It is this control over the amounts of assets and liabilities on its balance sheet that allows the Fed to have a direct impact on interest rates and, consequently, economic activity.

In the role as lender of the last resort, central banks play an increasingly important role in the provision of credit to financial firms (specifically banks) during financial crises. During the worldwide 2008 financial crisis originating as noted in the U.S. as a result of the defaults of the mortgage-backed securities, the U.S. Fed immediately stepped in and took on the vital role of helping the U.S. avoid a deeper economic recession. Cecchetti (2009) explains one of the critical jobs for a central bank during a financial crisis is to provide "liquidity" to financial institutions. As described above, this was particularly necessary in this most recent crisis, given the nature of the event and its origins in the quality of assets found on the balance sheets of financial institutions. As the crisis evolved, bank capital shrank and they became less willing to lend money. The Fed responded immediately to increase financial liquidity through aggressive monetary policy by cutting the discount and federal funds rates to banks. In addition, as Cecchetti (2009) details, the Fed carried out several nonconventional types of monetary policies by allowing commercial banks to take out longer-term loans (longer than overnight) of bank excess reserves and by providing a bailout to Bear Stearns, an investment firm that had suffered considerable financial losses as a result of mortgage-backed securities. In addition, the Fed ultimately approved the takeover of Bear Stearns by JP Morgan Chase. That these actions directly benefited investment firms and not commercial banks, and that the Fed's loan to Bear Stearns was made without an appropriate level of collateral, made these monetary policy actions particularly unconventional. These efforts were combined with the U.S. government's fiscal policies designed to increase the amount of liquidity in the financial markets and to provide some tax relief in order to increase personal consumption. It should be noted that the underlying largely Keynesian theory behind these central bank actions was that with the collapse of private investment, household consumption, the only way to re-stimulate aggregate demand would be for government stimulus (fiscal policy) and efforts by central banks to increase market liquidity to re-stimulate investment and consumption.

One of the central bank's policies to stimulate financial recovery during the crisis, the Economic Recovery Act, which passed in late 2008, contained the Troubled Asset Relief Program (TARP), which purchased $700 billion of the subprime mortgages from financial institutions. While the Fed also extended a line of credit to the ECB, some European countries had already taken steps to protect their financial systems from crisis. For example, Sweden learned lessons from its 1990s banking crisis and created "bad banks" to clean out its system and now has a stable and profitable banking system, even though the regulations imposed extremely high capital requirements (see *Case 5.3* on p. 189). The ideal structure of a central bank involves several different dimensions. Reis (2013) lays out several tasks when designing a central bank "from scratch," beginning with definition of the central bank's mandate. While this might seem straightforward, a clear mandate can be illusive. For example, the U.S. Federal Reserve Act of 1977 established the "dual mandate" for the Fed to control inflation and maximize employment. Aside from the fact these goals are ill defined, they will potentially conflict and the achievement of either will ultimately require trade-offs to be taken. Indeed, another dimension acknowledges the need for such trade-offs and explores whether the central bank should focus its monetary activities on the nominal interest rate measure or directly focus on a measure of real activity like national output and/or employment. As Reis (2013) explains, attention on real economic activity acknowledges the potential for an inverse relationship between unemployment and inflation (the so-called "Phillips Curve" shown in *Figure 5.3*) and that loosening up on inflation targets can lead to more stability in the economy. The move from 5 percent to 3 percent unemployment rate could be due to an increase in economic activity which lowers the unemployment rate but potentially puts pressure on price levels. However, this relationship depends on how much slack there is in the economy.

The appropriate mandate may then require weights to be assigned to the conflicting goals. The choice of the head of the central bank is another critical dimension of central bank operations to consider. For example, the U.S. Fed is headed by the Fed chair (a woman now), but the Federal Open Market Committee (FOMC) makes many of the decisions regarding monetary aggregates, nominal rates, and real economic activities. The FOMC is composed of seven members from Washington, DC, and five heads from 12 of the regional Federal Reserve banks from across the nation. The significance of this structure is that decisions can appear to be more decentralized, resulting in some sharing of the cost/benefits across the individual regions and states. Some research has been carried out on the optimal size of central bank committees (reviewed in Crowe and Meade, 2007). However, the current committee sizes in two of the major central banks—the U.S. FOMC and the Governing Council of the ECB—as well as a majority of central banks throughout the world are considerably larger than the theoretically determined "optimal" size. Like the FOMC, the committee size of the ECB is driven by membership of individual countries (in the FOMC, the states/regions) in order to get a decentralized decision-making process.

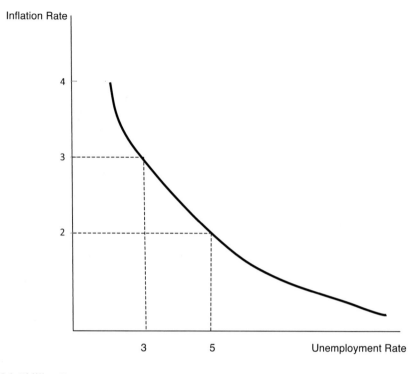

Figure 5.3 Phillips Curve

Case Study Central Bank Independence and Transparency

Central banks are in an excellent position to use strategic monetary policies in order to achieve the twin goals of price stability through the control of inflation and economic growth/stability. The critical element in general economic stability and/or growth is through the impact of monetary policy on interest rates. Given their significance, there is a temptation for government officials to pressure central banks to employ monetary policies for political gains. Indeed, it is the central bank's role as a lender of last resort that can open up the possibilities for political uses of monetary policies. However, central banks work most effectively when they are independent from such political influences and the decisions that are reached by central bank officials are transparent to the public.

The degree of central bank independence and the level of the transparency of its decisions vary considerably across countries and over time. An example of weak independence and lack of transparency can be found with the Reserve Bank (FRB) of India. The FRB requires banks to give it 4 percent of their deposits as well as to invest nearly a quarter of their deposits in government bonds. The central bank requires the commercial banks to direct 40 percent of their loans to support specific sectors of the economy such as agriculture, and that leaves about 60 percent of bank deposits to support the Indian government's agenda. The Argentinian government has used the central government to monetize its public debt, largely created by populist regime increases and expenditures on the poor and middle-class voters. In turn, the Argentinian central bank has controlled the measure of the country's inflation to make it appear much better than its true measure.

Stanley Fischer (former professor of economics at MIT, chief economist of the World Bank, former governor of the Bank of Israel, and most recently nominated by President Obama to be Vice-Chairman of the Fed) defines central bank independence as having two key aspects—instrumental and goal independence (Mishkin, 2013). Instrumental independence determines the central bank's ability to use the available monetary policy instruments, and goal independence determines the central bank's ability to set the monetary policy goals and/ or mandates described above. Both types of independence are clearly affected by its relationship to the government. As described, less developed financial systems may involve state-owned banks or otherwise government influenced banks which will act to monetize government debts and lend to favored sectors and clients. Given the power of a country's central bank, this lack of independence between the central bank and the government creates even greater problems associated with monetary policy mismanagement. State regimes often take actions to pressure their central banks to achieve excessive monetary policy outcomes (either to cover budget deficits or perhaps to generate a "political business cycle"), which often fuels inflation.

Central bank independence can be measured along several dimensions, including the process of appointment and tenure of the central bank chair and board members, the ability of the government to review and even overturn central bank decisions, and the presence of a clear mandate for the central bank (Crowe and Meade, 2007). A greater level of independence is assumed if the central bank governors are not directly appointed by government officials or if they could be dismissed by these officials. Long terms of office for central bank governors that potentially overlap the political terms of the government officials also increase independence. Prohibiting state officials from borrowing directly from the central bank is also critical to reduction or elimination of the ability of the state to use monetary policy to finance public budgets. Again, the goal is to keep fiscal and monetary actions and accounts separate. Finally, a clear as well as uncomplicated goal (e.g. price control) helps to create independence as well as transparency (discussed below). Using various measurable proxies for the dimensions, these characteristics can be quantified and combined into a single measure of independence. Using this empirical technique, Crowe and Meade (2007) found that the ECB and Sweden's Riksbank had the highest measures of independence. Indeed, the ECB has a higher degree of independence than individual European country central banks had in the 1980s. They also found that central banks in developing countries and in emerging market economies increased their independence over the past 20 years, reflecting the evolution of more mature financial systems in those countries. Poland had seen a considerable increase in central bank independence. However, this independence created restrictive monetary policies which were counter to the Polish government's (and many of the citizen's) fiscal interests. Such contrary actions are normal for independent central banks and indicate they are actually doing their job. Political regimes often respond by trying to reassert control. In response, for example, the government created regulations that would weaken the central bank's control, creating frictions between central bank independence and the government (*Economist*, 2006).

A perennial question is whether greater central bank independence leads to lower inflation? The appropriate empirical test involves an examination of the relationship between some measure of central bank independence and the level of the country's inflation. In their review of the research examining the impact of central bank independence, Klomp and de Haan (2010) found an inverse relationship between central bank independence and inflation, particularly when considering the more industrialized economies and to a lesser extent in developing countries. They noted that low inflation rates and central bank independence are by-products of a strong financial system and not necessarily related to one another empirically.

A key aspect of central bank independence and effectiveness in carrying out the goals is to have an appropriate level of transparency and accountability. These attributes reduce the uncertainty surrounding central bank policies and provide critical information to the economic agents; by reassuring the public, they can also assist the central bank in achieving its goals of inflation control and maximum employment. Understanding why and how financial decisions are made by the central bank provides information regarding monetary policy decisions and can be a source of stability for an economy. The recent unconventional monetary policy actions taken by the U.S. Fed beginning in 2008 were clearly announced to the financial sector and general population in an attempt to provide stabilization. The general rule is openness of the central bank's clarity of its mandate, procedures to arrive at particular decisions, information used to generate these decisions, and that the actual decisions deliver critical information to the economic actors and provide for a healthier financial sector.

Central bank independence is related to this degree of transparency through the revelation of any relationship between the central bank and the government. Some economists argue for monetary policy rules that would send a clear signal to the financial markets of central bank monetary policy actions. For example, Friedman's (1968) call for a constant rate of growth of the money supply was an extreme example of such a monetary rule. Other proposals discussed in Reis (2013) try to weaken the potential for this relationship by giving central bankers long (and generally nonrenewable) terms that might stretch over different political administrations, thereby limiting political threats to remove them from office. Some degree of transparency can be achieved by clear and accurate reports of monetary policy outcomes—e.g. periodic reports on inflation. Press statements, news conferences, public governmental hearings, and central bank committee transcripts could all be used to increase the amount of information and transparency to the financial markets and general public. Reis (2013) lists one additional dimension of central banking and that is "accountability." Of course, transparency is critical for accountability, since it is important to understand what policies the central bank has carried out in order to determine the effectiveness of these policies. Accountability requires political oversight and may generate a gray line between review and punishment. The creation of decentralized decision making, through a large and interest diversified monetary policy committee, and central banker terms of office that overlap with the terms of different politicians can help to clarify the lines between monetary policy and political influence.

In Crowe and Meade's (2007) review of the literature relating central bank transparency and inflation (82 countries in the sample), they found an inverse relationship between them. They examined changes between 1998 and 2006 in measures of central bank transparency across several countries. They found, as noted, that the ECB had a higher level of transparency than the central banks from the individual Euro-area countries. They also found that the ECB recorded a transparency level below the average level of the "inflation targeting" countries composed of Australia, Iceland, Israel, Korea, New Zealand, Norway, Sweden, United Kingdom, Brazil, the Czech Republic, Hungary, Indonesia, Mexico, Poland, South Africa, and Turkey. Many of the countries in their sample saw significant declines in the measure of transparency during the study period, with significant declines recorded in China and Russia. Perhaps unexpectedly, they did not find much statistical evidence for a relationship between higher inflation and lower central bank transparency.

Application of Policy Analytic Frameworks: Quantitative Easing Policies and the Financial Crisis of 2008

Growth depends on adequate prices for producers and sufficient credit to firms and households to invest and consume. Public regulatory and fiscal policies can ensure that competitive structures exist so that prices and credit flow smoothly. When the commercial banking systems of many countries around the world froze up in 2008, the flow of credit was interrupted and incomes plummeted. Even at adequate prices, firms and consumers could not borrow enough to invest and consume. This seemingly required governmental policies to fill the gap to try and stimulate aggregate demand in standard Keynesian fashion.

Applying our technical framework at the first level reveals that the empirical links between public sector credit to banks and greater demand is not straightforward at all. As in all cases of policy analysis, much depends on the problem definition. If the crisis-driven growth problem was mainly lack of demand, then increasing the supply of credit by providing bank funding would be unlikely to make a difference. The U.S. Federal Reserve focused on loans from banks to business which were actually expanding in 2008 rather than the contraction in consumer credit and lending by other financial institutions. If more banks had failed, the supply of credit would have declined further. But this likely would not have affected demand for credit, which had evaporated along with household wealth and desire to borrow due to the crisis. Thus, one policy option was to let the banks fail and stimulate credit demand by more flexible debt instruments and equity (*Economist*, 2014: 71). Otherwise, the policy premise was the unlikely sequence that additional credit supply would create credit demand. This line of empirical work challenged the orthodox view that the financial crisis led to diminished bank lending which if continued would lead to collapse and a major worldwide depression. The orthodox view was that reduced demand for credit was a function of decreased loan availability. It also suggested that, even if the unorthodox problem definition was correct, remedies would require medium-term institutional, legal, and financial efforts when time was of the essence.

One innovative response by central banks based on the orthodox view of the problem was the development and use of quantitative easing (QE) policies. At the macroeconomic level, monetary policies in response to low growth have varied in design and so have the empirical results. The central banks of Japan, England, and the U.S. adopted stimulus policies of quantitative easing, or purchasing government bonds with newly created money. The intent was to counter deflationary tendencies and encourage growth expectations by stimulating demand through artificial creation of inflation. The policies were designed according to the standard theory of monetary economics. But the European Central Bank (ECB) and German Bundesbank opposed QE, arguing that existing labor market rigidity, excessive taxation, and repressive regulations were structural or supply-side problems and could not be corrected by monetary policy which was focused more on demand. Nevertheless, the three economies applying QE policies have grown steadily without inflation increasing; the Euro area did not and German growth has stalled.

Moving to the second level of political economy, it was clear that institutional knowledge together with a legal system that supported bank regulation favored the orthodox policy view. That led to credit expansion and the use of other tools such as quantitative easing (QE) to generate mild inflation and prevent deflation/depression in the financial markets and economy. Political economy analysis of institutional constraints in Europe suggests that structural reforms are long-term policies while QE policies, like changes in tax policies, could work quickly to restore confidence. The successful monetary stimulus policies of these three countries suggested that QE could compensate for overly tight fiscal policies and still keep deflation at bay (*Economist*, 2015b: 69). In fact, a growing comparative literature exists on the fiscal and monetary policy impact on growth, much of it in response to the Great Recession or economic collapse of 2008 (e.g. Baldacci and Gupta, 2009).

At the third level, the question is where these policy lessons can be applied? Technical/empirical work has been confined so far to the OECD countries which were most affected by the crisis. Lesson applicability to transitional/developing countries would depend on the strength of monetary policies and their linkage to the commercial banking systems. Their effectiveness would also depend on whether the fiscal/monetary policies of particular countries were linked mainly to state banks with the inevitability of politically driven credit. In India, for example, public sector banks make 75 percent of the loans and are unionized; 65 percent of the population lacks banking accounts; and about 11 percent of all state bank loans are non-performing (*Economist*, 2013b: 69–70). This suggests that lessons of fiscal policy responses such as stimuli and central bank responses as QE would have little effect in stimulating allocation of increased credit supply to deserving borrowers or increasing demand among a population disconnected from the banking system altogether. Many transitional/developing countries have these constraints which would limit the comparative applicability of financial crisis lessons from OECD countries. Nevertheless, depending on whether the focus is strategic or operational, the international policy toolkit should include both the comparative and political economy frameworks to analyze the results of policies and where their lessons might be applied.

Conclusions

The importance of a strong financial sector to a country's economic development lies in its primary responsibility to link depositor funds to businesses, increasing investment and economic growth. This responsibility is the key to the profit-making activities of banking institutions. However, the presence of asymmetric information, specifically adverse selection and moral hazard, creates a potential need for government to provide the necessary regulations. The occurrence of asset price bubbles leading to financial crises reflects financial imbalances and reinforces the need for effective financial regulation and oversight. Although the developed countries have created institutions to mitigate the risks of financial crises, the developing and emerging market countries, particularly with increased globalization, are still vulnerable to financial crises.

A developed financial structure includes critical regulations designed to protect individuals, private firms, and the general economy. As described in this chapter, many of the policies in the financial markets are created to separate the financial markets from public sector and political regime influences. Two general models guide relations between governments and their financial sectors. The OECD countries take efforts to have the financial sector be more independent from the influences of governmental institutions and policy. The primary state role in these countries is to provide regulations and enforce laws that increase the amount of information available in order to reduce adverse selection and moral hazard problems. That is, it needs to provide and enforce the legal and regulatory framework. Much of the rest of the world blurs the line between the government and the financial sector. Weak regulations and/or a weak financial system can increase the chances of adverse selection and moral hazard problems, creating greater opportunities for loan defaults. And as we have seen, financial liquidity may dry up as more bank capital is required to cover these liabilities. The resulting bank runs, fire sales, and contagion will cross borders further weakening financial systems.

As described, the problems of adverse selection and moral hazard weaken the financial system and the best way to avoid crises is to make sound loans in the first place. The failure of loan origination criteria that had existed for almost a century in the U.S. allowed the creation of toxic mortgage stocks. The loans should not have been granted in the first place because of the high probabilities for default. Nevertheless, larger perverse incentives encouraged banks and other financial institutions to make the loans, securitizing them and selling them for profit. Rating agencies and auditors were also complacent in accepting superficial figures that hid these risks without conducting their own due diligence. Properly designed internal controls in both public and private organizations can guard against systematic fiduciary losses by separating functions, i.e. loan evaluation from the signing of contracts and issuance of checks.

The recent reform focus has been on requirements to prevent banks from engaging in the riskiest activities. For example, European ring-fencing and U.S. regulatory efforts such as the Volcker Rule can prevent banks from taking customer (depositor) money and investing in stocks, bonds, and derivatives. This in theory should shield depositors from trader losses. The EU would separate depositor funds from other bank liabilities. To balance deposit liability, banks could only hold less risky capital assets such as cash, government bonds, and loans to individuals and firms. But for this to work, mortgage origination risk assessment and controls would still need to be in place, especially for commercial property. Other proposals would require banks to hold more equity on the asset side to manage risk. Still other proposals include requirements that banks balance debt-equity. The need is for both regulators as well as markets to make rules with proper incentives to help banks act prudently. At the least, this requires more vigilant rating agency efforts to focus on the substance of balance sheet figures and risks to creditworthiness. Paradoxically, countries that rely on credit rating agencies for both public and private sector creditworthiness may mean more of an arms-length relation with their main credit rating institutions and smarter public sector regulation.

Cases and Exercises

1   Read *Case 5.1* on China and answer the questions following:

Case 5.1 Chinese State v. Commercial Banking

Source: *Economist*, 2013a

At first sight, China seems to have a superb banking system. Its state-controlled banks, among the biggest and most profitable in the world, have negligible levels of non-performing loans and are well capitalized. That appears to suggest that the country's approach should be applauded. Not so. For one thing, though China's banking system is stable, its banks are not as healthy as they seem. The credit binge of recent years has left them with far higher levels of risky loans than they acknowledge. The banks find their biggest depositors have turned to bond markets. As a consequence, the country's Big Four banks—Industrial and Commercial Bank of China, Bank of China, Agricultural Bank of China and China Construction Bank—will no longer make easy money by merely issuing soft loans to state-owned enterprises (SOEs).What is more, that vaunted stability has come at a high price.

China's policy of financial repression, which forces households to endure artificially low interest rates on bank deposits so that subsidized capital can be lent to SOEs, is a cruel tax on ordinary people. The size of China's banks may seem impressive, but in fact it is a sign that the economy is excessively reliant on bank lending. And the incentives encouraging the risk-averse Big Four, whose bosses are leading figures in the Communist Party, to funnel lending to cronies at inefficient SOEs have starved dynamic "bamboo capitalists" of credit.

China's new leaders have acknowledged that the old approach has led to excesses, notably overcapacity in state industries. That is not enough. For a start, China should end financial repression. If deposit rates were gradually freed, banks would be forced to compete with each other for depositors and free to win back customers now lost to the shadow banking system. Most Chinese banks have no clue today about customer service, risk management or credit assessment. Miserable returns on bank deposits encourage punters to plough money into real estate and other riskier investments, so paying decent deposit rates might help prick the property bubble, too.

Second, China needs to go beyond banking. In many developed economies, non-bank firms and financial markets vie with banks to issue credit, but in the Middle Kingdom banks still dominate. In recent years Chinese firms raised nine times as much money from banks as they did on the country's stock exchanges. The corporate bond market has grown quickly of late (and big banks no longer gobble up most of the offerings). This growth should be encouraged.

Third, China must separate banking from crony state capitalism. The best way to do this is privatization. Smaller banks like China Merchants and China Minsheng, in which private investors have significant stakes, lend much more energetically to small businesses and households than do the state-controlled goliaths. Privatizing the Big Four would help, though it would make it harder for the state to manage any future banking crisis. And as long as sheltered, oligopolistic SOEs exist, banks will lend disproportionately to them because they enjoy implicit state backing.

a   Why do you think China is reluctant to allowing more foreign investment into the financial sector?
b   What evidence is there that banks facing market competition will be more effective in the Chinese economy?
c   How would you suggest that the Chinese banks learn about customer service, risk management, and credit assessment?

2   Read *Case 5.2* on India and answer the questions following:

Case 5.2 Indian Financial Sector Liberalization

Source: *Economist*, 2013d

Raghuram Rajan, the new governor of India's central bank, has championed financial-sector liberalization as a way to boost growth and help the poor. There are several well-run private banks, such as HDFC. But public-sector banks (most of which are listed but under state control) make three-quarters of all loans. Foreign banks' market share is 5 percent. Unlicensed moneylenders thrive, hinting at lots of unmet demand for credit. The Reserve Bank of India (RBI) is now fairly independent and no longer sets the rates of interest banks charge, but it still manipulates the flow of credit to assist the government and, at least notionally, the poor. Banks must invest 23 percent of their deposits in government bonds, and park a further 4 percent with the RBI. This creates a captive market for public debt, the bulk of which is owned by banks. Some 40 percent of loans must be directed towards "priority sectors", mainly agriculture. Taken together these rules mean that 58 percent of the deposits the banking system raises are deployed according to the government's preference.

The truth is that this hybrid system may now promote social inequality and financial instability—the twin evils it is meant to eradicate. For a start, after decades of state direction only 35 percent of adults have bank accounts. This perpetuates poverty and makes it hard to collect taxes. About 11 percent of state banks' loans have soured. The reserves they hold are low and their capital levels are mediocre. Because of India's weak legal system, banks dislike forcing firms into bankruptcy. The state banks have been pressed to roll over credit lines to troubled but well-connected big firms that most private banks steer clear of. This sort of cronyism makes the banking system less stable.

The hybrid system is complicit in a borrowing binge by the government: the budget deficit is running at 7–8 percent of GDP. Since bond yields are held down artificially by the RBI, which buys bonds itself and forces banks to, politicians can borrow heavily without fear of a buyers' strike.

Low interest rates and fast-rising prices mean the return savers get on deposits is below consumer-price inflation. Some people buy shares instead, but many bypass the formal financial system and buy gold, straining the balance of payments. Over half of the current-account deficit of 4.8 percent of GDP in the year to March 2013 was due to bullion imports. The vicious cycle of borrowing, inflation and gold partly explains the 22 percent slump in the rupee between May and August.

The rules that force banks to buy government debt will be relaxed "in a calibrated way". Rajan's unspoken hope is probably that state banks will be fully privatized and forced to raise their game. India's politicians like the power they have over these lenders. Private banks, meanwhile, are not charities. Some struggle to gather enough deposits, limiting their growth. A huge expansion in the number of branches would help, but might not be profitable. These institutions prefer to lend to yuppies than to farmers and infrastructure projects.

a   What policies would you suggest that could increase the India central bank independence?
b   Do you think India's politicians will allow private shareholders to own a majority of state banks?
c   Will expanding the number of bank branches achieve greater competition?
d   What determines the profitability of the additional bank branches?

3   Read *Case 5.3* on Sweden and answer the questions following:

Case 5.3 Swedish Banking Profitability

Source: *Economist*, 2013b

On September 24th Sweden sold its remaining 7 percent stake in Nordea, Scandinavia's biggest bank, a legacy of the country's 1990s banking crisis. That crisis—in which Swedish authorities swiftly wrote down bad assets, moved them into a "bad bank" and recapitalized the remaining "good bank"—informed many of the bail-outs in the 2008 financial crisis. Since then Sweden has again taken a lead on regulation. It has imposed some of the highest capital ratios in the rich world, with minimum levels of core tier-1 capital (the best sort) set at 12 percent from 2015, compared with a minimum of 7 percent by 2019 under Basel 3. In late August it proposed to ratchet capital levels yet higher, with plans to add up to 2.5 percent to the capital ratio as a counter-cyclical buffer. It has also interpreted risk-weightings far more strictly than many peers. It has tripled the amount of equity that banks have to use to fund mortgages; it may tighten further. Yet even these punitive levels of capital seem easily within reach. Many of the country's biggest banks already have capital ratios of about 12 percent under the new rules (and close to 15 percent under the old Basel 2 regime).

You might think such stiff regulation would lead to weak earnings. In fact Sweden's banks have been earning respectable profits, are able to pay dividends and have seen their share prices soar. Nordea's shares were up by 28 percent this year, just before the government sold its last stake. Those of smaller rivals such as Swedbank and SEB are also up by 20–25 percent. Swedish banks are generating among the highest returns on equity among rich-world banks. Number-crunchers at Citigroup reckon that the big Swedish lenders will be generating returns of about 15 percent over the next few years. That compares with forecast returns of 10–12 percent at other European banks such as Deutsche Bank, Barclays and Société Générale.

---

a   One reason for the strong profitability of Swedish banks is their careful control of costs. "Australian and Nordic banks are the most cost-efficient … in the world," Citi's bank analysts wrote in a recent report, citing among other factors their use of technology to get customers to bank digitally instead of using branches. They are also helped by the fact that they operate in a bit of an oligopoly and can thus pay measly rates on deposits. Yet their high capital ratios may also play a role. Credit-default-swap spreads for Sweden's big banks, a measure of default risk, are significantly lower than for many of their peers, suggesting that their borrowing costs are much lower, too. The solidity of their balance sheets seems to have proved attractive to investors who may still be wary of buying bank stocks. How does an oligopoly determine the profit maximizing output? What could be done to break the oligopoly up?

b   How do the Swedish reforms compare with the types of financial market bank reforms that were carried out in the U.S. after the 2008 financial crisis?

4   Suppose three individual assets are part of a portfolio. Each of the assets has a 10 percent probability of default. What is the overall default rate for the portfolio? Suppose the three assets are put into three tranches. What is the probability of default for the "senior" tranche?

5   Considering the characteristics of central bank independence described in this chapter, propose some measures that could be used to quantify central bank independence.

6   Read *Case 5.4* on Brazil and answer the questions following:

Case 5.4 Brazilian Fiscal and Economic Crisis

Source: *Economist,* 2015e: 67–68

Brazil does not look like an economy on the verge of overheating. The IMF expects it to shrink by 3 percent this year, and 1 percent next. (The country has not suffered two straight years of contraction since 1930–31). Fully 1.2m jobs vanished in the year to September; unemployment has reached 7.6 percent, up from 4.9 percent a year ago. Those still in work are finding it harder to make ends meet: real (ie, adjusted for inflation) wages are down 4.3 percent year-on-year. Despite the weak economy, inflation is nudging double digits.

If fast-rising prices are simply a passing effect of the real's recent fall, which has pushed up the cost of imported goods, then they are not too troubling. But some economists have a more alarming explanation: that Brazil's budgetary woes are so extreme that they have undermined the central bank's power to fight inflation—a phenomenon known as fiscal dominance.

The immediate causes of Brazil's troubles are external: the weak world economy, and China's faltering appetite for oil and iron ore in particular, have enfeebled both exports and investment. But much of the country's pain is self-inflicted. The president, Dilma Rousseff, could have used the commodity windfall from her first term in 2011–14 to trim the bloated state, which swallows 36 percent of GDP in taxes despite offering few decent public services in return. Instead, she splurged on handouts, subsidized loans and costly tax breaks for favored industries. These fueled a consumption boom, andwith it inflation, while hiding the economy's underlying weaknesses: thick red tape, impenetrable taxes, an unskilled workforce and shoddy infrastructure.

The government's profligacy also left the public finances in tatters. The primary balance (before interest payments) went from a surplus of 3.1 percent of GDP in 2011 to a forecast deficit of 0.9 percent this year. In the same period public debt has swollen to 65 percent of GDP, an increase of 13 percentage points. That is lower than in many rich countries, but Brazil pays much higher interest on its debt, the vast majority of which is denominated in reais and of relatively short maturity. It will spend 8.5 percent of GDP this year servicing it, more than any other big country. In September it lost its investment-grade credit rating.

The alluring real rates of almost 5 percent ought to have made reais attractive to investors. Instead, the currency has lost two-fifths of its value against the dollar over the past 12 months. It is this pattern of a weakening currency and rising inflation despite higher interest rates, combined with a doubling of debt-servicing costs in the past three years, that has led to the diagnosis of fiscal dominance. The cost of servicing Brazil's debts has become so high, pessimists fear, that rates have to be set to keep it manageable rather than to rein in prices. That, in turn, leads to a vicious circle of a falling currency and rising inflation.

The central bank could print money to buy government bonds. But such monetization would itself fuel inflation. Either way, spooked investors would surely dump government bonds for foreign assets, speeding the currency's fall and inflation's rise.

Brazil has been caught in such a trap before, most recently just over a decade ago.

The situation today is different, Mr Blanchard stresses. Real rates are less than half what they were in the early 2000s and only about 5 percent of government debt is denominated in dollars, compared with nearly half back then. The central bank's reluctance to raise the Selic further may have more to do with the impact on output than with fiscal concerns. Currency depreciation, too, could be down to general gloom about the economy rather than fear of default or money-printing. It has also made Brazil's $370 billion in foreign reserves more valuable in domestic-currency terms—a handy cushion.

---

a   What are the dimensions of the Brazilian fiscal/economic crisis?

b   How did the "trap" of falling currency values and high inflation occur?

c   How is the central bank's "fiscal dominance" being introduced and what should the current political regime do to get control of the public finances and to stimulate growth?

References

Baldacci, Emanuele and Sanjeev Gupta, "Fiscal Expansions: What Works," *Finance and Development*, 46, 4 (December 2009): 35.

Cecchetti, Stephen G., "Crisis and Responses: The Federal Reserve in the Early Stages of the Financial Crisis," *Journal of Economic Perspectives*, 23, 1 (Winter 2009): 51–75.

Classens, Stijn and M. Ayhan Kose, "Financial Crises: Explanations, Types, and Implications," IMF working paper, January 2013, International Monetary Fund, Washington, DC.

Crowe, Christopher and Ellen E. Meade, "The Evolution of Central Bank Governance Around the World," *Journal of Economic Perspectives*, 21, 4 (Fall 2007): 69–90.

Economist (2006) "Central Banks Under Fire: Out of Bounds," September 14. Available online at www.economist.com/node/7915358.

Economist (2013a) "Banks in China: Too Big to Hail," August 31. Available online at www.economist.com/news/leaders/21584342-chinas-banking-behemoths-are-too-beholden-state-it-time-set-finance-free-too-big.

Economist (2013b) "Swedish Banks: Tips from an Ageing Model," September 28. Available online at www.economist.com/news/finance-and-economics/21586839-where-banks-are-both-safe-and-profitable-tips-ageing-mode.

Economist (2013c) "Infrastructure: The Road to Hell," September 28. Available online at www.economist.com/news/special-report/21586680-getting-brazil-moving-again-will-need-lots-private-investment-and-know-how-road.

Economist (2013d) "Financial-Sector Reform in India: Bridging the Gulf," November 30: 69–70. Available online at www.economist.com/news/finance-and-economics/21590928-financial-system-intended-promote-equality-and-stability-no-longer.

Economist (2014) "The Opposite of Insurance," May 17, p. 71.

Economist (2015a) "Better Than It Looks," June 13, pp. 24–26.

Economist (2015b) "The Money Trap," August 22, p. 69.

Economist (2015c) "Bank Regulation in China: Letting Go," October 31, p. 69.

Economist (2015d) "Interest Rates in America: Buckle Up," December 12, pp. 67–68.

Economist (2015e) "Brazil's Economy, Broken Lever," October 31, pp. 67–68.

Friedman, Milton, "The Role of Monetary Policy," *American Economic Review*, 58, 1 (March 1968): 1–17.

Klomp, Jeroen and Jakob de Haan, "Inflation and Central Bank Independence: A Meta-Regression Analysis," *Journal of Economic Surveys*, 24, 4 (September 2010): 593–621.

Mishkin, Frederic S. (2006) *The Next Great Globalization: How Disadvantaged Nations Can Harness Their Financial Systems to Get Rich* (Princeton: Princeton University Press).

Mishkin, Frederic S. (2013) *The Economics of Money, Banking, and Financial Markets*, 10th ed. (Boston: Pearson).

New York Times, "Erosion of Argentine Peso Sends a Shudder Through Latin America," January 25, 2014. Available online at www.nytimes.com/2014/01/25/world/americas/argentina-eases-currency-controls-but-citizens-are-not-reassured.html.

Reis, Ricardo, "Central Bank Design," NBER working paper #19187, July 2013, National Bureau of Economic Research, Cambridge, MA.

World Bank, "World Development Indicators," The World Bank, Washington, DC. Available online at http: //data.worldbank.org/data-catalog/world-development-indicators.

World Economic Forum (WEF), *The Financial Development Report 2012*, World Economic Forum, New York. Available online at www3.weforum.org/docs/WEF_FinancialDevelopmentReport_2012.pdf.

6 Educational Policy

Introduction

Like health, social assistance, and transportation discussed previously, the provision of primary and secondary education is one of the fundamental governmental functions. Since World War II, educational expenditures have been the fastest-growing area of public spending in OECD countries. Educational importance on national agendas is reflected not just in budgetary outlays. The most important values and interests of a society are represented in education policy (Adolino and Blake, 2011: 321). Defining such basic interests has been a matter of great controversy across the globe. For example, in 2000, representatives from 164 countries met at the World Education Forum in Dakar, Senegal, and pledged six education goals to be achieved by 2015, including expanding early childhood education; increasing access to and improving the education for all citizens, particularly for girls and the poor; providing equal access to education; improving literacy by 50 percent; and eliminating education disparities between boys and girls. Two education goals to be accomplished by 2015 also appear among the eight United Nations Development Program (UNDP, 2012) Millennium Development Goals. One is the attainment of universal primary education, and the other goal targets the elimination of gender disparity in all levels of education.

The achievement of these goals will require significant governmental involvement. According to a recent UNDP (2012) progress report on those goals, the developed regions have seen significant increases in overall enrollments, with 97 percent of children who are at the official school age for primary education enrolled in primary or secondary school in 2010. The increased participation has led to improved literacy rates in these countries. Although significant gains have also been reported by several countries in the education of girls and, as a result, a reduction in the incidence of gender-based disparities, significant education gaps in developed countries remain. One uncertainty associated with reported gains in female education is they may be considerably overstated, as enrollments contain students who have been held back, thereby increasing the numbers enrolled in particular grades, and/or the number of girls enrolled is often purposely inflated by school officials or teachers. Using an alternative measure—net enrollment—which considers only those students who are age-appropriate for the grade, Glewwe and Kremer (2006) reported lower percentages enrollments in primary school across the various world regions, relative to the developed countries—e.g. 56 percent in sub-Saharan Africa, 84 percent in Northern Africa, and 93 percent in East Asia. A bright spot can be found in Latin America with 97 percent net enrollment, comparable to the OECD countries. Smaller secondary school enrollment percentages are recorded. A larger portion of citizens of the less developed countries have not attended schools or, if they did attend, were exposed to severely inadequate resources.

International assessments reveal large cross-country differences in student academic achievement. The Progress in International Reading Literacy Study (PIRLS), an international exam of literacy given to fourth graders, reports average literacy scores are highest in the developed countries, ranging between 310 in Morocco to 571 in Hong Kong. An alternative international examination, the Program for International Student Assessment (PISA) is administered every three years by the Organization for Economic Cooperation and Development (OECD) and tests 15-year-old students' mathematics, science, and reading literacy. The results from the 2012 PISA, shown in *Table 6.1*, also reveal a wide distribution in overall country performance.

Assessments range from 613 in Shanghai-China to 368 in Peru in the mathematics exam, 580 in Shanghai-China to 373 in Peru in the science exam, and 570 in Shanghai-China to 384 in Peru in the reading exam.

This chapter will: (1) describe some of the issues all governments face in the provision of primary and secondary education and the progress that has been achieved in solving these problems; (2) review spending levels on education and any student outcomes; (3) outline three of the primary goals of government provision of education—equity, adequacy, and productivity; (4) review several important educational reforms found throughout the world, including assessment and private provisions; (5) explain the importance of government fiscal and management decentralization in the provision of education; (6) explain the differences in results from policy responses by referring to the framework in *Chapter 1*; and (7) draw lessons for policy and operations management using several cases to highlight these lessons.

Government Expenditures on Education and Progress in Transitional and Developing Countries

An important issue in education policy is who controls the education system. This question breaks into: (1) what type of delivery system should be used? and (2) should the system be controlled by government or the private sector? First, in federal systems such as Canada, Australia, and the U.S., systems are more decentralized with delegation of important policy, administrative, and financing decisions to the local level. In unitary systems such as France and Japan, educational decision-making authority is more centralized and most strategic and operational decisions are made at the national level. Nevertheless, in all industrialized countries, the trends have been toward more decentralization of authority to public schools, and various forms of state-supported schools such as charters that give more authority to local officials (Adolino and Blake, 2011: 322). That positve trend might be characterized as: normative centralization of national and regional standards and operational decentralization over the methods and tools of learning to local officials. The second part of the issue relates to private–public educational service delivery. Because education can be and certainly is provided by the private sector in many developed and developing countries, and this provision is "excludable" by charging tuition and/or other fees, education is not a "pure" public good. Even so, governments continue to be the primary provider of education in most countries, particularly with primary and secondary education, as they recognize many critical benefits to a country from an educated citizenry. The government's financial commitment to the provision of primary and secondary education varies considerably worldwide. These cross-country government spending differences across mostly OECD countries are displayed in *Tables 6.2* and *6.3*. *Table 6.2* lists public expenditures on elementary and secondary education as a percentage of the country's GDP, ranging from 5.0 percent of GDP in Iceland to 2.3 percent of GDP in the Russian Federation.

Table 6.1 Performance on the 2012 PISA Examination: Mathematics, Reading, and Science

Country	Mean Math Score	Share of Low Achievers in Math	Share of Top Achievers in Math	Mean Reading Score	Mean Reading Score
OECD average	494	23	12.6	496	501
Shanghai-China	613	3.8	55.4	570	580
Singapore	573	8.3	40	542	551
Hong Kong-China	561	8.5	33.7	545	555
Chinese Taipei	560	12.8	37.2	523	523
Korea	554	9.1	30.9	536	538
Macao-China	538	10.8	24.3	509	521
Japan	536	11.1	23.7	538	547
Liechtenstein	535	14.1	24.8	516	525
Switzerland	531	12.4	21.4	509	515
Netherlands	523	14.8	19.3	511	522
Estonia	521	10.5	14.6	516	541
Finland	519	12.3	15.3	524	545
Canada	518	13.8	16.4	523	525
Poland	518	14.4	16.7	518	526
Belgium	515	19	19.5	509	505
Germany	514	17.7	17.5	508	524
Viet Nam	511	14.2	13.3	508	528
Austria	506	18.7	14.3	490	506
Australia	504	19.7	14.8	512	521
Ireland	501	16.9	10.7	523	522
Slovenia	501	20.1	13.7	481	514
Denmark	500	16.8	10	496	498
New Zealand	500	22.6	15	512	516
Czech Republic	499	21	12.9	493	508
France	495	22.4	12.9	505	499
United Kingdom	494	21.8	11.8	499	514
Iceland	493	21.5	11.2	483	478
Latvia	491	19.9	8	489	502
Luxembourg	490	24.3	11.2	488	491
Norway	489	22.3	9.4	504	495
Portugal	487	24.9	10.6	488	489
Italy	485	24.7	9.9	490	494
Spain	484	23.6	8	488	496
Russian Federation	482	24	7.8	475	486
Slovak Republic	482	27.5	11	463	471
United States	481	25.8	8.8	498	497
Lithuania	479	26	8.1	477	496
Sweden	478	27.1	8	483	485
Hungary	477	28.1	9.3	488	494
Croatia	471	29.9	7	485	491
Israel	466	33.5	9.4	486	470
Greece	453	35.7	3.9	477	467

Table 6.1 continued

Country	Mean Math Score	Share of Low Achievers in Math	Share of Top Achievers in Math	Mean Reading Score	Mean Reading Score
Serbia	449	38.9	4.6	446	445
Turkey	448	42	5.9	475	463
Romania	445	40.8	3.2	438	439
Cyprus	440	42	3.7	449	438
Bulgaria	439	43.8	4.1	436	446
United Arab Emirates	434	46.3	3.5	442	448
Kazakhstan	432	45.2	0.9	393	425
Thailand	427	49.7	2.6	441	444
Chile	423	51.5	1.6	441	445
Malaysia	421	51.8	1.3	398	420
Mexico	413	54.7	0.6	424	415
Montenegro	410	56.6	1	422	410
Uruguay	409	55.8	1.4	411	416
Costa Rica	407	59.9	0.6	441	429
Albania	394	60.7	0.8	394	397
Brazil	391	67.1	0.8	410	405
Argentina	388	66.5	0.3	396	406
Tunisia	388	67.7	0.8	404	398
Jordan	386	68.6	0.6	399	409
Colombia	376	73.8	0.3	403	399
Qatar	376	69.6	2	388	384
Indonesia	375	75.7	0.3	396	382
Peru	368	74.6	0.6	384	373

Table 6.2 Public Direct Expenditures on Elementary and Secondary Education (as a percentage of gross domestic product, by country): Selected years, 1995–2009

Country	1995	2000	2005	2007	2008	2009
OECD average	3.5	3.4	3.5	3.3	3.5	3.7
Australia	3.2	3.7	3.4	2.9	3.0	3.6
Austria	3.8	3.7	3.5	3.5	3.5	3.8
Belgium	3.4	3.4	3.9	3.9	4.3	4.3
Brazil	---	---	3.3	4.0	4.1	4.3
Canada	4.0	3.3	3.3	3.1	3.6	---
Chile	---	3.2	2.7	2.5	3.0	3.3
Czech Republic	3.4	2.8	2.7	2.5	2.5	2.6
Denmark	4.2	4.1	4.4	4.2	4.2	4.7
Estonia	---	---	3.5	3.3	3.8	4.1
Finland	4.2	3.5	3.8	3.6	3.8	4.1
France	4.1	4.0	3.8	3.7	3.7	3.8
Germany	2.9	2.9	2.8	2.6	2.6	2.9
Greece	2.8	2.7	2.5	---	---	---
Hungary	3.3	2.8	3.3	3.2	3.0	3.0
Iceland	3.4	4.6	5.2	4.9	4.9	5.0
Ireland	3.3	2.9	3.3	3.4	4.0	4.6
Israel	---	4.5	4.2	3.9	4.0	3.8
Italy	3.2	3.2	3.2	3.0	3.2	3.3
Japan	2.8	2.7	2.6	2.5	2.5	2.7
Korea, Republic of	3.0	3.3	3.4	3.1	3.4	3.6
Luxembourg	4.2	---	3.7	3.1	2.8	3.2
Mexico	3.4	3.3	3.7	3.1	3.1	3.3
Netherlands	3.0	3.0	3.3	3.3	3.3	3.7
New Zealand	3.8	4.6	4.0	3.5	3.8	4.5
Norway	4.1	3.6	3.8	3.7	5.0	4.2
Poland	3.3	3.7	3.7	3.4	3.4	3.5
Portugal	4.1	4.1	3.8	3.5	3.4	4.0
Russian Federation	1.9	1.7	1.9	3.4	2.0	2.3
Slovak Republic	---	2.7	2.5	2.3	2.2	2.7
Slovenia	---	---	3.9	3.3	3.4	3.6
Spain	3.5	3.1	2.7	2.7	2.9	3.1
Sweden	4.4	4.4	4.2	4.1	4.0	4.2
Switzerland	4.1	3.8	3.9	3.5	3.8	3.8
Turkey	1.4	2.4	---	---	---	---
United Kingdom	3.8	3.4	3.8	4.1	4.2	4.5
United States	3.5	3.5	3.5	3.7	3.8	3.9

---Not available.

Source: Organization for Economic Cooperation and Development (OECD), Online Education Database; and *Education at a Glance,* 2007 through 2012. U.S. Department of Education, National Center for Education Statistics, *International Education Indicators: A Time Series Perspective, 1985-1995* (NCES 2000-2012). (This table was prepared June 2012.)

Table 6.3 Gross Domestic Product Per Capita and Public and Private Educational Expenditures Per Student (in constant 2011 dollars, by country): Selected years, 2005–2009

| Country | Elementary and secondary education expenditures per student | | | |
	2005	2007	2008	2009
OECD average	$7,775	$8,035	$8,542	$9,012
Australia	8,226	8,234	8,163	9,582
Austria	10,869	10,804	11,486	12,247
Belgium	8,415	9,040	10,140	10,258
Canada	8,954	9,100	9,399	---
Chile	2,417	2,266	2,345	2,763
Czech Republic	4,720	5,112	5,471	5,888
Denmark	10,363	10,250	10,896	11,632
Estonia	4,303	5,031	6,325	6,448
Finland	7,614	7,829	8,429	8,717
France	8,588	8,755	8,942	9,290
Germany	8,107	7,857	8,210	8,948
Greece	6,327	---	---	---
Hungary	4,638	4,742	4,833	4,725
Iceland	10,153	9,708	10,181	9,760
Ireland	7,384	8,453	9,314	10,082
Israel	5,806	5,799	6,039	5,729
Italy	8,534	8,430	9,477	9,377
Japan	8,458	8,692	8,672	8,914
Korea, Republic of	6,494	7,228	7,024	8,516
Luxembourg	18,349	16,901	17,666	18,891
Mexico	2,333	2,349	2,386	2,452
Netherlands	8,115	9,299	9,665	10,517
New Zealand	6,519	5,917	6,786	7,923
Norway	11,490	11,776	12,611	13,600
Poland	3,645	4,127	4,891	5,417
Portugal	6,503	6,398	6,557	7,641
Slovak Republic	3,156	3,575	4,186	5,012
Slovenia	8,137	7,883	8,938	9,091
Spain	7,384	8,322	8,903	9,246
Sweden	9,055	9,517	9,951	10,180
Switzerland	12,348	12,695	14,392	14,061
United Kingdom	7,934	9,354	9,579	10,068
United States	11,252	11,682	11,488	12,404

Note: Includes all expenditures by public and private education institutions (such as administration, instruction, ancillary services for students and families, and research and development) unless otherwise noted. Postsecondary non-higher-education is included in elementary and secondary education unless otherwise noted. Data adjusted to U.S. dollars using the purchasing-power-parity (PPP) index. Constant dollars based on the Consumer Price Index, prepared by the Bureau of Labor Statistics, U.S. Department of Labor.

Source: Organization for Economic Cooperation and Development (OECD), *Education at a Glance,* 2008 through 2012. (This table was prepared June 2012.)

Real per pupil expenditures (in 2011 U.S. dollars) listed in *Table 6.3* is a common measure of the government's involvement in education. These data reveal similar spending differences across countries, ranging from nearly $19,000 in Luxembourg to about $2,500 in Mexico. Significant differences are also found in education spending across less wealthy countries.

In addition to these inter-country differences, there are also significant intra-country differences in spending that can, in part, be attributed to the decentralization of revenue and expenditure responsibilities down to the subnational governments found in many countries. A notable example of this can be found in the U.S. primary and secondary education system. The U.S. federal government contributes about 10 percent of total education spending, with state and local (counties, cities, and school districts) governments splitting about evenly the other 90 percent of funding. As a result of this decentralization to the states and local governments, the U.S. faces large within-country differences. In 2010, the average primary and secondary educational spending per pupil on instruction in the U.S. was $6,526 and ranged from the low of $4,154 in Utah to a high of $12,676 per pupil in New York. Since this is spending on instruction, the variance does not reflect differences in operation and administrative expenditures and it is too wide to be explained by cost of living differences across the states. Instead this spread reflects differences in state-level demand for educational expenditures in state and local governments. It is this characteristic of keeping spending decisions closer and more responsive to the demands of the local citizens that is one of the benefits of the decentralized governmental structure (discussed in greater detail below).

Why does government assume the financing of the bulk of education in most countries, particularly when the private market has proven capable of providing this service? Government spending on education could be seen as a correction for the private market's failure to allocate education "efficiently," generally described as a "market failure." One type of market failure is the presence of beneficial externalities or spillovers. These types of externalities arise when the benefits from a private market transaction are received by individuals who are outside of the normal "market" transaction and private compensation for the receipt of those benefits is not possible. As a result of this inability to charge a price for these external benefits, the private market price system will not allocate the good efficiently and will provide too little of the good than is socially optimal.

Figure 6.1 illustrates the effect of this market failure on the inability of the market to achieve the socially efficient optimal output level. Where the curve representing the marginal private benefits of consumption (MB) equals the curve that represents the marginal private costs (MC) associated with the production of this good is where the perfectly competitive market will be in equilibrium at Q_{PRI}, designated as the "actual output." The presence of a positive externality creates marginal external benefits, represented by the MEB curve, which must be accounted for in order to reach the "socially efficient output" level, Q_{OPT}, where the marginal social benefits (MSB=MB+MEB) equals MC. Since the definition of externalities means there are no private market incentives to take into account the MEB, then the competitive market will produce Q_{PRI} and not Q_{OPT}, the socially optimal output level. In other words, the competitive market will produce too little of this good than is optimal and it will be inefficient.

The presence of externalities in the educational context means the benefits from education extend to individuals beyond the educated student into the community. For example, education can be an important component in educating a country's citizens to be full participants in a society and if this education causes that person to be a "better citizen," then educational programs will potentially benefit all the country's citizens. It is in the role of citizenship-builder where one might expect education to be important in teaching the student about the country's basic governmental structure and the society's history, customs, and norms.

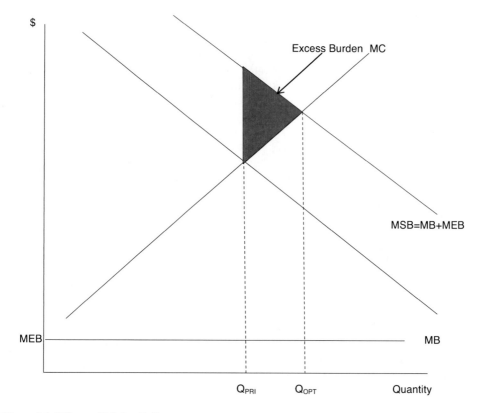

Figure 6.1 Effects of Market Failure

However, education has been used by authoritarian regimes to support the government's power. A World Bank (2003) report cites the Indonesian President Suharto's use of the education system to promote the five principles of *pancasila*, which is the country's official philosophical foundation. A related aspect is the role education plays in socializing immigrants into a country. Another potential externality is that an educated citizen is also seen as crucial for the adoption of new technologies, creating economic benefits extending beyond the educated individual. Finally, there is considerable evidence that education and crime are inversely related. Consequently, positive external effects are possible if an educated citizenry creates a reduction in crime and social disruptions. Governments value the links between education and several important developing and emerging market country outcomes, including increased productivity and income as well as improved country economic growth. However, even if these externalities are present, they may not require the type of universal education created by government intervention.

There may be other justifications for public sector provision of education. Governments may try to correct for parental underinvestment in education. If parents do not fully appreciate the personal or social value of educating their children, then governments will act paternalistically to correct for this underinvestment. Such values are clearly identified in recent international efforts in the education of girls in many developing countries. In his launch of the UN's education millennial goals, the Secretary General of United Nations Ban Ki-moon described education as "the basic building block of every society and a pathway out of poverty. More education means less vulnerability to extreme poverty and hunger. [Education provides] more opportunities for women and girls, more health and basic sanitation, more power to fight HIV, malaria, cholera, and other killer diseases." (See www.un.org/apps/news/infocus/sgspeeches/search_full.asp?statID=1676.)

Basic Education Finance

The standard method of allocating education expenditures in many countries is by "per student financing," or capitation-based funding which allocates funding to schools based on the number of students in the school. This is the education finance formula commonly found in the U.S., UK, and throughout the EU. The local school systems in many U.S. school districts employ a version of this formula funding system. For example, the *foundation* level of local expenditures in the Washington, DC, primary and secondary school system is determined by the *Uniform Per Student Funding Formula*, which mandates all public school students receive equal amounts of core education or foundation spending. In DC and in other U.S. states, the foundation amounts are then adjusted, generally in an *ad hoc* upward way, to account for particular students defined as "at risk," including students from low-income families and with limited English proficiency. Similar foundation weights are applied to account for the education of special education students.

Other countries have implemented alternative types of funding allocation mechanisms with far less effectiveness than the per student formula. One type is historic funding or incrementalism, where schools receive the same level or some modest incremental increase in the level of funding based on the previous year's level. Another common funding strategy is where schools are subject to the whims of a central funding agency either by being forced to bargain each year for funds or just by being subjected to the central government administrator's judgment as to the appropriate funding level. Judgmental approaches such as this are obviously the most unstable sources of funding and make it difficult for school-level officials to plan classes and teach them for the next school year. Changes in the demographic circumstances have necessitated modification to the way education is financed and require that they adopt the basic per student education funding formula.

Examples of these changes are found in Europe and Central Asia. As several of the countries emerged from communist control, they experienced changes in their demographics, specifically a decreasing fertility rate and the out-migration of its citizens. A World Bank (2011) study examined the policy responses of six of these countries—Russia, Lithuania, Georgia, Estonia, Poland, and Armenia—as each switched their education funding from a centralized finance system of historic/incrementalist funding to a decentralized per student formula in the wake of significant demographic shifts. This critical reform was part of a general movement in these countries to promote local government institutions as a way to diffuse the central government's political power. As described in the World Bank report, between 2000 and 2007 the school age population fell by 21 percent in Estonia, 20 percent in Armenia, 19 percent in Poland, and 12 percent in Lithuania. As expenditures were previously determined by a historic funding/incrementalist system, the schools in these countries did not immediately experience a reduction in their finance allocation even though they had plummeting class sizes, an excess number of teachers, too many schools, and an inefficiently high level of per pupil spending. Decentralization and the switch to a student capitation funding formula forced the schools in these countries to increase class sizes, reduce the number of teachers, and close many schools. Armenia reduced the number of teachers by 35 percent. There was also consolidation of schools—Poland reduced by 10 percent the number of schools and Lithuania went from 808 primary schools to 114. This shift created a more decentralized financing formula and diminished the role of the centralized allocation process and increased potential for better student outcomes as the most effective teachers were retained. Moreover, this deconcentration of financing from the central government provided opportunities for increased efficiency by introducing more competition among schools. To the extent that it also gave local governments the authority to link finance decisions to assessment mechanisms, the reform was an actual decentralization (as opposed to deconcentration of authority from the center to local units of the central government) which increased operational level accountability and transparency for parents.

Government Education Goals

Since education policy represents the most basic interests and values of a society, definition of actual goals and objectives is controversial. Because of the perceived gap between school system promise and wider performance in generating socioeconomic development, near universal calls for educational reform echo across the globe. That is because education reflects the most basic goals of a society in creating: individual success, social harmony, and competitiveness. The first two interests or goals are clearly social; the others are more narrowly economic. Nearly everywhere there are calls for reform. Reform successes, for example, are determined by access to good schools on the assumption that schooling will serve as a leveler as opposed to more stratified systems that perpetuate existing social or economic divisions (Adolino and Blake, 2011: 321). Opponents of equal access argue that such policies squander resources, especially at the secondary-school and university levels, thereby restricting achievement for all pupils by spreading funds around too thinly (ibid., 2011: 321). Note that the social value of equal access also merges with economic objective of equity. From the economic perspective, the equal access goal can be broken into three broader goals of achieving: educational equity, ensuring funding adequacy (or sufficient service coverage), and operating efficiently. Each of these goals either focuses on the inputs to education or the particular education outcomes, and/or the relationship between these inputs and outcomes. The achievement of *equity* will generally result in equal amounts of educational resources provided across different groupings—local school districts, school boards, schools, and/or students. Ensuring *adequacy* requires a definition of "adequate" education, with an emphasis on determining the level of resources necessary to achieve a predetermined education outcome, such as targeted levels of test scores and/or school graduation rates. To operate *efficiently* means achieving educational outcomes at the lowest cost in addition to understanding what education inputs as well as what input proportions best achieve the desired outcomes. Although these goals may ultimately be related (particularly the equity and adequacy goals), because of the inherent trade-offs involved, it is difficult to achieve all three goals simultaneously. In addition, each of these goals will probably require policies originating from different levels of government, necessitating a further discussion of the issues underlying fiscal federalism.

Goal 1: Equity

A basic governmental education goal is to achieve greater "equity" of education resources. Equity can be defined over two dimensions. Horizontal equity or the equal treatment of equals requires that students who are "alike" be provided equal amounts of educational resources. This dimension of equity is defined by a measure of the equality of the "inputs" into the education process measured across school districts, schools, or students, including teacher quality (often defined by teacher salaries, experience, and education), capital expenditures, class sizes (generally measured by simple student–teacher ratios), curriculum materials, other basic education inputs, and, probably the most commonly used input measure, per pupil expenditures. Of course, if governments employ a version of the "per student" funding formula described above, then horizontal equity across schools is achieved by definition. However, horizontal inequities arise in two other ways and cannot be easily solved by this per student funding formula. In many developing countries, where universal education is not as common as found in more developed countries, horizontal inequities can arise across a variety of student classifications, specifically gender, race, and socioeconomic status. As described in the introduction above, the United Nations' and other international agencies' call for universal education is an attempt to highlight and correct inequities in education provided to boys and girls. Horizontal inequities are also created in systems where the revenue and expenditure responsibilities have been devolved from the central government to the subnational or local governments. With a decentralized educational financing system, resource inequities can arise across the subnational governmental units (e.g. states, provinces, regions, cities, counties, and/ or school districts) as citizens from the different governments make different expenditure decisions.

Standard measures of educational resource inequality across these aggregate units are similar to those used to measure income and/or wealth inequality. The most basic equity statistic is some form of expenditure "range"—i.e. the simple difference between the top measure of the resource value input and the bottom measure. The closer the range is to zero, the more equal the distribution of inputs across the units. The primary advantage of the range is the ease of calculation and interpretation. One of its disadvantages is that the range does not reveal any of the inequities that occur between the high and low measures.

Table 6.4 lists two different hypothetical sets of average per pupil expenditures across nine different school districts. The range is equal to $4,290 in both sets of data. However, there are clear differences in the amount of inequality found across both groups of schools. A cursory review of the two groups suggests the second set has a more equal distribution of spending than the first set, as seven of the nine schools have an identical expenditure level that is relatively close to the highest level of spending. Another disadvantage with the range measure is its sensitivity to the effects of inflation. Consider that an inflation rate of 10 percent raises

Table 6.4 School District Equity Example

School	Local Revenue Per Pupil #1	Local Revenue Per Pupil #2	Local Revenue Per Pupil #1 X 10%
1	2,800	2,800	3,080
2	3,045	6,500	3,349.5
3	3,250	6,500	3,575
4	3,500	6,500	3,850
5	3,900	6,500	4,290
6	4,100	6,500	4,510
7	4,475	6,500	4,922.5
8	5,445	6,500	5,989.5
9	7,090	7,090	7,799
Range	4,290	4,290	4,719
Coefficient of Variation	0.306	0.195	0.306

all of the expenditure levels by the same percentage, as shown in column 3. Because all expenditure levels are raised by 10 percent, then inequality is not actually affected. However, the calculated range for these expenditures is $4,719, indicating an increase in measured expenditure inequality.

Two other inequality measures address these deficiencies. The coefficient of variation (CV) is a straightforward measure of the spread of the expenditure data. The CV measures the percent variation about the mean of the observations. The CV's two primary advantages over the range are that it uses all of the observations and does not change over time as a result of inflation.

The CV is calculated by dividing the standard deviation of the observations by the mean of the observations or

$CV = (Std\ Dev)/(Mean)$, where

$Std\ Dev = \sqrt{\sum_1^N\{(Observation - Mean)/N\}^2}$

Mean = the simple average = $\sum_1^N Observation$

and Observations = 1…..N

CV varies between 0 and 1 or, equivalently, between 0 percent and 100 percent, with lower numbers representing greater equity and zero equaling perfect equity or a uniform distribution. The primary disadvantage of CV is that since 0 will not be likely, the ideal standard CV is a value judgment. The calculated CVs for the two examples are reported in the bottom row of *Table 6.4*. A smaller CV of 0.195 or 19.5 percent for the second group indicates a more equal distribution, as compared with the 0.306 or 30.6 percent. This is expected, given the seven equal and relatively high expenditure levels inside the extreme observations.

Another inequality measure that uses all of the observations is the Gini coefficient. Although it is a commonly used measure of wealth and income inequality, in the education context, the Gini measures the extent to which the distribution of education expenditures among schools (or other areas like school districts, counties, states, regions, or cities) deviates from a perfectly equal distribution. The primary disadvantages of the Gini are that it is a much more complicated inequality statistic to compute than the CV and more difficult to interpret. A perfectly equal distribution of resources requires a match between the cumulative percentage of schools (beginning with the poorest school) and the cumulative percentage of resources (e.g. the first 10 percent of schools receives 10 percent of total expenditures, the next 10 percent of schools receives 10 percent, etc.). Calculation of the Gini coefficient begins with the Lorenz curve, created by plotting the actual cumulative percentages of total education expenditures received against the cumulative number of schools, starting with the poorest school. The Gini coefficient measures the area between the Lorenz curve and the hypothetical line of absolute equality, expressed as a percentage of the maximum area under the line. It ranges between 0, measuring perfect equality, where the Lorenz curve is equivalent to the line of equality, and 1, where one school receives all of the expenditure and the other schools receive no funding. As with the CV, the "ideal" Gini coefficient is also a value judgment.

Assuming the resource equities across these units can be accurately measured, then any policies designed to improve horizontal equity will require redistributing input measures across the local school units—school districts, cities, regions, and states/provinces. Consequently, any improvement of equity needs to be addressed at a higher level of government than the local units. Wealthy lower-level governments will not voluntarily give up resources to less wealthy lower-level governments in order to improve overall equity. A major source of inequity is caused by the reliance of local financing based on wealth, such as local property taxes. Several Canadian provinces adopted policies in the mid-1990s designed to undo the inequities inherent in local property tax funding systems by moving financing from the local municipalities to the provincial level beginning with the British Columbia enactment of a provincial-based educational funding system in the early 1990s (Herman, 2013). The province of Alberta is a good example of the types of funding systems that followed. It assumed all of the funding responsibility by centrally setting the local government property tax rates, which then became uniform across the province, and required that local governments send the money upwards to the provincial government. The Alberta School Foundation Fund (ASFF) was created to collect these funds and combine them with general revenue from the provincial sources and then dispense the funds on a per pupil basis to the local "school boards" (equivalent to U.S. school districts), resulting in improved education finance equity. The ASFF budget is designed to be separate from other provincial governmental financial duties, which makes it a source of educational finance transparency to the Alberta citizens. The categories of students receiving more support extended beyond the simple poverty measures used in the U.S. and incorporated the parents' education, whether there were two parents, as well as other "at need" factors. Although these changes appeared to reduce the amount of local control, the Alberta education act allowed the local governments a greater degree of budgetary discretion (as long as it did not violate the general requirements of the act). The province of Ontario also passed a similar provincial-centered funding system.

If the focus is solely on the "equality" of expenditures across these aggregate units, then the level of equality may be unimportant, since it could be achieved but with all units, or certainly the previously higher spending local districts, ending up with an equal but lower amount of expenditures. In 1971, the California State Supreme Court case [in *Serrano v. Priest*] declared the California system of funding its schools unconstitutional because of severe funding inequalities across the school districts. The legislative remedy was to require the California state government to impose an equal system of school district education funding, and 20 years after the court's decision and this equity remedy was imposed, all equity measures indicated greater equality. However, during that same period, California's education spending fell by nearly 25 percent and its state ranking for per pupil spending fell from eleventh among all states to thirtieth. Moreover, although the Canadian provinces of British Columbia, Alberta, and Ontario generated a more equalized system and performed well on the PISA, Husted and Kenny (2000) found that state-average university admissions examination results from U.S. high school students were inversely related to the amount of increase in equity across the states, suggesting an equity and efficiency (measured by student performance) trade-off.

Goal 2: Adequacy

The second educational goal is the achievement of adequacy or for public spending on education to be sufficient for pupils to reach some predetermined education outcome goal. This focus on both educational inputs and the educational outcomes represents a clear improvement from singular focus on the equality of resources found with the equity goal. An input focus involves the determination of the curricula, instruction/teacher resources, and capital sufficient to achieve the defined educational standard. By contrast, the outcome-side focus represents the measurement of that standard in order to determine the effectiveness of these inputs. The first step toward the achievement of this goal is the definition of an appropriate measure of educational adequacy, which usually involves the achievement of a certain level of test scores and/or graduation rates. Because of their ease of collection, the most common outcome measures used are generally periodically administered assessments such as government-administered exams. In the U.S., every state is required to have annual assessments of their primary and secondary students in order to measure the progress made toward the goals in the federal government's education policies of *No Child Left Behind*. These assessments are often used to measure the goals of adequacy. The state of Kentucky defined education adequacy much more broadly to include "sufficient oral and written communication skills," "sufficient knowledge of economic, social, and political systems," "sufficient understanding of government processes," "sufficient grounding in the arts," as well as "sufficient levels of academic or vocational skills to enable public school students to compete favorably with their counterparts in surrounding states." Central governments continue to devise methods to measure the success of all the local schools in reaching these goals and to apply possible sanctions on those schools that fail to reach them.

A critical step in achieving the adequacy goal involves determining the amount of funding necessary to reach the defined adequate outcome. This step is made more complicated as a result of differences among the student population. The adequacy goal is related to vertical equity or the unequal treatment of unequals. Achievement of education adequacy will require more resources allocated to those local schools with the greatest needs (more at-risk and special education students) because such students need relatively greater support. For example, students from lower-income backgrounds or with physical and mental disabilities will necessarily require greater inputs to reach the adequate outcome. Adequacy is achieved with the provision of curriculum and instruction with adjustments for special needs (e.g. at-risk students and special education) that is sufficient for all students to perform at a high standard.

Goal 3: Efficiency

The third educational policy goal is the achievement of "efficiency" in the production of education outcomes. This goal of education efficiency is grounded in the general theory of economic production. Specifically, education outcomes are produced efficiently with the least cost combination of inputs. Many studies examining the efficient production of education have applied the straightforward "input–output" production function relationship. Following the techniques used in the standard production relationships of "regular" industries (e.g. cars, steel, and electricity), the focus of these studies is not on what specifically goes on inside the schools.

There are some significant differences between the estimation of a standard production function for the standard industries and the educational production function. One difference is that important educational production inputs originate from sources outside the school policy-maker's (i.e. the school and/or government administrators identified as "producers" in the education production relationship) control. For example, family contributions (resource or otherwise), non-school learning, neighborhood and peer influences, and the student's innate ability all contribute to the student's education and cannot be directly controlled by the policy-maker. The main educational inputs under the policy-maker's control include the employment of teachers, as well as the provision of books, computers, curricula, and capital spending. The standard set of inputs used to explain any chosen output in an education production function model include pupil characteristics (e.g. innate ability, time or effort in school work), family characteristics (e.g. parents' education, income, number of books in the home, computers in the home, non-school activities), and school and teacher characteristics (e.g. per-pupil education expenditures, teacher experience, teacher education, teacher training, classroom curricula and materials, technology) that can be changed by the school and/or government.

Standard empirical production function models require a measurable output which is clearly identified in the standard industries. The second critical difference between these standard production functions and the educational production function is the inability to identify an "output" and an appropriate educational outcome. The most common measures used include student achievement, generally measured by test scores and/or graduation rates. A common criticism of this approach is that the singular focus on test scores potentially misses a considerable amount of alternative education outcomes. Many subjects that are taught in primary and secondary schools like art, performing arts, and other qualitative subjects or even key concepts like citizenship are not easily summarized by an assessment exam. Thus, it may be easier to gauge educational results or "outputs" from standardized tests and graduation/ promotion rates than outcomes (see *Figure 1.2*) or quality of education measured in more subjective ways such as rates of later employment and satisfaction surveys.

As government support for primary and secondary education increases worldwide, it is interesting to examine whether this increase in resources has led to improved educational outputs. There have been hundreds of empirical studies in the U.S. and other countries attempting to identify the school and non-school inputs with the greatest impact on improving student outputs. The approach is to estimate the input–output relationship using standard regression techniques. The estimated coefficients on the explanatory variables indicate the impact of each of these inputs on the education output (e.g. exam scores), accounting for the other inputs or holding them constant. The key contribution of this education production function research is the empirical examination of the relationships between the school and teacher characteristics and the education outputs. Hanushek (1997) describes the modeling underlying input–output research on the impact of school resources on student outcomes. He finds that overall, school inputs (those under control of the policy-maker) are generally insignificantly related to student achievement. He also lists the common statistical problems that can arise with the estimation of these models, including statistical bias of the estimated effects due to the omission of important inputs from the model and the potential for measurement errors. If important variables are omitted from the statistical model and they are related to the included variables, then the included variables will incorporate the effects of those omitted variables and their results will be biased, further weakening the relationship between the school inputs and student achievement. Errors in the measurement of the output and/or input variables are always a potential problem in empirical research. These problems are obviously exacerbated by the weaknesses in the agency infrastructure designated as the collector of these data in lower-income countries.

Although not universally accepted, the findings point to a lack of a clear or strong relationship between education resources and student achievement, particularly from the hundreds of papers that focused on the developed countries (generally the U.S.), after accounting for the student and family backgrounds. Greater amounts of school inputs (e.g. lower class sizes, increased teacher salaries, and greater teacher education and experience levels) evidently do not lead to greater student performance. Many of these studies have been carried out in the U.S. in an effort to explain the concurrent increase in education expenditures and the decreasing or stagnant performance on all types of student assessments. As described above, the 2012 international PISA examined 15-year-olds from 65 countries worldwide on mathematics, science, and reading literacy. The average score for students in the U.S. in all three literacy areas fell in about the middle of the 65 countries. The U.S. mathematics score was 481, which was lower than 29 countries and higher than 26. The score had not changed appreciably from the three previous exam periods (PISA is given every three years). At 497, the U.S. science literacy average score placed it lower than 22 countries and higher than 29 and was also not appreciably different from the previous exam periods. The average reading literacy score of 498 placed the U.S. lower than 19 countries and higher than 34 and not appreciably different from previous exam years. The relatively low performance of U.S. students and the continued lack of improvement over time on PISA as well as similar results in other international and national exams have raised concerns. Goldstein (2013) describes some of these concerns. He also provides a note of caution about thinking the current set of proposed educational reforms will necessarily result in any improvements, raising questions about the impacts of income inequality, child care, health care, and school organization on exam results (see *Question 4* at the end of the chapter).

In addition, the lack of relationship between the inputs under the control of the school policy-maker and student achievement has been particularly true in countries from the developing regions where government support has increased the most. Glewwe et al. (2011) reviewed the more recent (1990–2010) studies that estimated educational production function models using data from countries in the developing regions. They identified 72 papers, including 43 "high-quality" papers that corrected for some of the possible empirical problems described above, published in journals or as working papers that met the requirements that the research was carried out on developing countries and incorporate school- or teacher-level inputs. When the authors reviewed the estimates from these studies, they found that, when included, the most common positive effects on student achievement were from the impact of textbooks and work books. As for the teacher inputs, teacher education had the largest effect of all of the included variables. However, teacher experience, a common important input in the U.S. data, was not as important to student outputs. Teachers with higher test scores on the subject they were teaching had a strong impact on student achievement. The key conclusions from this literature were first, unsurprisingly, that education was important, and second, that the teacher's gender and whether he/she had any in-service training did not seem to have a consistently strong impact on student achievement measured by test scores.

Several curious issues arise when considering the relationship between educational resources and outputs, particularly as developing countries attempt to institute universal education. The first is the expected empirical relationship between inputs and student performance when more, and potentially less well prepared, students are introduced to formal education system. How does that affect achievement? Although it might be expected that increased school enrollment brings in students who are not as prepared for formal education, reducing the impact of the increased government provided resources, Glewwe et al. (2011) found reduced student performance in some countries (e.g. Argentina and Brazil) that experienced increased spending but which had only experienced small or moderate increases in enrollment. Another simple but interesting comparison is found in *Table 6.1* among countries with similar populations. Although Uruguay generally performed better on the PISA than Argentina, Uruguay spends slightly less than Argentina on education. Yet while Uruguay compares well to neighboring Latin American countries on PISA performance (*Table 6.1*), Argentina is among the lowest scorer, of all Latin American countries. Another example is the difference in performance between the U.S. and Canada. Both countries spend about 3.5 percent–4.0 percent GDP on education and yet Canadian students perform better on the PISA. Finally, while female students tend to have higher average scores than the male students in most of the OECD countries, severe problems remain in the education of girls in the countries from the developing regions, which will affect country performance as universal education policies are applied.

Of course the three goals of equity, adequacy, and efficiency are interrelated. The clearest statement of this interrelationship often cited in economics is the inverse relationship between equity and efficiency. That is, as policies are developed to make resources more equal, these same policies will negatively affect the efficiency of the delivery of those resources, which will be reflected in the measures of education output like achievement. The universal education reforms listed in the UN's education millennial goals are potentially more redistributive as they will benefit the children who have historically been left out of many countries' education systems, typically the poor and girls. However, the introduction of these new and perhaps less well-prepared students into the education system can potentially reduce significantly the common summary measures of academic performance, which can reduce country education efficiency.

Other educational reforms are focused on improving the education system for the existing students. Although the underlying theory suggests you cannot achieve "something for nothing," this does not have to be the case if the current expenditure levels are reallocated to more efficient uses.

Application of Policy Analytic Frameworks: Educational Goals and Reforms

Many countries with poor student performance on PISA tests in reading, math, and science have undertaken major structural reforms of their educational systems. Reforms also target school productivity, e.g. teacher and student attendance and graduation rates, as well as the problem of youth unemployment that constrains economic growth and suggests the need to link workplaces and schools more closely through apprenticeship programs. Reform lessons are flowing across continents, within them at the regional level, and between developed and developing countries and back. The flow of applied lessons from actual reform experiences is brisk, and many changes have been made in response to improve school performance. At the same time, reforms to increase competition and school choice by parents as well as to increase selectivity of students by schools have met serious political opposition from leaders as well as union groups representing teachers and other school workers. Nevertheless, the transferability of many of these applied lessons is largely universal, constrained only by the usual factors of local professional standards, political culture affecting student curricula, and even attendance, levels of poverty, and school resources.

Thus, at the first technical level, studies are largely consistent on the benefits of particular reforms. Where reforms target multiple problems with solutions tested in other similar countries, the acceptance may be more difficult by traditional political groups such as teacher unions and school administrators. For example, Italy is attempting a seven-part reform: (1) financial rewards for best teachers; (2) increased collaboration between schools and workplaces; (3) teacher stipends for books, software, and students' visits to museums; (4) devolution of authority to school heads to pick and reward teachers; (5) allowing parents to earmark a portion of their taxes to support particular schools and receipt of tax credits from donations to schools; (6) increase state funding for Catholic schools; and (7) eliminate "supply teachers" which have been hired for years as part-time teachers by giving permanent posts to many and dismissal of unqualified ones (*Economist*, 2015a: 44). While all these reforms have been tried elsewhere and succeeded under particular circumstances, presenting them as a unified package creates the problem of animating multiple opposition groups that can eliminate or water down the overall reform.

Two common reforms that have been attempted and studied extensively are smaller class sizes and higher teacher pay. While both of these reforms require greater resources, each could be achieved by reallocating or even reducing rather than increasing expenditures. As described above, common measures of school inputs in education production studies are class size and teacher characteristics like education, experience, and salary. GEMS Education

Solutions created an international "efficiency index" as a measure of the relationship between education spending and student outcomes in 30 countries (*Economist*, 2014). Specifically, the country's rank on the index is determined by its performance on PISA relative to its expenditures on teacher salaries, which account for the largest percentage of total education expenditures, and the average class size, which when low creates needs for more teachers (and their salaries) and school buildings. Finland and South Korea are ranked as the top two efficient countries based on their relatively high PISA scores, moderate teacher salaries (Finland is slightly higher and South Korea is more than 10 percent higher than the average U.S. teacher salaries), and high pupil–teacher ratios. In other words, the countries' high PISA performance levels are not the result of high education expenditure spending. Achievement of high "output" at relatively "low cost" is the measure of economic efficiency. What might be more remarkable is that other than having high levels of "efficiency," Finland and South Korea are largely disparate education systems. Teachers in the Finnish system are autonomous and there is no national testing until late in the schooling. There is also an emphasis on a balanced education, including a significant arts focus. Students in South Korea are subject to many examinations and there is, like many of the Asian schools, an emphasis on science and mathematics. The Czech Republic and Hungary rank third and fourth on this index and have teacher salaries considerably less than half the U.S. average salary.

Like Tolstoy's unhappy families in *Anna Karenina*, the inefficient countries also are extremely different. The cluster of bottom half of the countries are composed of less developed countries like Brazil (30) and Indonesia (29) but also high-income OECD countries Germany (25) and Switzerland (28). The OECD countries ended up near the bottom because even though they had relatively high PISA scores, they had average teacher salaries between 30 percent in Germany and 65 percent in Switzerland (the highest average of the 30 countries in the list), higher than the U.S. average, while the salaries in Brazil and Indonesia are only 35 percent and 6 percent of the U.S. average. The conclusion from this study of generally weak relationships between the largest inputs—class size and teacher salaries—and student assessment performance follows much of the educational productivity research literature.

An additional lesson to learn from this efficiency measure is that the quality of the teaching staff rather than the quantity (represented by class size) seems to have the greatest impact. Indeed, many countries have extreme cases of low teacher activity or teacher dysfunction, which means the quantity or workload indicators will overstate significantly this input measure. Examples of dysfunctional teacher quality can be found in most countries, but are quite prevalent in the less developed countries. *The Public Report on Basic Education in India* (PROBE) documents this dysfunction in the Hindi-speaking states of northern India. In the ten years, 1996–2006, advances were made in universal schooling. Attendance rates for the elementary-aged students went from 80 percent in 1996 to 95 percent in 2006, and these improvements went across the various subgroups—boys/girls and religions. This improvement was attributed to an expanding infrastructure as well as an increasing provision of textbooks, school uniforms, and school meals. However, even during ten years of improvement in attendance, and maybe because of this expansion, the incidence of low quality or even no teaching effort did not improve much. According to PROBE, in 2006 "close to half the schools had no teaching activity . . . some teachers were absent, others were found to be sipping tea, knitting, or whiling away time simply chatting." Of course, the expansion of the educational infrastructure and increase in attendance requires more teachers and they will necessarily be recruited from a weaker pool of applicants. This is a problem common to any policy designed to decrease class size, even in developed countries.

Other policies can be designed to increase the accountability of the teachers and school administrators. Since the most common method of education provision, including the hiring, training, and promoting of teachers, is through public provision, teacher accountability efforts are a government responsibility. These efforts have intensified in the developed world, particularly in the U.S., and are beginning to appear in the developing countries like Mexico. There is no ideal government structure that leads to universal education and high-quality teaching with strong accountability measures. A cursory glance of the 30 countries ranked on the GEMS list by efficiency does not show a particular type of structure differentiating countries at the top of the list from those at the bottom. What appears to be important is how the system can encourage citizens of a country to hold politicians responsible for education performance, how transparent are the governmental education decisions made, and the direct teacher training and accountability measures for schools and education systems. Since any effective system will probably be a combination of these characteristics, it follows that no one education system is "best." A critical condition to reach success is the establishment of a clear set of education objectives and goals. However, given the multiple constituencies of politicians, parents, administrators, teachers, and others involved, this clarity is difficult to reach. For example, while "democracy" is not a necessary condition to achieve these conditions (indeed, as described, the world's largest democracy, India, has extremely dysfunctional teaching conditions), government accountability and transparency are key aspects of education system performance. A democratic system provides an avenue for citizens to express opinions about the education goals and assessments where authoritarian regimes impose goals set by politicians. This relationship is not guaranteed, however, as countries with strong democracies like Germany, Switzerland, and Brazil are at the bottom of the list of efficient education systems and other countries with "flawed" democracies such as South Korea and Hungary are at the top of the list. One country not on the GEMS list is Cuba, which is known to have an education system that produces good and perhaps even "efficient" results.

Thus, lessons of reform are well-documented at the technical level from attempts to establish empirical linkages between policy inputs (e.g. expenditures and other resources), outputs (e.g. equalization and workloads), and outcomes (e.g. performance measures such as PISA and school-level tests, promotion, and graduation rates). Future research might broaden the input measure to include related services and influences at the pre-school level, which influence outcomes in multiple ways. For example, the Inter-American Development Bank (IDB) found that in Latin America, more spending for public educational programs may harm the youngest students, especially when targeted at building large day-care centers. The centers have been mostly holding pens where children are not stimulated to play or learn all day. By contrast, a program in Jamaica provided weekly visits to poor mothers at home by health sector workers to teach them parenting skills and encouraged them to play with their babies. Two decades later, their children had higher IQs, were better educated (i.e. higher outcome levels), less violent, and on average received 25 percent more than the control group whose mothers did not receive the visits (*Economist*, 2015b: 36). Note the broadening of inputs into the educational production of outcomes by resources from the related health sector.

At the policy level, structural changes that incentivize teacher performance, increase school choice by increasing competition for students, and financing that targets attainment of results by administrators, students, and teachers, have made important differences to educational productivity and student access around the world. Applied research on performance financing, for instance, reveals the conditions under which lump-sum transfers to equalize school resources versus conditional formula matching grants can make important differences in school and student performance. Such findings reveal the variables that can explain educational outcomes at the political economy, or second level of analysis. For example, Germany and Italy are European pioneers of these kinds of performance equalization grant programs. Other countries have experimented with redefining fiscal roles and responsibilities between levels of government. As will be described below, this involves modification of intergovernmental fiscal relations to improve the performance of educational programs at the local level. Countries such as France retain normative financial and administrative discretion and control at the center. Others such as the UK have devolved much fiscal and administrative authority to local levels and to alternative units such as charter schools and NGOs operating schools. This shifts fiscal and operational authority to the local level while retaining some capacity to set and maintain national standards at the center. Devolution of authority to alternative units such as charters provides an additional explanatory variable for gauging adequacy and efficiency of outcomes. Charter schools are state-financed schools that have been given more operational autonomy from regulations constraining innovative teaching and curricula while maintaining policy accountability through reporting requirements. Applied research found that poor, non-white students in urban areas fared better in charters than traditional public schools (Dynarski, 2015). Successfully reforming countries include Israel, Chile, Canada (especially Alberta), and Sweden. City level successes include Newark, New York City, and Dallas.

At the third level of analysis, policy and operational level lessons have been transferred around the globe almost irrespective of political cultures or traditions. This can continue, informed by first- and second-level applied research. As noted, at the second level, many of the same institutional and financial constraints to reform can be found in rich and poor countries alike and across different cultures. Despite these problems, the applied lessons can be successful at least in part. The eagerness of school systems to adopt them suggests that problems and constraints around the world are similar enough that officials are motivated to introduce operational lessons from international educational policy research.

Fiscal Federalism

National and subnational governments can be roughly divided into three levels—central (national), intermediate (state, provincial, or departmental), and local (municipal). One suggested reform is to decentralize educational efforts from the central government to lower government levels. A federal system of government assigns responsibilities for providing goods and services to two or more independent levels of government (e.g. Switzerland, India, Mexico, Canada, Germany, and the U.S.). Unitary governments, by contrast, diffuse or deconcentrate central authority over subnational units that are dependencies of the central government (e.g. the UK). In many countries, these expenditure assignments are primarily made at the central level although a federal system devolves or decentralizes fiscal and management authority and resources to the two lower subnational levels. Refer back to *Chapters 2–3* for further discussion of fiscal decentralization in relation to national fiscal policy and provision of urban public transit and infrastructure.

Most policy discussions of fiscal decentralization assume that tensions normally exist between national–subnational levels and that for optimal efficiency the balance should eventually be in favor of more decentralization to ensure accountability and responsiveness (refer back to *Figure 3.1*). These assumptions are largely correct now but they have not always been so. One tends to forget that historically, evolution around the world occurred from decentralized subsistence societies of bands and tribes to chiefdoms. Driven by the complex needs of growing population densities and facilitated by advances in agriculture that permitted sedentary lives and economic specialization, the simple villages based on reciprocal exchanges evolved into complex, redistributive economies that allowed savings, storage, and allocation of goods by centralized chiefdoms. Around the world, chiefdoms evolved into centralized states based on non-egalitarian practices. The leaders or chiefs, of course, ranged from wise officials to kleptocrats as they still do. The main advantage of centralized states then and now was the monopoly of force that prevented murders and other violence. They also developed conflict-resolution institutions such as courts, laws, and police. So the long-term trend was from small, non-centralized, kin-based societies toward large, complex societies, culminating in states (Diamond, 1999: 264–270). The point is that historically, how to establish centralized states to govern, protect, and provide services to large population clusters was the problem. It took centuries of trial and error practice to learn that once the preconditions of effective governance were established, the balance now needs to be shifted toward more accountability and responsiveness to those populations not residing in the capitals and central cities. That is where the debate on the proper design and optimal arrangements of fiscal decentralization should begin: with the understanding that a strong central state is a precondition. Decentralizing authority and power away from weak or failed states that lack service coverage for its population is unlikely to achieve either responsiveness or accountability for order, protection, and basic services.

Drawing from concepts introduced in Oates (1972), Fisher (2007) described the conditions underlying "optimal" governmental decentralization. The "correspondence principle" referred to the condition where public goods and services are appropriately assigned to the lowest level of government where there are no external or effects outside that particular level. Macroeconomic stabilization policies, income redistribution, and national defense responsibilities are generally assigned to the highest level or central government because of the nature of the available revenue instruments and/or the possibility for major external effects. Central governments are assigned macroeconomic policies because they require large fiscal and monetary instruments typically not available to subnational governments. Relatively generous income redistribution by subnational governments would encourage the in-migration of lower-income individuals into those local areas and out-migration from the higher-taxed higher areas with high-income residents. Defensive actions by potentially losing jurisdictions could create large externalities spilling over into neighboring districts, which would mean that non-residents of the defended area could benefit from the spending without paying taxes. On the other hand, governmental service responsibilities like police and fire protection, waste management, urban transportation, and education are often assigned to the lowest subnational governments, where the benefits are contained and do not generally spillover to the neighboring governments (again, refer back to *Figure 3.1*). The primary benefit associated with the correspondence principle is that the lowest level may employ information to provide amounts of the public good or service that best matches different demands for these goods across a diverse country. As Oates (1972) held in his classic "Decentralization Theorem," more efficient "levels of consumption are provided in each jurisdiction than any single, uniform level of consumption maintained across all jurisdictions."

While a decentralized fiscal system of goods and service provision is well-established throughout the U.S. with individual states (and local governments), other federal systems' similar decentralization reforms along with political decentralization have recently been implemented in countries from developing regions. In addition, even long-established unitary systems such as the UK have had to implement radical fiscal decentralization reforms to deal with political and economic tensions faced by both its local governments (councils) as well as to redefine core relations between its four component units: Northern Ireland, Scotland, Wales, and England. In exchange for instituting elected mayorships (only London now has one though city managers were created several decades ago in several large cities), local councils will receive much more fiscal, management authority. As is known, different governmental levels have different revenue instruments to fund these goods and services, including federal and subnational taxes (e.g. income, sales, property), intergovernmental grants from higher governmental levels (central and/or intermediate), and debt. Each revenue source has advantages and disadvantages, particularly when considering the fiscal relationships between the national and subnational governments.

Fiscal Federalism and the Government Provision of Education

The basic educational financing structure in many countries can be characterized as decentralized or a mix of central and local government control. The structure of this decentralization varies and was motivated by different goals. Schools in the U.S. have historically been operated at the local level—sometimes sub-metropolitan or school district level—with local entities taking up the bulk of financing and state financial involvement through intergovernmental grants (i.e. fiscal transfers). However, legal actions in the early 1970s led to greater state fiscal responsibility. Concerns over inequities as a result of local government reliance on property taxes led to federal court decisions focused on equal opportunity. The U.S. Supreme Court ultimately found no federal constitutional role in the provision of education, affirming that the responsibility for education on the state governments. This decision led to several successful individual state "equal protection" or equity cases. Recent cases have changed the focus of these cases away from equity concerns to the adequacy outcomes (goals 1 and 2). However, whether the focus has been on equity or adequacy, the state cases have re-centralized financial responsibilities from the local school districts to state governments in order to achieve greater fiscal equity or adequacy goals. The decentralization of education responsibilities in other parts of the world has worked in the traditional way by shifting financial and administrative responsibility for education from central/federal government to subnational governments, creating systems to evaluate individual teachers and schools, and forging public–private relationships. These reforms were put into place to achieve greater responsiveness over a diverse population, to foster competition among all types of schools, and to provide more efficient program administration leading to lower costs.

Latin America provides several recent examples of educational decentralization efforts. Chile implemented several reforms beginning in 1981 to decentralize responsibility for education and to promote competition among the providers. Decentralization efforts started with the transfer of management from the central government to the municipalities. In an unusual measure, the central government provided equal per-student intergovernmental transfers to both public and the private schools. As might have been expected, students left the public schools and enrolled in the private schools. The central government was able to reduce its overall fiscal responsibility for education caused by these reforms through substitution of private school fees for direct government transfers.

The primary advantage of a decentralized system is that proximity of service provision to citizens can improve governmental effectiveness and political accountability to the generally heterogeneous population found in these smaller governments. The impact of decentralized decisions on expenditure size is ambiguous, as several different and potentially conflicting effects are possibly created. One effect is generated by spending decisions made by a local school district or subnational government in pluralist democratic systems. The "decisive" or "pivotal" voter in such decisions has the median level of preferred spending in each district (the so-called "median voter"). That is, relative to extreme positions, the median spending level gets the most electoral support. Consequently, the average central government education spending level is the average "median" or the weighted spending average across all subnational districts. It follows that the difference in spending between a decentralized system and a centralized system depends on the differences in median voters. The pivotal voter with the central government's median desired level of expenditure may be different from the average median voter's desired expenditures across all of the subnational governments. If the subnational governments have homogeneous spending levels, then the average of these medians will approach the overall central average. However, because of differences in revenue raising abilities, homogeneity is probably not going to be the case, so the ultimate comparison is not known theoretically.

An alternative way to understand the impact on expenditure levels is that decentralization may create a more competitive system where the subnational governments are attempting to provide a given amount of local services in the most efficient manner—that is, at the least cost—and this improved efficiency can result in overall reduced spending at all government levels. Finally, the shift of education responsibilities closer to the affected citizens may establish and maintain a closer connection to a desire for funding, particularly during economic downturns. The central government may have more competing demands on its revenue sources, which could force austerity budgetary choices and reduce expenditures on education, particularly in bad economic times. That suggests expenditures would not necessarily decrease with decentralization, since state and local levels might make up the difference. However, no matter how much total expenditures are affected, the centralization of educational expenditures, taking advantage of its scale to reduce spillovers on national public goods, allows for a correction for inequities across the local governmental units created by decentralized expenditure decisions.

Local taxes link the demand for locally provided goods and services to the local pivotal voter's willingness to pay for them. The same set of revenue sources are available for the funding of all government expenditures—i.e. taxes on income, wealth, and sales—and can be used to fund education. A particular source will be used depending on the available tax base and the level of government. One problem might be that a robust set of local taxes would not be available or is insufficient to fund fully the goods and services. Given the ability of citizens or businesses to avoid taxes by moving as well as competition among subnational governments, income and value-added taxes (VAT) are generally assigned to the central or intermediate governments.

The VAT is found primarily in Europe and other countries outside the U.S., which has resisted its adoption. The basic structure of the VAT is similar to a sales tax. However, rather than the tax rate being applied to purchases made at the retail level (or the last stage) of production, the tax is applied at each stage of the production process. The base of the tax is determined by how much "value" is added at each stage and equals the difference between the cost of the inputs used at that stage and the amount received when the processed output is sold to the next stage. The VAT is calculated by the percentage charged against this measurement of value added.

Because of the similar structure, the economic inefficiency created by the VAT is similar to that created by a sales tax and will depend on how responsive the consumers' demand for the taxed good is to changes in its price. Specifically, if, as expected, the price of the taxed good increases with the VAT, and the quantity demanded for the good does not change much as a result of the increase in the tax, then the loss of efficiency may be small. There have been concerns about the ability of local governments to administer more complicated taxes such as VAT. That leaves land, property, and vehicle taxes as the primary sources of local revenue with which to finance education in most countries. Property taxes meet some of the disadvantages associated with income or VAT taxes—the property tax base is immobile, and it is highly visible and straightforward to administer. Taxes on vehicles are also highly visible and easy to administer. According to Daughters and Harper (2007) in their review of decentralization in Latin America, Argentina, Brazil, Chile, and Colombia have assigned considerable tax authority to their local governments.

Central Government Grants-in-Aid

Intergovernmental transfers from central governments to subnational/local governments continue to be an important source of local revenues. These transfers are critical for funding the goods and services assigned to the local governments in this fiscal decentralization, particularly in those situations where the local tax base is insufficient to support total spending. Intergovernmental transfers can also be used to correct for externalities that may occur at the lower level of government and cross into surrounding jurisdictions and are a source of market failure and economic inefficiency. They can also be used to fix fiscal imbalances or horizontal inequities that may occur as a result of differences across local governments in natural resources, industry, tax bases, or any other activities used to generate local tax revenue.

Intergovernmental grants or grants-in-aid can be categorized as either conditional or unconditional. Conditional or categorical grants are designated by the granting government for specific local government spending. There are three types of conditional grants. The matching "open-ended" grants require the recipient government to match the grant with some amount of local spending (e.g. dollar for dollar matching) for any amount of the central government's grant. Under that grant system, every dollar of spending costs the local government less than a dollar, depending on the match rate. For example, suppose a matching grant is provided by the federal government equal to $1 for every $1 spent by the local government? This means the local tax cost to the local government's pivotal voter for an additional $1 of expenditure on the activity (e.g. education) from all government sources is only $0.50 (half from the federal government and half from the local government). A matching "closed-ended" grant puts a ceiling on the amount the central government will grant and any spending beyond that ceiling will be entirely from the local government, limiting the local government's cost benefit. Finally, non-matching central government grants are lump-sum grants designated for a certain expenditure category with no expectation of a local government match.

Unconditional grants place no restrictions on the recipient government's use of the funds by the granting government. These lump-sum grants are used by central government to provide some minimum amount of revenue to local governments to use for basic services. For example, the Canadian provinces are responsible for the major social services—health, education, and social welfare. However, large differences in revenue-raising abilities in the provinces potentially exacerbate these national inequities. The Canadian federal–provincial fiscal equalization system was created in 1957 to address the large differences in provincial revenue-raising efforts. These lump-sum payments from Ottawa to the provinces out of federal general tax revenue are based on the provincial fiscal capacity or its ability to raise a certain level of tax revenue at the average provincial tax rate (i.e. revenue per capita). Not all provinces receive these payments and the total equalization payment amounts to less than 1 percent of Canadian GDP.

Since recipient governments are not required to use the grant funds for specific purposes, they should be allocated by the central government according to some formula based on conditions which are exogenous to the recipient government's actions such as population or income levels, perhaps as a way to alleviate poverty. The alternative system of basing grant formulas on factors that can be adjusted by the recipient government (e.g. the level of local spending) can create perverse incentives. Additional problematic incentives associated with these formulas can be created for the grantor government as well. Daughters and Harper (2007) described the common grant formula used in Latin America as shares of central government tax revenue. Since income and VAT tax collections are based on economic activity (as opposed to property and vehicle taxes, which may be relatively more stable during economic downturns), the lack of linkage between revenue source and the local revenue needs means that these subnational governments are potentially subject to central government expenditure demands and central government crises associated with downturns. That means more funding uncertainties with unstable and sporadic delivery of services such as education. As a result, Daughters and Harper (2007) suggested that the most effective transfer system is one where the central governments have little discretion. They analyzed measures of central government discretion and found that Bolivia, Ecuador, El Salvador, and Peru moved toward more formulaic transfer systems with broad grants of discretion, while other Latin American countries reduced discretion of subnational officials to allocate funds. One commonly used modification of the general grant is the "block" grant, which is a grant to local governments designated for broadly defined functional or sectoral expenditure categories like "education," "transportation," or "community development." Each of these broad categories consisted of a large number of specific expenditure items that could qualify for funding support.

Although it is one of the primary intentions of the central government to use grants-in-aid as a way to increase the recipient government's general expenditure and/or expenditures on specific categories, is there any reason in theory to believe that will happen? That brings to mind the old economist joke: the policy may work in practice, but can it work in theory? For example, while the recipient government could use the donor conditional grant to increase government spending by the full amount of the grant, such grants also allow the recipient government to lower its own taxes and use the grantor government's revenues to replace recipient revenues. Alternatively the grant might allow freeing up of certain recipient budgetary expenditures and use them for other non-programmatic government categories, e.g. salaries. Assuming local government expenditures are determined through a representative democratic process, then such analysis would be based on the theoretical grant impact on demand for services by the recipient government's "decisive" or "median" voter (Fisher, 2007).

First, all grants-in-aid, both conditional and unconditional, add directly to the recipient government's resources. This resource increase creates an "income effect." The income effect will generally increase the decisive voter's demand for these expenditures and the recipient government's expenditures are expected to increase. In the case of a general grant, this is the full effect of the grant on recipient government spending. In the case of a conditional matching grant, the grant-in-aid has the secondary effect of lowering the local price for the targeted expenditures demanded by the local government's decisive voter, relative to the other untargeted expenditure categories. This lower price is expected to increase the quantity demanded of this government program by the local government's decisive voter or create a "price effect." As the grant-supported government activity becomes cheaper relative to other government activities, then the recipient government's pivotal voter will substitute away from the relatively more expensive activity toward the relatively less expensive activity (i.e. the one supported by the matching grant). As a result, this effect is also positively related to the government expenditure level.

Although both effects are expected to influence positively the expenditure decisions made by the recipient government, the total impact is expected to be larger with one of the matching grant types than with an equally sized (the recipient government could select the same expenditure) lump-sum grant. That would be due to the presence of both an income and a price effect with the categorical grants and only an income effect with the lump-sum-type grants. However, the ultimate sizes of each effect depend on the responsiveness of the pivotal voter's demand for these grant-supported government activities to changes in income and to changes in the relative price of the expenditure. If a closed-end matching grant is used, then this can potentially reduce the price effect. The comparison with lump-sum grants becomes a bit more complicated when these matching grant restrictions are imposed, but in general, matching grants are still thought to have a large effect on recipient government spending. The effects of differences in grant types on educational expenditure are summarized in *Figure 6.2*.

Subnational borrowing for purposes of funding local goods and services is generally discouraged for the standard reasons. Increased indebtedness for current services violates the "golden rule" that borrowing shall be limited to capital needs and can threaten macroeconomic stability of the entire government and lead to government fiscal instability (see *Chapter 2*). For this reason, fiscal decentralization to increase local fiscal autonomy typically includes monetary and purpose limits on local borrowing, often a low percentage of past year revenues for only capital items such as schools, hospitals and other infrastructure. In some countries, such as the UK, performance transfers or grants are used for health, urban transport, and education. They are typically disbursed on according to an efficiency formula, such as operating cost/passenger mile in transport; cost/student output; cost/type of treatment rather than gross patient amounts (or services rather than capitation to try and decrease service costs).

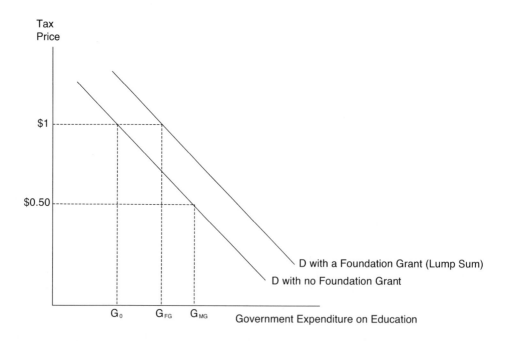

Figure 6.2 Effects of Grant Types on School Performance

A Foundation Grant shifts the D for government expenditure on education through an income effect only, keeping the marginal tax price of an additional dollar of expenditure at $1. As a result, the amount of government expenditure increases from G_0 to G_{FG}. A Matching Grant of 0.50 lowers the marginal tax price of an additional dollar of expenditure by 0.50 and increases the quantity demanded of education expenditures to G_{MG} through income and substitution effects.

Comparative Reform Evaluation

As described above, concerns have been raised about the quality of primary and secondary education in many countries around the world. In response, some of the more notable reforms introduced in many countries have been associated with the private market or with relaxation of the regulations applied to public schools. Policies drawn from the theories and practices of the private market have been commonly introduced into education systems as a way to increase the amount of choice and market competition. The basic idea has been that competition will make the education systems more economically efficient. As described above, probably the most common way competition has entered is through the decentralization of education revenue and expenditure responsibilities, incentivizing intra-governmental competition. Another method is the development of school choice through the use of school vouchers. Rather than funding schools directly, vouchers are attached to the students, who can use them to attend any school of their choosing. The key idea with vouchers is that this choice among "competing" schools is expected to improve overall school performance. However, there is not much evidence of increased performance as a result of the introduction of vouchers because several program complications potentially reduce the potential effectiveness. For instance, competitive effectiveness requires a true choice of schools and this is only likely to be true in the urban areas of the country. Private schools may also be available in urban areas for greater choice (if the government is willing to provide public funds for private education). Charter schools were created in the U.S. in 1992 that increased the public school options available for students. What was unique about these public schools, as noted above, is that they were allowed release from certain governmental regulations, such as requirements for hiring unionized teachers or for using predetermined school curricula. One additional requirement to maximize the benefits associated with competitive effectiveness is that adequate (ideally "full") information exists so that the best choices can be made.

Recent assessment measures allow for some of this information. There is extensive assessment of students in countries throughout the world. The most well-known student assessments such as the Progress in International Reading Literacy Study (PIRLS), the Program for International Student Assessment (PISA) (see the 2012 scores as reported in *Table 6.1*), and the Trends in International Mathematics and Science Study (TIMSS) are not going to be helpful for internal school choices to be made. However, several countries have created exams that are used for internal assessment purposes. The U.S. federal government's No Child Left Behind Act of 2001 (NCLB) required all public schools to administer an annual state-wide assessment to all students. These assessments scores can be used by parents to make basic comparisons of student achievements and general education performance.

Have any of these reforms been successful? The basic complication of measuring the impacts of these education reforms and summarizing their overall performance is that they are not consistently carried out to the same degree and or assessment level. Because of the general inability to determine a strong link between the school policy-makers' inputs and the education outcomes, the impact of many educational reforms is unclear. Impact measurement largely depends on governmental reform goals. In the U.S., for example, the emphasis has been on the equity of resource inputs and the necessary levels of inputs to reach certain student achievement levels. But there has been little assessment of such adequacy efforts after the policies were put in place. Educational outcomes are important in the context of the standard types of decentralization and privatization reforms that have taken place in Latin America. Gershberg et al. (2012) review the literature evaluating the reforms taken in Chile, Nicaragua, and Colombia. As noted, the Chilean central government decentralized school management to the city level in the early 1980s. An unusual reform at that time was to create a voucher system giving the same amount of per student funding to public and private schools. Given the usual view by parents worldwide that private schools are superior to public schools, the predictable result of this policy was a significant drop in the numbers of students attending public schools in Chile—78 percent of enrolled students in public schools in 1981 dropped to 43 percent in 2008. The benefits of increased choice were not immediately realized because parents did not have objective measures of school quality until 1995. But Gershberg et al. (2012) cite research indicating that parents did not use these assessment measures and instead chose schools based on "the availability of school equipment and cleanliness or the composition of the student body." The overall effects of these reforms on student performance in Chile were minimal. Objective measures of student assessment were stable over this time and, even though there may have been some increase in grades, perhaps not unexpectedly there was some evidence that schools engaged in grade inflation in order to attract students and the associated funding. Any differences found between private and public schools could probably be attributed to student selection.

Another example of significant education reforms involving decentralization occurred in Colombia in the 1990s (Gershberg et al., 2012). The central government of Colombia created a "Concession School" model that devolved the provision of education to the municipalities and allowed these local governments to contract with private agencies to provide school services or to manage the schools. On the assumption that private providers are more effective than public suppliers of educational services, the central government used this model to get quality education to the lowest income population. Preferences for enrollment in these schools were given to poorest students. The new schools instituted longer school days and had greater instructional resources. They also provided a range of social services (e.g. health care, meals, and counseling) which should lead to improved performance measures. In order to determine the effectiveness of the Concession Schools, one should compare student outcomes with the traditional Colombian public schools. There was evidence that the schools did perform better than the traditional public schools and some enrolled the poorest students. However Gershberg et al. (2012) described "creaming" of the best students or denying enrollment by at-risk students that may have unfairly benefited the Concession Schools.

School reforms in Nicaragua were also implemented in the early 1990s but were eliminated after the 2006 Presidential election. Educational decentralization created school-level councils that were charged with passing the budget, curricula, and evaluations. The councils consisted of school personnel and a voting majority of parents. Greater school autonomy combined with the high degree of parental control over the most important budgetary and curricular aspects of the school created opportunities for improved student performance. Indeed, there was evidence that student performance improved after the reforms were instituted. However, as pointed out by Gershberg et al. (2012), the results suffered from methodological weaknesses in the educational reform evaluations. The biggest problem was that schools participating in the program were not selected randomly, which biased the results used to make the comparison.

More recent educational reforms have been designed to measure directly the performance of teachers, administrators, and schools in an effort to strengthen greater accountability. Such performance evaluations typically use student test-based assessment measures to evaluate and identify weak teachers, administrators, and failing schools, with the ultimate goal of using the assessments to improve student performance. For this assessment system to work effectively, countries must collect examination data and have an understanding about how to analyze them. Examination results are best taken every year, so that "value added" can be measured. Since the education process is cumulative, a student's academic achievement is determined by the current teacher (by school) as well as all the previous teachers (at the same schools). The purpose of trying to determine value added is to try to isolate the impact of a particular teacher or school on the student's performance. In order to identify the teacher's value added, students would ideally be tested at the beginning of the school year and at the end. Most evaluations are not conducted this way. The standard practice is to estimate a "likely" score for the student using the student's previous year's assessment score and other relevant information. This predicted score is then compared with the student's actual score to determine how much the teacher has added achievement value to the student's assessment performance.

In the U.S. and many other countries, assessments have been introduced as part of a larger set of education reforms, including many of the private market reforms. For example, in addition to the decentralization measures described above in Chile, the central government replaced a teacher salary system based only on "experience" with an assessment system (National Evaluation System of Publically Financed Schools) that was used to supplement teacher salaries in schools with the highest achievement levels ("high stakes") and with the greatest improvements ("value added"). Teachers unions have generally resisted these "high- stakes" reforms, particularly teacher assessments using student exam scores leading to tenure and salary decisions. Many individual U.S. cities (e.g. Washington, DC, Los Angeles, and New York City) have adopted value added measures as part of their overall teacher assessments. Scores vary considerably across the districts that use them. Although the assessments predate her tenure as chancellor of the Washington, DC, public schools (DCPS), Michelle Rhee is often credited with igniting the assessment movement in the U.S. when she put into place in DCPS a system that uses, in part, student assessments to evaluate teachers in DCPS for promotion, retention, and salary adjustments. Although there is a long way to go, these assessments have been credited with improving the performance of DCPS teachers and schools. One effect of the evaluations is to change the incentives for such problems as teacher absenteeism that, as noted, is also a major problem in developing countries. Basing pay in part on teacher performance that includes (obviously) showing up to teach class increases the level of professionalism and tends to improve student performance scores as well. For that reason, second-level analysis of institutional incentives is critical for explaining differences in educational outputs and outcomes—as well as explaining why some reforms work and others do not. As indicated, the biggest challenges to these assessment reforms come from the teachers and their unions. Recent educational reform efforts by mayors in Los Angeles and NYC met resistance by the teachers unions. Referring back to *Figure 1.3*, this underscores the importance of lack of top level regime support, political opposition, and major institutional constraints as explanations for the difficulties in reforming educational systems. In fall 2013, the Oaxaca, Mexico, teachers union called on the 70,000 state teachers to strike in opposition to new assessment rules for teacher hiring, promoting, and retention. Teachers from this extremely poor state struggle with students unprepared for formal education. It had resisted the Mexican national standardized exam (Puig, 2013).

Conclusions

Primary and secondary schooling issues create critical political conflicts over issues such as financing equity, adequacy of services, productivity of education resources, access to basic education services, and the quality of the provision. The basic school structure for K–12 educational services is similar worldwide. However, there is widespread variation across countries in education inputs and the overall student performance results.

Comparative international performance can be measured by results from international exams like PISA. They indicate that while generally more spending as percent of GDP translates into higher scores, the exceptions (e.g. Japan, Shanghai, Germany) suggest that culture and institutions matter as much as money. For this reason, researchers have focused on the determinants of performance, especially access, governance, and financing variables. Access varies widely from culturally set rules (e.g. girls schooling in Muslim countries, and poverty in poorer countries requiring work instead of schooling). Policy efforts have focused on such operational reforms as conditional cash transfers to encourage attendance in exchange for cash payments. This has worked in many countries such as Peru and Brazil. Other reforms have focused on design of fiscal transfers or intergovernmental grants to change incentive effects. Grants can be designed according to rules that favor equalization of district finances, improved student performance, or some combination of the two. Substantial amounts of research in the U.S. have been done on the incentive effects of lump-sum versus matching grants with evidence that the greatest multiplier effects on schools and students flow from matching or cost-sharing grants.

The levels of financing and how money is spent also affect performance. German lander and cities spend 90 percent of total country funds but much of it is provided by central government transfers; by contrast, U.S. schools spend monies that are raised from states (48 percent) and local (43 percent) tax sources with only about 9 percent from the central government. The central government in France (Ministry of Education) provides 70 percent of the financing and all of the rules on school management, personnel, curriculum, standards, and spending choices. Some school districts with relatively low levels of financing are able to leverage or target funds better than those with more funds. This may be due to managerial autonomy, and fewer restrictions on spending the funds. In other cases, more restrictions or conditions on spending may lead to better performance, i.e. where funds would have been stolen or spent on higher salaries or more administrators instead of teachers.

In this rich context, reform programs have proliferated across the world from national and local levels. The focus on choice and performance dominates countries and particular provinces such as the U.S., Alberta (Canada), Chile, UK, and Sweden. The Swiss and German approach continues to be tough, centrally set standards; early student performance tracking, with emphasis on teacher pay and quality; and many options for apprenticeships and vocational choice. The Japanese approach is similarly focused on rote learning of facts and emphasis on test performance. But it offers fewer alternatives to those tracked out early. The Anglo-American model differs broadly from this in its effort to provide greater access and repeat opportunities for advancement along more traditional paths. This model focuses on alternative delivery systems, school decentralization, and incentivizing performance with transfers. Within the U.S., cities have experimented with pay for performance (e.g. Dallas and Chicago) and school closures for failing performance (e.g. Detroit, NYC, Washington, DC, Newark, Providence) as well as the expansion of choice through voucher funding, charter schools, and performance transfers based on tougher central standards (e.g. the No Child Left Behind and Race to the Top federal programs). In the U.S. and elsewhere, standoffs with teachers unions have been an important determinant of results. School unions often act as a brake on student results, focusing instead on teacher employment security. Often improvement of teacher quality is impeded by union rules. Reformist regimes in such cities as NYC, Chicago, and Washington, DC, successfully forced unions to change their rules in favor of teacher pay for performance schemes that exchange more funds for less security. All reforms have been controversial, and comparative policy research offers a rich library of best and worst practices for reformers around the world who seek to improve educational performance.

Cases and Exercises

1   Read *Case 6.1* on London school design and answer the questions following:

Case 6.1 School Design in London

Source: *Economist*, 2013

As the summer holidays approached, the Greenwich Free School (GFS) recently celebrated the end of its first year with a trip to the seaside at Broadstairs. Everyone enjoyed it: London is blistering and GFS, which was launched under a scheme to liberate schools from local-authority control, has only a small patch of grass outside its huddle of temporary classrooms. But for a dozen of its 11-year-old pupils the trip was especially wonderful, because they had not seen the sea before. The school is in a tough quarter. In the grounds of a derelict nurses' dormitory—which will be converted into classrooms over the holidays—it is close to the Shooter's Hill housing estate, one of London's grimmest. Over a third of GFS's 100 pupils receive free school meals because their parents are poor. Many came from such "chaotic backgrounds", in the careful phrase of Lee Faith, the 35-year-old headmaster, that they barely knew how to eat, talk or otherwise behave in public.

Remarkably, given that the school gave a place to every pupil who wanted one, including some pretty troubled children, this has only happened twice. No pupil has been expelled and, even with the riot of adolescence approaching, Mr Faith does not expect any to be. Most pupils see the sense of the discipline. Every child was involved in class and cajoled, to form judgments and ask questions—even if these were sometimes, as on a noticeboard in the science classroom, rather lavatorial: "Why is bird poo white?" "Why do you throw up sometimes?" GFS is too young to be inspected by the government watchdog, Ofsted— so it arranged an extraordinary inspection. The inspector said he had seen more "awe and wonder" in two days at GFS than during two years of inspecting schools. If only every local child could experience that. But GFS is now six times oversubscribed.

No wonder advisers to Michael Gove, the dynamic Conservative education secretary, rave about this school. His academies program, which has given autonomy to over half of England's 2,000 secondary schools, is one of the government's most touted reforms. And start-up free schools such as GFS are where the innovations it is designed to encourage are most evident.

GFS's originators, a trio of concerned Londoners, selected Shooter's Hill as an area of great need, then set about designing the perfect school. For this they visited schools in Sweden and America, where similar reforms are long-standing, and across Britain. They then rewrote the national curriculum. A class on computer skills was dropped in favor of computer programming; citizenship was replaced by politics, philosophy and economics—a course associated with Oxford University, which is where many of GFS's pupils say they intend to study. They also lengthened the school day by fully three hours. In their seven years at the school, Mr Faith estimates, his pupils will therefore have the equivalent of two extra years of teaching.

It cannot be replicated everywhere. Yet GFS is providing a useful example for other schools.

a   What is the evidence on the length of school day and academic performance in the U.S.?
b   Do you think this increased discipline would have a significant impact on student achievement in the U.S.?
c   Has "competition" of any type improved student achievement?

2   Read *Case 6.2* on Newark below and answer the questions following:

Case 6.2 Newark School Reform

Source: Economist, 2012

Newark's public schools are dreadful. Although they have been under the supervision of New Jersey's state government since 1995, there has been little improvement since then. Only 40 percent of students read to the standard prescribed for their age, and in the 15 worst-performing schools the figure is less than 25 percent. More than 30 percent of pupils do not graduate. Few of those who do are ready for higher education. As a result, fed-up parents are taking their children out of Newark's public high schools and placing them in independent charter schools. Many public-school buildings now stand half-empty. The best teachers often leave in despair.

Things might now start to change. Members of the Newark teachers' union approved a new agreement with the district which, it is hoped, will help to retain good teachers. It introduces, for the first time in New Jersey, bonus pay. Teachers can now earn up to $12,000 in annual bonuses: $5,000 for achieving good results, up to $5,000 for working in poorly performing schools, and up $2,500 for teaching a hard-to-staff subject. Newark will be one of the largest school districts in the country to offer bonuses. The idea was made palatable to the union, which had been reluctant to accept it, because the evaluation process will unusually be based on peer review, though the school superintendent and an independent panel will still make the final decision on each case. Chris Christie, New Jersey's governor, and Joseph Del Grosso, the head of Newark's teachers' union, both agree that Newark's contract could serve as a model for other school districts. These will take some convincing. The New Jersey Education Association, the state's largest union, which is not affiliated with Newark's, is adamantly opposed to bonus pay. The new salary and bonus scale could be replicated, but not every district has the funds Newark has.

Newark is not alone in using collective bargaining to achieve reform. Baltimore, Boston, Cincinnati, Cleveland and New Haven have all taken much the same route. Nor is it the only district to introduce merit pay. New York experimented for a few years with schoolwide, rather than individual, performance bonuses, but abandoned the idea in 2011. Denver has a programme where teachers receive extra pay for working in hard-to-staff schools. Bonus pay began in 2010 in Washington, DC, which like Newark gets useful extra money from private donors. But Mr. Petrilli notes that the District has yet to improve its worryingly high teacher-turnover rate. Performance-based pay is still controversial. Chicago's teachers, who went on strike in September, were opposed to merit pay.

a   Why might school-wide merit bonuses be more successful than individual teacher bonuses?

b   How would you suggest the measurement of teacher performance?

c   Is there evidence that these types of bonuses improve productivity in other industries?

3   Drawing on the set of common countries in *Tables 6.1* and *6.2*, use simple correlations to determine if there is any relationship between country per pupil spending and average literacy scores. If you were going to do further analysis, what other characteristics should you account for? How might the measure of per capita GDP provided in *Table 6.2* be incorporated into your analysis?

4   Read *Case 6.3* on PISA scores and answer the questions following:

Case 6.3 International Student Assessment and PISA Scores

Source: Goldstein, 2013

The Organization for Economic Cooperation and Development released the 2012 scores for the Program for International Student Assessment, commonly known as PISA. The United States did not do well: Compared with their peers in the 33 other OECD nations around the world, American teens ranked 17th in reading, 21st in science, and 26th in math. The top-performing region was Shanghai. While these results always make news, this year there is an added tempest in the teapot of the education policy world. But the truth is that the lessons of PISA for our school reform movement are not as simple as they are often made out to be. PISA results aren't just about K–12 test scores and curricula—they are also about academic ability tracking, income inequality, health care, child care, and how schools are organized as workplaces for adults.

To figure out what PISA results really tell us, let's first look at what's on the test. PISA is quite different from the mostly multiple-choice, fact-driven state exams American kids take annually. The idea of PISA is to test students' ability to handle words and numbers in real-world situations. One math activity asked students to compare the value of four cars, using a chart showing the mileage, engine capacity, and price of each one. American kids were especially bad at problems like this, in which they were not provided with a formula, but had to figure out how to manipulate the numbers on their own. A reading activity asked test takers to read a short play, and then write about what the characters were doing before the curtain went up. The challenge is that the question prompts students to envision and describe a scene not actually included in the text itself.

Yet we shouldn't be surprised that our 15-year-olds are stagnant on PISA. Nations that track their math instruction by ability, like the U.S., do worse on these tests, because fewer kids—especially poor kids—are exposed to the deeper conceptual thinking that becomes more important as the grades progress and tests get harder.

Test results and education policies are too often considered in isolation from other social and economic realities. Of course, one goal of education reform is to make sure that the decent opportunities that *do* exist in our economy are equally accessible to kids who grow up disadvantaged. PISA shows that with about 15 percent of the U.S.

achievement gap attributable to poverty, we are smack in the global middle in terms of the effect of socioeconomics on educational achievement. That makes us similar to the U.K., Singapore, Shanghai, Denmark, Spain, Poland, Germany, Brazil, and Argentina, and it means we're doing better by our poor children than France, New Zealand, Portugal, and Chile.

In Norway, Iceland, Korea, Japan, and Canada, poverty and immigration status have less of an effect on kids' academic performance than here in the U.S. But these nations also tend to provide children with more social supports outside of K–12 schools, like universal pre-K and health care, both of which help students perform better academically. It's important not to forget the other lessons of the PISA results: that out-of-school social supports matter, teachers should be empowered, and *all* kids ought to be exposed to the most challenging material.

a   How does this information in this case affect your answers about important characteristics in *Question 3*?
b   What factors prohibit the types of reforms in Norway, Iceland, and the other countries from happening in the U.S.? Do you think they would fix the U.S. weak academic performance?
c   What efforts have been taken to address the achievement gaps in the U.S.?

5   Consider the following table of per pupil revenue levels by school.

School	Local Revenue Per Pupil
1	6,624
2	6,839
3	7,030
4	7,216
5	7,466
6	7,840
7	8,103
8	8,476
9	9,445
10	11,090
Range	4,290
Coefficient of Variation	0.306

a   What is the value of the "range" across these schools?
b   What is the value of the coefficient of variation?
c   Suppose there was money given by the central government that raised each of the schools' revenue by 5 percent. What is the new value of the range?
d   How does that increase change the value of the coefficient of variation?

References

Adolino, Jessica and Charles H. Blake (2011) *Comparing Public Policies: Issues and Choices in Industrialized Countries* (Washington, DC: CQ/Sage Press).

Anuradha, De and Jean Dreze (1999) "Public Report on Basic Education in India," Oxford, UK: Oxford University Press.

Daughters, Robert and Leslie Harper, "Fiscal and Political Decentralization Reforms," in *The State of State Reform in Latin America*, Eduardo Lora, ed., Palo Alto: Stanford University Press, 2007: 213–261.

Diamond, Jared (1999) *Guns, Germs, and Steel: The Fates of Human Societies* (New York: Norton).

Dynarski, Susan, "Where Charter Schools Outperform," *New York Times*, November 22, 2015, p. 6.

Economist (2012) "Merit Pay for Teachers: Bonus Time," November 24. Available online at www.economist.com/news/united-states/21567105-new-contract-teachers-shaking-up-new-jerseys-largest-city-bonus-time.

Economist (2013) "Bagehot: Let a Thousand Flowers Bloom," July 20. Available online at www.economist.com/news/britain/21581984-inner-city-school-provides-plenty-hope-british-education-let-thousand-flowers-bloom.

Economist (2014) "New School Values," September 13. Available online at www.economist.com/news/international/21616978-higher-teacher-pay-and-smaller-classes-are-not-best-education-policies-new-school.

Economist (2015a) "Schools in Italy: A Class Divided," May 23, p. 44.

Economist (2015b) "Bringing Up Better Babies," October 31, p. 36.

Fisher, Ronald C. (2007) *State and Local Public Finance*, 3rd ed. (Mason, OH: Thomson South-Western).

Gershberg, Alec Ian, Pablo Alberto Gonzalez, and Ben Meade, "Understanding and Improving Accountability in Education: A Conceptual Framework and Guideposts from Three Decentralization Reform Experiences in Latin America," *World Development*, 40, 5 (2012): 1024–1041.

Glewwe, Paul and Michael Kremer, "Schools, Teachers, and Education Outcomes in Developing Countries," in *Handbook of the Economics of Education*, vol. 2, Eric A. Hanushek and Finis Welch, eds., 2006: 945–1017, Elsevier B.V. Amsterdam, The Netherlands.

Glewwe, Paul, Eric A. Hanushek, Sarah D. Humpage, and Renato Ravina, "School Resources and Educational Outcomes in Developing Countries: A Review of the Literature from 1990 to 2010," NBER working paper #17554, October 2011, National Bureau of Economic Research: Cambridge, MA.

Goldstein, Dana, "The PISA Puzzle," *Slate*, December 3, 2013. Available online at www.slate.com/articles/double_x/doublex/2013/12/pisa_results_american_kids_did_not_do_well.html.

Hanushek, Eric A., "Assessing the Effects of School Resources on Student Performance: An Update," *Educational Evaluation and Policy Analysis*, 19, 2 (Summer 1997): 141–164.

Herman, Juliana, *Canada's Approach to School Funding*, Washington, DC: Center for American Progress, May 2013.

Husted, Thomas A. and Lawrence W. Kenny, "Evidence on the Impact of State Government on Primary and Secondary Education and the Equity-Efficiency Tradeoff," *Journal of Law and Economics*, 43, 1 (April 2000): 285–308.

Oates, Wallace E. (1972) *Fiscal Federalism* (New York: Harcourt Brace Jovanovich).

Puig, Carlos, "The Oaxaca Teachers' Union," *New York Times*, October 9, 2013. Available online at http: //latitude.blogs.nytimes.com/2013/10/09/the-oaxaca-teachers-union/?emc=eta1&_r=1.

United Nations (2012) Millennium Development Goals and Beyond, United Nations Development Program. Available online at www.un.org/millenniumgoals.

World Bank (2003) *World Development Report 2004: Making Services Work for Poor People*, Washington, DC: World Bank.

World Bank (2011) *Reforming Education Finance in Transition Countries: Six Case Studies in Per Capita Financing Systems*, Juan Diego Alonso and Alonso Sanchez, eds., Washington, DC: World Bank.

7 Energy and Environmental Policies

Introduction

Energy and environment/natural resources are both core budgetary functions of national governments. Relevant policies seek adequate production of local energy sources for generation to meet national demands. Governments attempt to make up energy deficits in the national accounts by encouraging imports of oil, gas, coal, and nuclear fuels and stimulating alternative energy technologies such as solar and wind. With the exception of some countries that can rely on hydropower, most country energy policies have substantial environmental costs. Emissions of air and water pollutants as well as solid wastes from energy production and consumption damage both the natural environment and human health—driving up both the costs and levels of public and private spending for health care services as discussed previously. Up to 500,000 people die prematurely in China each year, for example, as the result of foul air largely from the use of coal in power generation that supplies 80 percent of its electricity. Thus, the sources of energy have costs that must be reflected in energy prices, and they should be smartly regulated to protect the environment and human health and ensure that economic growth continues.

The International Energy Agency (2009) calculated a 10 percent increase in the world's average per person energy use between 1990 and 2008. This increase varied significantly across the world's regions, with the largest growth rates occurring in China (111 percent), Middle East (79 percent), and India (42 percent) and the U.S. and European Union near zero growth. These increases in energy use have been driven by increases in economic growth, particularly in the largest developing countries of China and India. Negative external effects of increasing economic growth have clearly affected the environment as a result of energy generation and distribution for consumption by firms and individuals. Growing demand has created opportunities for a growth in alternative energy sources away from the largest sources of oil, coal, and gas, as the primary sources of environmental disastrous greenhouse gases. Nuclear, natural gas, and the broad category of renewable energy (e.g. water, wind, and solar) represent smaller but growing sources of the world's energy. Such alternative energy sources can reduce the disastrous impacts on the environment as a result of the large energy production and consumption from oil, coal, and gas. The purpose of this chapter is to describe the "sources" of energy in the world and the consequences on the environment associated with the "uses" of this energy.

This chapter will: (1) describe growth of energy demand and discuss some of the issues governments face in providing energy subsidies; (2) provide an overview of the negative environmental impacts associated with this growth in the demand for energy; (3) discuss externalities generated by energy production and environmental effects; (4) review options for policy responses to environmental externalities, e.g. command and control policies, effluent charges, and tradable pollution permits; (5) discuss the use of cost–benefit analysis within the context of evaluating environmental externalities; (6) explain the differences in results from policy responses by referring to the framework in *Chapter 1* using examples from global warming; and (7) provide lessons for policy and operations management. As indicated in the *Cases and Exercises* section at the end of the chapter, we draw on several cases to highlight these lessons.

Energy Demand

Laderchi et al. (2013) list three broad determinants of energy prices—"prices, regulations, and investments." International energy prices have increased significantly over the past years and the impact of the price factor is determined by the dependency of a country on international sources of energy. Increased energy industry regulations focused on, for example, emissions control will generally increase operation costs and prices. Finally, investments on the energy grid undertaken to reduce the possibilities for energy shortages will increase energy prices while increasing protections against disruptions. The exception to this general trend has been the production of shale oil largely from U.S. "frackers" that has reduced the price of crude oil to a new normal of around $50 per barrel (*Economist*, 2015a). Laderchi et al. (2013) describe the extensive grid investments that have taken place in the Balkans, Slovenia, and Turkey. The general increase in the cost of energy to households and industry has had a tremendous adverse economic effect.

Governments attempt to reduce the adverse effects of price increases on demand by providing subsidies to the energy producers and/or consumers to make energy more affordable. These subsidies are in place in all regions of the world, amounting to about $700 billion in 2008 (Commander, 2012). De Moor (2001) defines subsidies as "measures that keep prices for consumers below market level or keep prices for producers above market level or that reduce costs for consumers and producers by giving direct or indirect support." Subsidies can either support domestic consumption by keeping domestic prices for energy below world market prices or they could be used to subsidize production by keeping domestic prices above the market level (see *Figure 7.1*). Either policy creates market distortions associated with overconsumption caused by lower consumer prices or overproduction associated with higher producer prices. In addition, environmental problems are often created by the increased energy production and/or consumption. De Moor (2001) found that production subsidies are generally found in OECD countries, in particular coal (he estimates about half of the total subsidies in Europe). Germany is a prime example of this use of production subsidies (Tait, 2010). It recently gained approval from the European Commission to extend subsidies given to loss-making hard coal mines until 2018. Production subsidies for fossil fuels are the result of several forces. Some governments argue that economic growth depends on the domestic economy and that maintaining employment is associated with fossil fuel or electricity production. However, some research suggests the opposite effect, i.e. that the efficient use of resource use and allocation is negatively affected by state promotion of fossil fuels. This efficiency loss is in addition to the reduction in pollution, generally CO_2 and SO_2, created by the decreased use of these fuels. Large consumption subsidies, sometimes near or greater than 50 percent, on coal, oil, gas, and electricity are more common in the non-OECD countries.

Using De Moor's definition, Badcock and Lenzen (2010) categorize energy subsidies as financial subsidies (e.g. direct subsidies, tax breaks, investment credits, and various trade policies), research and development funding, and external costs (explored more in detail below). While demand for energy is growing generally, it is affected by recessions and use patterns. For instance, demand peaks for natural gas at certain times of day and different seasons of the year. Northern European demand peaks in the winter and southern Europe's in the summer. Failure to integrate the European market means that because supplies are largely fixed and demands variable, prices are higher than they should be. In addition, energy sources often follow the subsidies—windmills and solar farms are often built where subsidies are high rather than in places with strong wind or abundant sunshine and cost-effective infrastructure connections (Varro, 2014: 25).

Energy supply subsidies are often detrimental to growth and development because they absorb funds that are needed for other programs such as poverty reduction. In Nigeria, for example, energy subsidies have become a breeding ground for graft and a drain on the public purse. It spends 1 percent of GDP or about $6 billion per year, about 50 percent of which goes for kerosene subsidies which are used by the poor for cooking and lighting. But subsidized kerosene is hard to find since it is swiftly resold to airlines as jet fuel. Gas, which is meant to sell at a subsidized price of 87 naira ($0.43 per liter), is smuggled to neighboring countries and sold at the higher world market price. Nigeria suffers from fuel shortages much of the year that forces residents to stand in line for hours and days. Traders on the black market do a brisk business by selling the kerosene at 200 naira per liter outside official stations (*Economist*, 2015c: 7). How officially sanctioned price floors and subsidized fuel programs lead to shortages is illustrated in *Figure 7.1*.

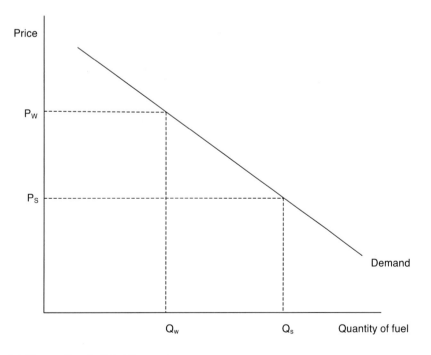

Figure 7.1 Energy Supply Subsidies

The Nigerian National Petroleum Corporation (NNPC) pays subsidies for fuel imports (P_W) and transfers funds (P_S) to the poor. The difference ($Q_S - Q_W$) is smuggled and resold resulting in fuel shortages.

Energy Supply

Energy is supplied to industrial and individual users through a supply chain of: (a) generation, (b) transmission, and (c) distribution. Generation occurs from the core sources of coal, nuclear, gas, oil, wind, solar, and thermal. Constraints to effective supply can occur at one or more of these linkages in the chain. Generation can be disrupted by nuclear disasters as in Japan, which also diminished interest in the source elsewhere such as Germany and England. Technical and economic improvements in alternative energy sources can increase alternate supplies. But these advantages can be diminished by constraints in transmission. As noted by Varro (2014: 25), each new transmission line faces heavy local resistance which diminishes capacity and keeps prices high to users and prevents efficient use of new generation sources. In many countries, resistance to new transmission lines threatens energy supply and artificially drives up prices to end users.

Assuming the transmission line problem can be remedied (e.g. through eminent domain, burying lines, or other methods), an alternative way to keep energy prices low is to increase the amount of alternative energy sources. This is done either by finding new sources of existing energy sources like oil or by converting resources into alternative energy sources like natural gas. The latter has created a new and potentially enormous source of world energy. As described in a report by the U.S. Energy Information Administration (2013), new techniques of horizontal drilling with hydraulic fracturing ("fracking") have made the extraction of oil and natural gas quite profitable in the U.S. This extraction process captures natural gas from layers of shale rock, which are areas that otherwise would be unreachable without this new technology. Fracking injects highly pressurized water, sand, and chemicals into the shale in order to create new natural gas extraction channels. Following initial hydraulic fracturing in Texas in 2000, several other companies joined in the natural gas drilling efforts in Texas and Arkansas. According to the report, this technology spread throughout the U.S., and shale gas production increased "from 0.3 trillion cubic feet in 2000 to 9.6 trillion cubic feet by year-end 2010," amounting to 40 percent of U.S. natural gas production. There are several hundred trillion cubic feet of technically recoverable shale gas reserves remaining. As the study points out, shale gas reserves are found throughout the world. Europe has nearly as much technically recoverable reserves. In that region, Poland and France have the largest amounts. Although Europe has considerable reserves, the countries have encountered problems in production. Governments own the mineral rights and receive all gains from successful exploration. There is also a lack of pipelines (or freight rail capacity) necessary to transport the oil and gas, and environmental concerns, which keeps the process of fracking banned in many of the European countries. The primary environmental concern involves the methane released from the extracted natural gas. Methane is a far greater threat to global warming than CO_2 emissions from coal burning and as a result could reduce the environmental benefits associated with the shift from coal to natural gas. The estimates of the methane leakage are uncertain and, in fact, its threat from the extracted natural gas has been downgraded by about 10 percent from original EPA estimates (Song and Morris, 2013). However, the remaining threats from leakage by the extraction equipment need to be addressed. Although many of these same problems exist in the U.S., particularly the environmental concerns and need for greater infrastructure and improved equipment, private owners have been able to extract considerable amounts of oil and natural gas from the shale formations (because as holders of subterranean oil rights they have more incentive to support mining).

The impacts of these new extractions on the supply of energy and its prices have been dramatic. This is particularly true for U.S. natural gas prices, as the gas retrieved from shale formations has been considerable. The impact on world oil prices of new extraction technologies alone has probably been less dramatic. Given the integrated world oil markets as well as the various factors contributing to world price, it is unlikely that dramatic increases in U.S. oil production would be enough to affect world prices. However, any significant increase in production, particularly domestic production, combined with lower worldwide economic growth has contributed to lower prices. One thing that may help to reduce the European resistance to fracturing methods is that most of these countries have Russia as their primary source of oil and natural gas. Given its market power, Russia acts like any monopoly—with ability to reduce quantity and/or increase prices. This was evident in 2014 as Russia flexed its energy monopoly status with Ukraine. It is also true to a lesser extent with the EU which threatens financial sanctions over annexation of Crimea and to deter further occupation of eastern Ukraine. Russia has at least two problems acting as an aggressive monopolist in the international energy market. First, Russian oil and gas provide 70 percent of its export earnings, and receipts from sales cover about 50 percent of its federal budget. The problem is less the supply dependence by Europe than Russian demand dependence on sales to its European clients. Second, to sell oil and gas, Russia like all countries relies on the international financial system: its firms must borrow on the bond market; trade their shares on international exchanges; and process payments in dollars, the currency in which almost all international energy transactions are priced (*Economist*, 2014b: 45). Financial sanctions applied by countries such as the U.S. can therefore deter monopoly behavior as well as preserve international order.

Another example of world demand for additional natural gas sources occurred in Japan. As a direct result of the earthquake/tsunami in March 2011, the country went from relying on nuclear power for 30 percent of its energy to no nuclear power at all. Even though there are industry pressures to reopen the damaged nuclear power plants, they have been blocked by the government's Nuclear Regulation Authority based on the risks of future earthquake damage. The lack of its core nuclear power source has caused the Japanese government and its citizens to sensibly search for replacements. One important option, of course, is renewed conservation efforts by the public. More significantly, the Japanese government is now importing the new natural gas extractions from shale formations in the U.S.

Environmental Problems

The potential for external effects as a result of increasing economic growth affects the environment as a result of energy generation and distribution for consumption by firms and individuals. In addition to the effects on air, water, and solid wastes that have been measured and documented for decades in many countries of all regions, the larger effects of climate change on the world's economy are potentially disastrous. One of the primary contributors to this climate change is the build-up of greenhouse gases (e.g. carbon dioxide (CO_2), methane, carbon monoxide (CO), nitrous oxide (NOx), perfluorocarbons, hydofluorocarbons, and sulphur hexafluoride) in the atmosphere. The build-up of several of these greenhouse gases (GHG) over time is illustrated in *Figure 7.2*. Excessive build-up of GHG keeps infrared heat from escaping the atmosphere and traps heat, potentially causing "global warming." Global warming has been cited by environmental scientists as contributing to increasing temperature levels, melting ice caps and rising sea levels, and changing weather patterns that can lead to greater incidences of extreme weather events causing significant property damage and loss of life. The United Nations Intergovernmental Panel on Climate Change (IPCC, 2014) in its 2013 fifth assessment report on climate change reported an increase of 41 percent in the level of carbon dioxide since the Industrial Revolution. That level is expected to double within

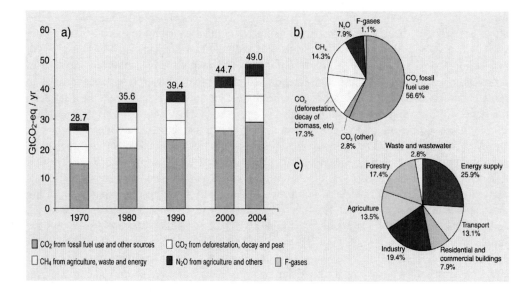

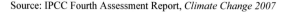

Figure 7.2 Build-Up of Greenhouse Gases

Source: IPCC Fourth Assessment Report, *Climate Change 2007*

decades, with a consequent increase of the world's temperature by five degrees. The effect of this warming is expected to alter rainfall and snowmelt. In turn, that will adversely affect agricultural conditions, possibly reducing crop yields in the affected areas.

Production of power dependent on hydroelectricity may also be adversely affected. Obviously the significance of these effects will depend upon a country's location, its dependence on agriculture for consumption and production, and its power supply. Countries closer to ocean coasts may ultimately experience greater flooding or more extreme weather events. Developing countries may see reductions in important agricultural production, reducing national income. However, even though there is considerable agreement among these scientists, there remain serious controversies surrounding the measurement and interpretations of these gases and their impact on the world's environment. For example, the number of stations responsible for the measurement of temperature over time has decreased and the remaining stations are located in generally warmer, urban areas.

Given these potentially devastating effects of pollution, particularly from excessive GHG emissions, there are obvious environmental advantages associated with individual countries' actions in pollution abatement. However, there are significant disincentives for individual countries to carry out these actions unilaterally, given the potential effect on competitiveness caused by additional regulations and fees on domestic firms. As a result, there have been attempts to pass important international agreements to reduce GHG emissions. Unfortunately, they have not been fully effective in reducing the world's greenhouse gas emissions, sometimes because of the inability to gain the cooperation of the largest world emitters—the U.S., European Union, China, and India. For example, nearly 200 countries, including the largest emitters, signed the 1997 Kyoto Protocol, which identified and directly addressed the reduction of greenhouse gas emissions. However, the U.S. was unable to obtain Congressional ratification of the Protocol. The follow-up 2009 Copenhagen Accord was not a binding agreement among the world's largest greenhouse gas emitters and countries would have needed to act unilaterally.

Externalities

Perfectly competitive markets are characterized as having a large number of perfectly informed consumers and producers, so that the actions by the individual suppliers and/or demanders will not affect the market price. The output from each of these many producers is homogeneous—that is, output from one producer is a perfect substitute to each of its rivals' output. Finally, there are no barriers to entry by potential rivals into or exit by existing firms out of the market. Under these basic conditions, the market is economically efficient. In the event that these characteristics do not hold, then the market fails to be efficient. Government intervention *may* be required to correct this market failure.

Positive or negative externalities are an example of when perfectly competitive markets may fail to reach an economically efficient market outcome. An externality is created when "the activity of one entity (a person or a firm) directly affects the welfare of another in a way that is not reflected in the market price" (Rosen and Gayer, 2010: 73). Because these effects are not appropriately "priced" in the market place, decisions made in the private market may not be economically efficient. The private market decision alone would create effects reducing the well-being of economic actors not directly part of this decision; then, in the case of a negative externality as indicated in *Figure 7.3*, too much of a damaging output would be allowed.

Where the curve representing the marginal private costs of production (MC) equals the curve that represents the marginal private benefits (MB) associated with the consumption of

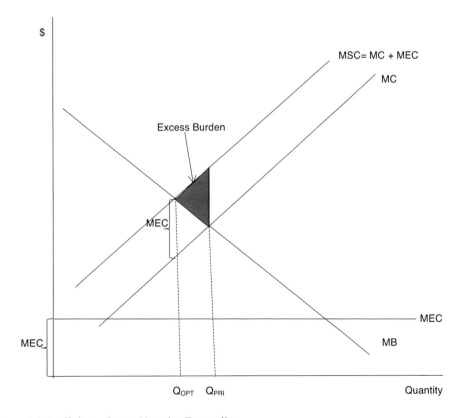

Figure 7.3 Inefficiency from a Negative Externality

this good is where the perfectly competitive market will be in equilibrium at Q_{PRI}. The presence of a negative externality creates a marginal external cost (or marginal damage), represented by the MEC curve. When this external cost is included with the private costs, then the "social" costs associated with the production of this good are calculated or MSC. The "socially efficient" output level, Q_{OPT}, is where the MSC are equal to the MB. Since the definition of externalities means there are no private market incentives to take into account these MEC, then the competitive market will not produce at Q_{OPT} and too much of the good will be produced as a result. The efficiency cost (or deadweight loss) to the economy of this overproduction is represented by the shaded area.

Greenhouse gases and other discharges from the private market consumption and production economic activities fall under the standard definition of negative externalities. The producers creating these externalities will not take into consideration the marginal damages when making their private production decisions. This means the private market will produce too much of the pollution-generating production output than is economically or socially efficient. Reaching the socially optimal level of output requires a measure of the marginal external costs or damages and then a mechanism to cause the private actors to consider them in their transaction. The first calculation is the determination of the marginal damages associated with pollution emissions. Aldy et al. (2010) review the studies which have estimated these damages. Marginal damages from warming of 2.5ºC above preindustrial levels amount to 1–2 percent of world GDP. Damages double to 2–4 percent of GDP with warming of 4ºC and then escalate to nearly 10.5 percent of GDP for warming of 6ºC. Needless to say, these estimates are imprecise. Estimates differ across studies based on what is included in the damages—market, nonmarket, and catastrophic effects.

Although several types of government mechanisms could be designed to address the consideration of externalities by the private market actors, government policy may not be required to correct the market failure. Coase (1960) presents the case for a private (i.e. non-governmental) solution to the standard externality-caused market failure. For example, the basic problem with pollution is that property rights to clean air/water have not been appropriately assigned, so the responsibility for the marginal damages is unclear. Once assigned, bargaining will take place in the private market and, if necessary, compensation will be paid. Coase shows the ultimate outcome of this bargaining will be the socially optimal equilibrium. Who is actually assigned the property rights is not important to achieve social efficiency but it will determine the direction of any compensation payments. The assumptions underlying this solution are that there is full information (the producer of the externalities can be identified) and the transactions costs associated with any bargaining between the parties are zero.

The obvious difficulties of a private market solution to the externalities problem come about when the Coase model assumptions do not hold—i.e. when information is not full and when transactions are costly. In those more standard cases, a government solution will generally be required to address the presence of externalities like pollution. These government policies include regulation and more market-oriented programs that affect either the market price or quantity.

Application: Comparative Responses to Global Warming

As mentioned above, reports from the United Nations IPCC describe the dire consequences of increased GHG emissions and resulting global warming. The most recent report described the emissions of GHG as "the highest in history" with historically recorded higher temperatures and diminished levels of snow and ice which result in rising sea levels. However, the very nature of negative externalities and the enormous costs involved in their control mean that no country can or will take into account all of the social costs of these effects. Even if a country wanted to, it is limited by the economic means to address the problem. As a result, any effective public policy to control global warming requires a coordinated international response involving both developed and underdeveloped countries. Structural changes to overcome the confederation problem of states acting individually to their common detriment by imposing unitary or federalist solutions have been proposed but usually fail because few countries will sacrifice economic sovereignty for common environmental benefit even if it is in their long-run interest, i.e. the classic commons problem. Several such international conferences have been held to try to secure these agreements, to various levels of incomplete success.

One of the primary difficulties to any international agreement is that the majority of GHG emissions and the external costs from global warming are not evenly distributed across countries. While the historical sources are the developed countries corresponding to their large economic growth, the largest developing countries are now responsible for the largest emissions of GHG. The greatest current GHG emitter is China, with about a quarter of the world's emissions. Rivers and soils in China are heavily polluted and the air pollution is described as "toxic" (*Economist*, 2013b). India has the largest recent growth in global GHG emissions. Historical differences provide the main arguments made by the underdeveloped countries for not aggressively adopting policies to reduce GHG emissions. That is, it is argued that the developed countries were also late to begin the process of pollution control after first experiencing significant economic growth. Like those countries, China and other countries now want to enjoy the benefits of economic growth before the burden of cleaning up. Although this analogy with the developed countries may seem persuasive, there are major differences in the time frame. The recent amounts of GHG emissions in China and India (as well as other developing countries) add to the large stock of emissions created by the previous growth of the developed countries like the U.S., Britain, and Japan and it is the cumulative effect of GHG that matters. Moreover, China has historically been an enormous consumer of energy, and most of this energy was generated through coal burning plants. As a result, the emissions of CO_2 in China are increasing and have recently exceeded the U.S. emissions (*Economist*, 2013b). Because of this cumulative effect, it can be argued that later emissions have a greater impact than earlier ones.

As the sources of GHG emissions are unevenly divided across countries, so are their economic and health impacts unevenly divided across the developed and underdeveloped countries. Although the overwhelming source of carbon emissions is from the poor and middle-income countries of the world, these countries, particularly the poor countries, face the greatest costs relative to income levels. The costs mount from reduction in crop yields, greater disease, and reduced water supply. Climate change also expands the areas where warm-climate, disease-carrying insects are able to survive. That will increase negative health outcomes associated with diseases like malaria, meningitis, and dengue fever, incorporating the densely populated urban areas of the less developed African countries. Rising tides and flooding are expected to have greater effects on the populations of developing countries, as "10 of the developing world's 15 largest cities (including Shanghai, Mumbai, and Cairo) are in low-lying coastal areas" (*Economist*, 2009). The poor populations of such countries are especially vulnerable because of their inadequate housing, limited health care, and subsistence incomes give them insufficient means to adjust to changing circumstances. India has suffered as a result of climate change. Crop yields and other advances from the Green Revolution have declined sharply (*Economist*, 2009). The supply of usable water in China has fallen dramatically, creating problems in agriculture in the rural areas as well as shortages of drinking water in the urban areas (*Economist*, 2013b).

There are clear benefits to pollution control policies. The Chinese government has responded with several anti-pollution laws and regulations and created a Ministry for Environmental Protection. It has reduced CO_2 emissions and invested heavily in renewable or green energy. However, the concerns of retarding economic growth remain. Although we have seen the move by democratic governments away from an alternative source of GHG-free power, nuclear power, in response to the public's discounting of future environmental costs for present day (relatively low risk) dangers (refer back to *Figure 3.7*), it is the case that public opinion ultimately forced leaders in the developed countries to address environmental damage. An argument could be made that the authoritarian Chinese government could force energy efficiency on the population. Indeed, China is building the largest number of new nuclear reactors in the world and the government has "bullied" the state-owned factories to adopt energy efficiency targets. That being said, the government and these state-owned factories rely on and benefit greatly from this large economic growth and coal will remain the main power source for it. Moreover, the local Chinese government officials who focus on economic growth advance in the political system more quickly than those officials who spend more time and money on environmental policies (*Economist*, 2013b). This is an interesting contrast to the original political parties of most of the new countries created after the breakup of the Soviet Union that were formed by groups brought together out of environmental concerns (*Economist*, 2013b). There is some optimism that new technologies and the, albeit muted, public response to this pollution will allow China to make important progress on emissions control.

Government—Regulatory Command and Control

States have controlled the externality of pollution in two basic ways. The regulatory "command and control" approach assigns a certain amount of pollution control, generally across all polluters. This assignment could either come in the form of a particular type of control technology that would achieve a given level of pollutant or it could be an actual level of pollutant allowed to be emitted (this could include zero) across all emitters, with the stipulation that firms have the flexibility to adopt any technology to achieve it. The basic problem with assigning the particular technology is that the mandated technology may not be the most appropriate or least-cost abatement method. The other regulatory method allows for profit maximizing firms to adopt the least cost methods and has a greater potential to be efficient. However, in neither case is consideration taken for the very likely possibility that abatement costs vary across the various polluters. Consequently, while potentially effective, the given level of pollution abatement will not be achieved at the lowest cost and will therefore be inefficient.

Government—Market Based

Alternative methods for government intervention in pollution control are through "market-based" pollution abatement instruments. Such instruments control externalities by forcing the polluters to "internalize" the externality—either by setting prices (taxes) for emitted pollution or by setting the optimal quantity of pollution and then issuing tradable pollution permits. The basic idea is that producers facing charges for pollution—either managed through taxes on pollution or through charges for pollution permits—will make a rational decision and select the least expensive alternative—either to self-clean up and pollute less or pay the tax/buy the permit associated with polluting. If set correctly, either method leads to the socially efficient level of output, and as a result, pollution control would be achieved in the least cost manner.

Although there are significant differences in each, the choice of instrument is often associated with the types of pollutants, political pressures, and/or with the ease of instrument implementation. Each of these market-based methods is described more fully below.

Market Based: Effluent Charges

A common market "price"-based method to control externalities was first proposed by Pigou in an early public finance textbook. Economic efficiency is achieved by establishing a "Pigouvian tax" for the damage caused to force the emitter of the externality to consider any external costs. The appropriate or "efficient" tax is set equivalent to the marginal damage caused by the pollution at the optimal or socially efficient level of production or where the marginal social benefit of production equals the marginal social cost (Sumner et al., 2011; Rosen and Gayer, 2010). For example, the government could levy a tax on the producer's output that is equal to the marginal damage caused by the pollution at the socially efficient level of production. If set correctly, the addition of this tax will force the producer to "internalize" the costs associated with pollution and, therefore, reduce output and the resulting pollution to the economically efficient level. *Figure 7.4* illustrates the use of a Pigouvian tax. The appropriate tax rate is set equal to the MEC at the optimal output level. Since this tax now must be considered along with the marginal private cost of production (MC), this raises the firms costs to the marginal social cost MSC (=MC + the MEC at Q_{OPT}). The polluting firms

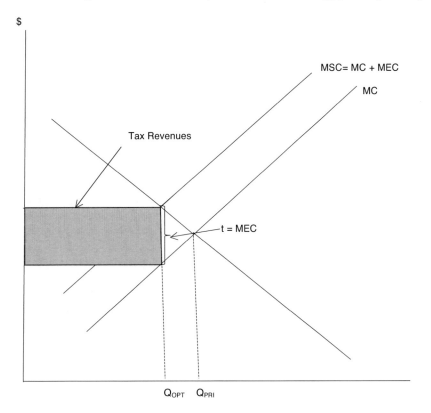

Figure 7.4 Incentive Effects of Pigouvian Tax

must then make the decision to either pay the tax on pollution emissions or install technology to reduce emissions and, unlike command-and-control policies, firms will now have the incentive to develop the lowest cost emissions reduction technology. This tax will then cause the equilibrium output to be reduced to Q_{OPT}, that is, if the emissions tax is set correctly, then the optimal amount of pollution will be reached, efficiency will be improved (e.g. deadweight loss eliminated), and cost savings can be realized. The tax revenues generated from this tax is the shaded area.

In practice, there are three basic questions that need to be addressed in order to implement a Pigouvian tax—the tax base, the tax rate, and the distribution of revenues. For example, consider the Pigouvian tax on carbon. The first decision is what should be taxed or what is the appropriate tax base? The government generally places carbon taxes on oil, coal, natural gas, and gasoline. A related decision is whether the tax is placed on "upstream" sources or "downstream" sources of pollution. Manufacturing firms purchase as an input energy source into its production (e.g. coal, oil, or another type) and then, as these energy sources are used, the firms emit pollutants during the production process. The government could control pollution by taxing the input sold by an "upstream" firm to a "downstream" manufacturing firm. The government could instead place the tax on the downstream firm based on its emissions caused by the use of that energy input. Placing taxes on upstream sources limits the collection points and affects the direct demands for the various types of energy sources by changing the relative prices for these inputs (e.g. taxes on oil and coal could be based on carbon content) (Parry et al., 2012). The next decision that needs to be addressed is the appropriate tax rate. It is the case that a unit of carbon will have the same impact on the environment no matter the source, so carbon taxes should not vary across the various pollution sources. However, often governments will apply different rates across different industries/pollutants or exempt industries entirely. This is another advantage of upstream taxes on the input rather than downstream on the firm's emissions. The final implementation decision is the distribution of revenues from the carbon tax. An obvious additional benefit associated with carbon taxes to control pollution is that they can generate considerable governmental revenue. These revenues could be used to reduce other, possibly relatively more inefficient, federal taxes or shifted over to fund environmental initiatives and tax policies to encourage the adoption of "green" technology. If revenue from the carbon tax replaces income or value-added taxes, then there could be some efficiency gains, as a result.

Two additional issues remain, focusing on the evaluation of carbon taxes—specifically the incidence of the tax and the ultimate impact on externality control. Stavins (2003) describes several examples of effluent charges/taxes on a variety of GHG primarily throughout the European countries and to a lesser extent in the United States. The U.S. EPA has placed user charges based on wastewater discharge by utilities. The general problem with a majority of these charges is that while they represent a good source of revenue for these countries (this was used as a reason to support them in the U.S.), they are usually set too low so there is no expectation of reaching the socially optimal level. Carbon taxes have been around for nearly 25 years. Finland was the first country in 1990 to use carbon taxes. According to Stavins (2003), several other OECD countries, including Denmark, Italy, the Netherlands, Norway, and Sweden, followed Finland's lead and assessed some form of carbon tax by 2000. China, Malaysia, some Latin American countries, as well as transitional economies or countries from the former Soviet Union like Bulgaria, Hungary, and Poland, have also introduced pollution taxes. Water pollution taxes are extensively used in the Netherlands, Germany, and France. These taxes have had mixed success with firm behavior and pollution reduction, generally because success is difficult to measure. Some of the countries include extensive exemptions that reduce coverage and effectiveness, taxes are set below the optimal marginal damage level, taxes are part of negotiation between the governments and the polluters, and enforcement mechanisms are weak. Smaller types of charges can be found throughout the world, for example on deposit-refunds on beverage containers, scrap metals, plastic shopping bags, and light bulbs. In addition, there is an extensive system of taxes throughout many developed and developing countries associated with transportation designed to address and control the pollution associated with the use of motor vehicles (gas and diesel) and airplanes. These include the heavy use of taxes on gasoline, tires, automobile batteries, and tolls.

Market Based: Tradable Permits

The alternative to setting pollution prices/effluent charges is to use a "quantity" instrument to set the desired quantity of pollution. The first step is to determine the socially optimal quantity of pollution and then develop a mechanism that encourages firms to reach that quantity by allowing firms to choose between cleaning up or buying a permit to pollute. The theory associated with tradable permits is similar to the theory of the effect of emissions charges. Once the optimal quantity of permits is established, then the polluting firms must compare the market price of those permits—which could be established in a type of commodity markets setting—to the cost of installing technology to reduce emissions. Once again, unlike command-and-control policies, firms will have the incentive to develop the lowest cost emissions reduction technology. Stavins (2003) breaks tradable permit programs into two basic types— credit programs, which reward firms that exceed the emissions target, or a cap-and-trade system (CaT), which sets the quantity and then distributes permits to pollute. In general, both types create a market for pollution permits where trading can, in theory, take place within, across, or even outside of the polluting firms. But the price must be right.

The U.S. has experimented with several incentive-based pollution credit programs. In these programs, credits are given to firms that exceed established emission limits, which can be used by the firm internally or traded to other firms. One of the first was the emissions trading program set up by the U.S. Environmental Protection Agency (EPA) through the Clean Air Act in 1974. Greenhouse gases including CO, SO_2, and NO_x were subject to emissions controls, and firms exceeding these limits received credits. Various mechanisms were created to allow firms to use these credits internally. Since the emissions limits were source-based and not on the firm, total firm emissions limits were set, and "netting" or "bubbles" were allowed so that the firm's total emissions sources were treated as under a single bubble—credits could be traded across the firm's sources within the bubble in order to achieve the least cost emissions control. The EPA eventually allowed firms to "bank" credits to use against future emissions or for future sale to other firms. Another example was the lead trading program. That program was designed to assist refineries as they were required to reduce the lead content in refined gasoline. After the lead phasedown was completed, the program was ended. Canada established emissions trading programs to control greenhouse gas emissions in the mid-1990s that covered CO_2, SO_2, and CO.

CaT programs work like the credit programs. Governments establish a target level of pollution (the "cap") and then determine how many and how the permits will be distributed (the "trade"). One of the largest and most important U.S. CaT programs is the SO_2 emissions program affecting electric power plants. The program was established under the U.S. Clean Air Act Amendments of 1990. The program had two distinct phases. The emissions goal of the first phase of the program was to reduce SO_2 emissions from 263 coal fired electric generating plants with the greatest emissions by 10 million tons (relative to 1980). The second phase of the program added 3,200 electric generating plants to the list of affected plants and a cap of 50 percent reduction (relative to 1980). Schmalensee and Stavins (2013) described the selection of the target level as resulting from politics, rather than by calculating the output level where social marginal benefits equals marginal costs. Although, as with emissions taxes, an opportunity was created to generate government revenue through the sale of these pollution permits or "allowances." Once the target reduction level was determined, allowances were given away to the affected industries. Firms then decided to use the allowances or sell them to other firms or bank them for future use by either reducing the pollution generating output or by using the appropriate pollution abatement technology in order to exceed the abatement goal.

By all measures, the SO_2 program was successful. According to an EPA acid rain progress report (EPA, 2010), SO_2 emissions were reduced by 67 percent compared with 1980, emitting 5.7 million tons of SO_2, which was below the cap of 9.5 million tons. Similar success occurred in the reductions of NO_x emissions. In addition, the firms saw significant cost reductions relative to the command and control regulations. Economists have measured these cost savings as double-digit. Profit-maximizing firms burned cleaner coal and developed better technology in order to meet and, in some cases, exceed the emissions requirements. As a result of these lower emissions, air quality (measured by lower annual mean ambient SO_2 and NO_x concentrations) improved significantly. Estimates suggest the benefits of this program through the improved effects on the environment have far exceeded the program costs.

The European Union (EU) Emissions Trading System covers the 28 EU countries as well as Iceland, Liechtenstein, and Norway. It is the largest CaT system, affecting more than 11,000 electrical generating and manufacturing plants, representing 45 percent of the EU greenhouse gas emissions from CO_2, nitrous oxide (N_2O), and perfluorocarbons (PFCs). Caps on these gases are designed to reduce emissions by 1.74 percent every year until greenhouse gas emissions reach 21 percent lower by 2020, relative to 2005. The program works similarly to the U.S. SO_2 program. Allowances are allocated free to the affected industries, and they are allowed to bank them for future use or to sell them to other firms. The EU system also places a cap on emissions from the aviation sector. Plans are underway to link this program with the U.S. program as well as others existing in Australia, New Zealand, Japan, and Switzerland.

Taxes v. Permits

Both permits and carbon taxes establish a price for pollution. Carbon taxes will have an obvious direct relationship to SO_2 and/or other emissions prices, which are set directly by the regulatory body. The quantity of emissions permits are set in a cap-and-trade system and a market price to trade these emissions permits is established as a result. As indicated in *Figure 7.5*, the equivalent market price results under either system. The optimal quantity and price of pollution abatement is A, where the MC of abatement is equal to the MB. This establishes the optimal quantity of pollution permits and also determines the optimal emissions tax. Prices always affect the producer's decisions regarding the production of pollution causing outputs and/or use of pollutant creating inputs. Consumer decisions will also be affected by the change in the relative prices of these taxed factors (e.g. gas and electricity).

Potential differences exist based on the distribution of the benefits and costs between the two market-based systems (Goulder, 2013; Rosen and Gayer, 2010). However, these differences could be minimal with certain program modifications. For example, under cap-and-trade, permits have trade value, and if these permits are auctioned off by the government, the trade value will be realized and paid to the government. The overall loss to the firms is identical to a government emissions tax. However, if these permits are initially allocated for

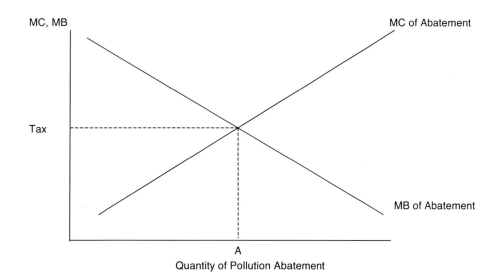

Figure 7.5 Equivalence of Optimal Emissions Tax and Pollution Permits Quantity

free, then firms will gain the surplus previously paid to the government. Firms that can achieve emissions reductions will possess valuable emissions permits which can be traded in the secondary market. Within an emissions tax system, exceptions given to firms could mimic the outcome under a cap-and-trade system with a free allocation of permits.

This does not mean that differences do not exist between these two types of systems. Institutional differences associated with the ease of administering the two programs are potentially large. Permit allowances must be tracked and registered. Permit trades and ownership must also be monitored. Where significant program differences exist is in the treatment of uncertainty. As indicated in Rosen and Gayer (2010), under certainty, the emissions price and quantities are identical under the two systems. Uncertainty creates the possibility of preference for a particular type of program. Under emissions taxes, the price is certain, set to equalize the marginal benefits and marginal costs of these emissions (as estimated by the government setting the emissions tax). The emissions output is potentially uncertain if the true marginal benefits and costs are associated with the emissions are different from those estimated. Similarly, under a cap-and-trade system, the quantity is certain, set to equalize the marginal benefits and costs of these emissions (as estimated by the quantity setting government). The emissions price is potentially uncertain if the true marginal benefits and costs associated with the emissions are different from those estimated. Environmental groups tend to prefer the certainty of the emissions quantity (e.g. cap and trade) over a certain emissions price. However, as with many economics questions, the appropriate system when there is uncertainty about the external costs associated with emissions depends upon relative elasticities. As indicated in Rosen and Gayer (2010), if the marginal social benefit function is relatively steep (inelastic) and costs are higher than expected, then an emissions fee results in too little emissions reduction and a cap-and-trade system is more efficient. However, if the marginal social benefit of pollution abatement is relatively flat (elastic) and costs are higher than expected, then the emissions tax is preferable to a cap-and-trade system. Several studies have found the marginal social benefit function to be relatively elastic, suggesting an emissions tax to be the more efficient policy.

Large questions remain surrounding the implementation of these market-based programs. As observed, these programs will not be implemented exactly like the ideal forms presented in the textbook graphs. For example, the emissions price is generally too low (or the permits are allocated for free across the polluting firms) to generate the socially optimal output level, particularly if the tax is designed as a revenue generator and not as an optimal policy instrument. The use of the revenue generated by this emissions tax is also uncertain but could be an important source of abatement, particularly if they are used for related environmental activities. They are less important to the environment if they are earmarked for the general government budget (as has been proposed as a way for the U.S. to address its growing public debt and associated fiscal deficit problems). In addition, the efficiency gains from a permit program require a large amount of market trading activity so that polluting firms are able to compare the efficient market price with the cost of abatement technology. This creates the additional problem that the price will not create the incentive for firms to develop the lower cost abatement technology, contributing to relatively low efficiency gains from these market-based mechanisms. It follows that these market-based programs will be most "effective" when emissions charges are accurately set (reflecting the marginal damage of the pollution) and, in the case of permits, trading barriers are low.

There are other "imperfections" as well which will affect the ability of these market-based programs to reach the optimal outcomes and reduce the potential cost savings and other program benefits associated with a more efficient market. The determination of the efficient price and/or quantity requires a large amount of data gathering to establish the social costs of these emissions. In general, these external damages may be difficult to calculate, which creates additional uncertainties regarding the achievement of efficiency cost savings. New monitoring and enforcement technology mechanisms may be required to reach these optimal levels. There are also the underlying motives of the various private and public actors which could undermine these market-based programs. Environmentalists in many countries may view these programs as somehow allowing pollution, as opposed to the use of environmental regulations that could be used to ban these activities outright. Politicians may view taxes of any form as harmful to the economy, and the industry polluters may see these taxes as an additional cost of doing business, even though ideally they provide incentives for the firms to achieve pollution abatement goals at the least cost. Indeed, these differences across the different interest groups (as suggested in our second level of policy analysis) could be one explanation for the different programs found across countries (Hahn, 1989).

Cost–Benefit Analysis

As any benefits of pollution reduction are expected to occur many years in the future, affecting future generations, the approach generally used to evaluate costs and, in this particular application, benefits that occur far into the future is cost–benefit analysis (CBA). CBA is widely used by government public policy officials as a decision-making tool for various capital projects. It allows a way to evaluate policies that have a stream of costs and benefits occurring at different points in time. It is also a frequently used technique to evaluate regulatory policies, the type considered within the context of pollution control. The CBA process is to put a monetary value on present and future costs and benefits of a proposed project/regulation. A comparison is then made between these costs and benefits and, in the event there is a net gain in social welfare, the project/regulation is approved. Alternatively, CBA could be used to rank-order the possible alternatives and the project/regulation that increases social welfare by the largest amount would be selected. Some of this was discussed in the context of urban transport capital projects in *Chapter 3*.

The first step in any CBA is to identify the costs and benefits of the proposed project/ regulation. A key part of this step is to determine the timeline of the project/regulation and, therefore, the timing of the project's benefits and costs. The second step is putting a monetary value on these costs and benefits. These would include "direct" benefits and costs as well as "indirect" benefits and costs or externalities. Care must be taken to compare the benefits and costs of a proposed project/regulation with the alternative of case without the project/ regulation, in order to isolate the benefits and costs which are associated with project. This can be a straightforward exercise, particularly if the goods are traded in the market and have prices. A major potential difficulty with the application of CBA is in the accurate identification of the project/regulation costs and benefits that are not traded in the market and have no prices attached, such as the general problem with externalities. This becomes potentially more problematic when the costs include morbidity and mortality effects, a clear issue in the evaluation of various environmental policies and regulations. These potential problems become particularly acute when there is uncertainty involving measurement and timing. The third step is to account for benefits and costs that occur at different times in the future. Standard discounting puts costs and benefits that occur in the future in present-day values. It is used to account for the fact that people prefer to have benefits more immediate than in the future. The discount rate or rate of time preference must be used to adjust these future costs and benefits, leaving the difficult decision of the choice of discount rate. The typical choice is to equate the discount rate to a market interest rate. The problem is the many available market interest rates.

The formal basic formula for net present value or discounted net benefits at discount rate r is:

$$NPV = \Sigma^T_{t=0} (Benefits_t—Costs_t)/(1+r)^t$$

The choice of discount rate is a crucial step in this process. Low discount rates favor projects with longer-term benefits. High discount rates will favor short-term benefits and are likely to discourage investment. Which rate should be used to calculate the discounted benefits? Some argue that the rate should reflect the opportunity costs of these funds or the rate of return these funds would have had if they remained in the private consumption or investment. For example, the opportunity cost of private investment is the rate of return or productivity of that investment, and the opportunity cost of private consumption can be measured by the rate of return on private savings. This is particularly true since one of the important assumptions underlying the use of CBA is that there is full employment in the economy. As a result, the discount rate should reflect the decrease in private consumption (opportunity cost of consumption), a decrease in private investment (opportunity cost of investment), or some combination of the two opportunity costs. However, even if it can be determined whether the decrease can be attributed to private consumption and/or investment, there still must be a decision to make regarding the choice from among the many private market interest rates consumers and investors face. Furthermore, there are considerable differences between the rates faced by the average consumer and those faced by the average investor, making the ultimate choice of the appropriate rate even more difficult. Furthermore, if the government funds are taken from a combination of consumption and investment, then an additional difficult decision needs to be made—the proportion of consumption and investment funding given up for the additional government spending. For example, the historical pre-tax rate of return on stock market investments has been about 7 percent while the average return on U.S. treasury bills has been about 1 percent. This enormous variation in rates of return to consumers/investors creates extremely large variations in the calculated present values of future costs and benefits.

There is an additional large division between those who argue that it is appropriate to use these historic values from the private markets and those who argue that instead of thinking that the project discount should reflect the opportunity costs associated with the private market, it should be considered on its own as to reflect the government's and its citizens' desires for these activities. The latter focus would probably lead to a discount rate substantially lower than the standard private rate, particularly if one is considering those historic rates of return drawn from private stock market investments. One of the primary justifications for using this alternative discount rate is because of the view that the use of a private market interest rate does not show an appropriate level of concern for future generations. Since most of the benefits from environmental policies/regulations are expected to occur far into the future, the discount rate is critical for determining their economic value. It also follows that some might argue for a lower interest rate than would be found in the private consumption or investment markets.

An example of the importance of the selection of discount rate can be found in the recent large-scale environment study the "Stern Review on the Economics of Climate Change" (Stern, 2007), which was commissioned by the British government and undertaken by Sir Nicholas Stern. In that review of climate change, Stern calculates large environmental damages as a result of the build-up of greenhouse gases. He employs a near zero discount rate in order to calculate the net benefits associated with reducing these greenhouse gases. As a result, he advocates a large government role in environmental protection. Nordhaus (2007) and Weitzman (2007) argue that this low discount rate is not appropriate and, as a result, the conclusions from the Stern Review (2007) are too drastic. Nordhaus (2007) presents an example on how this low discount rate affects monetary decisions based on numbers from the Stern Review (2007). Using this low discount rate, he calculates that $30,000 billion would be needed to be spent today to fix damages estimated to be 0.1 percent of net consumption beginning in 2200 (!). He urges sensitivity tests to determine the outcomes from using different discount rates. Furthermore, the extremely low discount rates mean that environmental costs from any future distance will be treated as if they occur today.

Once the benefits and costs have been discounted, the final steps are to create a decision rule. One of three standard rules is typically applied to determine the socially optimal project/regulation. The first is to use the NPV formula directly. A positive NPV supports undertaking the project/regulation. A second approach is to employ the ratio of discounted benefits to discounted costs.

$$\text{Benefit–Cost Ratio} = (\Sigma^T_{t=0} \text{ Benefits}_t /(1+r)^t)/(\Sigma^T_{t=0}\text{Costs}_t/(1+r)^t)$$

A ratio greater than 1 supports undertaking the project/regulation. The third possible rule is to calculate and use the project's internal rate of return (IRR). The IRR is the calculated rate of return where the NPV is 0.

$$\text{NPV} = \Sigma^T_{t=0} (\text{Benefits}_t - \text{Costs}_t)/(1+\text{IRR})^t = 0$$

The IRR is then compared to the proposed project discount rate and if the IRR $> r$, then the project/regulation would be socially beneficial.

Given three possible decision rules, is there a best one? The rule most closely aligned to the actual decision is to select the project with the highest NPV. The other two decision rules have serious drawbacks. The benefit–cost ratio can be misapplied if the benefits and, particularly, the costs are not accounted for correctly. Problems can occur if certain "costs" are added to the denominator or subtracted from the numerator. This will obviously affect the size of the ratio but will have no effect on the NPV calculation. While this is thought to be a small problem, there is no reason to use the cost–benefit ratio when there is a chance for a problem and a more accurate method is available. The IRR has potentially larger disadvantages. If discounted net benefits fluctuate negative and positive over time, then the IRR may not be a unique value.

Application of Policy Analytic Frameworks: The Adoption of Nuclear Power

At the technical level, it is critical to empirically demonstrate the linkages between proposed policy or program inputs in resources with the outputs in energy units produced per dollar and the outcomes in terms of wider costs and benefits. The latter needs to be linked to the inputs directly in, for instance, environmental costs/benefits. Then it needs to be compared with other energy policy options. Most countries perform this kind of basic input-output analysis and supplement it with comparative cases and data from other countries and energy policy information sources. Most countries also use a mix of energy sources in addition to nuclear. For example, Hungary has five nuclear plants which produce 42 percent of all its electricity; France, 58 nuclear plants producing 75 percent; Japan 54 plants producing 29 percent, and the U.S. 104 plants producing 20 percent. These figures indicate the value placed on other sources such as hydroelectric (e.g. Brazil relies on hydropower for 70 percent of its electricity; Switzerland, 60 percent; and Costa Rica, 80 percent); coal; oil; gas; and renewables such as wind, solar geothermal, and biomass. Costa Rica alone now produces 100 percent of its energy from renewable sources!

At the first level of analysis, the known facts and established costs are presented as well as the known outputs and forecasted outcomes. For example, it is known that demand for energy is likely to hold up thanks to growth in emerging economies. IEA predicts it to increase for the next 25 years by 37 percent. In countries such as China, increased investments in new clean coal power generation (stack emissions scrubbed of nitrogen and sulphur), nuclear and renewable energy, and long-distance transmission lines means greater efficiency (outputs) but also increased consumption from billions of new devices that will be hooked up to the "Internet of things" (*Economist*, 2014a: 5). Thus, the demand will increase for more energy from the most cost-beneficial sources.

Referring back to *Chapter 3*, note that the method for capital project/plant evaluation matters. Cost-effectiveness analysis assumes the worth of the benefit (e.g. running water) and seeks out the least costly alternative for producing it (Michel, 2001: 79). The costs are known and the benefits are given, with volumes of benefits forecasted (e.g. demand for water). By contrast, benefit–cost analysis seeks costs and benefits to society. Electricity worth can be an assumed benefit like running water but not necessarily if produced by nuclear energy. Since nuclear plants are long-term capital investments, their costs require discounting (net present value) to determine the actual cost of capital. The rate of interest used (discount rate) represents the high upfront construction costs together with the risks and uncertainty of accidents, delays, changes in the regulatory environment, public opposition, decommissioning costs, and location issues. Costs of capital are high, and discounted returns low. For example, an initial $4-billion plant investment over a 40-year lifespan would require an 11 percent discount rate (for risks) and translate into a $17-billion investment over the life of the loan. That makes the option uneconomic without state subsidies. Nuclear is now the most heavily subsidized energy industry per kilowatt hour behind wind and solar. The nuclear option becomes economic only if external costs of fossil fuel plants would be internalized into real costs through a carbon tax, e.g. $100 per ton would make nuclear competitive with natural gas.

As indicated, the burning of fossil fuels, particularly coal, to produce electricity represents the primary contributor to the creation of GHG, resulting in global warming and negative environmental consequences. The cost of coal mining is going up. Global oversupplies have leveled the price at $80–$85 per ton, which barely covers mining costs of capital. Paradoxically, the production of coal in countries such as Germany is the highest in decades in order to cover the shortfall from the gap in nuclear production. It is paradoxical because Germany is still the greenest country in Europe! Japan is also relying on coal to meet its nuclear energy shortfall despite health costs and contribution to GHGs and the evidence that mines require costly subsidies or face closure. A new $5.2-billion taxpayer-supported plant in Mississippi incorporates the latest technology. But at $6,800 per kilowatt hour, it is the costliest power plant ever built! A gas-fired plant in the U.S. costs $1,000 per kilowatt hour (*Economist*, 2014c: 56).

Based on best available energy technology, there are several market-based or incentive-driven public policies that can be and have been used to reduce the use of these fossil fuels, to encourage a more efficient generation of electricity, to clean up more effectively the emissions from these sources, and to develop alternative renewable energy sources. All of these approaches have factors that complicate achieving the goals of reasonably priced energy sources with minimal environmental damage and contribution to global warming.

Nuclear power is now responsible for about 20 percent of the world's electricity generation. The largest producers of nuclear power are the U.S., Japan, Germany, France, Russia, and South Korea. Two important advantages of nuclear power are low costs and low emissions. First, in the U.S., the average cost of generating electricity from a nuclear plant was only 2.4 cents per kilowatt ($24 per megawatt hour). That is cheaper than gas or coal-fired power but disguises wide variations. The least efficient plants have higher operating costs per unit of electricity than coal or gas. Since the main cost of nuclear power is building the plant in the first place, the narrowing gap in operating costs is ominous for the industry. And in the U.S. (as elsewhere in the world), gas prices are still plunging. In Sweden, electricity prices have often fallen below nuclear plant operating costs (*Economist*, 2015d: 59). Second, nuclear plants have no CO_2 emissions and therefore represent a source of "clean" energy. France recorded the largest drop in GHG emissions when it moved more significantly into nuclear power as a source of energy production (*Scientific American*, 2013).

However, even though most of the individual countries from the developed world have goals to reduce GHG emissions, either created internally or as part of a regional or international agreement, the worldwide use of nuclear power is decreasing considerably. Only one new nuclear power plant is planned for the U.S. (Watts Bar plant in Georgia was recently licensed). Some replacement plants are being built, and in Europe, only Hinkley Point in Britain has been proposed with required high public subsidies and high fixed electricity prices to make the project "economic." There is widespread political and public resistance to the expansion of nuclear power and even a desire to reduce its use. The main resistance comes from a public that has several concerns described below that, combined with the heavily discounted future benefits from pollution reduction, do not favor the expansion of the nuclear energy option. Even France mandated that its share of nuclear energy drop from 75 percent to 50 percent within ten years (*Economist*, 2015d: 59). Both countries promise that the nuclear shortfall will be made up with renewable sources, mainly wind and solar. Still, new nuclear plants are planned in the Czech Republic, China, Taiwan, India, Japan, and South Korea.

Three issues arise that must be addressed before the expanded use of nuclear power can be considered. Until they are resolved, they will increase the discount rate for risks and continue to make the nuclear option uneconomic. The first issue is about safety. Events in the U.S. with Three Mile Island, in Russia with the Chernobyl reactors, and the recent disaster in Japan caused by the impact of the tsunami on the Fukushima Nuclear Power Plant have increased safety concerns. Although the incidence of accidents is rare, the impact is potentially devastating and creates negative reactions from the public, which has ultimately caused the reduction in the nuclear power industry in most developed countries. The second issue is about nuclear waste. Although nuclear power does not create CO_2, its production does generate spent fuel and radioactive waste streams that are themselves environmental hazards and are dangerous to present as well as future generations. Decommissioning costs are high. Perhaps the most important issue is the risk to worldwide security created by nuclear proliferation. The technology required to create nuclear power and the spent fuel from this process are elements in the creation of nuclear weapons. Thousands of nuclear warheads exist in the U.S., France, Britain, and Russia, with other countries possessing the materials and technology to create such weapons in countries like India, Pakistan, and Iran, creating potential military instabilities. These security concerns raise another complication in support from the developed countries in expanding nuclear power.

The evidence indicates that the costs of alternative energy sources to nuclear are dropping: coal prices have decreased 80 percent in the U.S. since 2008; costs of solar and wind (though subsidized) have declined; political pressures have grown against coal. It provides 40 percent of world electricity but 75 percent is of the dirtiest kind, which emits 75 percent more CO than the most advanced and costly coal plants that burn powdered coal (*Economist*, 2015b: 65). The electric energy problem is that nuclear and many fossil fuel options are becoming uneconomic. Oil and gas prices have dropped dramatically and the new normal consensus is around $50 per barrel or half what most large firms need to break even on exploration and government oil exporters estimate as revenues to balance their budgets. Shale producers can break even only at around $55, meaning the squeeze is on even against them. Meanwhile, electricity demand is increasing and green alternatives of wind and solar are still not economic or reliable. Large scale solar capacity to generate depends to some extent on extension of transmission lines from plants far away from population centers. That causes intense environmental opposition and project delays that will reduce the reliability of electricity supplies to fill the shortfall created by loss of nuclear and coal options in many countries.

In short, the concept of energy "cost" should be narrowed to include subsidies and the overall effects on energy markets. Solar and wind farms produce more expensive energy than coal or gas on a "levelized cost" basis, which includes construction costs. Once the solar farm is up, the marginal cost of power output is close to zero, meaning solar energy is free at the margin. Refer back to the discussion of marginal costs in *Chapter 3*. Because it is free at the margin, green-power producers offer it for next to nothing in the wholesale markets. They often make money from subsidies known as "feed-in tariffs." The energy companies start by accepting the lowest bids for the day's requirements. The surge in wind and solar power (with high subsidies such as in Germany) pushes down the clearing price for all energy bidders (nuclear, coal, gas). The effect is to raise the cost per watt of electricity produced by coal and gas. Given the currently intermittent nature of renewable energy supply, the result is likely to be blackouts as fossil fuel plants are unable to meet their costs with revenues, largely from charging high user fees. For instance, German feed-in tariffs are guaranteed for 20 years; German consumers pay twice as much as French consumers for a kilowatt hour of electricity (*Economist*, 2015a: 7–8).

Nevertheless, the nominal cost of electricity from solar is plummeting; it is now between $90 and $300 per megawatt hour. The renewable power capacity China installed in 2013 was larger than combined new nuclear–fossil fuel capacity. In 2013, wind turbines were responsible for 33 percent of Denmark's national energy supply and 20 percent of Spain's. Breakthroughs in storage also promise to increase the reliability of renewable energy supplies (*Economist*, 2014a: 6–7). Thus, nuclear may not become as viable an option as renewables in meeting the projected shortfall from fossil fuel production. These linkages are well researched, and the costs and benefits of all energy options are relatively agreed upon. Thus, at the strategic and operational levels, the energy policy function gains from having valid and reliable data and information on which to base policy decisions. At the second level of political economy analysis, nuclear energy must deal with three sources of strategic opposition: financial/ economic costs, public opposition, and green environmental reviews that delay projects and increase costs. At the operational systems level, the systems depend less on political contexts and cultures than technical environments, e.g. sun and wind. Nuclear energy is now plagued by high upfront costs and uncertain risks of construction, operation, and decommissioning. Fossil fuel prices are dropping on average because of oversupply. That could change with strong world growth and increased demand. But public opposition to nuclear risks from real accidents and health impacts (e.g. Japan) and corresponding skepticism during environmental reviews increases the costs of nuclear energy even more. The public support and financial incentives for green alternatives, e.g. solar subsidies (EU), rebates (Germany), and mandates (California), combined with successes in dropping unit costs to near economic break-even levels, make renewables the favored option. As noted, improvements in storage capacity offer hope to the 2.5 billion people in the world that are "underelectrified" (*Economist*, 2014a: 8). In short, the technology largely drives the solutions and as long as they are not too costly (in financial terms), regimes worldwide favor them as cheap, efficient means of electricity generation.

Capital markets frozen after the 2008 financial crash are again financing investments on the basis of future revenues. Solar energy offers a predictable income stream that draws in real money. A rooftop lease can finance an investment of $15,000–$20,000 with monthly payments that are lower than the customer's utility bills. The growing number of energy service companies (ESCOs) pay for installation in such cases, bundle the revenue, and sell bonds on the expectation of future income streams. This lowers the cost of capital for the solar industry 200–300 basis points below that for utilities (*Economist*, 2014a: 12). Technology has created a virtuous circle with the help of financial markets and supportive public policies worldwide. Thus, technological, public, and regime support variables can explain the particular mix a country adopts to meet its energy needs and to fill the shortfalls faced by each.

Thus, the third level of comparative analysis for energy and environment can be conducted largely at the operational level of energy source systems performance. Much data and information are available to conduct technical comparisons and provide country policy options that fit local needs and demand. For instance, emissions trading systems and models for water and air pollution abatement have been transferred across country boundaries for decades. And advances in wind, solar, and traditional fossil fuel generation sources can and have been transferred across national boundaries by governments and private investors and used to increase national installed capacities.

Conclusions

The increased availability and use of energy alternatives has led to varying degrees of pollution. Environmental policies, some based on economic models, have been proposed to reduce the negative impacts on health and quality of life associated with increased pollution. Energy policies are driven by resource availability in particular countries, creating over-consumption of coal and oil in many countries. Economic models have shed some light on the appropriate market-based policies that could be used to affect the demand for energy as well as to provide incentives to guide the market to more efficient outcomes. Political forces have kept many of these models from being fully realized. Alternative energy sources have emerged to replace use of certain energy sources considered most detrimental (e.g. nuclear and coal) or as an attempt to reduce the reliance on foreign sources of energy (e.g. shale oil fracking leading to greater natural gas production and wind/solar energy). However, the alternative sources of energy may lead to additional serious environmental problems. As it is often said in policy analysis, all solutions lead to new problems ...

Cases and Exercises

1 Read *Case 7.1* on "Carbon Taxes Make Ireland Even Greener" and answer the questions following:

Case 7.1 Irish Carbon Taxes

Source: Rosenthal, 2012

Over the last three years, with its economy in tatters, Ireland embraced a novel strategy to help reduce its staggering deficit: charging households and businesses for the environmental damage they cause. The government imposed taxes on most of the fossil fuels used by homes, offices, vehicles and farms, based on each fuel's carbon dioxide emissions, a move that immediately drove up prices for oil, natural gas and kerosene. The Irish now pay purchase taxes on new cars and yearly registration fees that rise steeply in proportion to emissions.

Environmentally and economically, the new taxes have delivered results. Long one of Europe's highest per-capita producers of greenhouse gases, with levels nearing those of the United States, Ireland has seen its emissions drop more than 15 percent since 2008. Although much of that decline can be attributed to a recession, changes in behavior also played a major role, experts say, noting that the country's emissions dropped 6.7 percent in 2011 even as the economy grew slightly.

By contrast, carbon taxes are viewed as politically toxic in the United States. Republican leaders in Congress have pledged to block any proposal for such a tax, and President Obama has not advocated one, although the idea has drawn support from economists of varying ideologies.

Yet when the Irish were faced with new environmental taxes, they quickly shifted to greener fuels and cars and began recycling with fervor. Automakers like Mercedes found ways to make powerful cars with an emissions rating as low as tinier Nissans. With less trash, landfills closed. And as fossil fuels became more costly, renewable energy sources became more competitive, allowing Ireland's wind power industry to thrive. The three-year-old carbon tax has raised nearly one billion euros ($1.3 billion) over all, including 400 million euros in 2012. That provided the Irish government with 25 percent of the 1.6 billion euros in new tax revenue it needed to narrow its budget gap this year and avert a rise in income tax rates.

The prices of basic commodities like gasoline and heating oil have risen 5 to 10 percent. This is particularly hard on the poor, although the government has provided subsidies for low-income families to better insulate homes, for example. And industries complain that the higher prices have made it harder for them to compete outside Ireland. Although carbon taxes in some ways disproportionately affect the poor—who are less able to buy new, more efficient cars, for example—such taxes do heavily penalize the wealthy, who consume far more. As with "sin taxes" on cigarettes, the taxes also alleviate some of the societal costs of pollution. Some of Europe's strongest economies, like Sweden, Denmark and the Netherlands, have taxed carbon dioxide emissions since the early 1990s, and Japan and Australia have introduced them more recently. Of course, new environmental taxes bring new pain. Gas, always expensive in Europe, sells here for about $8 a gallon, around 20 percent more than in 2009 because of tightening market supplies and the new tax.

a   Do you believe the emissions tax is set "optimally"?
b   How would you be able to determine the optimal level?
c   If it is not optimal, is there too much or too little pollution being emitted?
d   Would you say this tax is progressive or regressive?

2   Read *Case 7.2* on "The Shadow of Fukushima, the World's Worst Nuclear Disaster After Chernobyl, Hangs Over Japan's Energy Future" and answer the questions following:

Case 7.2 Fukushima and Japan's Energy Future

Source: *Economist*, 2013c: 59

The closure of Japan's last nuclear reactor was supposedly for routine maintenance and safety checks. Yet no firm date is in sight for reopening the Oi reactor or any other of Japan's 50 others, shut in the wake of the triple meltdown at the Fukushima Dai-ichi plant. Before the earthquake and tsunami of March 2011 turned so much of Japan's world upside down, the country counted on nuclear power for 30 percent of its electricity—one of the highest proportions in the world. Now it is entirely without nuclear power for only the second time since 1970. The industry ministry says that the need to import extra oil, gas and coal to fire conventional power stations will have cost Japan an extra ¥9.2 trillion (about $93 billion) by the end of 2013. A sharply weaker yen and higher oil prices have not helped, and Japan is now running trade deficits for the first time in three decades. Businesses and consumers face much higher electricity costs in Japan than in many countries.

While the community of electricity utilities, bureaucrats, academics and heavy industry, known in Japan as the "nuclear village", is urging a restart of the reactors, Japan is preparing for other long-term energy supplies. Since 2011 the number of independent power producers tapping renewable sources, such as solar power, has tripled, thanks in part to a new "feed-in" tariff system for renewables. Including hydro-electricity, renewables now represent 10 percent of the energy mix, leading to hopes that they might one day replace the share that nuclear power once claimed. But the power grids are still owned by the big utilities, which can find excuses to deny access. For a long time to come, therefore, Japan will turn to oil, gas and coal to make up most of the nuclear shortfall. In May the government won American approval for imports of cheap shale gas from the United States. That could handily slash the cost of energy imports and alleviate concerns about energy security.

The cranking-up of fossil-fuel power stations, many working at well under capacity before March 2011, is one reason why the predictions of widespread black-outs never came about after the Fukushima scare. But another reason was the room for conserving energy. Tokyo alone has slashed electricity consumption by a tenth since 2011, according to the Japan Renewable Energy Foundation. The demand for power-saving devices has leapt. Sales of light-emitting diodes have shot up from 3 percent of all Japanese bulbs sold in 2009 to over 30 percent today. Long-overdue proposals to liberalize the electricity market may do much to diversify energy sources and lower electricity bills. If the reform succeeds, says Hiroshi Takahashi of the Fujitsu Research Institute in Tokyo, the share of nuclear power in the energy mix would fall as new, non-nuclear providers won customers. It would, at long last, give the public some say over Japan's energy choices.

a How has Japan (in particular, Tokyo) achieved this significant reduction in electricity consumption?

b How do you expect the introduction of competition to the electricity market will affect the price of electricity? What is the evidence that competition in this market has reduced prices?

3 Read *Case 7.3* on "The Cost del Sol" and answer the questions following:

Case 7.3 Spanish Solar Energy Policy

Source: *Economist*, 2013a

Angel Miralda had 320 solar panels providing 56 KW of clean energy bought with a $735k bank loan and retirement funds. The government promised a 10 percent annual return on such projects. That was in 2008. Five years later, after subsidies were cut on July 12th for the third time since 2012, his income is down by 40 percent and he is struggling to repay the loan. Mr Miralda is the victim of a bungled, overambitious renewables program. Governments everywhere want to turn green and create environmentally friendly jobs. But as Spain shows, good intentions are not enough. If the policies are wrong, the benefits are wasted, the jobs disappear, the costs remain—and business investors bear the brunt.

In 2007 Spain had just 690 megawatts (MW) of installed capacity of solar photovoltaic (PV) panels. That was the year global PV prices started to fall, thanks to booming production in China. Hoping to stimulate a new green industry, for which sunny Spain seems ideal, the government increased the prices it paid for solar power to 12 times the market price for electricity. Renewable-energy output doubled between 2006 and 2012.

At that point, Spain had the fourth-largest such industry in the world. But costs exploded, too. Subsidies to solar energy rose from €190m in 2007 to €3.5 billion in 2012 (an 18-fold increase). Total subsidies to all renewables reached €8.1 billion in 2012. Since the government was unwilling to pass the full costs on to consumers, the cumulative tariff deficit (the cost of the system minus revenues from consumers) reached €26 billion, having risen by about €5 billion a year. This would have been unaffordable at the best of times: €8 billion is almost 1 percent of GDP. But as the euro crisis overwhelmed Spain's finances, reform of the renewable-energy bonanza became inevitable. On July 12th the government unveiled its latest cuts. It lopped €2.7 billion off the overall bill, of which €1.4 billion were cuts to subsidies for renewable energy and €1.3 billion cuts to other revenues of utility companies.

The changes have turned renewable energy into a fully-regulated business. Companies used to be able to choose between getting market prices plus a premium, or to agree on long-term contracts that guaranteed a set margin above their costs. The government scrapped the first option earlier this year and has now scrapped the second. Instead, it will estimate the value of companies' assets and cap their pre-tax profits at three percentage points above ten-year Spanish government-bond yields. The changes have infuriated everyone. They are retroactive—affecting current operations as well as new ones—so there will be a deluge of lawsuits challenging their legality. Some firms will face problems servicing their debts and the government is in talks with banks to forestall bankruptcies. Outstanding loans for renewable energy are reckoned to be €30 billion. Five of the biggest utilities estimate that the reforms will jointly cost them €1 billion a year. The share prices of companies most affected—Iberdrola, EDP Renewables and Acciona—nosedived.

a What were some budgetary options for the Spanish government during the boom times for renewables?

b Why do you suppose the Spanish government failed to cut the energy subsidies during that time?

c What other options are available rather than putting a cap on pre-tax profits? What are the advantages and disadvantages of these alternatives?

4 Given the following information on net benefits for two different construction projects (A and B), calculate the NPV at three different interest rates—3 percent, 5.2 percent, and 8 percent—using the formula presented in the chapter.

Project	Net Benefits in Year		
	0	1	2
A	-500	0	605
B	-500	575	0

a Which construction project would you recommend at each interest rate?

b How would you summarize the relationship between the interest rate and the timing of these net benefits? Why?

5 Read *Case 7.4* on "A Canal Too Far: Water Consumption" and answer the questions following:

Case 7.4 Chinese Water Consumption

Source: *Economist*, 2014d: 44–45

A new water way near Hualiba village is part of the biggest water-diversion scheme in the world: the second arm of what is known as the South-North Water Diversion Project. This is designed to solve an age-old imbalance. The north of China has only a fifth of the country's naturally available fresh water but two-thirds of the farmland. The problem has grown in recent decades because of rapid urban growth and heavy pollution of scarce water supplies.

In 1952 Mao Zedong suggested the north could "borrow" water from the south. After his death China's economic boom boosted demand for such a scheme and provided the cash to enable it. In 2002 the diversion project got under way. An initial phase was completed last year. That involved deepening and broadening the existing Grand Canal, which was built some 1,400 years ago, to take 14.8 billion cubic metres of water a year more than 1,100km northward from the Yangzi river basin towards the port city of Tianjin.

In late October the second, far more ambitious and costly route is due to open. This new watercourse, over a decade in the making, will push water more than 1,200km from the Danjiangkou dam in the central province of Hubei to Beijing. The transfer will supply about a third of Beijing's annual demand. Even if people use less water, population growth, the expansion of cities and industrialization will increase China's overall demand. By lubricating further water-intensive growth the current project may even end up exacerbating water stress in the north.

Shifting billions of cubic metres across the country has caused huge disruption. The government says it has moved 330,000 people to make way for the central route. Some argue that the number uprooted is at least half a million. The financial cost is also high. Mr Sun puts the cost of the project at more than $62 billion—far higher than the original $15 billion price tag. His estimate does not include the running of the project or the building of 13 new water-treatment plants to clean the water.

By increasing supply, the government is failing to confront the real source of the problem: high demand for water and inefficient use of it. Chinese industry uses ten times more water per unit of production than the average in industrialized countries largely because water in China is far too cheap. In 2014, Beijing introduced a new system that makes tap water more expensive the more people use. But prices are still far from market levels. Officials turn a blind eye to widespread extraction of un-tariffed groundwater by city dwellers and farmers, despite plummeting groundwater levels. Raising the price would cut demand and encourage more efficient use. It should also help lure industry away from water-scarce areas where prices would be set at higher rates. Arid areas that are forced by the government to pipe water into desiccated cities like Beijing could offset their losses by charging higher tariffs.

The above case deals with how the economics of pricing trumps large public capital diversion schemes in dealing with water scarcity in China. China is the case, but the problem of project evaluation without careful economic analysis of pricing (a basic level-one empirical problem; see *Figure 1.4*) is common around the world. The new Chinese Communist Party policy of letting market forces allocate resources in land, water, and electricity is in force. So the questions are:

a   How were pricing principles and the economics of proper project evaluation ignored here?
b   What will be the likely impact of these methodological flaws?

6   Refer back to fiscal policy addressed in *Chapter 2* to answer questions related to *Case 7.5* on "The Nigerian Economy: Well Below Par."

Case 7.5 Nigeria's Economic and Fiscal Crisis

Source: *Economist*, 2014e: 68

When the price of oil tumbles, you should worry about a country that relies on the stuff for 75 percent of government revenue and 95 percent of exports. That country is Nigeria, Africa's biggest economy. Earlier this year oil was selling at well over $100 a barrel. It is below $70 now. Nigeria's currency the naira is diving; the central bank is shedding foreign exchange reserves in its defense. On November 25th it hiked interest rates by a percentage point to 13 percent (the first increase in three years) and said it had reduced its target rate for the naira (against the dollar) by a further 8 percent. That will not be the end of the story.

Since 2014 the Nigerian economy has expanded at an average rate of 7 percent a year—faster than the West African average. High oil prices spurred the boom: Nigeria exports 2m barrels a day, much of it especially prized by refiners for its low sulphur content, which makes it easier to meet environmental rules. Unfortunately, most of the extra 3m barrels of daily production America has added since 2011 (e.g. shale oil) have been low in sulphur too. As a result, low sulphur oil has fallen even more dramatically in price than other sorts. The Economist Intelligence Unit (EIU), a sister company of the *Economist,* reckons that in 2015 Nigeria's oil exports will bring in $67b, an 18 percent drop from last year, even though its output is rising.

As oil revenue has dropped, the naira has taken a beating. This year, it has fallen by a tenth against the dollar and in recent weeks the slide has grown even more rapid. The central bank has tried to stem its fall by selling foreign exchange reserves; these have dropped by nearly 20 percent in the past year and are now sufficient to cover just six months of imports, compared with 15 months a few years ago.

Nigeria's long-term economic prospects are good. In recent years, industries other than oil, including manufacturing and communications, have begun to thrive. But according to Deutsche Bank, Nigeria needs an oil price of $120 a barrel to balance its budget—far above the current level. Big spending cuts would harm the economy. The likelier outcome, with an election looming in February, is that the government will run even higher fiscal deficits which will probably stroke inflation, currently 8.1 percent. That would put the naira under more pressure.

a   What are the dimensions of the fiscal and energy crisis for Nigeria? How would you compare them to similar countries such as Russia?

b   How does the fall in oil price affect its fiscal position?

c   What is the effect of devalued naira on consumption and growth?

d   What fiscal policy options look most feasible? Would an MTEF have helped?

e   What are the options for ring-fencing oil revenues to hedge against inflation and stabilize the currency and the economy? Are the stabilization fund options used by Chile (copper), Norway (oil), and Mexico (oil) potentially transferable to Nigeria?

7   Refer to *Case 7.6* on "Electricity Firms in Japan: Solar Shambles" and *Case 7.7* on "German Utilities E.ON and E.OUT" and answer the questions following:

Case 7.6 Japanese Solar Energy Subsidies

Source: *Economist*, 2014f: 59–60

Mr. Sato's solar power company says it can produce electricity for about 700 households. But the local power utility is refusing to buy more than a quarter of it. Japan set one of the world's highest tariffs for renewable energy in 2012, as part of a bid to live without atomic power following the Fukushima disaster. Electricity companies were ordered to pay ¥42 a kilowatthour (kWh) to novice producers like Mr Sato. The promise of such a high guaranteed price triggered more than 1.2m applications, mostly for solar power installations. Japan's power utilities say they are overwhelmed and have revolted. Most have begun blocking access to the transmission grid.

Kyushu Electric, which supplies electricity to 9m customers in Japan's sunny south, was the first to balk, in September, after 72,000 solar power producers rushed to beat the deadline for a cut in the guaranteed tariff to ¥32 a kWh. The company says it will accept no new applications to join the grid until it has settled concerns about the reliability of supply from the new producers. The Ministry of Economy, Trade and Industry (METI) is backing the utilities, and mulling a further tariff cut.

The utilities' objections have added to doubts about Japan's plan to increase renewables' share of electricity output to 20 percent by 2030, almost double its pre Fukushima share. If all the projects for which METI has had applications went ahead, Japan could leave most of its nuclear stations switched off, notes Mika Ohbayashi of the Japan Renewable Energy Foundation, a think tank. But so far just 12 percent of them have been installed, and much of the rest may prove uneconomic, she says, given that in less sunny parts, solar panels' output will be more sporadic.

The utilities say they want to avoid blackouts.

Germany triggered a similar stampede of small producers in 2009–12, by offering them guaranteed prices for 20 years and priority access to the grid. That has helped push clean energy's share to nearly a quarter of Germany's power consumption, but driven up electricity bills: subsidies cost consumers €16 billion ($21 billion) last year. And some power utilities are suing the government, saying their business has been damaged by the subsidies. METI should have learned from Germany's mistakes by being less generous with its guaranteed tariffs for renewables producers and by ensuring that the transmission grid was modernised to prepare for their arrival. Ideally the ministry should have created a separate grid operator, independent of the big power utilities, says Tom O'Sullivan, a consultant in Tokyo. At present the utilities own everything and have little incentive to let independents on to the system.

Japan may have to spend $60 billion over the next two decades subsidizing the preferential tariffs for renewables producers. Since Japan switched off its nuclear plants, the cost of importing fossil fuels has soared, to $250 billion a year.

Case 7.7 German Energy Transition Policy and Utilities

Source: *Economist*, 2014g: 76

Germany's biggest utility, E.ON, will split itself up in 2016 into a new company which will include its power generation from nuclear and fossil fuels, as well as fossil fuel exploration and production. The rump—which will keep the E.ON brand—will make money from renewable energy.

Germany's *Energiewende,* or "energy transition" policy, has hammered the country's utilities. The government aims to shut down all nuclear plants by 2022, a decision made after the Fukushima disaster in Japan. Renewable energy sources, on the other hand, are heavily subsidized. Operators are paid well above market rates for each kilowatt hour of power they feed into the system, and renewables are given priority on the grid over conventional sources. This policy has caused a stampede into renewables, with the ever growing subsidies funded by ever rising surcharges on electricity bills.

Big incumbents, including E.ON as well as RWE, EnBW and Vattenfall (a Swedish firm with German operations) had invested heavily in conventional generation before the renewables rush began. The resulting overcapacity caused wholesale electricity prices to tumble. Some conventional plants cannot make enough money to cover fuel costs and are being shut down.

Many observers took E.ON's decision to hive off the fossil fuel and nuclear generation business as the creation of a kind of "bad utility"—like the "bad banks" created to house toxic assets after the financial crisis. Others think that cynics have it wrong. Rejecting the "bad bank" analogy, they note that the new firm will be born debt free and have provisions to cover the exit from nuclear power (currently €14.5 billion, or $18 billion). Shareholders can expect respectable cash dividends, paid for by profitable operations, even as net profits look bad.

---

a   What energy subsidy policy lessons were not learned by Japan given the experience of Germany?

b   What is the energy "policy triangle"? How does German *Energiewende* contradict one or more of the three sides: stability, cheap supplies and prices, and climate friendly? What are the perverse incentives and effects of German policy in the near term and probable long term?

c Devise a decision matrix for comparative analysis: decisions taken, consequences for consumers, public budgets, production of each energy source. Apply this decision matrix for Japan using Germany as the baseline for energy policy.

References

Aldy, Joseph, Alan J. Krupnick, Richard G. Newell, Ian Parry, and William A. Pizer, "Designing Climate Mitigation Policy," *Journal of Economic Literature*, 48, 4 (December 2010): 203–234.
Badcock, Jeremy and Manfred Lenzen, "Subsidies for Electricity-Generating Technologies: A Review," *Energy Policy*, 38, 9 (September 2010): 5038–5047.
Coase, Ronald H., "The Problem of Social Cost," *Journal of Law and Economics*, 3, 1 (1960): 1–44.
Commander, Simon, "A Guide to the Political Economy of Reforming Energy Subsidies," IZA Policy Paper Series #52, December 2012, Institute for the Study of Labor: Bonn, Germany.
De Moor, Andre, "Towards a Grand Deal on Subsidies and Climate Change," *Natural Resources Forum*, 25, 2 (May 2001): 167–176.
Economist (2009) "A Bad Climate for Development," September 17. Available online at www.economist.com/node/14447171.
Economist (2013a) "The Cost del Sol," July 20. Available online at www.economist.com/news/business/21582018-sustainable-energy-meets-unsustainable-costs-cost-del-sol.
Economist (2013b) "The East Is Grey," August 10. Available online at www.economist.com/news/briefing/21583245-china-worlds-worst-polluter-largest-investor-green-energy-its-rise-will-have.
Economist (2013c) "Power Struggle," September 21. Available online at www.economist.com/news/asia/21586570-shadow-fukushima-worlds-worst-nuclear-disaster-after-chernobyl-hangs-over-japans-energy.
Economist (2014a) "Special Report: Energy and Technology," January 17, pp. 1–12.
Economist (2014b) "Conscious Uncoupling," April 5, pp. 43–45.
Economist (2014c) "Coal: The Fuel of the Future Unfortunately," April 19, pp. 55–56.
Economist (2014d) "A Canal Too Far: Water Consumption," September 27, pp. 44–45.
Economist (2014e) "The Nigerian Economy: Well Below Par," November 29, p. 68.
Economist (2014f) "Electricity Firms in Japan: Solar Shambles," November 29, pp. 59–60.
Economist (2014g) "German Utilities E.ON and E.OUT," December 6, p. 76.
Economist (2015a) "Special Report: Energy and Technology," January 17, pp. 1–12.
Economist (2015b) "Coal Mining: In the Depths," March 28, pp. 65–66.
Economist (2015c) "Special Report: Nigeria-Opportunity Knocks," June 20, pp. 1–16.
Economist (2015d) "The Future of Nuclear Energy: Half-Death," October 31, pp. 59–60.
EPA (2010), Clean Air Markets, Progress Reports, United States Environmental Protection Agency. Available online at www.epa.gov/airmarkets/progress/ARP09_1.html.
Goulder, Lawrence H., "Carbon Taxes v. Cap and Trade: A Critical Review," NBER working paper #19338, August 2013, National Bureau of Economic Research, Cambridge, MA.
Hahn, Robert W., "Economic Prescriptions for Environmental Problems: How the Patient Followed the Doctor's Orders," *Journal of Economic Perspectives*, 3, 2 (Spring 1989): 95–114.
International Energy Agency (2009) "Key World Energy Statistics, 2009." Available online at www.iea.org/publications/freepublications/publication/KeyWorld2013.pdf.
IPCC (2008) *Climate Change 2007: Fourth Assessment Report of the Intergovernmental Panel on Climate Change* (Geneva, Switzerland: IPCC).
IPCC (2014) *Climate Change 2014: Synthesis Report, Fifth Assessment Report of the Intergovernmental Panel on Climate Change* (Geneva, Switzerland: IPCC).
Laderchi, Caterina Ruggeri, Anne Olivier, and Chris Trimble (2013) *Balancing Act: Cutting Energy Subsidies While Protecting Affordability* (Washington, DC: World Bank).
Michel, R. Gregory (2001) *Decision Tools for Budgetary Analysis* (Chicago: Government Finance Officers Association).

Nordhaus, William D., "A Review of *The Stern Review on the Economics of Climate Change*," *Journal of Economic Literature*, 45, 3 (September 2007): 686–702.

Parry, Ian, Rick vad der Ploeg, and RobertonWilliams, "How to Design a Carbon Tax," in "Fiscal Policy to Mitigate Climate Change: A Guide for Policymakers," Ian W.H. Parry, Ruud de Mooij, and Michael Keen, eds., 2012, Washington, DC: International Monetary Fund: 28–47.

Rosen, Harvey S. and Ted Gayer (2010) *Public Finance*, 9th ed. (New York: McGraw-Hill).

Rosenthal, Elizabeth, "Carbon Taxes Make Ireland Even Greener," *New York Times*, December 28, 2012. Available online at www.nytimes.com/2012/12/28/science/earth/in-ireland-carbon-taxes-pay-off.html.

Schmalensee, Richard and Robert N. Stavins, "The SO_2 Allowance Trading System: The Ironic History of a Grand Policy Experiment," *Journal of Economic Perspectives*, 27, 1 (Winter 2013): 103–122.

Scientific American, "How Nuclear Power Can Stop Global Warming," December 12, 2013. Available online at www.scientificamerican.com/article/how-nuclear-power-can-stop-global-warming.

Song, Lisa and Jim Morris, "Study Delivers Good News, Bad News on Methane Leaks from Fracking Operations," *Inside Climate News*, September 16, 2013. Available online at http: //insideclimatenews.org/news/20130916/study-delivers-good-news-bad-news-methane-leaks-fracking-operations.

Stavins, Robert N., "Experience with Market-Based Environmental Policy Instruments," in *Handbook of Environmental Economics*, vol. 1, K.G. Maler and J.R. Vincent, eds., 2003, Amsterdam: Elsevier Science: 355–436.

Stern, Nicholas (2007) *The Economics of Climate Change: The Stern Review* (Cambridge: Cambridge University Press).

Sumner, Jenny, Lori Bird, and Hillary Dobos, "Carbon Taxes: A Review of Experience and Policy Design Considerations," *Climate Policy*, 11 (2011): 922–943.

Tait, Nikki, "Germany to Win Coal Aid Deal," *Financial Times*, December 9, 2010. Available online at www.ft.com/intl/cms/s/0/87308c76-02f2-11e0-bb1e-00144feabdc0.html#axzz40LiI8oe9.

U.S. Energy Information Administration, *Annual Energy Outlook 2013 with Projections to 2040*, April 2013, Washington, DC: U.S. Department of Energy.

Varro, Laszlo, "Greener Europe," *Finance and Development*, 51, 1 (March 2014): 24–25.

Weitzman, Martin L., "A Review of *The Stern Review on the Economics of Climate Change*," *Journal of Economic Literature*, 45, 3 (September 2007): 703–724.

8 Summary and Conclusions

Targeting International Policy Problems

The list of opportunities for international policy analysis and transfer of comparatively appropriate lessons seems to grow each day. In health care, for instance, most policy-makers want to know how to avoid the mistakes in design and implementation of the U.S. Affordable Health Care Act to expand coverage and control costs. Poverty policy experts want to know how to design a conditional cash transfer program to achieve the maximum impact on poverty reduction in widely different regions and cultures. Though these commonly designed programs seem to work well in all regions and contexts, under which conditions to they work best and least? To reduce congestion and maximize impact on local economic development, subnational (i.e. urban) policy-makers still want to know whether to install rapid bus or light rail transit systems. And policy analysts in the U.S. and the E.U. work assiduously to empirically establish the points and trajectories where fiscal austerity programs weaken economic growth. Answers require verification of the links between basic variables from fiscal policies to macroeconomic results in comparative contexts. So far, this has not really achieved. It is hoped that this book stimulates more of the path-breaking research efforts that have been undertaken across a wide range of sector policies.

The Three Levels of International Policy Analysis

To review, our comprehensive policy analysis framework presented in *Chapter 1* (see *Figure 1.4*), the three types or levels of analysis that are required. At the first level, one must figure out what is happening—the statistical and empirical relationships between inputs, outputs, and outcomes. If these basics cannot be established, as for instance the linkages between fiscal stimuli programs and return of economic growth, it makes little practical sense to move to the second level. If they can be, as in health care or education, it is important to ascertain how and why the linkages are occurring. That is the task of our political economy framework. As indicated in *Chapter 1*, four clusters of variables had to be combined into comprehensive explanations of what works and what did not (see *Figure 1.3*). Institutions in the form of formal and informal rules play an important part; so does the politics of financing of policies and programs through budget systems; and economic methods are most important in developing rigorous tests of hypotheses, providing analytic methods and developing operationally useful studies. One must include the regime type and the political structure of the country to assess top-level policy support for implementing programs and policies. Federal systems are more complex than unitary systems for some policies; presidential systems vary from parliamentary systems in the discipline they can bring to policy implementation. Finally, we noted that political culture remains the critical glue that holds the other three sub-variables together. Political culture in the form of values and attitudes that affect political and institutional behavior serves as a constraint or opportunity to policy results and reforms in all countries.

More recent studies have excluded political culture and focus on institutions, politics, and economics alone (Allen et al., 2013). We believe this is a flaw and will result in unpleasant surprises and wasted funds later. Needed are studies of which elements of the political culture can be changed or not changed through differing institutional incentives. Other studies explicitly reject the comparative approach and focus instead on a "core set of universally relevant and standards and dimensions of systems" (DeRenzio, 2013: 146). The problem with this (for analysis of public financial management systems as well as sector policy systems such as health, education, or transport) is that it is simplistic and avoids the need to find out which standards can be obtained in different contexts. It presumes the ability to agree on universal standards across cultures, which could be useful only in the broadest sense without comparative inputs. For instance, advocating the lack of evaluation studies to find out which activities combined leads to which outcomes in different contexts (Klitgaard, 2013: 408) might explain general failure. From another perspective, it merely restates the problem of finding out what doesn't work and studying the trials and errors of applied remedies. That is why comparative policy analysis is needed.

Ideally then, the international policy practitioner would analyze policies using the three-level framework, which can also serve as a threshold. First, the need at the technical level is to ensure that policy expenditures are tailored to the expected results. For simpler program designs such as conditional cash transfers to eliminate poverty while attaining social objectives such as immunizations and school attendance, the links are relatively straightforward. The only variables are how to target the clients better and ensure that they receive payments while preventing fraud. Cell phone transfer systems and bank accounts are needed but have been provided for hard to reach populations in rural India and Mexico. Urban transport projects such as BRT are also technically simple and the linkages between design, expenditures, construction, operations, and results are quite clear in the 100-plus systems in all regions of the world. More complex policies such as fiscal consolidation/austerity and health care have more confounding variables at this basic level. The threshold for austerity for fiscal deficits and debts is still debatable and the links between types of austerity and effects on growth (some positive; some negative) are also dependent on study context. Multiple health care policy models are used with variable results. Until the links between variables such as mandatory payments, health care exchanges, medical coverage, and employer/insurer responses are clarified, the basic linkages will remain controversial at both technical and political levels.

As noted, there is little point in conducting full political economy or comparative applications analyses if first level policy basics between design and implementation have not been agreed upon. This requires rigorous statistical and econometric analysis of the most quantitative measures of inputs, outputs, and outcomes for each policy issue. For in the second level of analysis, the practitioner would apply the political economy approach. This would assist in explaining how and why similar well-tested policies had variable results in differing institutional, regime/political structure, financing, and cultural contexts. For example, the impacts of grants programs to schools to equalize income and maximize student performance (common programs around the globe) depend on examination of specific marginal costs, tax prices, and marginal benefits, often in an econometric model (meaning "taking a theory and quantifying it" (Ouliaris, 2011: 38)). Institutions such as rules and degree of local school fiscal and managerial autonomy are critical. But failure to include culture, such as local values to exclude girls from the educational system, would vitiate any comparison—except with similarly restrictive cultures. In the area of school and student performance reform (again, occurring in most regions of the world at national and local levels), linkages between recent reforms and results are relatively clear, even in widely varying socio-cultural contexts. Most studies find empirical evidence for the influences of school competition, student choice of schools, teacher incentives, management control of school performance, and school-level administrative discretion on student performance, often labelled loosely as an output or outcome (not the same as distinguished in *Figure 1.2*). In health care, as noted in countries like India, the relation between spending for latrines and sanitary systems is confounded by cultural practices of public defecation. How can this cultural practice be modified to improve the effects of sanitary systems? If they cannot be, the well-known link between such spending and positive results in other regional countries such as Pakistan is broken. Applying the second political economy framework in contexts implementing well-tested policies allows for focus on the cultural-institutional obstacles that must be modified to prevent program or policy failure and wasted funds.

Third, once explanatory propositions and lessons are generated, the issue is where they can be used or at least adapted at the operational level (*Figure 1.4*). The need is to identify similar contexts and then measure the differing performances of target policies, programs, or systems across boundaries. The critical factor is to ensure the similarity of important contextual variables. We employed a simple method, which is widely used for international comparison (Xavier, 1998). On a national basis, it is used to compare results for different targets, e.g. prisoners. Since they can be identified, controlled, and measured to ensure similarity, how they respond to remedial approaches can be easily compared. To measure comparative effectiveness at the program level, with UK Social Impact Bonds, for example, remedial programmatic outcomes are linked to payments to those organizations (often NGOs or private firms) that propose policy solutions. Their efforts are financed by bonds sold to individuals and charities for social purposes that believe (in this case) that reduction of prisoner conviction rates is important. The results can be measured and traced back to characteristics of prisoner cohorts in the UK, its regions, and localities. These results can then be applied to similar cultures (i.e. Commonwealth countries and some U.S. states) that will use lessons for adaptive design and implementation of similar programs. An important pre-condition to application would be to those countries with well-developed financial sectors (including at least rudimentary capital markets, with rule of law for contract enforcement). Beyond these two regions, then, we would include selected Asian countries such as India, the Philippines, Malaysia, and China, and Latin American countries such as Chile, Brazil, Costa Rica, Uruguay, and Mexico. Analysis of lessons must include contextual constraints that impeded or facilitated results. The incentive for getting the method and comparative lessons right in the instance of Social Impact Bond programs, then, is that payouts to investors are based on measurable results from pre-selected indicators in performance contracts.

Again, applications at the operational level may be easier despite ostensibly incomparable or hostile cultural and institutional contexts. Examples include IFMS systems, conditional cash transfer systems, budget transfer rules that incentivize MOF and line ministry management to achieve better program performance, and urban transport systems such as BRT. What this suggests is that for effective implementation of a complex policy such as health care, it may be more feasible to hive off an operational-level portion of it and implement it. This will among other things demonstrate the value of the policy and may contribute to incremental modification of cultural and institutional contexts to allow for full policy implementation.

For the future, we can expect more analyses at the technical level, investigating the variables that affect policy performance and deriving practical lessons. It may be that as systems converge and become more professionalized, there will be less need to be concerned about cultural and institutional differences that now affect policy performance. That would mean even less concern about transferable contexts for lessons, because those generated at the technical level should be applicable universally—roughly like lessons from systems at the operational level today.

International Policies

Macroeconomic and Fiscal Policy

Despite the apparent precision of macroeconomic concepts and public expenditure measures, the many empirical studies performed have multiplied policy options rather than narrowed them. Basic studies at the technical level have examined fiscal policies in different contexts for impacts. Contexts are important, for example, in that the banking or financial sector may be entwined with the fiscal sector, such as in the recent crisis derived from Grecian state insolvency. Banking systems in EU countries where in at least one case (Ireland) failed performance forced the government out have required significant fiscal austerity measures that have been largely successful. OECD countries offer similar institutional and political contexts that allow for basic measurement of fiscal responses on macroeconomic variables. Policy responses to similar crises in similarly developed countries have provided important lessons. While there is still little technical or political consensus on results, especially where there are major structural constraints to economic growth, there is general agreement on the efficacy of particular fiscal stimulus programs. For example, the IMF conducts ongoing reviews of what has and has not worked in fiscal adjustment and consolidation efforts in a wide range of countries (e.g. Cottarelli et al., 2014; Fiscal Monitor, 2011; Cangiano et al., 2013) and the World Bank similarly examines impacts of differing mixes of stimuli programs in middle-income transitional and developing countries (Dethier, 2010).

International fiscal policy analyses are probably most needed because the crises have been severe internationally (e.g. the Great Recession of 2007–2009 and related financial sector meltdown) and the variations in responses have been substantial across countries. But as noted, consensus has been elusive on the most effective options and their linkages to results. Policy responses to the financial crisis of 2007–2009, for example, were often based on weak definition of the underlying problem. The savings glut from countries such as China and Germany had forced a credit bubble onto financial, especially real estate markets, that burst, leaving substantial unpayable mostly private debts. The orthodox response of public sector fiscal austerity blamed the evident regulatory weaknesses of the public sector on overspending and fiscal deficits, which were often simply not the case. Until this point, separation of financial sector from monetary and fiscal policy had been standard theory and practice. Monetary financing of fiscal deficits, for example, threatened reserves and breached a firewall between public spending/taxation and financing from monetary reserves and the banking system. It was consistently scored by IMF and other international policy institutions as the wrong practice for any country. But more recent advice recommends breaching this wall: under conditions of weak demand and stagnation, rely on permanent budget deficits financed by central banks. This would force central banks to match their deposits with safe government bonds, reduce the risks of bank crashes, and encourage healthier reliance on equity finance. Economists such as Martin Wolf argue this would be a safer way to sustain spending than private asset booms and busts. If done responsibly, it would not cause inflation (*Economist*, 2014g: 86). Such analyses integrate formerly separate policy fields, simplifying underlying complexities while making advice even more conditional. How would the regulatory architecture ensure that all the pieces balance? Where would such recommendations be taken seriously outside the U.S. and UK? The ECB …?

For such reasons, it may be more feasible to focus at the operational level for transferable lessons. As one might expect, in the narrower sense of public financial management systems (PFM), much more has been done comparatively. As noted, Xavier (1998) did an important comparative study on Australia and Malaysian PFM reforms that illustrated his simple comparative methodology as well as lessons for particular reforms of PFM systems in different countries with similar contexts. Additionally, in-depth studies of particular PFM functions such as procurement, capital planning, accounting, internal controls and audit systems, debt/cash management, and budgeting have been performed, again often by IMF and World Bank. Fiscal deficit and debt levels are taken seriously by policy-makers around the world to ward off inflation and improve macroeconomic stability. The latter is needed for poverty reduction and sustained service delivery and to induce foreign investment for development and growth. An important lesson in debt management, for instance, is to avoid currency mismatches. Governments or firms with costs or debts in solid currencies (e.g. dollars or euros) but sales to customers and liabilities in depreciating ones (e.g. Argentinian pesos or Turkish lira) are squeezed and this can threaten fiscal discipline and macroeconomic stability.

In the sub-field of public financial management or PFM, budgeting is considered a synonym for PFM and serves as the lead function. It leads PFM because it is tied directly to the political and technical arena of resource allocation (Hemming, 2013: 18). The fiscal survival of countries depends on this function, which then is both a narrow PFM sub-function and the central incentive mechanism of the political system. The standards for good fiscal policy and budgeting everywhere are generally fiscal discipline, allocational efficiency, and technical efficiency. Specifically, policy-makers need to know when and how to achieve all three standards in differing contexts. As noted, political leaders and some policy-makers are often more interested in crude cuts to achieve austerity objectives. Reliance on traditional object of expenditure budget formats for this purpose allows cuts to line-items such as salaries, supplies, and capital spending. But it is hard in any government to make incremental cuts without shutting down whole departments, programs, or services. Much of government consists of fixed costs. In most cases, simply thinning the number of staff or line officials paradoxically results in productivity and results falling faster than costs. And across-the-board cuts reward bloated, inefficient operations and penalize those that have taken steps to cut costs and achieve greater productivity. More problematic is that often costs are hidden and/or, as in the case of infrastructure cuts, shifted to future generations. Economic conditions such as recession and low economic growth often argue against simplistic fiscal austerity remedies. The cost dilemma underscores the need for results-based budgeting systems to improve allocational efficiency. Case studies have pointed to technical lessons for sequencing and establishing priorities. Others have tried to compare country reform efforts in similar contexts (i.e. South Asia) pursuing similar policies, e.g. fiscal decentralization (Guess, 2005).

The relevant technical, political economy, and comparative lessons from the fiscal policy chapter are:

1   Structure the problem to be solved and respond accordingly on the scale of policy complexity. Balanced budget objectives can be met with straight accounting solutions; if

the objective is to provide services and balance, more nuanced solutions are called for that may include use of cutback techniques and results or zero-based budgeting types of analyses. If the problem is severe and multi-faceted, complex policies and risks are required to avoid making the economy worse.

2   Ensure that program analytic systems are in place to call in if cuts are required (or additional funds become available). This avoids rewarding inefficient programs and penalizing efficient ones with concomitant disincentives for further analytic initiatives in each government unit. Such information is useful to legislators, the media, and community stakeholders that need to know the probable consequences of alternative budget choices.

3   Focus on the size of the state in relation to the nation. Fiscal crises invariably call into question the size and strength of states. They should both be considered. The size of states (spending and or taxation in relation to GDP) is important if the private sector is being squeezed out of credit markets. Here, the payroll size per capita, number of civil servants per capita, and the degree of structural and functional redundancy in the state should be considered for reforms. The strength of states is important in that states that may be too small or also too weak to control or defend the country and to provide service coverage (e.g. Pakistan at 19.5 percent GDP spending and India at 27.2 percent GDP spending). Ideally, stronger and smaller states should be preferred, e.g. Chile (21.1 percent GDP spending). But that is a function of longer-term civil service reforms and experimentation with different incentive systems by sector. Few leaders want to spend the political capital on such efforts as their payoffs are often minimal.

4   Focus on structural constraints to growth. Balancing budgets through austerity might work on paper but result in further economic damage and leaves structural impediments intact. Overregulation facilitates corruption in public finance (e.g. multi-stage budget approvals for purchasing) as well as commercial enterprises (e.g. customs bribery). Regulations are used to protect guilds, unions, and monopoly industries and ensure access to subsidies, tax breaks, and other leakages from the treasury that harm fiscal balances and service results. Such structural constraints as evidenced in contemporary Italy in this chapter's case study (*Case 2.2*) are critical intervening variables between fiscal policies and macroeconomic results. In all countries, regulations and subsidies are held in place by powerful political interests and are thus hard to eliminate.

5   Design culture into reforms. Given cultural and political constraints to patterns of spending and taxation, fiscal policy reforms transfer from one context slowly if at all. One cannot, for example, import the Canadian budgeting system into the U.S. because of its parliamentary institutional setting and less adversarial and litigious culture. Many Canadian reforms have been imbedded in U.S. rules in the past (e.g. up or down party votes) but have been derailed by the intensity of the U.S. adversarial system (see *Case 2.3*). But in Central and Eastern European contexts, more akin to the Canadian rule-respecting culture, if financed by international donors, budget and PFM reforms that proceeded in fits and starts were scaled down to what was possible within the local context and were successful. It should not be surprising that most PFM reforms proceed incrementally given their complexity. Use a stages approach and allow for significant inputs through such tools as participatory budgeting. Cultural practices may amount to constraints, where, for instance lack of deferred gratification and religious opposition to girls in schools damage well-traversed links between policies and results. But defining micro-cultures that affect only those policies can allow policy-makers to design incentives to incrementally make changes that allow policies to perform as they have in other contexts, e.g. performance transfers to schools and local governments for girls' enrollment

in Pakistan incentivized officials to try and protect girls and to support their retention and promotion in schools.

Urban Transport and Public Infrastructure

As a major opportunity for international policy analysis, the needs and contexts of urban transport infrastructure are converging and becoming more similar each day. Problems that had seemed unique for the U.S., Europe, or Asia are becoming common. For example, the U.S. buys all its metro and light rail cars from Canadian, European, or Asian manufacturers. To some extent, their technical specifications and requirements influence the design and operation of U.S. systems. The U.S. buys its cars and trucks from all over the globe to populate its massive bridge, tunnel, and highway system. In all OECD countries, infrastructure quality determines export performance and overall economic growth. But the problems are also converging. In OECD countries, infrastructure quality is declining and the spending required to maintain facilities is not keeping pace with maintenance requirements or economic needs. Germany spent only 0.6 percent of GDP in 2011, less than France, Britain, or Canada, which face their own infrastructure deficit problems (Birnbaum, 2014). The infrastructure bottleneck to growth is evident in many OECD countries now, especially Germany, which is geared toward exports. It needs to spend $9.7 billion more just to maintain the existing network, which in many parts of the country is crumbling. Fifty percent of its bridges and 20 percent of its highways are in poor condition (Birnbaum, 2014). If investments are not made now, in 10–15 years infrastructure will be in worse shape than in southern Europe. According to the World Economic Forum, from 2006 to 2013, Germany slipped from third to tenth place in terms of quality of overall infrastructure. The U.S. slipped from eighth to nineteenth place in the same period (Birnbaum, 2014).

While the contexts and bottleneck problems are converging, so are the constraints. In Germany as in other EU countries and the U.S., the guiding rule is fiscal austerity and balanced budgets. The German public sector borrowing requirement of $9.7 billion threatens its self-imposed austerity requirements, which view borrowing (debt = guilt = *schuld*) as a sinful practice. In the U.S., similar political arguments have paralyzed spending for infrastructure and virtually eliminated tax increases as a financing option. Other countries will face austerity requirements from EU or the IMF as their spending outpaces revenues. Since capital is a long-term asset that should be financed at least in part by debt, there should be no conflict with balanced operating budgets (as in U.S. state–local governments). Nevertheless, many countries consolidate their budgets and make few distinctions between capital and current spending.

Fortunately, solutions to the problem of infrastructure financing are also converging. Fees and tolls are being increased to finance roads, tunnels, and bridges. Ports and airport landing fees are being increased. Municipal bonds continue to be used in the U.S. and many countries to finance revenue-producing facilities. Local financing shares require only dedicated taxes or fees to pay back interest and principal on bonds. Some countries have not assessed risk properly and use local debt to finance dodgy real estate investments rather than infrastructure for public purposes. For instance, according to Chinese official and UBS reports, subnational debt to finance infrastructure and real estate developments has jumped 67 percent since 2010. Local government debt in China jumped from 8 percent of GDP in 2008 to 33 percent GDP in 2013. Since few of these projects will cover loan repayments, the risk of default and threat to central government finances is growing (Samuelson, 2014). Consolidated national debt has climbed to 250 percent of GDP (compared to around 75 percent in the U.S.) (*Economist*, 2015), which could threaten its banks and macroeconomic stability in the future.

Controls over local borrowing need to be strengthened either through central government strictures or transparent fiscal data evaluated regularly by independent credit agencies, e.g. Fitch or Moody's. But even here, the threats to capital financing are well-known as comparative cases of defaults and bankruptcies at the municipal and state level are well-studied (e.g. Spiotto, 2012). Private financing alternatives are also in use around the world to cover cutbacks in public budgets. Their comparative successes, weaknesses, and requirements have also been well-studied (e.g. Dannin and Cokorinos, 2012).

In the forced solutions category, one positive result of infrastructure deterioration and fiscal austerity in many countries is that capital improvement planning (CIP) processes are now taken more seriously in promoting the most efficient and productive capital projects. This appears to be happening across the developed (OECD) and transitional country world. In addition, more innovative financing (if risky) methods are being tried. Past efforts to leverage private financing to build, operate, and maintain road projects have now been extended to urban public transport projects in states such as Maryland and Colorado. Other states are attempting to remedy the issue of stabilization clauses and revenue guarantee measures ("adverse action" and "compensation event clauses") that for financing projects such as the Indiana Toll Road protect investors but put the longer-term public interest at serious risk. In that case, weak and careless state bargaining allowed the contractor to interfere with public road safety and to be reimbursed for its costly obstruction by taxpayers.

Smarter and harder bargaining by the public sector with contractors, e.g. requiring contractors to carry insurance, could save public monies and make privatization more effective (Dannin and Cokorinos, 2012: 734). The risks of private bankruptcy illustrated by the South Bay Expressway project in California resulted in costly and time-consuming claims and counterclaims by developers, operators, and other stakeholders (ibid., 2012: 747). Despite the relatively successful examples from the UK where infrastructure is treated as a regulated monopoly, and long-term capital leasing examples from Australia, Canada, and selected EU countries, it may be that for many subnational governments in the U.S., the least expensive way to finance infrastructure in the future is through taxation rather than reliance on private investors (ibid., 2012: 746). For instance, to finance the depleted Federal Highway Trust Fund, an increase in the tax rate of $0.15 per gallon would raise $150 billion over ten years to finance deteriorating roads, bridges, and related infrastructure. Since many drive more efficient vehicles, another tax could be based on miles driven (*Washington Post*, 2013). Such efforts would reduce desperate moves to rely on private finance for public projects. If greater reliance on public capital financing is the future, additional efforts to improve and apply rigorous CIP methods to capital programs and projects at the state and local levels will be required by legislators as well as executive officials. Lack of a comprehensive capital process or budget for the federal government means that state and local reforms will occur from the bottom up (Marlowe, 2012: 664) with continued variation in quality and standards across federal systems such as the U.S.

Application of the technical, political economy, and comparative frameworks can be illustrated by the international urban transport system: bus rapid transit or BRT. These are "surface subways" that combine the speed and capacity of LRT and metros with the simplicity, flexibility, and lower cost of bus systems. BRTs serve 166 cities worldwide with 55 alone in Latin America. The first one was in Curitiba, Brazil (1974), and there are systems in Jakarta, Indonesia, Johannesburg, South Africa, and an attempted implementation in Amman, Jordan. At the technical level, they function as planned along fixed routes. The technical systems, rolling stock, and signaling are straightforward as is the construction and maintenance during operations. Needed to build and operate BRT are basic systems of administrative management, contracting and procurement, and CIP to plan projects properly. Where these basic elements are present, the systems work as planned and 27 million passengers ride them worldwide, of which 17 million are in Latin America.

However, though the technical links for service outputs are clear, the linkages between public investment and wider economic or outcome benefits and costs are not. Many BRT projects are justified to voters and officials on wider bases than mobility, i.e. induced investment, employment, and higher local incomes. There is substantial variability in the economic impact of BRT and system cost recovery. Once the lessons of individual systems performances are measured and analyzed, they can be compared for transferability to other regions. As noted, BRT systems have already been transferred to other regions such as North America, South Africa, and Asia successfully at the technical–operational level. It cannot be said that there is a basic system and routing plan that will lead to development and cost recovery because the 166 cities are all quite different geographically, demographically, and jurisdictionally, e.g. metro governments, city managers, and authority deconcentrated from national and state level political institutions. Lack of a proper legal and regulatory framework and financial institutions in Jordan can explain why that BRT there has had serious difficulty in becoming operational. At the strategic policy level, devolution of financial/political authority is essential, e.g. Brazil, Ecuador, and Mexico; and internal audit institutions must be stronger to counter the powerful tendencies to corrupt the contracting and implementation processes normally associated with larger public capital projects. These too have been developed in Latin America to ensure implementation successes; they have not been in regions such as the Middle East or countries such as Jordan, which explains the lack of BRT success there.

At least five sets of international policy lessons can be derived from this chapter:

1 *Comparative Method:* To generate useful lessons, urban transport illustrates the importance of targeting similarities or like cases first. That is relatively easy to do: cities deliver most of the service; they can be distinguished by size and region. In addition, the modes are clear—rail, bus, BRT, LRT; the conditions affecting service costs and results are also clear, e.g. severe weather. Finally, cities deliver transit through a variety of clear governmental and non-governmental units and structures. Their authority to manage and borrow for capital acquisition is also clear and can be differentiated. Defining the similarities then allows focusing on the transit system management and policy-making variables that affect costs and service more clearly.

2 *Culture:* Urban transport systems are often closed, technically designed, and managed activities. This means the chances of routines and repertoires being modified by local cultural practices and affecting results significantly are perhaps less than for other programs in health and education. The importance also of comparing systems in particular regions would mean that culture would play even less of a role—it would affect all units about the same. One might conclude that culture is more important where cultures are widely different from the West, e.g. the Middle East.

3 *Governmental Structures:* Much is made of organizational structure and legal processes. While these are important, participants often adapt to them or are able to circumvent them in non-systematic ways (e.g. political influence channels). Thus, the effect of government structures is hard to measure. For transit, use of differing structures such as city enterprises versus city departments has not been shown to make a substantial difference to design or system performance.

4 *Institutions*: The formal and informal rules that guide behavior for urban transport project planning, contracting, and financing are critical. The rules for financing and contracting are critical to transport project design and implementation and service performance.

5   *System Design and Implementation*: It is important that lessons from other system designs and implementations be absorbed during the planning phases of transport projects. Lessons are often ignored or denied because of turf–ego–power problems that prevent learning. For these reasons, the wrong LRT cars or BRT systems may be procured; and for such reasons, obvious implementation constraints are ignored and stakeholder analyses that could have been performed during appraisal are not.

Health Care Policies

The framework used for energy policy may also usefully serve as a description of policy responses to the demands of international health care. As indicated in *Figure 8.1*, in what might be termed the *generation phase*, demands for more access to health care based on needs comes from individual patients (including retired, disabled, and special need). The demand is specifically for health care, generally for social safety net access. For this reason, it is hard to distinguish in other than an administrative program sense the difference between needs and requirements for social assistance, elderly care and nursing home, special need clients, and the multiple kinds of primary and secondary medical needs from outpatient eye and emergency care to secondary treatment of cancer and other serious diseases.

In response to these needs, firms manufacture medical equipment and engage in research to improve the technology for diagnostic and intervention devices and drugs. Universities train and educate personnel and conduct research in laboratories. This is the context of health care in all countries; it is the set of givens from which they must decide what they will do and how they will respond on a national basis. An assumption is that competition in freer markets works best to generate the quality products needed to respond to needs and serve employment and growth needs as a local drug products industry. Temporary palliatives such as import substitution industrialization work only at the early stages of industrialization. The case of Brazil in the 1970s–1980s illustrates that tariff policies only retard industrial growth that can really supply local needs and compete with international firms. In short, policies should encourage competition so that industries such as pharmaceuticals and energy companies can grow and compete. Once their products are for sale, smart government regulatory policies need to ensure that they meet health, safety, and welfare objectives.

In what might be termed the *transmission phase*, countries translate these contexts into policy based on problem definition, review of feasible options, and ensuring effective implementation of laws, policies, and operating regulations. This takes place at two levels: (1) legal and regulatory and (2) institutional, cultural, and structural. All countries would maximize coverage to accommodate health needs and minimize costs of production, delivery, and access to provide general health, safety, and welfare. As in the first phase, there are a number of given problems which all countries face. Demand for services is always greater than supply, which requires allocation of scarce personnel and financial resources. Costs of equipment, drugs, and personnel are always greater than the income level of society to pay for them. Only in an ideal society without institutional costs could costs and income abilities of all members of society be balanced. In the context of legal and regulatory rules, policy-makers must allocate the scarce resources given these constraints by providing income subsidies; producer subsidies to ensure that drugs and equipment are available; direct funding to ensure that personnel and equipment are allocated; regulatory structures to ensure that subsidies are monetized and targeted; eligibility requirements for safety net programs that are reasonable; insurance programs that function as intended and do not maximize profit at the expense of health objectives; and audit institutions that ensure fiscal leakage and corruption is minimized.

As noted, health care firms need to be regulated to ensure health, safety, and welfare objectives are attained. An important international regulatory policy issue in health care is drug pricing. Drugs are invented and produced by private firms. But they are public goods in that they prevent epidemics and enable people to be more productive in the economy. Innovation and research constitute most of the costs of many drugs. Drugs constitute a growing proportion of health care costs and spending in many transitional countries, e.g. 44 percent in India and 43 percent in China. They amount to much less in wealthier countries such as the UK (12 percent) and U.S. (12 percent) (*Economist*, 2014: 10, 46). The problem is that patents on intellectual property can allow companies to profit at the expense of populations that cannot pay for them, either in poor countries or in wealthier countries where such costs are not covered in national health care programs. The issue is how far regulatory agencies should go to restrict compulsory license privileges to epidemics. Intrusions on patents would restrict innovation. "Tiered pricing" by firms, which sell expensive drugs at substantial discounts in some poor countries, opens up the black market problem. Developed country allowance of tiered pricing for firms (perhaps in exchange for continued patent protection) pushes the issue down to poor countries. The issue then is pushed down to the country level where local regulators would have to be able to control the resulting corruption. Public drug pricing policies offer many second or third best options and no unequivocally preferred option to go forward.

Policies are made and financed in contexts of what political processes determine are the collective values in this area. It may be that regimes and elites determine only a few shall be covered at high cost or that the many will be given only basic services and the few may pay for their own access. Policies are financed in the context of tax and spending policies constrained by fiscal sustainability criteria. As we have seen, much of this turns on whose definition prevails: those who focus on short-term accounting balances or long-term growth and economic development. In a narrower sense, this relates to the issue of defining how many resources shall be allocated to preventive care versus treatment after illness occurs. Health care policies are also constrained by competing needs in education, defense, transport infrastructure, energy, and other functional areas.

At the second level, needs and resources are translated into actual care by running through "black boxes" of their political systems. These are the particular cultural constraints such as religious norms against treatment of or by women in many Middle Eastern Islamic countries or irrational fears of immunization and inoculation programs. For example, armed opposition by conservative Muslims to WHO and other official efforts to administer polio vaccinations in northwestern Pakistan has been driven by fear that the campaign is a Western anti-Islamic plot. With a sharp increase in polio cases and recognition by Pakistani officials that without vaccination certificates, workers will not be able to travel abroad, they have moved in response: providing police protection to health aid workers and enlisting celebrities to stamp the vaccinations as both safe and consistent with mainline Islam (Constable, 2014). With such efforts, cosmopolitan values can overcome dangerously provincial conservatism in the political culture, allowing proven medical technology to function as it does anywhere. Many other cultural constraints have been cited in this book that affect policy performance. It is worth noting that many of the "constraints" are viewed as "opportunities" or "rights" by those advocating them. For instance, those schools designated as Irish language schools in Northern Ireland are exempt from technical formulae for closure that are based on current student enrollments and recent past trends (*Economist*, 2013d: 87). This might stimulate interest in the language but spread already scarce resources for implementation of the standard education curriculum as well as any health services provided schools. It also reinforces segregation in the name of a cultural "right."

Particular policy designs are also filtered by political structures. Federal (or federation) system policies are in constant redefinition of where authority and responsibility lie not just in a constitutional sense by what also makes economic sense as well. Implementation of the national U.S. Affordable Care Act illustrates that pooling responsibilities to pay for maximum coverage makes good economic but not political sense in federal systems where states view this as federal intrusion. Statist systems in the former Soviet Bloc provided high-cost/lower-quality health services to most people while providing mostly excellent but high-cost services to party functionaries and their families. Unitary systems such as the UK have better capabilities to enforce basic levels of services at maximum coverage but are often unresponsive to specific needs. As with niche alternatives to public education such as charter schools, smaller private clinics can provide on-demand quality services to enhance overall health care quality.

At the micro level of transmission are the institutional rules that affect both cost and quality objectives in the first phase as well as the actual *distribution of services* and level of real access. As suggested in *Figure 8.1*, for instance, the distribution of all health care and safety net is determined by rules such as procurement and contracting for which services, eligibility requirements for access to government programs, staffing and quality of hospitals, licensing of clinics, and inspections of alternatives to existing systems such as neighborhood outpatient clinics and drug store clinics for minor problems. Procurement and contracting rules in many policy areas can favor insiders and low-quality producers. This wastes scarce available funds and lowers actual coverage and quality expected in designed policies. Failure to review and control health care cost increases caused by leakage and *clientism* severely damage policy results. It is in the review of distribution and allocation of resources related to access needs that models of health care delivery are tested. Some countries still use pure statist models, e.g. Belarus, North Korea, and Ukraine. They provide poor quality services at highly subsidized cost. A few countries such as France emphasize state health care delivery, transmission,

Generation	*Policy-Making and Transmission*	*Institutions, Culture, and Political Structures*	*Distribution and Access*
Demand: patient demands for safety net, primary-secondary care, special needs, and elderly care	*Problems:* demands greater than supply capacities; costs greater than supporting income levels; requirements that coverage be maximized and costs minimized	*Culture:* religious norms; irrational fear of public health programs	*Access Points:* hospitals, clinics, private dispensaries such as drug stores and boutique services, e.g. eye care
Supply: equipment and technology, drugs, medical training and education, research and development	*Policy–Responses:* income and producer subsidies; direct expenditures for programs and services; regulatory structures to ensure cost, expenditure, and quality control	*Government Structures:* federalism, unitary, elitist–populist systems	*Evaluation:* performance audits of cost and quality to determine if health care model is effective
	Constraints: fiscal sustainability, political values on who should be covered, at what level and who shall pay	*Institutional Rules:* procurement, contracting, internal audit, and control systems	

Figure 8.1 Framework for International Health Care: Problems and Responses

and allocation but maintain high-quality services—though at high cost. Elitist and populist systems, such as Venezuela, socialize health care to the extent that most receive poor quality while a narrow elite controls access for itself. Most countries have adopted middle-range or mixed solutions, i.e. those that allocate private and public spheres that may be flexibly breached based on changing needs and technological advancements.

Financial Sector Policy

Public policy analyses often downplay the fact that in most countries it is the private sector which generates the savings, jobs, and incomes through their profit-making activities. The tendency instead is to focus on tax policy disincentives to profit and productivity. But the influence of an unregulated financial sector can be just as dangerous for private firms and the economy. Two general models guide relations between governments and their financial sectors. The Anglo-American model attempts to keep the banking and financial sector at arms-length from governmental institutions and policy. The government intervenes via independent examination and regulation of the sector. The rest of the world beyond Commonwealth (including Singapore and Hong Kong) and U.S. borders encourages cooperation and mutuality to govern relations. Allowing for local design variations, the EU, China, and many transitional and developing countries follow this second model, including state banks. In times of crisis, competent and conservative bank management is able to overcome financial and regulatory problems better in the first model rather than the second. In the context of the second model, banks face pressures for political lending that invariably violate economic and financial norms.

In all contexts, the banking and financial sectors attempt to intermediate depositor funds to investor loans in order to increase the flow of savings and investments and to spur on economic growth. Historical recurrence of bubbles and financial crises reflect imbalances in the political economy that require governmental regulation at arms-length to preserve the integrity of both the economy and the public finances. Recent events starting with the Great Recession of 2007–2009 suggest that crises will recur and that independent regulation of the financial sector based on best international practices and norms is necessary to fit each particular context. It should not be forgotten that the low interest rates and lax federal regulation of the housing market allowed banks and financial institutions to set up alternative financing that included subprime mortgages. Securitization and derivatives in the form of collateralized debt obligations (CDOs) and bundled mortgages were largely the conduit rather than cause of the crisis. Banks sell receivables such as claims to mortgage payments in order to boost capital to loan ratios which allows them to lend out more money. But if the receivables packages have not been reviewed for creditworthiness, the result is high risk of insolvency and bankruptcy. Weak regulation of the financial sector allowed this opaque system to set lending standards and prices (Pearlstein, 2014). Regulatory failure could allow a new property bubble and foment another worldwide financial crisis. Loan origination standards and bank capital requirements have been tightened (*Economist*, 2014a: 11). Regulatory requirements that parties creating new securities must retain some exposure to the underlying credit should also decrease the risks of future meltdowns while stimulating capital growth and more lending.

An important determinant of financial as well as public sector financial stability is the due diligence of loan origination. If public CIP processes fail to winnow out bad projects, funds are spent on assets that do not contribute to growth or welfare. Because of its size and threat to the world economy, China is an important example of this problem. If private mortgage and loan applications are flawed, superficially reviewed, or approved because of perverse incentives (i.e. securitization, resale, and rated with legitimate loans all generating more profits), loans from banks to these creditors will jeopardize the financial system with toxic loans for property. If the banking system is tied to the public financial system directly through state banks or indirectly through state enterprises as in the second model, the risk to the entire economy grows. Weak banks in Ireland and Cyprus, for example, tipped both countries into bailout programs. EU funds already have been spent to recapitalize Spanish and Greek banks and concerns over Italian lenders have grown as its economy deteriorates.

As indicated previously in *Figure 5.2*, banks attempt to intermediate between savers and lenders. They stay in business by having enough capital to cover their depositor liabilities. But bank shareholders want returns to cover potential future losses, forcing them to invest in higher return but riskier assets. This creates an inherent instability in all Western banking systems between its operating requirements and regulatory concerns for macroeconomic stability. Soviet system banking, as is known, viewed bank balance sheets in reverse. Deposits were "their" assets which they kept safe to cover the loans which they were ordered to make by state plans and directives. So, to Soviet bank managers, loans were liabilities. This perversity has been carried forward into financial repression or financial socialism when governments restrict depositor access to their deposits, as has been done periodically in Argentina, Brazil, and China (*Economist*, 2014f: 9). Nationalization converts bank liabilities into state assets—a portion of deposits are made unavailable to their owners to prevent banks from collapsing with risks to the macroeconomy and to ensure the continued flow of loans to state firms and other favored clients. Under such statist systems, credit to the private sector is minimal and given low official priority. To avoid such perverse perspectives from taking hold, Western international banking rules have long required banks to hold minimum capital to cover liabilities. But capital has been hard to define, i.e. how much safer cash and government bonds should be held versus loans of varying degrees of risk? (*Economist*, 2013c: 75). As discussed in this chapter then, banking assets are the receivables from loans to government and firms. The loans may be internal to the state banking system or state firms (e.g. BNDES in Brazil) or to other governments (e.g. purchase of Greek sovereign bonds).

Capital asset totals need to balance deposit liabilities or a banking liquidity/solvency crisis (or run) can occur. If debts are called in faster than assets can be sold, insolvency looms (*Economist*, 2013b: 80). For instance, the largest bank in Cyprus, the Bank of Cyprus (BOC) is deposit-based with little debt issued to bondholders. But in 2013, 53 percent of its loans were non-performing (payments by debtors more than 90 days overdue) as property values collapsed and incomes dropped with which to pay mortgages. The hole in BOC balance sheets grew: loans were 45 percent greater than deposits. As arrears and defaults on poorly culled loans increased, more capital was required to balance liabilities, i.e. EU emergency funding and/or state treasury funds. That meant more capital relative to total assets (see *Figure 5.2*). Nevertheless, the downward cycle often continues as returns on investments, loan repayments, and equity values all drop as confidence in banks diminishes further and jobs and incomes disappear from firms unable to sustain them without orders. Declining aggregate demand for products from firms by individuals and other firms in the supply chains reduce overall orders. At the same time, firms are unable to repay old loans or negotiate new ones at higher interest rates. Nor do firms have much interest in new loans with the markets in flux and aggregate demand collapsing. In this context, modern governments that had little directly to do with the financial sector crisis except failing to ensure vigilant regulation are often constrained from investing to try and stimulate demand through more savings and investments. They are constrained by fiscal rules and political majorities fearful of current deficits and future debts. Again, this is paradoxical in that the cause of financial sector failure was largely private sector debt and flawed loan origination controls.

In many countries, then, the financial, banking, and governmental sectors are tightly entwined. Such countries follow the second model as an alternative to the less intimate and more ruthless Anglo-American regulatory model. And the second model works well when the economy is growing or stable. When parts of the system fail, the repercussions affect all sectors quickly. In the EU, for instance, without a banking union and controls over bank capital, bad loans brought down both sectors requiring country banking system bailouts from EU. Measures to strengthen economic and financial architecture such as banking unions with access to public resources as a backstop are needed to "break the vicious cycle of mutually reinforcing distress in the banking and public sectors" of Europe (Berger and Schindler, 2014: 21). Depending on public sector accounting rules, they can create either a contingent liability through loan guarantees, or a direct one which contributes to deficits and debts. By contrast, Sweden learned lessons from its 1990s banking crisis and created "bad banks" to clean out its system. Today, its banking system is profitable, cost-efficient, and stable despite one of the highest regulatory core capital ratios in the world (7 percent–12 percent) (*Economist*, 2013a: 70). EU countries failed to learn the lessons from Sweden and suffered financial crises beginning in the mid-2000s and extending to Greece in 2013–2014. While the earlier financial crisis originated in and threatened the U.S. economy, rapid increases in banking capital, higher quality controls, and new loan standards led to damage controls that allowed the U.S. system to regain growth by 2013. Again, in the U.S., the Troubled Asset Relief Program (TARP) for real sector and banking bailouts ($700 billion) was implemented with a program of stress tests and tighter regulation of the mortgage and financial sector. The result has been a net gain of $25 billion to the government for the interim bailout loans.

It is clear that regulatory failure to control official incentives to provide subsidies and loans to special interests allows distorted incentives to persist. This weakens the financial sector and, depending on the structure of firewalls and controls between sectors, can also threaten the public finances. China is the current example of this breach: state banks guarantee local government loans for uneconomic commercial real estate developments. According to Chinese official and UBS reports, subnational debt to finance infrastructure and real estate developments jumped 67 percent since 2010. Local government debt jumped from 8 percent of GDP in 2008 to 33 percent GDP in 2013. Since few of these projects will cover loan repayments, the risk of default and threat to central government finances and the state banking system is growing (Samuelson, 2014). While consolidated national debt is 250 percent of GDP (compared to 75 percent in the U.S.), the threat to banks and macroeconomic stability could be severe. Given diminishing economic growth, the current state of subnational indebtedness, and the risks posed to the banking and public finance systems in China, when such reviews are performed, the risks posed by subnational debt are very important and should be included and heavily weighted. More comparative research is needed into the causes of modern financial sector crises and on the effectiveness of policy responses on growth, employment, and stability.

Four sets of recommendations were proposed to strengthen the financial sector and protect the public finances from further deterioration:

First, consistent with discussions of this under Macroeconomic and Fiscal Policies (*Chapter 2*), it is important for PFM integrity, transparency, and control that risks be minimized. Risks to the public finances take many forms. Larger risks are evident in many countries from loan guarantees and special-interest-driven subsidies. Sugar and honeybee subsidies in the U.S. are obviously wasteful. These are costly and unneeded but backed by bipartisan district support in Congress. When oil prices were higher in 2013–2014, subsidies cost 5 percent of GDP in Jordan and 14 percent in Egypt. They absorbed 8 percent of governmental revenues worldwide.

With lower oil prices now, such oil-importing states save and have more money to waste on subsidies! But subsidies regardless of oil prices are regressive and benefit mainly the wealthiest: 43 percent of the subsidies in poor countries flow to the rich (*Economist*, 2014c: 63). To the extent that the financial sector follows subsidies in with more special-interest-driven loans, the macroeconomy is threatened. Other major risks derive from concessions and PPPs to replace public funding with private funding of infrastructure projects. These transactions as well as the trail of their formal benefit–cost evaluations need to be made public and recorded in "credit budgets" and other documents for later use by auditors.

As noted in the second chapter, the notion of infrastructure privatization as an alternative to public financing is appealing. The U.S. and many countries are faced with deteriorating infrastructure but often lack the will to design and impose taxes that could finance this essential component of growth. Dannin and Cokorinos (2012) reviewed the results of large infrastructure privatization deals done thus far. They noted that at present, decisions on whether to privatize infrastructure in the U.S. and other countries are often based on minimal and often faulty cost–benefit analysis. The financing question is whether this approach is better than the traditional one of issuing new debt, subsidizing fares, and operating the system itself. At this late date, basic comparative questions still need to be answered on the results of PPP financing from Canadian, European and other U.S. LRT systems such as Denver. For example, what happens if the firm goes bankrupt? Are state payments to the firm for borrowing costs counted against state debt levels? Serious problems also relate to conflicts of interest with "revolving-door" relationships between financial advisors and governments that often lack the expertise to evaluate either contracts or the implications of proposed projects on users, citizens, and bond-holders in the longer term. In their pursuit of narrow financial objectives, contract provisions such as revenue-guarantee or stabilization clauses may give contractors quasi-governmental status. This allows them in some cases to claim damages from governments but remain immune from accountability, disclosure, and oversight when projects (e.g. highways) fail to generate forecasted revenues and other expected benefits. Despite the appeal of private financing of public projects, it is clear that in many countries infrastructure privatization schemes are leaving an unexpected legacy of lawsuits as the validity of various concessions and contracts continue to be tested.

Second, to guard itself from risks of selecting uneconomic and wasteful projects for either public or private financing, governments need to strengthen their CIPs (detailed in *Chapter 3*). This is an important component of institutional weakness in many countries that encourages not only politicized and wasteful spending but also corruption. High-speed rail lines in Spain, China, and other countries that are a favorite of engineers and visionaries but less so passengers and fiscal managers that have to pay for maintenance and rehabilitation are a good candidate for better CIP reviews. Once these very high-cost projects begin to draw upon higher subsidies, rollover of existing loans, and more loans (to state and quasi-state firms) to meet operating costs, in countries with state banking systems they threaten the competitiveness of the commercial banking sector, increase the risks of state bank failure, and add to the fiduciary risks in overall political economy.

Third, while the focus has been on managing risk and ensuring sufficient capital exists to cover sudden shocks to the financial system, the best way to avoid crises is to make sound loans in the first place. The failure of loan origination criteria that had existed for almost a century in the U.S. allowed the creation of toxic mortgage stocks. The loans should not have been granted because of the high risk of default. Nevertheless, larger perverse incentives encouraged making the loans, securitizing them, and selling them for profit. Rating agencies and auditors were also complacent in accepting superficial figures that hid these risks without conducting their own due diligence. Properly designed internal controls in both public and private organizations can guard against systematic fiduciary losses by separating functions, i.e. loan evaluation from signing contracts and issuing checks. Elaborate schemes occur of course that integrate these separate financial transaction functions in wider plots and conspiracies to defeat sound internal controls. Nevertheless, textbook design and vigilant enforcement of these controls is essential to prevention of further credit-driven crises. With further improvements in regulatory strength and experience in managing financial crises, one means of managing bank risk is to once again use securitization to bundle loan assets and sell them to outside investors. This improves bank capital ratios by shedding assets: increasing the ratio of owner equity to loans (A to B in *Figure 5.2*). New requirements that those involved in creating securitized products must retain a portion of the risk can reduce overall systemic risks of failure caused by the financial "Frankenstein's monsters" of the recent past, e.g. collateralized debt obligations secured by other securities secured by other securities and so on (*Economist*, 2014b: 60). Of course, just as we noted in *Chapter 7* that alternative energy sources can create new environmental problems, the modified financial policy could create new risks as well.

Fourth, the reform focus has been on requirements to prevent banks from engaging in the riskiest activities. For example, European ring-fencing and U.S. regulatory efforts such as the Volcker Rule can prevent banks from taking customer (depositor) money and investing in stocks, bonds, and derivatives. This in theory will shield depositors from trader losses. The EU would separate depositor funds from other bank liabilities. To balance deposit liability, banks could only hold less risky capital assets such as cash, government bonds, and loans to individuals and firms (*Economist*, 2013b: 81). But for this to work, mortgage origination risk assessment and controls would still need to be in place, especially for commercial property. Other proposals require banks to hold more equity on the asset side to manage risk by increasing leverage ratios. A leverage ratio limits a bank's loans and investments to a certain multiple of its capital, often without considering how risky they are. But 70 percent of European banks have less than 3 percent of their assets available to absorb future losses (*Economist*, 2014d: 29). Requirements that banks hold more loss-absorbing capital as equity in proportion to their assets are controversial. But previous efforts to risk-weight assets have been even more subjective, i.e. banks have lost on many supposedly safe assets such as mortgages. Banks complain that holding redundant equity could reduce lending needed for economic recovery (*Economist*, 2013b: 81). In the European Union, if banks could meet reasonable leverage ratios of 5 percent–8 percent of assets, investors would likely trust them more, allowing banks to finance themselves in capital markets instead of through the European Central Bank.

Still other proposals include requirements that banks balance debt and equity. One way to do this is for banks to sell contingent capital. These are IOUs that act like bonds in normal times and pay dividends. But in bad times, they convert from debt into equity which is less risky to the banking system (ibid., 2013b: 81). The need is for both regulators as well as markets to make rules with proper incentives to help banks act prudently. At the least, that requires more vigilant rating agency efforts to focus on the substance of balance sheet figures and risks to creditworthiness. Paradoxically, in Anglo-American countries that rely on credit rating agencies for both public and private sector creditworthiness, this may mean more of an arms-length relation with their main credit rating institutions and smarter public sector regulation.

A final way to strengthen the commercial banking system is ironically to retry securitization. Stronger regulations in the wake of the 2007–2009 financial sector meltdown have reduced risks of bundling loan receivables such as mortgages and credit cards and selling them to outside investors. As noted, those involved in creating the securitized products must now retain some of the risk of the original loan. To the extent that these and other reforms work to reduce systemic risks by eliminating the over-engineered, Kafkaesque products of the past, the use of securitization allows banks to increase their capital–loan ratios. This is what banking and financial regulators are seeking in the U.S. and EU, and in the context of lower yields worldwide, it would be one means of reducing risks to the financial system.

Education Policy

To a greater extent than even urban transport or health, more people are affected by educational system performance because they have children or can identify with schooling when they were young themselves. Primary and secondary schooling issues are tangible and become daily flashpoints for political conflicts over issues such as financing, districting, access, and quality. In more areas, because of cultural practices, security efforts to respond to school or student violence are also major educational issues. Schooling is structured similarly around the world, with students advancing along a 12-grade trajectory often from pre-school programs. Beyond the similarity in frameworks, there is widespread variation in curriculums, standards for advancement and graduation, teacher background and quality, delivery systems, management autonomy over rule-making and enforcement, financing, and overall student performance results. This has made education a ripe area for comparative international policy research and much empirical work has been done. Despite the variation, many reform programs have focused on the same variables and achieved similar results in many different contexts.

As noted in *Chapter 6*, international performance is often measured by PISA scores. They indicate that while generally more spending as percent of GDP translates into higher scores, the exceptions (e.g. Japan, Shanghai, Germany) suggest that culture and institutions matter as much as money. For this reason, researchers have focused on the determinants of performance, especially access, governance, and financing variables. Access varies widely from culturally set rules (e.g. girls schooling in Muslim countries, and poverty in poorer countries requiring work instead of schooling). Policy efforts have focused on conditional cash transfers to encourage attendance in exchange for cash payments. This has worked in many countries such as Peru and Brazil. They have also focused on design of fiscal transfers or intergovernmental grants. Grants can be made according to rules that favor equalization of district finances, improved student performance, or some combination of the two. Substantial amounts of research in the U.S. have been done on the incentive effects of lump-sum versus matching grants with evidence that the greatest multiplier effects on schools and students flow from matching or cost-sharing grants.

Governance also varies widely across the globe. Education is delivered within unitary and federal systems that are centralized or decentralized and that include market versus public sector delivery systems. It is believed that variation in student performance has much to do with the differences in these delivery system models. The levels of financing and how money is spent also affects performance. German lander and cities spend 90 percent of the funds but much of it is from central government transfers; by contrast, U.S. schools spend monies that are raised from states (48 percent) and local (43 percent) tax sources with only about 9 percent from the central government. The central government in France (Ministry of Education) provides 70 percent of the financing and all of the rules on school management, personnel, curriculum, standards, and spending choices. Some school districts with relatively low levels of financing are able to leverage or target funds better than those with more funds. This may be due to managerial autonomy and fewer restrictions on spending the funds. In other cases, more restrictions or conditions on spending may lead to better performance, i.e. where funds would have been stolen or spent on higher salaries or more administrators instead of teachers.

In this rich context, reform programs have proliferated across the world from national and local levels. The focus on choice and performance dominates countries and particular provinces such as the U.S., Alberta (Canada), Chile, UK, and Sweden. The Swiss and German approach continues to be tough, centrally set standards; early student performance tracking, with emphasis on teacher pay and quality; and many options for apprenticeships and vocational choice. The Japanese approach is similarly focused on rote learning of facts and emphasis on test performance. But it offers fewer alternatives to those tracked out early. The Anglo-American model differs broadly from this in its effort to provide greater access and repeat opportunities for advancement along more traditional paths. This model focuses on alternative delivery systems, school decentralization, and incentivizing performance with transfers. Within the U.S., cities have experimented with pay for performance (e.g. Dallas and Chicago) and school closures for failing performance (e.g. Detroit, NYC, Washington, DC, Newark, Providence) as well as the expansion of choice through voucher funding, charter schools, and performance transfers based on tougher central standards (e.g. No Child Left Behind and Race to the Top federal programs). In the U.S. and elsewhere, standoffs with teacher unions have been an important determinant of results. School unions often act as a brake on student results, focusing instead on teacher employment security. Often improvement of teacher quality is impeded by union rules. Reformist regimes in such cities as NYC, Chicago, and Washington, DC, successfully forced unions to change their rules in favor of teacher pay for performance schemes that exchange more funds for less security. All reforms have been controversial, and comparative policy research offers a rich library of best and worst practices for reformers around the world who seek to improve educational performance.

Energy and Environmental Policies

In general, environmental policies are a response to energy uses and misuses. The uses of energy alternatives produce varying degrees of pollution. Environmental policies should respond to those misuses and attempt to redirect generation, transmission, distribution, and consumption to reduce negative impacts on health and quality of life. Environmental policies to achieve these purposes conflict with interests in production profit and growth. Many of these conflicts have been shown to be illusory as proper designs of incentives have made the requirements of profit and environmental regulation consistent. For this reason, environmental and health policies are tightly linked in many countries

Energy policies are driven in the first instance by resource availability in particular countries. Not every country has coal or oil; not every country will allow nuclear power generation anymore; every place wants wind and solar energy but few will allow heavy transmission lines to accommodate these alternative sources. Some countries can grow sugar for ethanol. But consumers may want low prices for consumption; producers want high export prices; prices for ethanol even with subsidies may not match prices for non-energy use. Shale oil and gas may revolutionize the geopolitics of energy use and provide enormous benefits to the U.S. economy. But it may also lead to serious water pollution requiring regulatory limits on profit-making for this source of energy. Like agricultural policies, energy policies are often driven by powerful producers that gain a wide range of subsidies from insider contacts in governments. This works against fiscal discipline, allocative efficiency, and consumer and citizen welfare.

Perhaps the most rational environmental response to an energy misuse problem has been automobile gas consumption. Over the past 50 years, regulations have forced and/or encouraged auto manufacturers to innovate beyond all expectation. Regulations also forced oil firms to remove lead for health reasons. Gas consumption is dropping; efficiency is increasing; autos now run on batteries, solar, natural gas, ethanol, and biodiesel. Air pollution from auto use has dropped significantly. International environmental problems remain in solid wastes; water pollution and scarcity; and natural resource management, e.g. forestry.

The international arena provides varied approaches to the problems of related energy–environmental policies. Many applied solutions have already been transferred successfully between countries and regions.

Constraints to the Adoption of Policy Lessons

To conclude, this book has little to say about how countries progress, become more civilized, reverse course and become underdeveloped, or fall into chaos as failed states. There is no teleological pattern to ascension or decline, nor is there much agreement on the ingredients of success. Nevertheless, guiding rules and propositions can be fashioned from experiences at the sectoral level on how a country might work if all sectors performed efficiently and effectively. The book offered some basic rules and systems that seem to work in a variety of contexts at the middle range in functional or sectoral policy areas, such as transport, infrastructure, health, and education. As noted in the first chapter, nearly 45 years ago, Holt and Turner (1970: 5) called for more cross-cultural research for theory-building. Riggs focused on comparison of "whole political systems" for this task, by which he meant government structures and their functions (1970: 80). Focusing on public policy, Holt and Richardson (1970: 39) called for less macro-theory building and more emphasis on generation of middle-range propositions. We have expanded their emphasis from simply bureaucracy and public administration to include cultural, economic, and institutional variables to try and explain successes and failure in sectoral policy areas.

We attempted to demonstrate that this requires the tools of economic analysis and the rigor of comparative methods applied to policies. Almost paradoxically, some failed states have particular sectors that function well despite constraints of weak and ineffective governance at the center. This was particularly evident in the Balkans during the transition of the late 1980s–early 1990s when countries with effectively no central government such as Albania were able to continue and avoid descent into chaos through social safety net provision (with vital advice from the World Bank). This suggests a rich area of middle-range policy comparison and analysis that can improve programs and build theory at the same time. Controlling for culture, institutions, and political structures, it can be said that successful models exist in all the functional areas covered in this book. Rigorous comparative analysis can refine the contexts in which these models and lessons can be made more applicable.

Returning to the questions posed in the first chapter as to why a country with major health needs would ignore or deny successful policy lessons from neighboring countries with similar populations, the book had little to say about why successful country policies are not adopted by other comparable countries or why failed policies are continually transferred from one country to another or to different regimes within the same country. The question is asked almost perennially: why do regimes ignore or deny the lessons of others? Despite decades of empirical evidence on what works and does not in applied policies, countries still do not adopt them. Unfortunately, there is no species learning or emergence whereby rules or lessons are encoded in nervous systems by biological evolution. Natural selection does not operate in the realm of culture and institutions to weed out regimes that engage in policy failure to prevent both these regime types and their policies from recurring. In the first chapter, we noted that the Nicaraguan press ran many editorials in the 1980s–1990s imploring policy-makers to adopt the successful health, education, welfare, and investment policies of neighboring Costa Rica, all to no avail. Recent responses to the Argentinian fiscal crisis have the same obtuse quality: never learning from its past mistakes. Now ex-President Cristina Fernandez de Kirchner followed the same populist policies of past regimes: unproductive, politicized public spending beyond any sustainability measures; heavy export taxes; strict import controls; and disincentives to foreign investors such as banning the sale of foreign currency (*Washington Post*, 2014: A20). Freezing electricity and gas prices in 2002 meant that grids have decayed from lack of maintenance and rehabilitation. While energy subsidies amounted to $11 billion in 2013 (*Economist*, 2014d: 29), the energy deficit is $9 billion and blackouts continue, diminishing industrial production. Such repeatedly failed policies of the past were pursued anew as the per-capita income of neighboring Chile soared in the wake of policies informed by empirical analysis and comparative examples. The same policy follies continue in other once-successful and wealthy regional Latin American countries as Venezuela.

In addition to Argentina and Venezuela, other states engaging in policy lesson denial include Turkey, blending economic nationalism with Islamic populism; Italy, which believes rating agencies and the IMF should count its cultural wealth as part of GDP to improve policy performance; California, which allows quick fixes through referenda that weaken both public finances and private sector performance; and Russia, immersed in aggressive nationalism and ruled by kleptocratic oil oligarchs (*Economist*, 2014e: 13). The same economic mistakes of closed economies, protection of inefficient industries, costly untargeted subsidies, political repression, and quick fixes that demonstrably do not solve problems all prevent these regimes from taking advantage of comparative policy lessons.

So why do countries pursue policies so obviously contrary to self-interest and demonstrated policy results in similar contexts? Why do they persist in error? Tuchman (1984: 7) asked these questions and concluded that governments have peculiar "wooden-headed" qualities that allow "self-deception" to take hold of leadership. This wooden-headedness is "also the refusal to benefit from experience." She noted that "no matter how often and obviously devaluation of the currency disrupted the economy and angered the people, the Valois monarchs of France resorted to it when they were desperate for cash until they provoked insurrection by the bourgeoisie" (ibid., 1984: 8). Popular explanations focused on international capitalism and dominant classes, i.e. dependency theses. But these were superficial in that they could not explain why other regimes such as Chile had done so well in the same context. The key seems to be regime quality, the peculiar institutional and organizational architecture of the governing class. Those "princes" that are "great askers and patient hearers of truth" (Machiavelli), those which become angry if "anyone has scruples about telling him the truth," those which refuse to "draw inferences from negative signs" will persist in error and "protective stupidity" (ibid., 1984: 383).

More recently, Horne (2015) focused on why generals and nationalistic political leaders delude themselves and make the wrong policy decisions in war and domestic policy. He argues from a review of six battles in the first half of the twentieth century that they dangerously delude themselves into thinking that they know better from combined delusions of hyper-nationalistic superiority and excessive self-confidence or hubris. From this it follows that policy solutions developed elsewhere, especially by unfriendly regimes and countries, are to be ignored. Like Tuchman, Horne noted that for the ancient Greeks hubris was the folly of leaders who through excessive self-confidence challenged the gods. It was always followed by *peripeteia* (a reversal of fortune), and ultimately nemesis (divine retribution). In short, leaders who experience triumphs overreach. The next generation of leaders then inherits this arrogance and complacency with disastrous results (*Economist*, 2015a: 79). Irrational policy denial then is the strategic and operational consequence of the turf–ego–power problem noted above.

Countries are not simply economies. Each sectoral policy will reflect voter preferences, special interests, cultural practices, and institutional rules that can combine to produce inefficient and ineffective results. The vagaries of state regimes have to be factored in. Other policy books concentrate sensibly on explanations from partisan politics. Just as banking systems intermediate between borrowers and lenders, political systems should mediate between needs, demands of public opinion, and resource constraints. But they often do not do this precisely because parties fight for control of governments by responding to their nativist populist bases. And populist bases often like to nostalgically revisit the failed programs and solutions of the past. Parties often pander and do not adapt well to economic change or demographic realities. How countries and regimes can protect themselves from failing to learn from comparative historical and current policy experiences is the question that should be tackled by social psychologists, political scientists, and economists. Until more satisfactory answers emerge, we remain hopeful that at the sectoral level at least, positive changes are still possible by initiating successful practices or adapting successful lessons from elsewhere. It can happen. More than three decades ago, one of us was told by a Cuban official working in Costa Rica that they were learning from their visits how to develop effective health and education policies. As noted in the first chapter, at least at that level, the transfer of policy lessons to Cuba was successful.

References

Allen, Richard, Richard Hemming, and Barry H. Potter (eds.) (2013) *The International Handbook of Public Financial Management* (New York: Palgrave Macmillan).

Berger, Helge and Martin Schindler, "A Long Shadow Over Growth," *Finance and Development*, 51, 1 (March 2014): 20–23.

Birnbaum, Michael, "A Bottleneck Ahead in Germany?" *Washington Post*, January 2, 2014, p. A4.

Cangiano, Marco, Teresa Curristine, and Michael Lazare (eds) (2013) *Public Financial Management and Emerging Architecture* (Washington, DC: IMF).

Constable, Pamela, "Persuading Reluctant Pakistanis to Trust Polio Vaccine," *Washington Post*, January 22, 2014, p. A8.

Cottarelli, Carlo, Philip Gerson, and Abdelhak Senhadji (eds.) (2014) *Post Crisis Fiscal Policy* (Cambridge, MA, and Washington, DC: MIT Press and IMF).

Dannin, Ellen and Lee Cokorinos, "Infrastructure Privatization in the New Millennium," in *The Oxford Handbook of State and Local Government Finance*, Robert D. Ebel and John E. Petersen, eds., New York: Oxford University Press, 2012: 727–756.

DeRenzio, Paolo, "Assessing and Comparing the Quality of Public Financial Management Systems: Theory, History and Evidence," in *The International Handbook of Public Financial Management*, Richard Allen, Richard Hemming, and Barry H. Potter, eds., New York: Palgrave Macmillan, 2013: 137–156.

Dethier, Jean-Jacques, "Measuring the Efficacy of Fiscal Policy in Stimulating Economic Activity in Developing Countries: A Survey of the Literature," unpublished paper, March 8, 2010, Washington, DC: World Bank.

Ebel, Robert D. and John E. Petersen (eds.) (2012) *The Oxford Handbook of State and Local Government Finance* (New York: Oxford University Press).

Economist (2013a) "Tips from an Ageing Model," September 28, p. 70.

Economist (2013b) "Schools Brief: Making Banks Safe," October 5, pp. 80–81.

Economist (2013c) "Schools Brief: Crash Course," September 7, pp. 74–75.

Economist (2013d) "In the Trenches of a Language War," December 21, p. 87.

Economist (2014) "The New Drugs War," January 4, pp. 10, 46.

Economist (2014a) "Securitization: It's Back," January 11, pp. 11–12.

Economist (2014b) "Back from the Dead," January 11, pp. 59–60.

Economist (2014c) "Energy Subsidies: Fueling Controversy," January 11, p. 63.

Economist (2014d) "Tensions in Argentina: Holding the Ring," January 11, p. 29.

Economist (2014e) "Bank Capital: A Worrying Wobble," January 18, pp. 12–14.

Economist (2014f) "The Parable of Argentina," February 15, p. 9.

Economist (2014g) "How to Fix a Broken System," September 6, pp. 85–86.

Economist (2015) "Local Government Debt: Looking for Ways to Spend," September 12, pp. 41–42.

Economist (2015a) "Military Hubris: Their Own Worst Enemy," November 6, p. 79.

Fiscal Monitor, "What Failed and What Worked in Past Attempts at Fiscal Adjustment," Appendix 4, April 2011, World Bank, Washington, DC.

Guess, George M., "Comparative Decentralization Lessons from Pakistan, Indonesia and the Philippines," *Public Administration Review*, 65, 2 (March/April 2005): 217–231.

Hemming, Richard, "The Macroeconomic Framework for Managing Public Finances," in *The International Handbook of Public Financial Management*, Richard Allen, Richard Hemming, and Barry H. Potter, eds., New York: Palgrave Macmillan, 2013: 17–37.

Holt, Robert T. and John E. Turner (eds.) (1970) *The Methodology of Comparative Research* (New York: The Free Press).

Holt, Robert and John M. Richardson, "Competing Paradigms in Comparative Politics," in *The Methodology of Comparative Research*, Robert T. Holt and John E. Turner, eds., New York: The Free Press, 1970: 21–73.

Horne, Alistair (2015) *Hubris: The Tragedy of War in the Twentieth Century* (New York: Harper).

Klitgaard, Robert E., Review of *The Limits of Institutional Reform in Development: Changing the Rules for Realistic Solutions* by Matt Adams, *Public Administration and Development*, 33, 5 (December 2013): 408–410.

Marlowe, Justin, "Capital Budgeting and Spending," in *The Oxford Handbook of State and Local Government Finance*, Robert D. Ebel and John E. Petersen, eds., New York: Oxford University Press, 2012: 658–682.

Ouliaris, Sam, "What Is Econometrics?" *Finance and Development*, 48, 4 (December 2011): 38–39.

Pearlstein, Steven, "Time to End the Mortgage War Against Fannie and Freddie," *Washington Post*, January 19, 2014, p. G1.

Riggs, Fred W., "The Comparison of Whole Political Systems," in *The Methodology of Comparative Research*, Robert T. Holt and John E. Turner, eds., New York: The Free Press, 1970: 73–123.

Samuelson, Robert J., "A Chinese Debt Crisis in 2014?" *Washington Post*, January 1, 2014, p. A15.

Spiotto, James E., "Financial Emergencies: Default and Bankruptcy," in *The Oxford Handbook of State and Local Government Finance*, Robert D. Ebel and John E. Petersen, eds., New York: Oxford University Press, 2012: 756–783.

Tuchman, Barbara W. (1984) *The March of Folly: From Troy to Vietnam* (New York: Ballantine).

Washington Post, "15 Cents a Gallon," December 27, 2013, p. A20.

Washington Post, "Argentina's Crisis," January 31, 2014, p. A20.

Xavier, J. A., "Budget Reform in Malaysia and Australia Compared," *Public Budgeting and Finance*, 18, 1 (March 1998): 99–118.

Index

Page numbers in italics refer to figures. Page numbers in bold refer to tables.

operational level xii, 8–9, 263; austerity programs
59; educational policy 203, 213; energy policy
250; financial sector policy 168; health care
137; macroeconomic and fiscal policies 265;
political culture 14, 16; public financial
administration 51; transferable lessons 65, 265,
269; urban transport and public infrastructure
110
operations and maintenance 40, 43, 44, 49
Oportunidades 148
opportunity costs: budget reviews 57–8; energy
and environmental policies 245–6; financial
benefits analysis 120–1; health care 144, 147;
telecommunications policies 2; urban transport
87
organizations 17, 64
outcomes: budget reviews 57; education 201,
203, 206–7, 211–12, 219, 220; evaluation
9–10, *10*; health and health care 137, 139, 156;
performance or program budget format 45
out-of-pocket medical expenditures 141, 156
outsourcing 89–90, 104, 107
own-source revenues 33, 100, 102, 130

Padoan, Pier Carlo 71
PAHO (Pan American Health Organization) 156
Pakistan: alternative institutions 30; education 5;
fiscal decentralization 34; health care 153, 154,
156, 271; informal economy 177; institutions
20; policy design and financing 21; political
culture 16
Panama 1, 89
pancasila 201
parliamentary systems 72
partisanship 64–5, 73–4
patents 160, 164, 165, 271
payables 36, *174*
pay-as-you-go financing 130
pay-as-you-use financing 131
penalty prices 106
pensions 56, 57, 165–6
per pupil expenditures **199,** 200, 202, 204,
204
performance budget 45, *46, 50*
performance measures 9, 10; budget formats 43;
education 212, 221; health care 152; urban
transport 90, 109, 116
performance transfers: budget reviews 57;
cultural practices 266; education 22, 219, 223,
279; health care 156; urban transport and
public infrastructure 90
permits, pollution *see* tradable pollution permits

Peru: educational policies 194, 218, 278; health
care 154; urban transport 85, 93–4
perverse incentives: financial sector policies 176,
177, 186, 274, 276–7; institutions 18; labor
laws 52; policy implementation 6; political
economy xiii; subnational government finances
54–5; urban transport 89
PETI program 148
PFM *see* public financial management
pharmaceutical prices 159, 164–5, 270–1
pharmaceuticals 159–60, 161
Philippines: fiscal decentralization 34; health care
154; policy design and financing 21;
telecommunications 2; urban transport 82
Phillips Curve 180, *181*
photovoltaic panels 253
Pigouvian taxes *239,* 239–40
Piketty, Thomas 32
PIRLS *see* Progress in International Reading
Literacy Study
PISA *see* Program for International Student
Assessment
PISA scores 278
pivotal voter 215–16, 217, 218–19
Poland: central bank 182–3, 184; education
202–3, 227; fiscal policies 64; health care 24;
market-based pollution control measures 240;
shale gas reserves 232
policing strategy xiv
policy conundrum 41
policy design xii–xiii; economics 12; education
211; institutional context 18; macroeconomic
and fiscal policies 62–3, 64; political culture
13, 15; political economy analysis 20–1;
political structures 271–2; problem definition
47; randomized control trials 10
policy lesson denial 280–2
policy process 5–7, *6*
Polish clinics 24
political culture 14–17, 262; fiscal policy 64–5;
health care 158, 271; information asymmetry
170; institutions 19–20; urban transport 109–10
political economy xii–xiii, 11–13, *12, 23,* 261–3;
background support 13–17; education policies
212–13; financial sector policies 273–4, 276;
fiscal policy 64; health care 158–9; institutions
17–20; monetary policy xv; policing strategies
xiv; policy design and financing 20–1;
quantitative easing policies 185; urban
transport 109–10
political regimes: fiscal policy 64; legitimacy 7–8,
13, 14; types **15,** 15–16; urban transport 109–10